DON'T SHOOT
THE YANQUI

DON'T SHOOT
THE YANQUI

THE LIFE OF A WAR CAMERAMAN

Erik Durschmied

GRAFTON BOOKS

A Division of the Collins Publishing Group

LONDON GLASGOW
TORONTO SYDNEY AUCKLAND

For my Vikings.
Living with me sometimes took more courage
than I needed to face the Viet Cong.

Grafton Books
A Division of the Collins Publishing Group
8 Grafton Street, London W1X 3LA

Published by Grafton Books 1990

British Library Cataloguing in Publication Data

Durschmied, Erik
Don't shoot the yanqui
1. Documentary films. Cinematography. Biographies
I. Title
778.5′3′0924

ISBN 0-246-13631-6

Phototypeset by Computape (Pickering) Ltd, North Yorkshire
Printed in Great Britain by
William Collins Sons & Co. Ltd, Glasgow

CONTENTS

PART ONE THERE IS A TIDE

	Prologue	3
1	Father, What Is War?	14
2	A Surfeit of Woes	39
3	Laterna Magica	54
4	Fidel Castro	65
5	James Mossman	85
6	The Head Cutters	92
7	The Jim and Erik show	109

PART TWO A LONG, SAD WAR

1	The New Bush-war	127
2	The Mills of the Gods	144
3	Hill 943	182
4	The Battalions of the Noble Duke	205
5	A Confederacy of Villains	214

PART THREE HOMECOMING

1	Cherchez la femme	233
2	The White Tribe of Rhodesia	240
3	Cambodia 1979	247
4	In the Name of the One	256
5	Dead Man's Zone	272
6	The Confession	285
7	Death in the Marshes	293
8	The Home Menagerie	307
	Epilogue	320
	Photo Credits	325
	Index	327

The greatest thing a human soul
ever does in this world
is to *see* something
and tell what it *saw* ...

Hundreds of people can talk
for one who can think,
but thousands can think
for one who can see.

To see clearly is
poetry,
prophecy,
and religion –
all in one.

John Ruskin, 1819–1900

PART ONE

THERE IS A TIDE

There is a tide in the affairs of men,
Which, taken at the flood, leads on to fortune;
Omitted, all the voyage of their life
Is bound in shallows and in miseries.

Shakespeare, Julius Caesar, Act IV

PROLOGUE

I was twenty-eight – and about to die … '*No maten al yanqui!*'

'Don't shoot the Yanqui!'

The scream came from somewhere behind me, as I was staring down the gun barrels of a firing squad, my drenched back pressed against the car. Then an angel in uniform appeared, with three stripes on his shoulder. To me, he looked a hundred feet tall – a saviour!

When I had left the village in my beat-up car, which had been hidden in a cluster of bushes for the past month, nobody had bothered to warn me that mine would be the first vehicle on the country's *carretera central* in more than three weeks. The highway had been shut down by a combination of rebel ambushes and soldiers' attacks. Sitting behind the wheel, I cruised along the road, giving little thought to why I saw no traffic. My mind was on other things. I was elated, singing as I drove through the steaming countryside. I had pulled off a major scoop, and my career in the media was established. Alongside the road I noticed a few rebel flags stuck in trees, the red-and-black colours with which I had become so familiar over the last few months.

By now the whole island had been torn apart by the revolution: law had ceased to exist, gangs roamed the countryside to settle old scores, and no one was called to account for murder. Fields were abandoned, houses gutted, people slaughtered.

Nothing moved in the jungle: even the birds had stopped their chatter. The heat was a heavy blanket, flickering along the tarmac like liquid fire up ahead. Outwardly all was quiet. Too quiet. Until I came to the bridge at Cauto Cristo. That's where the four Cubans jumped me. There was a little one, a small, olive-skinned mestizo, unshaven and smelling of garlic. A nasty one, with a dirty uniform shirt of indistinguishable colour draped over bony shoulders and a frame like a scarecrow. One with an ugly grin and a rash of mosquito bites on his forehead, and baldhead, the sweating sergeant.

The snaggletoothed one ran out into the road, raising his rifle. I slammed on the brakes, as two more rushed in from the side. The nasty scarecrow one wrenched open my door, then grabbed my shirt and pulled me out. When I did not move fast enough, he hit me in the stomach with his rifle butt. I doubled over, retching bile. They were standing over me, screaming, kicking, until Scarecrow put his rifle to my head. '*Arriba*,' he shouted, and his gesture needed no translation. I tried to get up, pushing on my arms while the little one pulled on my shirt collar. Somehow I got up, aching. I was much taller than the members of this vicious gang, and certainly much broader. But they had the guns. Little men with big guns, a vivid reminder of rule of survival number one. What do you call a hoodlum with a gun? Answer: 'Sir!' I was facing a whole collection of Sirs. Four of them. Baldhead strolled up to the car. He took his time checking the vehicle. Not for booby traps, but for booty.

The boot was closed, so he put his pistol to the lock and blew it off. The lid sprang open. How lucky I was to have taken certain precautions. All I had with me were my clothes, and a bottle of Ron Anejho. The clothes went on to the ground. Clutching the bottle in his hairy fist, he smacked the bottom with the flat of his hand and the cork popped out. He took a long, satisfying swig, and his Adam's apple rose and fell until a third of the yellow liquid had disappeared. He burped, and passed the bottle to his cohorts.

In no time the bottle was sucked dry. Before the baldheaded sergeant swayed ponderously towards his motley detachment, he peed into my car. Then he said something, which must have been very funny, for there were howls of laughter. He made sure I caught the joke. He pointed his finger at me, clicked his fingers, and smacked his lips: 'ppphh!' The sign is international, it doesn't really need translation. 'Finish him and dump him next to his car, make it look like an ambush by the rebels.' Or something like that ...

My mind went blank. I vaguely knew that this was Christmas Eve, and that Christmas occupied a special place in my life. I was born on Christmas Day, now I would die at Christmas. Strange. I thought of cold snow and turkey ... turkey and guns ... guns, turkey, snow-covered pines ... candles and guns. It was difficult to concentrate. Think, think, there must be a way. Everything always came back to the guns. I stared at guns, I thought of guns. Fear, cold fear at the wrong end of a gun. They pushed me against my car. All was quiet, except for the hum of one particularly unpleasant fly buzzing around my head. I dared not chase it away. I knew that the moment I lifted my arm, they'd shoot. I could feel the sweat running down my spine. What shirt was I wearing? Did it really matter what I would look like when I was found? Christmas trees and candles and guns ...

And even those few thoughts went. I was drained of any emotion. A command. In the absence of any other sound my subconscious registered the click. Just the click. Another moment and then ...

Scarecrow must have made a good suggestion, because they all nodded their heads, and then Garlic-face walked up to me and pushed his hands into my pockets. A few pesos, and a fifty-dollar bill. Jubilantly he waved the greenback. The treasure of the Sierra Maestra.

Kaleidoscopic pictures, like a bad movie, only there are no super-stars acting heroically – this is stark reality. Now I am going to die, there is no magic bolt of lightning to strike down the bald head. I am dead. And I want so very much to live. While their attention was on the money I was safe, but that moment has passed. Ugly-grin says something, and Scarecrow kicks him in the balls. The little man goes to the ground, screaming. In the confusion, Garlic-face grabs the fifty-dollar bill and starts running. Baldhead pulls out his gun, points it at the back of the escaping figure, and: boom! The rum has affected his marksmanship and the bullet strikes a tree. But it brings Garlic-face to a sudden halt. Terrified, he turns, waves the money with a sly grin, a stain spreading on his trousers where he lost control of his bladder. He hands the money to the sergeant, who stuffs it in his sweaty shirtpocket before smashing the culprit in the teeth with his gun. Garlic-face sinks on to his knees, his face a bloody mask. Their hate turns back to me and they raise their rifles. Am I worth only fifty dollars? Is that what life is all about?

But the sound of the shot has a side-effect: it brings on the scene my angel with the three stripes. 'Don't shoot the *yanqui!*'

'Oh, my Lord,' I silently pray, 'did You forsake me when I lost my faith in You? But please, please, let this one be the man in charge.' The Lord must have heard my prayer.

'Don't shoot the *yanqui!*' he yells, pulling up his trousers as he stumbles across the ashes of burnt sugar-cane.

'Don't shoot the *yanqui!*' he keeps on yelling. Out of breath, he reaches the group, a big gun in his hand. He grabs me, propels me towards the open car door. Slowly, like a chorus from afar, I start to register shouting. He screams at me: '*Largate!* Get going!'

I must be alive because I can feel pain. Mechanically I turn the starter. Nothing ... flooded ... please make the car start ... coherent thought seeps back into my body, the black void of my mind changes into panic, raw fear. I crank the starter, once, twice, three times. A cough, a splutter, the engine fires. My capacity to react has returned, my senses are sharpened by the aching terror. Gently, ever so gently, the car starts to roll. I dare not turn my head. I can smell their fury, that of hunters deprived of their game. They will probably kill their officer for spoiling their fun with the terrified, wounded animal. They are on the road, four behind me, one in front: Scarecrow. Like a wounded turtle my car creeps towards that solitary figure with his eyes narrowed to slits, the veins on his forehead bulging. My stare is riveted to a single point, the black hole of a muzzle pointing at my head through the glass, and his finger on the trigger. As I roll past, his gun barrel grates along the side of my car. Nothing else, just the noise of metal on metal and a sneer through foul teeth. Little men, with big guns. Will I get a bullet in the back of my neck?

And then a strange thing happens. A thing which is to change my life for ever. Deep inside me, something snaps – I do not know what it is, I can only feel it, it is there, getting stronger by the second, stronger, stronger, I grind it out through my teeth: 'You don't frighten me!' – *I have shed the terror, lost my fear!*

Defiantly, I turn round, face their stare. They have not moved, legs planted, rifles at the ready, framed in the iron girders of a rusty bridge ... then I hit the accelerator ... on my next glance they have become black silhouettes rapidly receding on a heat-shimmering tarmac ... I reach a turn in the road.

They have disappeared, and I am alive.

There is a high death rate among combat cameramen. In the past this was due to inadequate equipment: First World War newsreels were not thought to have a significant effect on the outcome of the conflict, and cameras remained primitive affairs.

In a typical First World War camera, a hand crank linked to a simple drive mechanism fed highly-inflammable celluloid over two sprocket wheels past a rotating shutter, which looked like a metal Camembert with a slice cut out of it. The camera would have a single lens, and two settings: bright, or hazy. The low-speed films of the period make it look as though the whole war was fought in sunshine. Housed in a wooden box, the whole apparatus weighed about twenty kilograms.

Standing fully exposed above a trench, the cameraman might have to point the lens at an onrushing bayonet charge. With his heavy camera and wooden tripod, he was a perfect target.

The inter-war years witnessed the dramatic rise of Hollywood, where special equipment was developed for making feature films. Optical refinements permitted the film-maker to smooth away the wrinkles from the face of a movie queen, or put stars into a paper moon. The Mitchell cameras ranged from large to very large, and were moved around the set by hordes of assistants.

Newsreel remained the poor relation, and there was little improvement in hand-held cameras. The British put the Newman-Sinclair into a shiny metal box, but it still had to be cranked. The Americans made a small step forward with the spring-wound, single-lens Bell and Howell. The first major developments were made in Munich by two young German engineers, Arnold and Richter, who produced the first electrically-driven camera with a reflex viewing system. The ingenious use of a rotating mirror allowed the cameraman to see exactly what he was putting on film.

During the Second World War, combat cameramen had the lowest life expectancy anywhere in the services, but this was because of their frontline positions – in the lead aircraft or tank – and not their inadequate gear. Their films were effective. In 1940 a German general announced, 'The nation with the best cameras will win the war.' The Americans put an annual budget of fifty million dollars into their wartime newsreel effort. Of the German combat photographers, a mere four percent survived.

The Korean War saw the newsreel format reduced from the old, reliable 35mm to 16mm. Not until the mid-fifties did a Los Angeles firm, Auricon, bring the first popular sound-on-film camera on to the market, and it was widely used until the mid-sixties, when it was displaced by a combination of 16mm reflex camera and portable tape recorder. This meant a quantum leap in quality and manoeuvrability, and gave cameramen a chance of survival: they could run, crouch, or dive into the nearest hole.

The basic mechanism inside the camera was still recognizably the same as that in the magic box invented almost a hundred years before. There was still a claw to pull the film in front of the aperture, and a pin to fix it for a split second while the shutter rotated. To make the moving image on the screen, this happened 24 times a second, and the camera exposed 36 feet of film a minute. The cameramen of the 'pin-and-claw' age did not need any advanced technical knowledge to be able to thread their film over two sprockets.

Television made a new system possible. With the development of electronics and magnetic tape, companies in Europe and America tried to put together a television camera and a tape recorder to make a video camera. Electronic tubes would translate light waves into electrical waves, which a magnetic head would transfer to fast-moving tape – all of which is much too complicated for a proper description (or the brains of a cameraman). The breakthrough came in the mid-seventies, when two Japanese companies, Sony and Ikegami, beat the competition to produce a workable model.

Electronic News Gathering, or ENG, as it was called, meant the end of the line for film cameras as far as television news was concerned. The decisive factor was the speed of transmission to the audience. Early video cameras were cumbersome, unreliable and heavy. They cost about $50,000 each – as opposed to about $500 for a basic film camera.

The combat cameraman had to cope with the umbilical cord which linked him to his sound engineer: rapid movement became almost impossible, and you could no longer hide behind a tree. In terms of size and weight, it was like going back to the First World War. Once more, the camera team was out in the open, a conspicuous target. In Beirut, the networks lost more crews in one week than in the final year in Vietnam.

At present we are stuck with an apparatus which is neither fish nor fowl, combining camera, video-recorder and built-in microphone. Because it is a one-man band, it is extremely attractive for network economics, but it is bulkier and heavier than anything we used twenty years ago. It has a voracious appetite for electricity, so the batteries are heavier as well. The whole thing weighs thirteen kilograms. The future promises miniaturized digital cameras, but there is a lot of life left in the old heavies. It still costs $50,000 to replace one, and for that kind of money a network can hire plenty of strong men willing to schlep.

Only two of my cameras have left marks on my films – one was a simple 16mm film camera in Vietnam, the other was a state-of-the-art electronic camera in the streets of Beirut. It isn't technical wizardry that makes films – it is the sensitivity of the person behind the camera. It doesn't matter if it's a spring-wound square box or an electronic marvel – to me, cameras are all alike.

In order to get a picture, the combat cameraman has to look for the sector under attack. A soldier can sit in a bunker and let the bombardment roll over him. A cameraman cannot take pictures from the safety of a dugout. He actually looks for the bullet. On the other hand, a cameraman is not a permanent fixture in a battle. After his moment of ultimate risk, once he has got his pictures, he can bid farewell to the danger. A soldier cannot. Cameramen do not behave like tourists on a sightseeing trip. When we delay unduly in a precarious situation, the chances are we will get hurt. 'Get in, get it and get out!' is our motto.

The drawbacks to the job are numerous. One is the boring routine.

A cameraman will spend more hours in the air than the average pilot, jog more miles than a marathon runner, schlep more boxes than a porter, and eat more bad food than anybody else. He will contract two diseases, diarrhoea and lumbago. Following a day's hectic activity he will sink into a bathtub and then fall into bed, too tired for sightseeing. Next morning, he will rush to the airport to fly to another bathtub in another hotel in another city in another country. And they keep telling me a cameraman's life is glamorous.

There are two sorts of reporter-cameramen. Those who go for the beautiful image, like the writer who has found a marvellous allegory and is determined to use it, no matter whether it fits the plot or not, and those who go for the jugular, the single image that says it all, no frills, no window-dressing. I definitely belong to the second category. Nothing is more foreign to me than the construction of an image in order to illustrate a thesis. Real events are significant in themselves, and I intend the viewer to be seduced by their power.

I never romanticize wars. Anyone who thinks wars are beautiful is mad. As far as I am concerned, war reports are one notch down from pornographic movies. But, let's face it, violence is sometimes unavoidable. I cannot just sit by and pretend conflicts do not exist: ignoring them does not prevent wars from exploding.

I have covered the Game of Nations for twenty-five years, collecting my personal impressions and sharing them with millions of television viewers. I have reported from places which are generally referred to as 'practically nowhere'. I have become cynical about politicians' wisdom, about propaganda's half-truths, and certainly about appearances. Because if ever there was an untruth to be exposed, I have learned that it is the idea that the camera never lies. The camera, handled by a professional, is without doubt the most flexible instrument invented by man for telling the perfect lie. With my camera I can make anyone look beautiful or ugly, human or inhuman. I can shoot circles around the truth. I can falsify the present and lead historians a generation into the future to believe that what they see on the screen, and what they will go on to write about, is what actually has taken place.

If this implies that the cameraman is a liar, he is not. The cameraman's problem is often to see through what appears as truth, but is in fact a well-prepared deception, a clever manipulation inducing us to take the only image we are offered, since it might well be the only picture brought home. Professional pride does not permit failure, or returning without a story, and so we present those pictures which we actually believe contain the truth.

Every day, cameramen are faced with the moral issue of what should be shown and what would best remain unreported. Such judgements are also made in the course of editing, but mostly the cameraman is forced to decide on the spot. Will the presence of a camera and cameraman start a riot – incite a crowd to violence, ending in bloodshed? I have seen it happen, many times. Can a camera really change natural behaviour? Ask yourself: when you tell children to smile and 'Say cheese!', do they act naturally? Politicians always shake hands and smile, before and after they do each other down.

Cameramen dig into the misery of others. We intrude into the inner sanctums of thoughts, pains, horrors. We juggle with pictures and emotions. We bare private feelings for public inspection. With the help of film and tape, we freeze the present into images for posterity.

Have I, as an observing, feeling, supposedly human being, become hardened to tragedy? I cannot pass judgement on myself, I must leave this to my peers, to all those who have shared this part of my life, who have endured equal hardship, who have observed me during moments of stress. I can judge others, see fear in their faces, but I do not carry a mirror for myself. I do not record myself, I record others.

I am trained to react to a situation. I do not reflect, I act. In Algiers, I saw a woman in the middle of the street. My experience warned me to keep my head down, but she walked blindly into a trap. The gunmen were in place, their fingers on the trigger. I did not know her, she was just someone about to get killed. When the first volley rang out, I raced across the street and pushed her into a doorway. My action was not planned, it was a reflex triggered by the noise of the guns.

Recently I participated in a television panel discussion about danger in the field, and the host asked: 'What was the most terrifying experience you've ever had?' I didn't think this line of questioning very bright, so I said the first thing that came to my mind. 'The wedding of Princess Beatrice. There were so many photographers and television crews fighting for a choice position, that I was almost trampled under in the rush.' The host winced. When I returned to my hotel, I tried to think of a more truthful reply, but I couldn't come up with one that would not have condemned me in the eyes of the audience for flippancy.

How does death affect me? I am not talking about a quiet sleep after a full life, but ugly, sudden death. The soldier with his guts torn out; the car wrapped around a tree; youth snuffed out by an overdose. I feel revulsion, and sometimes hate. But I must look at drama with the eyes of the cameraman. I find it obscene when people stop at the side of a highway to gawk at a car crash victim. Only when on a specific assignment do I take a picture. That's all. Why is death such an aphrodisiac to the viewer? Audiences are repelled by horror, and yet irresistibly fascinated by the tragedy of others. They can see that there is someone even worse off than they are. I deliver this thrill. I induce bad dreams, a morbid power I do not fancy. I do not wish to imply that I have a strictly clinical interest in drama. I have emotions like everyone else, although perhaps mine are under better control than some. I start to reconstruct the events which have led to the tragedy, I thank the Lord that it isn't me who is lying there. I exclude dark thoughts from my mind. Like anybody who is used to facing danger, I know about it, yet I do not think about it. Such thoughts would distract my concentration, and lack of concentration invariably leads to disaster. Like a survivor of the bullring, the only veteran camera-man is the cautious one.

We seldom discuss tragedies: we know they exist without having to spell them out. We are far from fearless. When the shit hits the fan we are far too preoccupied with our professional duties. Our thoughts are channelled into the single task we are expected to perform: shooting pictures. There are no sideroads, there is little room for an acceptable exit. Some cameramen have tried to operate under dangerous con-ditions, standing out in the open with shells flying all over the countryside. They panicked and froze. There is no dishonour in refusing an assignment.

I would not want to overstate the importance of the cameraman, but today's media-conscious world has revolutionized accepted values. We have entered the age of an international war of images, a war fought without pity, and at great cost. That these pictures are effective, there can be little doubt. We are but a portrait of ourselves.

Each night television bombards the societies of the world. The image has started to replace the written word and in this new phenomenon a vital contributor is the image-taker.

This book is the story of one such cameraman, myself. I am not a voyeur in search of sensations. There is a screen between myself and reality. My protective shield is the lens. It is a wall of glass. I see, but I do not touch. Nothing seems real, all is but a passing image. I prefer not to look at my films. I do not wish this image to become reality.

1

FATHER, WHAT IS WAR?

(VIENNA, 1930–1945)

' ... war brings out the best, and the worst, all at
the same time.
The worst is what we are here to do, and the best
is what we are fighting for ... '

Letter from my father to my grandmother,
Austro-Italian front, 1916

It was a magnificent Christmas Day.

The city was covered in snow. The bells of St Stephen's Cathedral called the people to prayers. Vienna was a very religious town, and history had left its imprint. Although the glories of the Holy Roman Empire were only a memory, Austrian people continued to live in their past. Vienna was the place where Mozart wrote *The Magic Flute* and Beethoven composed his 'Ode to Joy'. Where, during the Middle Ages, the burghers had successfully stood up to the mighty Turk, and where, during the dancing congress, Prince Metternich had divided up Europe. Long before any other great city, Vienna had waltzed to the 'vulgar and popular' airs of Johann Strauss. Now, Vienna meant Freud and Klimt and Gustav Mahler. The traditional capital of central Europe was haunted by a parade gone by. Now the Viennese had to live with what was left, empty palaces and cold monuments, and no empire. In 1919 the peace treaty of Saint Germain had truncated Austria, and had turned Vienna into a big city in search of a country.

A people can lose an empire, but they will never lose their faith in God. And on this very special day of the year they hurried through the snow-covered streets towards the hundred steeples of Vienna's christendom. Candles from a thousand Christmas trees helped to guide them towards their churches to hear the good news about the birth of the Holy Child. Joy to the world.

Our house was in a suburb of the city, where the vineyards of the Kahlenberg reach down to the baroque houses in narrow lanes. It was near the place where Beethoven had composed some of his symphonies. Ours was a comfortable house, not very tall, the interior warm with memories and its thick exterior walls still painted in imperial yellow like most houses in the neighbourhood. In the back was a small garden with apple trees, which were now covered with a pristine blanket of snow. Further up our lane was a gas lamp, which threw its blue light on the snow and made the crystals sparkle like myriads of diamonds: nature had put on its tiara. A thousand bells had rung out the eventide message: *Peace, peace, tonight the Saviour is born.* Now the city had returned to its peaceful calm. Once in a while the passing sound of a horse-drawn carriage, the clop-clop of horses' hoofs, and wheels crunching through thin ice. The doctor's car was outside our house, inside all was quiet: only the chime of the grandfather clock and some laboured breathing interrupted the silence. My father was not at home. Luckily for me, my mother was. This holy night I was born.

The following day on a Tyrolean ski slope a telegram was delivered, brief and to the point: NOTIFY DURSCHMIED: IT IS A BOY. STOP. But even the fact that an heir had been added to the family circle did not stop my parents from a messy divorce, a mere six months after my birth.

The next few years I spent growing up. Looking back, life in those distant days is only a vague blur of everyday events. There were long lines of cold and tired-looking people waiting patiently at the public soup kitchens. I didn't understand the meaning of their suffering, because at home we had always enough to eat.

'When people are hungry they will act.' That's the way my father put it. In 1934 they did act, twice in the short space of three months. One day, I saw soldiers in the streets, there was a lot of shooting, and we had to close the windows. My aunt said that the workers had started a revolution. I pulled the covers over my head when I saw flames lighting up the night sky. It was the night the Karl-Marx Hof housing estate burned and a thousand people died.

It ended, like most popular uprisings, with the army in command, and more firmly entrenched than before. But the tension continued to mount, and a few months later another revolt erupted, more shots were fired, and the Bundeskanzler, Dollfuss, was killed. Once again I dived under the blankets. By now I could feel that my father was getting extremely worried. From time to time we had guests in the living-room, and they talked until late into the night. The following morning we would have to open the windows to let out the smoke from their smelly cigars. Once a general visited us, in a green uniform with red stripes on his trousers, and when he lifted me up for a kiss on the cheek, I touched all his medals. He stayed late into the night, and after an overdose of wine and cognac, his commanding voice, completely off key, roared into the night a popular melody of the time, but with the lyrics slightly changed:

> *... Adieu, mein kleiner Gulaschoffizier, lebwohl,*
> *und vergiss mich nicht, und vergiss mich nicht ...*

followed by howls of laughter.

Most of the time I was alone. Once, when I sneaked into my father's study and opened a drawer, I discovered a collection of coloured ribbons and shiny medals. It made me very proud to know that my father was also a soldier and had a uniform with red stripes, hidden in some closet. He never talked about the Great War, or about the glory that had been Austria. As far as I know, he had never been involved in politics or intrigues, unquestionably the favourite pastime of the Viennese. At all times of the day, the burghers of the city sat around in the coffee-houses to read newspapers and discuss the failure of this year's wine harvest, the football game between Italy and Hungary or how to bring back the monarchy. My father, an expert skier, was most interested in which team would represent our country in the forth-coming Olympics, to be held in the small German resort town of Garmisch. Of course, Austria was favoured for the gold medal.

For Christmas in 1935 my father gave me an electric train set. It came all wrapped up with a card that my aunt read to me. It said: 'To my son, a Merry Christmas and a Happy Birthday.' Because of my failure to cling to my mother's womb for a few additional days, I always received combined gifts. My father asked my aunt (a real aunt) to take me for a walk. I put on snowboots with metal clasps, she wrapped me in scarves and hat and gloves, and we strolled along in the crisp snow. I tried the ice slide other kids had made in the middle of the street, and promptly fell, ripping my trousers and hurting my elbows. My aunt picked up the screaming five-year-old bundle and we continued our stroll through the festive, decorated streets of the Habsburg capital. We passed a Christmas market, with marzipan and toffee-apples and magic sparklers. I ended up with a stick of candy-floss, which stuck to my face like frozen whiskers on a cat. Our walk ended in front of a magnificent building with many lights and a lot of people queuing, stamping their feet. My aunt told me to wait to one side and not to get lost. I stared at the photographs in the windows, and I was particularly impressed by a man in a Boy Scout hat, sitting on a horse.

Inside it was warm, much too warm for all my scarves and sweaters. We entered a large hall; one wall had a beautiful gold frame with lots of little angels stuck to it, and in the middle was a red velvet curtain. An organ was playing – that was nice. A lady pointed us to a row of chairs. My aunt unwrapped me and told me to sit on the pile of clothes, so that I could see better. I didn't know what I was supposed to see, but I looked in the same direction as everyone else, towards the front. Then the lights went out, not suddenly, like at home, but dimming slowly until the room was dark. Then music started and there where the red curtain had been, appeared a flickering picture of the man I had seen in the photograph, riding on a horse. All very strange. He still wore his oversized Boy Scout hat, and then he yodelled:

'*I'll be calling you, youhoohoo, youhoohooo.*' Then came this pretty blonde woman and they were smooching, and he sang: '*Oh Rosemarie I love yooooo.*' By this time, a woman with a spray was walking up and down the centre aisle, to spray smelly stuff all over us. Memories are funny – I cannot recall the film clearly, but certainly remember the smell.

What an exciting day it had been. Now I wanted to get home and play with my new train. In our living-room I found a collection of uncles crawling around on the carpet. Under the supervision of my father, who was sporting an Imperial Austrian Railways station-master's cap and blowing a whistle, they were busy changing loco-motives to catch up on the schedule of a delayed Orient Express. The dining car had just left Innsbruck, as the freight train from Linz made its entry into Vienna's West Bahnhof, and fell off the track, because Uncle Leopold had forgotten to change the signal. The locomotive ended under the piano. I was given hot chocolate and bundled off to bed. I did finally play with my electric train, but not until after Christmas.

In this long gone time, now generally referred to as 'The Years of the Great Depression', my father played tennis and proudly presented his offspring to a never-ending stream of instant 'aunts'. I never realized how many aunts I had. Without exception they came from far off places and didn't speak Viennese. They had one thing in common: they were wealthy, brought me presents, and took my father on trips. I got postcards from Monte Carlo and Venice and Paris. In 1936 he went to Berlin to watch the Olympic Games. He didn't like what he saw and came back in a dark mood. 'There were too many flags' was all he would say.

I was only five when I started school. My father knew the principal of the local school. 'Son, it's time to learn, let's go.' He took me by my tiny hand, and we walked into the office of the school director, who jumped up from behind his pencils, and saluted my father:

'Selbstverständlich, of course we'll take him.' I had to pass an exam, which was much too basic for a growing genius like me. I had to point out red and blue and green and put a puzzle together. In those days such a test was a daring novelty. The first day in class was frightening and I tried to fade from sight by disappearing in the last row, next to my wicker basket with an apple and a knockwurst sandwich.

'Durschmied, I want you to sit in front.' My teacher's voice terrified me, I kept my eyes on the floor as I moved to centre stage. All the other children were staring at me. I had been singled out for special attention, and that was bad. Also I was the youngest and as usual I was beaten up by my elders. During lunch break when we played marbles, some boys cheated and took my loveliest pieces, clear glass balls with colourful veins. I quickly learned to fight for myself as best I could and discovered ways of revenge. I poured ink on the benches of my persecutors. When they returned home with inkstained trousers, they in turn received a thrashing from their parents. Whenever the class went on a school picnic, and the teacher counted heads, there was invariably one missing – me. He would find me sitting under a tree, staring into the sky, searching for eagles. I had disappeared into a dreamland which I built around me, and had never heard his whistle.

The day before I was to leave for the summer holidays, I fell into the Danube and was rescued by a passer-by. It was no great feat of heroism on his part, he only reached down from the shore and pulled me out, wet and frightened. He turned out to be one of the army of unemployed who had taken up permanent residence under a bridge. I was scared and didn't dare tell my father. The Samaritan solved my dilemma when he rang our door bell to demand his reward. My father gave him some money. In the meantime I had escaped on vacation.

My parents' arrangement was that my father kept me throughout the school year, and mother had to suffer me during the summer. She took me to the Tyrol. There I played with a number of big cows, and the boys who looked after them. The husky country boys took great pleasure in proving their superior intelligence by beating up the scrawny kid from the city. It was during this summer that I discovered a pair of eagles. Every day, I climbed the high slopes to watch them at play. To be near them became an important ritual to me. On rainy days, I climbed up to sit in a hayshed, and wait for their performance. Afterwards I slid down the steep slopes on the seat of my pants. Thus I spent the summer, with muddy trousers, and bruises, and also dreading my reception on returning home.

My father was gentle about the Danube incident. He gave me a lecture about the fact that I had hidden the accident from him: 'Remember, it is better to face responsibility and to tell the truth, than to try and hide it. This will save you lots of worries, because in the end everything comes out.'

On my sixth birthday, my father gave me a pair of skis. These were made of ash with leather bindings. After the first careful paces in the Vienna woods my father took me into the high mountains, where one of our friends owned a ski lodge. It was a large wooden mountain hut, and we were about twenty people, all grown-ups except for me. Our friend had been a member of the Austrian alpine team: he was an excellent instructor, and he took me under his wing. Each morning we would climb a different mountain. To help us climb, we attached strips of sealskin to the skis. Once on top, we took off the skins, and then sat down with a sandwich and hot tea from a Thermos. It was marvellous, up there in the 'great white', looking at the magnificent Alps, discovering a new world. To me, this was poetry and religion.

Then we set off downhill. Skiing was a thrill, and I quickly proved a natural talent. I easily picked up the principle of Christiania turns and before long I was actually faster than the grown-ups. In the evenings I crawled into bed, my father lit a fire in the grate, and before the first flames had a chance to warm the room, I was asleep.

I was in my second year at school when an event occurred which had consequences far beyond the borders of Austria. On 13 March 1938, our teacher ordered the whole class to the Ringstrasse to hail the new saviour of Austria, a man called Hitler. He was expected to make his triumphal entry into Vienna that very day. I did not consider our outing important enough to inform my father about it – a mistake I was to regret for many years.

Dressed in lederhosen or dirndls, our class piled into the tram, and off we went. When we got there, we were confronted by masses of people lining the street, all talking excitedly. An army of policemen waved their arms to direct the eager newcomers to their appointed areas. Built on the foundations of the old city walls, the Ringstrasse was the circular parade road of imperial Vienna, a wide avenue lined by chestnut trees. It had witnessed generations of Austrian emperors parading on their white chargers. Many songs had been written glorifying the beauty of springtime in Vienna. Pink candles of chestnut blossoms were shooting up on the trees. The mood was one of festive expectation.

We had been directed to a spot near the Hotel Imperial and installed in front of the excited grown-ups, when along came a group of older boys wearing brown shirts, black neckerchiefs and red armbands with a black cross in a white circle. They looked nice. What caught my attention were their small swords. They handed each of us a red flag with the same black cross in a white circle, and told us to wave and cheer. I knew it wasn't an Austrian flag, since I had seen a lot of these in Vienna's stadium during a football game to which my father had taken me. The Austrian flag was red, white and red and had an eagle in its centre. I was quite certain of that. Here I was, in my lederhosen, waiting with all the other seven-year-olds. It was a long wait and I was getting tired, and then I wanted to pee, but we weren't allowed to leave. I listened to the grown-ups behind me.

'It can't be any worse than what we've got now.'

'At least he's going to clean up the mess.'

'I'm glad he's finally coming.'

'I wonder what he looks like, the Führer of all Germany.'

Along came a black car with a movie camera. It came to a halt right in front of us. There were four men on a platform, one directed the camera towards us, and the other three told us to shout with joy, and wave our flags. We did a lot of screaming. We were to be featured as part of the unstaged 'joyous reception by the whole Austrian nation of the German Führer.' That day was my first close encounter with a movie camera, which may be why I remember it in such great detail.

An hour later a cavalcade of motorcycles raced down the Ringstrasse. I could hear rumbling, a growing thunder carried by a wave of voices, screaming 'Heil! Heil!' The crescendo reached us and with it a monster of a car with six wheels, and a man in a brown shirt standing in it, looking proud and stiff, his right arm stretched out in salute. He wasn't very tall and had a black moustache. The crowd roared. We went wild, screamed 'Heil!' and waved our flags. That was the first and only time I came close to Hitler.

When I returned home, my father was waiting for me in our salon. He had been listening to the events over the radio and a worried look crossed his face. 'Where have you been?' he asked sternly.

'I went to see our Führer.'

'He isn't our Führer.'

'But they all say so.'

He stared at me, so very sad. I shall never forget his words that day: 'Son, people are blind, they like to believe in miracles. There are no miracles. All this is going to end so terribly for us Austrians.' He was trying to convince his son, the only person he really loved. Of course, I didn't believe him.

That evening my father made me listen to a radio broadcast by Chancellor Schuschnigg, who ended his speech with the words: '*Rot-Weiss-Rot, bis in den Tod* ... Red, white and red until death.'

My father switched off the set. He turned to me and looked me straight in the eye. 'My son, always remember the twelfth of March 1938, the day when Austria died.' I still didn't realize what the flag

that I had so vigorously waved that afternoon really represented. In
time I was to find out.

That night, Frau Blumiger, an old Jewish lady who had always plied
us kids with sticky candy, took sleeping pills and died. Next morning
men in black uniforms came and took away Herr Stern, who owned
the shop where we bought our pencils and schoolbooks. They put him
into a car and I never saw him again. In the afternoon, the same men
came back and threw all Herr Stern's books out into the street. I ran
down and picked up some coloured pencils, which they gave away.
Then they put up a large flag like the one I had seen on the
Ringstrasse, and with white paint wrote on the window: *NSDAP
Blockleitung*. A schoolfriend told me that this was now the local
headquarters of the National Socialist party of Adolf Hitler. The day
after these events, we had to assemble in the courtyard of our school. A
new man, one I had never seen before climbed on a chair:

'*Jungmannen, Heil Hitler*! You have finally returned into *Grossdeutsch-
land*, the Great German Reich. You are no longer Austrians, you are
now Germans. This is a great honour, and we must all be proud. You
will all join the Hitler Youth, and serve our Führer, Adolf Hitler, *Sieg
Heil*!'

We screamed *Sieg Heil* several times. A lot of my classmates had
tears in their eyes, that's how stirred they were to be German. Two
boys in our school, both Jewish, had not shown up for class. They
never returned to school.

After the excitement of March '38, Vienna once more turned to its
sleepy state. We no longer started off the school day with the Lord's
Prayer, but with a poem about being 'a German boy who loves and
obeys his Führer.' For us, the deity had changed names. We had to
address our teacher with 'Heil Hitler!' instead of the Austrian '*Grüss
Gott*!' Our priest, the one who had been giving us religious lessons,
wasn't there any longer; we now had a man in a black suit, black tie,
with a red party pin in his lapel. He taught us all about a great German
hero, Horst Wessel, who had been assassinated by the Jewish-
Communist conspiracy. We were given a paper which our parents had
to fill in. It was the '*Arierausweiss*', a proof that we were all pure-
blooded Aryans from way back, and not subhuman rats called Jews.

In order to keep me in school, my father had to buy me the Hitler Youth uniform and I had to go on hikes with the rest of the gang. We had a small triangular flag, a *wimpel*, and we marched behind it through the streets, singing with utter conviction:

'*Denn heute gehört uns Deutschland* … Today Germany is ours, and tomorrow the whole world will belong to us.'

It was an exciting time. We were taught to be tough German boys, we were told that Germany was the centre of the universe, and our newly-issued history books clearly provided us with proof that this was true. We were shown that the real border between Germany and our neighbour to the north, Czechoslovakia, was not at all where we had previously been told it was. Finally, German troops crossed into the country to free the Germanic tribe of the Sudeten. When that liberation had been achieved we had to march in a victory parade on the Ringstrasse. If the song about *Deutschland* was to be believed, a new portion of the world now belonged to us, and part of Czechoslovakia became the Sudetengau.

A month later our teacher showed us films of massacres the Poles were perpetrating on defenceless Teutonic families in areas which, according to our new school maps, rightfully belonged to the German Reich, but had been illegally annexed by Poland. It was our sacred duty to help to free these ill-treated Germans from the Slavic yoke. He then asked all those who agreed to raise their hands; we all did, and agreed that it was Germany's sacred duty to liberate the poor families.

It was during this time that my father brought home a lot of travel literature. I loved looking at the pictures. There was a statue of a big woman with a star-shaped crown and a torch in her raised hand, it was called the *Freiheits Statue*. Some photographs showed buildings so tall that I couldn't imagine how they could stand up. We had nothing like that in Vienna. My father called me into his study. 'How would you like to go to America?'

For me America was Cowboys and Indians and little else. 'Will I get a horse when we get there?'

'Not in the city. I have written to Aunt Susan, she has a big house in Connecticut, and I have asked her if we could come and visit her.'

'For how long?'

'Perhaps for a very long time … ' We never received an answer from the good aunt, whom I vaguely remembered as one of the many nicely-dressed ladies I had been presented to during the summers gone by. She had been a very nice aunt, she had taken me to the Prater and let me ride on the Ferris wheel. Then my father had left on a long trip with her. When he returned to Vienna he was alone.

Perhaps my father was too Austrian to leave his country, or he hedged his bets too long, and then it was too late. On a day towards the end of our summer holidays, 1 September 1939, my father arrived at our alpine lodge to announce that Germany had declared war.

'*Krieg? Vater, was ist Krieg?*' What is war to an eight-year-old boy?

'War is something where a lot of people die.'

'But the Germans will defeat the world and win great victories.'

'I am not sure that the price is right.' He must be wrong. The teacher had told us that Germany was invincible, and that its might would conquer the world. I was in for another shock. I found my mother worried, and my father in uniform. He was caught in the dilemma of an officer who had sworn his loyalty to the Habsburg empire and the Austrian army. Austria was now called the *Ostmark* and the Austrian army had become the *Deutsche Wehrmacht*.

'I have pledged my allegiance to the Austrian Kaiser, not to this contemptible little corporal.' This was a rash statement, especially in front of a snotty kid, who by now had been utterly convinced that *unser Führer*, Adolf Hitler, would deliver Germany from the Jewish-Communist enslavement, whatever that was. Furthermore, my Gruppenführer in the Hitler Youth had issued strict orders that anyone who blasphemed against the Reich, or the Führer, had to be denounced. The sheer monstrosity of this command, the thought that it is possible to corrupt the mind of a child to the point where he will sacrifice his own father on the altar of an idol, is horrible beyond description.

This was the most shameful period of my life. I was a child, influenced by evil, shown falsehood and taught to hate. I dread the thought of what other parents in countries with totalitarian regimes have gone through, faced with similar circumstances. I know from too many examples, some of which ended terribly, that I was no exception to the rule. The warped mind of a child can conjure up damage beyond description. My father was saved from such disgrace when he was ordered to command a fighter unit, won victories, and sent his son a few postcards. That's what changed my mind: after all, I could hardly denounce a hero.

In class we were shown pictures of great battles and heroes who had helped to achieve victories. We were given photographs of tanks and planes and burning cities, which we collected and glued into our notebooks. 'I'll swap you a Colonel Moelders for a General Guderian.' It was the time of a seemingly unstoppable drive to crush the enemies of the Third Reich, and German columns spearheaded deep into enemy territory. Every time we heard the tune of Liszt's *Les Préludes* we knew that it would be followed by the customary victory bulletin issued by the German High Command:

Das Oberkommando der Wehrmacht gibt bekannt:

Heute um 10 Uhr morgens haben deutsche Truppen die Stadt Amsterdam erobert ... The victory message was followed by a radio address from the man himself, Adolf Hitler, which started: '*In dieser historischen Stunde* ... In this historic hour of the German Reich ... ' It brought tears to our eyes and our chests burst with pride to be part of this monumental event in history. On it went, the victorious merry-go-round. Poland had succumbed in two weeks, the German armies were pushing towards Paris, London was crumbling under a hail of bombs. The newspapers were full of glad tidings about the iron will of the Führer, and the supremacy of the whole German nation. There was only one leader, the military genius Adolf Hitler: he would take us on to the Great Final Victory. The rest of the world was overcrowded by the lower species who would have to be subservient to Germany so that it could achieve global greatness. These were heady times for a ten-year-old.

A man in the black uniform of the SS walked into our classroom, accompanied by the director of the school. We jumped to attention. '*Heil Hitler!*'

In chorus we answered: *Heil Hitler!*

'One of you has been chosen to enter the German officer school. This is a great honour for our whole *Gymnasium*. Durschmied, step forward.' I couldn't believe it! Me! What a great honour. And yet I was not big and tough, I was small and forever scared, certainly not the steel from which future heroes would be forged. I basked in the limelight for two days, and then they took me away and stuck me into the most famous of Austrian military academies, the Theresianum. There I was given tests, which I passed with flying colours. Had I only known what was in store ...

On 22 June 1941, Hitler ordered 220 German divisions to invade Russia, pushing reason – and Germany – over the brink, and altering the global balance forever. The day the culling of nations started was no different for the ten-year-old Hitlerjunge Erik, still convinced of the invincibility of the German master race. Since my father's division had been moved from Norway I had had no news from him. Life at the military academy was hard, unreasonably so. We were being groomed to be the future elite of the Thousand Year Reich. Nobody explained to us why this meant we had to get up before dawn, fold the blankets to a precise size and make the beds, wash with cold water and stumble into the courtyard every morning at six for exercises.

Between the dawn jog and the sunrise breakfast, we were allowed five minutes to visit the loo. As there were more boys than holes, the allocation per hole was thirty seconds. Even on the crapper, our time was rationed. We spent so much time doing physical push-ups that we were constantly hungry. The food was monotonous – boiled potatoes, dried fish or brown sauce on a slice of bread. Punishment for the slightest offence was swift and harsh. We had daily inspections for clean fingernails and clean socks and clean rooms. That normally happened at three in the morning. Woe to the room that was not perfect, for the boys would be deprived of weekend leave and school felt like a prison.

During my first year in school I made my first bad strategic appraisal when I should have seen the need for a diplomatic compromise. We were on a ski exercise on the Zugspitz mountain when my class was challenged by a cadet school from Saxony to decide the superiority between the skiers from 'Prussia' and the Ostmärkler with a race. Austrians were always considered inferior in physical achievements, especially on the battlefield or in a sports stadium. The test was to be a parallel slalom. Each school had to provide five skiers. I was picked as the last runner. Two tracks were laid out next to each other, and the winning school was to be established by process of elimination. While waiting for the start I stood next to one of the Germans, blond crew-cut and obnoxious. '*Bruder Schnürschuh*,' he said to me, definitely the wrong thing to say, since this referred to the laced shoe of the Austrian army, considered a joke by German generals, who preferred the uncomfortable jackboot, 'we are going to pick your feathers.'

'Ski, and talk afterwards, Prussian jackass,' was my swift, and furious reply. The boy went red and went to see his leader. I was called to appear before my captain.

'*Jungmann* Durschmied, you will never again talk in this manner to the son of the Gauleiter of Saxony. Furthermore, make sure he wins.' The second wrong thing to say. The race started. The first Austrian won, the second lost. After four skiers the score was tied at two all. The decision was now up to the two of us, Gauleiter Junior versus me. The son of a bitch jumped the gun. Before the flag had dropped, he was already into the first gate. I raced after the Gauleiter's boy, and just before the finish line I passed him. Victory! The laced-shoe brothers had proved their superiority over the master race.

It was not to be. I was disqualified for having started before the flag came down. But what was worse, I was publicly disgraced because I had disobeyed the order of my captain. That was my first ski race, perhaps the most important in my life, and it taught me a lesson. Punishment followed, and our team was ordered to climb a steep slope three times following the race. Forced on by my fury over the blatant injustice, I collapsed with exhaustion and high fever. They rushed me to a hospital where I remained for ten days. During my first night's delirium I started to babble about SS dragons and my father's conviction that Nazis were evil men, bent on the death of Austria. The person who saved my family from arrest was the doctor who looked after me. He was a Viennese, who happened to belong to my father's tennis club. When he found out about my raving, he had me transferred into an isolation ward. There, one of the few remaining religious sisters kept vigil, efficient, and – silent. When my condition improved, and I could sit up in bed, the doctor paid me a visit. '*Guten Morgen*, Erik, how do you feel?'

'*Danke*, Herr Doktor, much better.'

'How is your father?'

'I don't know. I haven't heard from him in two months.'

'You gave us reason for concern, you've had some bad dreams.'

This struck like lightning – one slip of my feverish tongue, one wrong phrase overheard …

'Did I say anything?' Vaguely I recalled my dreams, my teachers, all Party members, dragons pushing me into an underground ocean; a devil with a black moustache riding around in a big car, raising his fiery hand in salute and screaming orders to drown me. And my father, in the role of a sports announcer, provided a running commentary at a football game, which pitched Germans against Russians, calling out the attack, and the defeat of our team. I wanted to go home.

'What did I say? Did I talk about my father?' I was terrified.

'No, no. Don't worry, everything's fine. We all have our dragons. Just take a few days' rest and everything will get back to normal.'

Normal, what is normal? What is he trying to tell me? Am I not normal? 'Herr Doktor … '

He interrupted, 'Call me Uncle Kurt. I have known your father for a very long time … ' his voice trailed off.

'Where did you meet my father?'

'We were in the same *Gebirgsjäger* unit in the last war, in Südtirol. He was a great officer.' I realized how little I knew about my father. I had never enquired, and he had never volunteered information about 'his' war.

'Please, tell me about the last war. I know so little about my father … '

'Why, don't you know?' exclaimed 'Uncle Kurt', quite astounded. Then he pulled up a chair. 'Well, there is a story which made him quite famous in the Austrian army. Your father seldom did things by the book, he let himself be guided by common sense. His main objective was always to save lives, especially those under his command. It was during the winter of '16, or '17, I can't remember. We were in trenches in the Dolomites, on sheer cliffs no one could climb. The Italians didn't manage to push into Austria, and we didn't even try to push the other way. This stalemate lasted for two years. In the centre of our front line was a bulge, a hill held by Italians. They shot down and we shot up. Since they were on top, they got the better of it. Our commanders tried to blow up the hill. Most of the mountain came down, but not the part with the Italians on it, and they continued to shoot down at us.

'That's when your father came up with an idea. He captured an

Italian *Gulaschkanone*, a field kitchen complete with cook, food carriers, and mules. An hour later, he and a troop of twenty Austrian mountain troops, dressed in the liberated uniforms, were on their way up the mountain. Since these were boys from the South Tyrol, they were fluent in Italian. Once they got into the Italian lines at the top, the Tiroleans served the Italians their rations, and while they were busy with their pasta, simply took them prisoner. Unfortunately, one of the Italian lookouts was missed, and he got off a shot which hit your father in the thigh. That's how I first met him. I patched him up enough for him to be able to hobble to Innsbruck to receive his medal from the *Erzprinz*. Your father is the only Austrian who has ever won a battle with goulash artillery, and he became known as the *Gulaschoberst*.' My father had kept his exploits with his catering-equipment version of the wooden horse of Troy a military secret from his son.

'When you see your father, give him my respects. Tell him I very much look forward to beating him on a tennis court,' he sighed, 'when all this is over … ' Three weeks later the doctor was sent to the Eastern front. My secret, that Hitler's dragons had haunted me in my nightmare, died with him in the snows of Kursk.

'All this' was far from being over – the war continued and the winters were getting colder. It was 1942, the year of the battle for Stalingrad. We were still bombarded with positive radio messages telling how the heroic German forces would hold out and defeat the attacking Mongol hordes, because such was the Führer's will. But the statements started to lack the conviction our teachers had displayed a few years before. One winter's day, my father returned on leave. It was a wonderful surprise to see him after such a long time, but I was shocked by how he had aged. He had added a few more medals to his collection. When he visited me in school, the director, a nodding, saluting colonel, took him through all the classrooms. Whenever my father asked one of his rare questions, the colonel would click his heels. That day I was very proud to be my father's son. I received permission to stay at home during the four days he could spend with me. In civilian clothes we walked up the Kahlenberg. A beautiful vista of imperial Vienna.

'Look at it, look at it well, my son, soon this will change.'

'How will it change?'

'The Allied bombers will come, Vienna will burn.'

'What about our fighter planes?'

'We haven't got enough, we have no spare parts to keep them flying, we have no more petrol, and, worst of all, we have no more pilots. Yes, the *Kriegsindustrie* continues some production in underground hiding places, but all we get are replacement planes, with crews that wouldn't have been allowed to drive a tractor on my land. Fools, why don't they stop it! *Mein armes Wien* … ' He cast his glance over his beloved city, as if to say goodbye. Then he put his arm around me and took me to the little chapel. Inside were drawings and battle plans of the great siege of Vienna by the Turks in 1683. 'Perhaps one of our ancestors stood on this very spot, looking down on his city. It happened on a Sunday. First they prayed, then they stormed down from here into the camp of the Great Turk. The battle lasted from mid-morning until nightfall, and Vienna was delivered from the Turkish host. This time, our city cannot hope for a miracle.'

We had no more wood. It was strange to see the fireplace of my childhood black and cold. We were sitting in our salon in heavy sweaters. It was the last evening of my father's leave. Everything appeared so unfriendly, even the photographs of my grandparents on the great oak desk were different – they were no longer smiling. The heavy velvet curtains were drawn across the windows, which had been painted black to conform to the black-out orders now strictly enforced by the people's air raid patrols roaming the streets. My father startled me by saying, 'Germany has lost the war.'

'But our teachers tell us we are victorious.'

'All make-believe. It has been one big lie right from the beginning. Once the Russian campaign got under way, we never had a chance. If this man had only asked for peace when there was a chance! When France had collapsed and England was down to its last plane. It was then he went mad, a megalomaniac who wouldn't listen to the experts. He thought that with his corporal's genius he could win all by himself. He is blind, and now he will kill us all.' I was stunned. Never before had my father been so direct and vehement. 'I buried my best troops in Narvik and outside Odessa. I get paper replacements, or men who haven't held a gun since the battle of Waterloo. And orders, stupid orders: hold this and stop that. Stop how? Three hundred Soviet T34s! And I have twelve Tigers with seventeen-year-old drivers and sixty-year-old gunners.'

He told me that the regular staff officers in the front-line units didn't believe in Hitler any longer, and that a number of highly competent army generals had been replaced by political commissars who had no idea what a fighting force was all about, nor how to conduct a battle.

'The army is losing, and the Party is winning. The sooner that maniac dies, or the Americans get into Europe and stop it, the better for all of us.' My initial shock was terrible, and I stared at my father, unbelieving and frightened. Granted, the Americans had joined the war, but they were nowhere near Europe. Our military instructor had shown us pictures of their navy's annihilation by our allies, the Japanese. In any case, they were no danger to the German army; our military instructors had assured us that they were terrible soldiers. Day after day, it had been drilled into us to believe completely in the invincibility of fascism, and yet ... I knew that my father would never lie to me. What was he really trying to tell me? Finally, he said it. 'Whatever happens to me, I want your promise that under no circumstances will you ever join the German army and fight. You are the last of our family, I love you more than anything on this earth. I want you to stay alive. When the time comes you will know what to do, but don't sacrifice your life for a lost cause.'

I was shattered. All my training in the academy had been focused on the one aim of becoming a German officer. And now this. I loved my father, and I could feel that he was extracting my solemn promise to preserve the life of his only son. When I had refused to believe the words of my own father, it was during the early days of the *Anschluss*. Recently, I had begun to ponder the morality of a German victory, and what it would do to my country. During a visit to the city, I had stumbled on an illegal flysheet bearing a jingle:

Wenn wir den Krieg gewonnen hätten ... dann wäre Deutschland nicht zu retten ... Had we won the war, Germany couldn't be saved and would resemble a madhouse.

Common sense questioned indoctrination. It didn't take much to recognize that the iron will of the German nation and its leaders was coming apart. The once invincible German armies had suffered a great defeat at El Alamein. The Afrika Corps was no more. In the snows of Stalingrad the Sixth Army of Field Marshal Paulus had been annihilated. Bombing raids were hitting German cities, and Marshal Goering's famous promise that no Allied plane would ever penetrate

German airspace was proved false every day. Hamburg, Cologne and Bremen had gone up in flames. Our food rations were getting smaller, and our homes colder. The U-boats were still mauling convoys on the Western Approaches, but all was not well on the high seas. My room-mate, son of a highly decorated submarine captain, had been called into the director's office to be told that his father had died a hero's death for *Führer und Reich*.

For the first time in my life I had serious doubts about the future. I must admit, it didn't come as a sudden flash from one day to the next: it dawned on me quite slowly. My father had pointed the way. The rest I discovered for myself. It took me months. I needed to be certain. Gradually I turned into the most anti-military person in my class. I hated school and, even more destructively, I hated the people who had been feeding me with untruths, my teachers. Never lie to a child; my pride in being German, in having been chosen as one of the future elite, turned into despair. I wrote a long letter to my father, explaining, and asking for his forgiveness. Fortunately I never sent the note, since my teachers would have intercepted it, and my fate would have been sealed.

There was no one I could turn to. I directed all my thoughts to one object: survival. I simply had to get away from that school. Following the invasion of Normandy, the political climate changed. The army commanders took second place to Party bosses, and my instructors took liberties they would have never dared before. I, the son of an army officer, became their favourite scapegoat. One of my instructors managed to put a stop to my home visits. He was a small-minded Austrian who tried to outdo the Germans. He was tall and peroxide blond, a self-proclaimed hero in Waffen-SS uniform. We nicknamed him Knopf and everyone loathed him. After a day's forced march in pouring rain, 'to toughen the future German elite', we arrived back in the Theresianum wet and tired. I slouched over my desk. Somebody slapped me. 'Durschmied, stand at attention when I talk to you!' Drugged by tiredness I tried to get up. '*Jawohl*, Herr Leutnant.'

'Look at your boots. You are a disgrace to this unit.' He woke all the others in my room. 'Just look at him, and this is supposed to be a German officer cadet.' My room-mates stood there, numb. 'Well, answer when you are spoken to.' He barked at them.

'*Jawohl*, Herr Leutnant. Jungmann Durschmied's boots are dirty.'

I feebly tried to put up a defence. 'Sir, we have just returned ... '

'Be quiet!' he screamed.

'*Jawohl*, Herr Leutnant.'

'This room will have latrine duties for a month.' This was the way he turned my room-mates against me. 'And for you, until further notice your weekend leaves are cancelled. Now you will stand out in the hallway, at attention.'

Tears came into my eyes. '*Jawohl*, Herr Leutnant.' I could see the great pleasure it gave him to see me suffer. He kept me standing there until nightfall. This was his personal vendetta, and the SS was achieving a cheap victory over the army at the expense of a child. He was a loudmouth, and when called up for front-line duty, he managed to disappear. Needless to say, his kind always survives.

If he could do it, so could I. I too learned how to survive. The first allied air raid unloaded hundreds of bombs on the baroque glory of the city. People were unprepared, and many lost their lives in these first attacks. A number of the bombs failed to explode. Dropped from high above the city, they impacted like old-fashioned cannonballs, penetrating but not igniting, and they stuck out of pavements and roads like obscenities from heaven. They had to be dismantled. An old sergeant, with medals and minus a leg, showed us how to defuse incendiary bombs.

'Be very careful, take your time, don't jerk when you unscrew the fuse. Just take your time.' He demonstrated how to take off the heavy metal base, and then pull out a flat fuse. The trick was not to get blown up. I was a quick learner. My aim was not to save some desperately needed war factory from burning to the ground, just to stay alive. Some of my comrades were not quite as selfish, or apt, and didn't make it to the end. I was scared, and that made me very careful. I probably hold the record for being the slowest bomb dismantler in Vienna.

Just after the school year ended, on that fateful 20 July 1944, a group of German officers made an attempt on Hitler's life. To a man, the class above ours was called up to die heroically for the Fatherland. We all knew that within a few months it would be our turn to join the slaughter. I was now fourteen, husky, well-trained in all martial arts. I knew how to put a detonator into a stick of dynamite and had been taught how to shoot to kill. I was just the right stuff for the new forces of the Waffen-SS. It was high time to think of a strategic withdrawal. Somehow my mother produced a health certificate which proved to the head of the cadet academy that I had contracted a highly contagious disease, and had to be confined for a long treatment. In September, when classes resumed, and all my *Jungmannen* colleagues returned with their cardboard suitcases, I stayed at home. It was a good arrangement all round: the school rid itself of the spectre of an infectious disease, and I obtained my freedom. It may come as no great surprise to the reader that my illness was cured by the second week of September, but I refrained from informing the school of my miraculous recovery.

Daily bombing raids became routine, and each morning we disappeared into the relative safety of our *Luftschutzkeller*, a dingy place, where the coal of centuries had covered the walls with black soot. Every day we emerged with hands and hair to match the cellar walls. During the attacks the electricity was cut off, which made our gloom gloomier. We sat in darkness, waiting for the unthinkable to happen. Our makeshift shelter harboured a collection of scared women. One was a girl of about twenty, who was married to a soldier at the front. She had not seen her husband for over two years. One day, when the hail of bombs was so close that bricks came down from the ceiling, and everyone expected this to be their final moment, she grabbed my hand and pulled me into the next cubicle. There she pulled down my trousers and put me on a coal heap. Then she pulled up her skirt, threw herself on top, impaled herself and raped me. Her moans, which turned into screams, were muted by explosions and the crumbling of houses, a bizarre love sound I shall never forget. In anticipation of our inevitable end, when that one bomb destined for us would hurtle through wafer-thin ceilings and blow us all to hell, we continued to copulate on our coal pile for weeks. It was that simple, and life didn't amount to much during the fading days of the Thousand Year Reich.

It was 15 January 1945, a beautiful midwinter's morning, exceptionally warm for that time of the year. At ten o'clock in the morning we heard the by now familiar announcement over the radio: '*Large enemy bomber formations from the south in direction of Vienna.*'

My grandmother had just started the washing up when the sirens blared: '*Grossmutter, Fliegeralarm!*' I pointed to the heavens. My grandmother was almost deaf and we had developed our private sign language; she was more fortunate than most in that she had been spared the terror – she simply didn't hear the bombers come.

'Go ahead, I'll finish the dishes,' she said, and sent me off into the basement. There was a whine, a rolling, the earth shook, I was lifted off my feet and smashed against the wall. Then the house came down on me. I don't recall what happened next, until I saw a ghost staggering towards me, covered in white as if dumped in a barrel of flour, with a red slash across the forehead. It was my grandmother: somehow she had survived.

'Erik – Erik! *Alles ist hin!* Everything's gone!' Our house was reduced to rubble and a few splintered beams, which, like broken fingers, pointed accusingly to the sky. My grandmother stared at what had been her home for seventy-five years. She had been born there and she had been married there. In this house she had given birth to my mother, had nursed her, and had given refuge to her grandson in a bed that was now buried beneath bricks and broken memories. The bomb had gone off in the cellar next door. Most of the women were killed instantly, including the one who had initiated me into love.

If ever there was any one precise moment when I started to hate wars, this was it. This was the first time I felt a total rejection of the sacrifice of human life for an ideal, be its guiding principles economic or religious, or worse still, a *Weltanschauung*. A heresy called *The Thousand Year Reich ruled by the Master Race*! A mere four years had sufficed to destroy everything my people had built in the last thousand. Vienna the beautiful was rapidly on its way to becoming Vienna the obscene. We were bombed, we were scared, we were cold and we were hungry.

Near the Opera lived an old aunt, who had a precious hoard of potatoes in her basement, soft and rotten, some with roots and some with white nightflowers, but food. I decided to see the old lady and to make her part with some of her treasure. Before I reached her house the first bombs had begun to fall. Until now the centre of the city had been spared, and the historic section was relatively unscathed. The crumps of exploding bombs were still far off, but then I could hear the whine of approaching plane engines. The nearest public bomb shelter was in an office block known as the Phillipshof. Beneath its solid structure were the city's ancient catacombs, which provided refuge for the inhabitants of the central area. I ran towards it, and just as I reached the Mozart monument, directly opposite the entrance into the shelter, I was hit by an appalling blast of sound and light, then dust. Three explosions shattered the Albertina, with its invaluable Dürer etchings, and the Phillipshof collapsed like a house of cards.

The blast must have thrown me into the protective shadow of the monument, because the first thing I noticed when I regained my senses was the silhouette of the bronze Mozart leaning over me. Everything else was covered in a choking cloud of pulverized brick. Like the waves of the ocean crashing ashore came the sound of glass cascading from shattered windows all across town. Then I heard the first scream, a quite inhuman sound. An old man wearing a shiny fireman's helmet came stumbling towards me. He was covered in red, and blood gushed from the stump of an arm. He stared into emptiness and mumbled: '*Tot ... alle tot ... ach Gott ... so viel Blut ...* ' He collapsed and was quiet. A woman, whose blouse had been torn off by the blast, and whose torso was blackened by the explosion, ran past with a high-pitched wail.

'*Hilfe! Hilfe!*' screamed people from beyond the curtain of dust. '*Der Phillipshof ... mein Gott ...* they're all dead ... '

At the time of the attack, an estimated eight hundred people had crowded into the cellars. One or more bombs with delayed action fuses had smashed through five storeys of masonry to penetrate the shelter overflowing with people. There they exploded. A water main had burst and was gushing down the exits into the cellar. The few that had escaped the blast were drowned. In the street a truck had been set on fire and oily black diesel smoke obscured the carnage. I looked at Mozart and noticed that he was full of holes, and that some of his stone cupids were gone.

The following days I passed in a state of shock. Finally came the dreaded message: I was called up to defend the Fatherland. At fourteen. The Russians were knocking on the doors of Vienna, and my sacrifice would not have made the slightest difference to the final outcome. My father had been right – Hitler, the man so many had cheered as saviour an eternity ago, had brought only misery, famine and death. The Apocalypse was upon us. For me, it was too late to admit this to my father, and to ask for his forgiveness. He was buried in a cold field somewhere, with a branch stuck in the soft mound, and a helmet on it. Not even a name.

Months earlier I had decided to follow my father's last wish, to take my chance and run rather than fight and die for what I now knew to be the Great Lie. From beneath the rubble my grandmother unearthed the little sailor suit I had worn to Holy Communion during happier days. It didn't make me look eight, but it did change my age, and it needed to. That night I set off on my escape from the devastated city. It was a trip through an inferno. Streets where I had played as a child had simply ceased to exist and were now unrecognizable heaps of rubble. In the park where I had kicked a football, I found a mangled tram among shredded trees which were punctuated with bomb craters. In the centre of what once had been a green, near the statue of the emperor, the one we had climbed on to ride the old man's bronze horse, I stumbled across graves. Above the freshly dug earth was a sign: 'It is forbidden to bury bodies in the park. By order: the city council.'

Fires danced ghostly shadows on the walls of ruins. And then I discovered the bodies, dangling from lamp posts, executed in a last-minute frenzy to stem the inevitable. I stumbled on blindly to get away from the horror, through a night alive with strange sounds, until I came upon one last shadow, slowly turning on a rope. He was lit up by a fire, his bloated face a horrible mask whenever it turned into the light. I was shaking, I wanted to scream and yet I couldn't utter a sound. His neck was twisted, his uniform soiled and around his neck was a piece of cardboard which read: '*I have betrayed Führer and Fatherland.*'

This was *Götterdämmerung* and I was inextricably linked to its horrors. As I stumbled on I could feel dead eyes following me. Think! Think! If you get caught … No, that can't happen. Think! Calm down! Plan your escape! Follow the open main sewer, the Wienfluss, which leads from the city! Finally I came to a bridge which I had to cross. There was no way round it. A patrol was coming up behind me and I could see their silhouettes against the burning city. For me, there was no way back. In the moonlight I stared at the corpses swinging from the girders above, and noticed an SS detachment stopping all passers-by. A group of five prisoners in torn Wehrmacht uniforms was marched off by two SS guards with submachine guns. A few moments later, the rattle of gunfire, then silence. Would this be my end? The bridge might be my final destination – I too would get caught, and my life would be snuffed out at the end of a rope as *ein feiger Deserteur!* There was no way to describe my terror. The pale moon and my fright must have made me look much younger. I approached the bridge, slowly walking up to the four SS guards. My knees were shaking. They didn't even look at me. I went right on, past them.

2

A SURFEIT OF WOES

Our life was but a battle and a march
And like the wind's blast, never resting, homeless
We stormed across the war-convulsed heath

Friedrich von Schiller,
Wallensteins Tod, Act III

I have not spoken of love. I didn't really quite know what it was. I had
heard people talking about it, I saw it in the movies, I read about it in
Heidi and other children's books, but I hadn't exactly been overwhelmed by it myself. I was the child of a broken marriage. I had been
passed from 'aunt' to 'aunt' and, when the war came along, put into a
school which I loathed. When fellow-students received parcels from
home, I could only stare at them enviously, not because of what was in
them – home-made cake or hand-knitted socks – but because others
were given a kind of attention that I could only dream about. This is
the typical outcome when two people beget a child and then decide
they cannot get along with each other, and it is finally left to an
uninterested judge to decide who should have the baby.

My father won the prize. I saw my mother very seldom. I am
convinced that she tried to be close to me, but for some unexplained
reason she was unable to manage it. She was a gentle woman, with a
job somewhere in the city, and every Friday she would come to visit
me. For a whole week I looked forward to the moment when our
doorbell would ring. Then I would rush out. She would stand there
and take me into her arms. Sometimes she looked after me over the
weekend. We took long walks in the Vienna woods, and there she
introduced me to all the wonderful flowers in the meadows, and

invariably we would end up at the zoo. She warned me of the tiger's teeth and the lion's bite and showed me the big, gentle, elephant. I wanted to have a mother. Everybody else had one, why couldn't I?

'Why don't you live with us, Mutti?' I kept asking, and her answer was always the same, 'Because I can't.'

My father loved me in his way. He was old Austria, straight-backed and correct, an out-of-place remnant from bygone days. He had been groomed to be an officer in a Vienna that was bright and sparkling, a member of a class that waltzed in glittering uniforms, and went to their castles in Hungary to slaughter grouse with the local gentry. In the Great War he marched into battle under the crowned double-eagle. He survived the cannons and the machine guns, proud and undefeated. His dreams had died with a peace treaty he felt to be a betrayal. For four years he fought to prevent the Italians from taking the Tyrol, and then the territory was handed to Rome by a signature on a conference table in Saint-Germain. What awaited him on his return was a new Vienna with a new flag and new loyalties, torn between workers' uprising, financial depression, inflation, and the birth of a kind of nationalism he neither understood nor wanted to be part of. His class had no place in this new society, and though he made an attempt to keep up appearances, he lacked the financial resources to succeed.

Our house became a shunting yard for lady visitors from overseas. Home was like a busy railway station with a precise timetable, and my father was its station master waiting for the train which brought a new 'aunt'. Arrival was followed by the established ritual of introduction to the heir and only son. 'Oh, what a lovely boy. How are you?' they all said, with a smile. Most of them didn't care for me, and I could feel their rejection. They were threatened by my very existence – I was someone they had to compete with for my father's affection. However the routine was always observed, a day of gifts and visits to amusement parks, and then I was returned to my siding. 'Goodbye, take good care of yourself,' my father would say. Then the woman would take him away, and I was sad. When he returned, after a week, or a month, he was alone, and soon after another 'aunt' would arrive in the paternal home. My life was a never-ending series of dreaded train departures, and desperately awaited arrivals.

Following the *Anschluss* his oath of loyalty as an officer forced my father to serve what he referred to as 'the upstarts of a new Prussia', but his heart was no longer in the army. Although I must have made him suffer by my refusal to comprehend his rejection of the New Order, he never forced me to bend to his own beliefs. Perhaps he knew that I would find my way back to him.

The boy who escaped under the guns of the Waffen-SS was no longer the little child he looked. I had been forced to grow up to the realities of life quicker than most generations. I may have looked young, but I had already wrapped myself in a protective carapace and would let nothing and nobody penetrate it. My face displayed little emotion. In my few years of life I had witnessed destruction and death to an extent which is hard to describe. It not only taught me, but gave me the will, to survive. The nights I had lain in my bed, when sleep wouldn't come, and imagined a marvellous tomorrow, always gave way to a dawn of realities. If I wanted to escape the juggernaut, I could count only on myself. In such a quest, love had no place.

After I had crossed the bridge in Vienna I was still a long way from safety. I had to reach the distant Alps, across four hundred kilometres of danger. The war wouldn't last much longer. At that very moment the Allied armies were avalanching towards a broken Germany, crushing it under their combined might. Any day now the Russians would overrun Vienna. There was only a thin line of defenders, my schoolmates, frightened boys with bazookas to try to stop a thousand Soviet tanks. The population was terrified of the Russians. Stalin had repeatedly announced that he would do nothing to prevent his soldiery from taking their share of booty and women. My city, my lovely Vienna of blooming chestnut trees and the giant Ferris wheel, was doomed, along with its people.

The countryside I passed through was crawling with commando units, trying in vain to stem the tide of soldiers running away. Simply because of my age, fourteen, I might be suspected of 'desertion in the face of the enemy'. If caught it meant a bullet in the neck. My child's clothes would not protect me from an overzealous SS captain and his squad of executioners, because they could not hide my growing body.

To begin with, in the familiar surroundings of the Vienna woods, I dared to walk in daylight, as there were enough hiding places in case I needed to crawl into a hole. But once I came down into the flatlands of

Lower Austria the real danger began. I knew from my holiday train journeys that between Vienna and safety there was one major obstacle, the River Enns. It was wide and had only two bridges. Both would be well guarded. From now on I walked mostly at night. When dawn broke I hid in barns. For safety and warmth I dug into the hay and covered myself, and let my worries drop. In one barn I found dried corn; I crushed the kernels into a chewy paste. It was food. In another, near Pöchlarn, I was discovered by a farmer's wife. I woke up with a start, but she just smiled and took me into her farmhouse, where she gave me boiled potatoes and lard. I ate so greedily that I threw up. The emotions of the last days and my empty stomach had sapped my strength and I couldn't continue. I crawled back under my hay. During the day I watched two SS patrols pass near by, but fortunately they didn't approach my hideaway. It became obvious that I could not delay. That night I continued my march, and by next morning I had reached the river. I found a hole in a thicket of bulrushes from where I could study the bridge.

In cadet school it had been drilled into us that any military operation needed careful planning, and that eventually there was always a way to success. I noticed a roadblock and a tank across the bridge, its ugly gun pointing in my direction. This time I couldn't bluff my way across. Although I scoured the river bank, I couldn't find a boat. I had not learned to walk on water. Perseverance, six hours of constant observation, and I found the solution. It was actually quite simple: the children from a village on my side of the river had to cross the bridge on their way to school. For the trip, some twenty kids piled on to a horse-drawn hay wagon and a farmer's wife shuttled them back and forth. I had to take a chance. I followed the woman to her house, knocked, and told her my story. She put me up for the night and early next morning, when all the children gathered in the village square and she arrived with her wagon, I climbed on, disappearing among the schoolchildren. I did earn a few surprised glances, but the children probably thought I was a new pupil in class. We reached the bridge. To the SS guards we were routine, just the daily wagon load. The woman was waved through. I wish I could thank her, but I cannot. In the last days of the war, Allied bombers tried to cut the retreat of the remnants of the German army. They went for the bridge, and hit the village.

From the river onwards progress became easier – I was running away from the Russians and approaching the American front which was pushing in from the south. I passed thousands of refugees, a ragged miserable sea of bundles and crying babies, all headed for some great nowhere. On a rise in the road between Linz and Salzburg the vista of defeat became apparent. Until now, I had been hiding in a stream of refugees who were all coming down from Czechoslovakia and Bavaria, fleeing in panic before the advancing Soviet forces. When we reached the top of this hill we saw, about a kilometre away, another flow of refugees, heading straight for us. They were coming from Styria and Carinthia, fleeing from the Americans. When the two masses collided there was a mêlée of great confusion.

None of the other refugees seemed to be headed anywhere in particular, but I had a destination, a valley in the High Alps where I had spent my childhood holidays. There I could count on help and would find familiar mountain trails. I reached the valley in three days. Only once did I have a close call. It happened close to Hitler's mountain redoubt. Because the Nazi bosses had taken refuge in the *Alpenfestung*, the mountain range where the Third Reich was to make its final stand was heavily patrolled. A convoy of trucks full of Waffen-SS men drove down the road. Fifty yards from where I was hiding behind a pile of rocks the vehicles came to a halt. The soldiers jumped from their trucks and headed in my direction. It was too late to run. Luckily, they stopped and, guffawing, opened their flies and peed. After which they returned to their vehicles and the convoy moved off.

When I reached my destination, the farmhouse where I had spent many happy summers, the door opened and the woman took me into her arms and led me into the warm room. A wonderful surprise was in store for me. My grandmother. Somehow she had managed to board one of the last trains from Vienna. It was an emotional reunion, and I allowed myself a good cry. The strain of the past weeks gave way to numbness. The old women fussed over me, stuffing me with black bread and hot tea laced with honey, and listening to my adventures. 'How did you get here?' asked my grandmother, adding: 'I never had any doubts that you would slip through.' They put me to bed and I slept uninterrupted for forty-eight hours. When I woke it was dark outside and I could hear a rumbling on the nearby road which led across a mountain pass towards Italy.

'What's that?' I asked.

'It's like that every night: the Prussians are running away.' To farming people, everything non-imperial and non-Catholic was Prussian. Austrians were loved, Prussians were not. 'They come in here quite often for water, or whatever else they hope to scrounge. You must go up into the mountains.' The village had an alpage about three hours' climb from the valley. These animal shelters were made of the only material available at such altitudes – solid rock. During the winter months deep snow and avalanches cut off access to them, but that was no obstacle for an expert skier like myself, as long as I could get a pair of skis. 'There are skis in the barn, take them. And here is a pair of boots. You will also need a sweater and heavy socks.' The woman was marvellous. Her husband no longer needed the things: they had buried him somewhere in Russia. My grandmother packed a rucksack with provisions, and I walked out into the cold, crisp morning. I lacked the seal skins I needed to climb and kept sliding back. Then I remembered a simple solution my father had once shown me: I peed on the skis, and the frozen result gave me a good grip.

To go by the direct route would have involved the danger of crossing the highway. Up the valley was a bridge, and by sliding underneath its concrete span, I avoided the long stream of fleeing convoys and crossed safely. When I reached the shelter it was dark, and I almost missed it. Using a ski as a shovel, I dug away the snow and uncovered the entrance. Inside it was damp and cold. I found dry wood, kindled a flame, piled dried cow dung on it, and within minutes had a fire roaring. It stank, but it was warm.

Outside more snow fell, which forced me to stay inside, but also covered my tracks from the valley. The driving snow flurries made it possible to light a fire in the daytime without having to worry about the tell-tale smoke. Luckily there was a lot of dry dung. My hair and my sweater were proof of that: I stank. My grandmother had packed sufficient rations to last me two weeks. When they ran out I ski'd into the valley. I set off late in the afternoon, and was back in the arms of my grandmother after dark. Just before sunrise I made my return trip, the rucksack on my back filled with potatoes and lard, a heavy jacket from the farmer's closet, a pair of field glasses and Jerome K. Jerome's *Three Men in a Boat*. I read that novel twenty times, and I made Montmorency, the dog, my imaginary Man Friday.

A constant fear of discovery had kept me from venturing far from my shelter, but the claustrophobic environment got to me, and started to drive me mad. I decided to take a chance and went for long trips through the woods. As long as I remained inside the snow-covered forest it was safe. The sun had melted the snow from the roof of the hut, and quite often I would lie up there, staring at formations of Allied bombers on their way north. They passed high over the Alps, only their vapour trails betraying their position. There were hundreds of them. I did not know where they were headed for, but I thought of the poor cities which were their day's target, and of the human destruction which they carried in their bellies. Sometimes I spotted circular trails around the formations, the few remaining fighter planes of the Luftwaffe putting up a feeble defence. One of the planes came down, trailing black smoke, while a parachute drifted into the valley. I saw it crash on a nearby mountain and decided to look for the plane. I did not have to worry about give-away tracks any longer – the slopes were sheets of ice and skiing left no marks. After a few hours of climbing, I reached the wreck. It had survived the impact and slid across the snow. It was smaller than I had expected a fighter aircraft to be. The wings were riddled with holes, and its propeller was bent. It had one item of interest, a clock, and with lots of patience and the help of my pocket knife I detached it.

During my last visit to my grandmother I had been given the sad news that Vienna had fallen, and that St Stephen's Cathedral had burnt down. There was no news from my mother. The first patches of earth peeked through the white, and in almost no time these were covered with a thick carpet of crocuses. My days were spent exploring nature and staring at large bomber formations. As I became more daring, my walks turned into mountaineering feats. It was on one of these excursions that I found myself stranded on a glacier, a dark speck in an ocean of white, with a plane diving down on me. It roared overhead, and I waved. I noticed the twin booms of a Lightning and white stars on its wings. It made a sharp turn, and on the return pass waggled its wings. Then it zoomed off into the blue and disappeared over a ridge. That was my first contact with America.

It was towards the end of April 1945. I had been in the mountains for four weeks when I noticed a long convoy of a type of vehicle I had never seen before creeping along the valley floor. I slid and stumbled to a precipice which perched like an eagle's nest above the village, an ideal position from which to spy without being spotted. I could make out a tank on the village square, with a white star. A Sherman, *Amerikaner*! I ran towards the valley, and as I rushed from the cover of the trees, 'they' were right in front of me. First they were startled, but when they saw that I was only a boy, they smiled. I was stunned and out of breath.

The enemy, this was the enemy. One waved. Timidly I went over. Their behaviour was a shock. They sat in front of their officer, and didn't salute or stand to attention when spoken to. They wore a funny kind of olive battle dress, had high brown leather boots and small automatic rifles. Their belts were made of webbing, hung with bottles and bullet pouches. And they wore a double helmet, two hats one on top of the other. A few of them were black, like the athletes I had seen in the newsreel of the Berlin Olympics. 'Hi kid.' What did that mean? I didn't understand Newyorkese.

'How do you do,' I managed to get out in a halting voice.

'Hey, the kid speaks a known language.' And with that he offered me a Hershey bar. It tasted wonderful – my first piece of chocolate in four years. They crowded around me, and I was treated like a lost pet. They gave me chewing gum and fruit cake and a Coca-Cola. 'Do you know this place?' asked the one with silver bars on his shoulder.

'Yes sir. I live here.'

'All right, bring me to the burgomaster.'

'Sir, he is dead.'

'Well, who's in charge?'

'Frau Huber at the inn.' I took them to the local inn, and found the publican's room overflowing with terrified village folk. They had converged there during the night when a German captain had told them that he was the last of the German army and that the dreaded *Amis* were only a mile behind. I interpreted the surrender of the village to the American forces. There wasn't much resistance from Frau Huber or the other women. They hung a white bedsheet from a window, and the ceremony was complete. We were now in the 'Liberated Zone Europe, American Sector'. That night everyone put a candle in their windows and, for the first time in many years, the bells rang to summon worshippers to church. The nightmare was over.

***

I was spared the confusion of the next months, and the malaise that swept Europe: one side celebrated while the other wept. For this, our village was much too isolated. My mother had finally joined us: we held each other and celebrated being alive. Since I was the only 'kid' in my village that spoke 'a known language' and the local hotel served as headquarters of an American division, I was railroaded into providing the good life. For the officers I arranged enjoyable evenings in nice company. For the sergeants I served mainly as go-between for deals involving girls and boxes of food. And for the enlisted men it was the village's left-overs in exchange for Hershey bars and chewing gum. For this service I was well fed, so much so that I had plenty to take home and feed the whole family.

I had to find a way to finish my studies, and this implied an end to my well-nourished existence and a return to the burnt-out shell called Vienna. I had no news from the city. I didn't know if there were still people who would give me shelter, or even if my school was still standing. Vienna was in the Soviet zone of occupation, and that meant crossing the demarcation line at the bridge at Enns. I jumped on a freight train which was taking back some of the thousands of refugees who had camped in railway waiting rooms or abandoned SS barracks. In the three days it took us to reach the city, I caught glimpses of the devastated countryside. It gave me a foretaste of what was to come, but I still wasn't prepared for what awaited me in my poor, poor Vienna. I walked to my own pile of rubble. I was counting on the one back room we had managed to save after the bombing. When I got to the boards that served as a door, I found a family of four installed there. An elderly man, wearing my father's coat, pushed me to the ground. 'Get the hell out of here, and if you ever come back we'll kick the shit out of you.'

After one night in the open, and having walked many ruined streets on foot, I ended up with a distant relative. She took me in and made me a cup of hot water on a tiny stove which she fed with pieces of wood the size of matchsticks. She had nothing to eat, but I wasn't even hungry, just tired and sad. My next week was spent on the most pressing items, such as getting ration cards, and trying to locate the temple of my future education. Most school buildings had been bombed or burnt during the fighting in the city. On a pile of rubble I found a sign directing me to another district of Vienna. This created a problem. The school was in the British zone, I was in the sector occupied by the Soviets, and before I could go to class I needed Allied papers to cross the line. I queued alongside many desperate and hungry people, all applying for dream permits. After a week I heard my name called and was handed a paper in four languages, telling every Hank, Tommy, François or Ivan that they were permitted to let a certain E.C. Durschmied, age fifteen, get on with his education.

The school was housed in a blackened building without windows. The principal was a nice old man, a survivor of World War One. 'Hm, Durschmied ... are you the son of ... ?' His jobs included teaching Latin, distributing ink and turning off the lights. I had no papers to prove that I had ever attended a school before. I thought it wise not to mention the Theresianum. I simply stated that I had been in a particular class in a school which had ceased to exist. I wanted to get into a class and was not above using any cheap trick – I had joined the ranks of the survivors. If I jumped one year from my previous grade, I could finish high school at seventeen, two years ahead of schedule. He accepted me at face value. As I said, he was a nice old man, trusting.

Classes were difficult, not because of stiff exams, which could be prepared, or cheated. But we were starving and one's attention is not at its sharpest when the body is racked by pangs of hunger. The class of '45 were tough kids, and we made it. I was still living in the Soviet zone, in the Leopoldsstadt, which happened to be on the wrong side of the Little Danube, and all the bridges were down. During the final assault on the city, a Soviet division and an SS division had confronted each other across the narrow waterway, and now the place looked like a moonscape. On one side of the water the Russians checked my papers, then I was allowed to cross on planks which had been thrown across the twisted girders of the blown-up bridge, to be welcomed by a British trooper with further scrutiny of my 'border paper'. School was not a simple affair.

My first few months were the toughest. But soon everybody had found a way to beat the system. Our teachers were understanding, as they were equally hungry, and word was out to close their eyes and allow as many as possible of the 'new Austria' to pass. Right now we represented the only future for our devastated country. Vienna was a blasphemy – under a hail of bombs and shells it had ceased to exist.

The city was in ruins, St Stephen's Cathedral a burnt-out shell. The 'Bummerin', a huge bell poured from 180 captured Turkish cannons, had come crashing down and lay shattered. The Prater park had burnt down: only the giant Ferris wheel was rising above the ashes. Whole districts were nothing but rubble, and on many *Schutthaufen* were little sticks with pathetic notices such as:

'The Tanner family lives now at Waaggasse 17.'

'Karli, we are waiting for you at Tante Poldi.'

'Trade small stove for bicycle tyre.' Or epitaphs: 'Little Charly, Leopoldine and Karoline Braunschweiger died in the air raid on 12 March.'

'*Vati*, please contact me at Uncle Georg. Anna.' Vati, meaning father, who was probably a prisoner of war in some camp in France or a gulag in Siberia. I saw men wandering through deserted streets, dressed in ragged Wehrmacht uniforms, with P.O.W. stencilled on their backs, asking passers-by or neighbours for the whereabouts of their loved ones. It was sad to see the lack of compassion shown to people's misery, but everyone was preoccupied with their own necessities of survival. The black market of *The Third Man* was flourishing, and fortunes were being made by some on the backs of their fellow-citizens. The price of a loaf of bread was a watch.

In late autumn, the new Austrian president, Renner, persuaded Stalin to allow free elections. In a talk with the Soviet dictator, the Austrian had predicted that the left would achieve a great victory and hold the majority in parliament. On the day of the vote, after all ballots had been counted, it became painfully clear that the communists had not gained a single seat in the national assembly. The hatred of everything Russian was just too overpowering. The rape of Vienna was not to be forgotten for a long time to come. In their fury over their loss of face, the Russians cut down on the already meagre rations, and the coming winter was very hard to live through.

We looked for ways to forget the hunger. I discovered music. Throughout the city musicians came up with ingenious methods of procuring instruments. One violinist went to the Technical Museum and found an odd-shaped box – the original synthesizer, which produced the right sounds. Others used military bugles and tubas, to produce brassy splendour. I was not talented at any instrument, and yet I found incredible delight in discovering partitas and cantatas, minuets and lieder, symphonies, rhapsodies and mazurkas.

The musical bastions of the city had fallen victim to the bombs or were now serving as garages to the Allied powers. Soloists, quartets and even the odd symphony orchestra played in factory halls without windows – sometimes without roofs. One orchestra found itself practising in the city's slaughterhouse. It was strange to listen to a symphony of the meathooks. During the winter months the artists and their audience wrapped themselves in army coats or blankets or whatever they still possessed against the cold. I remember the performance of one particular string quartet, where the lead violin wore a German air force parka, the viola-player a Russian padded jacket, the second violin a sweater which had been knitted from several leftover socks of various colours, and the cellist an overcoat sewn together from two women's winter coats heavy with Chinese embroidery. They produced sweet, wonderful music.

For me a new world was opened. Every day I queued, sometimes all night long, to be told in the morning that all tickets had been sold out – or requisitioned by our Allied protectors. I was famished for anything on the menu, from *Zauberflöte* or *Fidelio* to an organ recital in a cold church or a jazz jam session in a cave. At school we traded tickets. 'What have you got?' was the standard question. 'I can let you have a fourth gallery standing room *Salome* with Welitsch.'

'All right, I'll trade you a Schubert's Fifth for next Sunday.' After our musical fraternity discovered that a classmate with a penchant for soccer had a father who was a ticket collector at the Theater an der Wien, which stood in for the burnt-out Opera, we queued up for football tickets, which were easier to come by since the Vienna stadium could take sixty thousand. It now became: 'I'll trade you two W.A.C. v. Rapid for two Lohengrins.' The football father let us into the magic of Mozart, Wagner and Verdi. I went almost every night – sometimes I could see, sometimes I found myself parked behind a pillar, but I could always hear.

During the Nazi years jazz had been frowned upon as a Negro subculture. For whatever you cannot get there is a hunger. American Forces Radio provided our first contact with the sounds of Louis Armstrong and Glenn Miller. From school I went to the football queue, from there to the opera, then to the jazz club, and back to school the next day. I had become so busy that I forgot I was hungry. When spring finally provided some warmth for our frozen bodies, I was well on my way to finishing the exams. Apart from music there were no distractions – no dances or amusement parks, and only censored films were given a permit for public showing. Most were of the sort where a single incredibly resourceful Allied soldier shot and killed a bunch of stupid Germans screaming 'Achtung' and 'Sauerkraut'. I had seen enough of the real war.

The country had regained a small measure of legality, and during the summer I succeeded in having the squatter family evicted from my family's pile of rubble. I spent every free moment fixing up the place to make it livable. No longer did I have to cross the Allied boundary to go to school. I had moved ten city blocks from the East to the West. In the winter of 1946 I noticed a small announcement in the newspaper of Austria's leading party, the Christian Democrats. There was to be a skiing competition on the outskirts of Vienna. I liberated a pair of skis and made my way to the hill, where I found hundreds of students, all eager to win the first prize – four pounds of flour. I won the slalom race, and was offered a spot on the party's Viennese ski team. This meant skiing over the weekends at a training camp in the Vienna woods, and slightly better food on Sundays. In February I won my first major race, the Viennese junior championships. From then on my rise in the skiing fraternity was assured.

Skiing came easy. I discovered that I had the one thing vital to any speed sport, a quick eye when it came to judging when to brake and when to let go. With the help of a coach who had been a member of Austria's 1936 Olympic squad, I also discovered that it mattered little how fast a racer came down a hill, as long as you arrived a fraction faster than number two. From then on I studied my competitors almost as much as the lay of the run. Compared with today's highly sophisticated equipment and training methods, we were rank amateurs. I had been given a pair of US army skis, which I stripped of their white camouflage paint, a pair of mountain boots studded with nails, and a leather tongue to strap me securely to my boards. The skis and I were thus inseparable, which meant that a fall at high speed was an invitation to disaster. During my career I broke my ankles several times. The races were run down steep gullies which had not been cleared of obstacles. Fallen trees, hidden rocks and sometimes even a wire fence only slightly covered by snow added to the danger.

There were no ski-lifts to the starting gate, only muscle to get us uphill. By the time we reached the top we were hungry, tired and cold, and it is amazing how many made it to the bottom without serious accidents. Granted, this was not at the breakneck speeds of modern racing, but if you hit a tree it doesn't make much difference whether you are doing fifty or ninety – the end result is much the same. The ski teams were fairly big, since half of their members would be sitting on the bench in plaster casts. Some races I won, and a lot I lost. When I won, that was wonderful.

During one victory celebration I met a girl – I was now seventeen, she was eighteen. My sexual initiation in the bomb cellar had not prepared me for instant love: my experience with girls was nil. In the post-war years it was difficult enough to subsist without any of the complications of amorous attachment. Her name was Ricki and she was very pretty, with black curly hair and very generous breasts. If I was nervous, she was not. She helped me along by opening a button here and putting up a roadsign there. When we were naked and she pulled me inside herself, she started to cry. I was puzzled. After all, she hadn't been a virgin. But she kept on crying, and then revealed her particular tale of horror.

Her handicapped father had failed to get the family away from Vienna in 1945. Shells were exploding all around her house. There were three dead Germans in her doorway, and a machine-gun firing across the street at the onrushing Russian troops. A brief silence, and suddenly, an urgent cry from her invalid father: 'Hide under the bed!' Quickly she crawled from sight and then she saw heavy nailed boots, and heard a voice: '*Frau, wo Frau?*' and then: '*Uri, Uri,*' and again '*Frau*'. Her father's voice, a shot.

Ricki started to whimper. An unshaven face peered under the bed, grabbed her ankle, pulled her out. Struggling only made things worse. One of the soldiers smashed a closet and took some of her father's ties. They spreadeagled her on the bed and tied her to the posts. Then they ripped off her clothes. All she could remember was the searing pain when the first Russian drove into her virgin body. First there were four, then there were six. They took turns. Her ordeal lasted for two days and two nights. Somehow she managed to free herself, and made it to the bathroom. When she opened the door, she found her father, with his dead eyes staring at her. A few days later some neighbours found her there. For a whole year she couldn't speak.

All of a sudden I had found four major interests in life. My studies, my music, the ski team, and a girlfriend. Things were definitely looking up. I had also joined several associations, like the Austria into the United Nations club and the American-Austrian Friendship Society. In July I passed my final high school exams. During a 'Canada meets Austria' festival, I was introduced to a woman from the Canadian consulate, who suggested I could apply for an immigrant's visa. Canada was opening her borders to certain categories. I went to the passport office and filled in the necessary papers. Where it specified profession, I wrote: ski instructor. Three months later I received a brief reply from a ski resort in northern Quebec. Armed with this letter I returned to the embassy, and received my immigration papers. Everyone chipped in to get me the $125 for the Atlantic crossing. I said goodbye to my family, and I still remember the parting words from my grandmother: 'My child, I know I shall never see you again. I also know you will come back one day a changed man. May the Good Lord protect you always.' The door closed on her tear-streaked face. That was the last time I saw her. Goodbye, Vienna.

Thus my childhood ended. My life was no different from that of most other children of my time: we all had to suffer, one way or another. Our generation was born into a war which almost devoured us. Most of the children who survived the war – with scars they would carry for the rest of their days – made it in life. I tell the story of my childhood not to justify my later conduct, but to explain where I found the roots of my philosophy, my reactions in the face of misery, and my instinct for survival. *Man is but a prisoner of himself. He cannot escape his upbringing, his environment, his native instincts.*

I was on my way to a new life in the New World. On that cold and foggy November night, as my ship, the Cunard liner SS *Samaria*, slowly pulled away from the quayside at Le Havre, and I stared down into the black waters that began to separate me from what had been, I threw my address book overboard. It was a futile but symbolic gesture. With it, I cut the link to my past. For me, there was only tomorrow.

3

LATERNA MAGICA

(CANADA, THE 1950s)

In order to understand a documentary report one has to understand the reporter, the cameraman. Films are made by individuals, and no one can escape his basic background, his upbringing, his environment.

My welcome to Canada was a cold wind from the approaching shore. On my way down the gang-plank I faced a moment of panic; here was I, a teenager, with only a bundle of belongings and twenty-five dollars in my pocket. I dragged my battered old suitcase to the bus depot, and two days later arrived in the ski resort, where I was handed an axe and told to cut trees down. After three days, I left and found another job, this time as a ski-lift operator, and later on as ski instructor. I won a few races and received the offer of a college scholarship which brought me back to Montreal.

To supplement my diet, I worked nights operating a hotel elevator, and in the summer I took a job organizing the wellbeing of guests in a resort hotel. I was given the grandiose title of social director, but my pay was only twenty dollars a week. On one hot summer evening I met a girl from Indiana. It was all so romantic: a hay ride, a harvest moon, a courtship that lasted three days, and then we got married. I was twenty-three and she was twenty-two. It never worked. No one was to blame, we were too young, too naïve, and too different. We lived in Montreal, not particularly well, mostly in vertical parking lots which were pompously referred to as 'Eagleview Terrace' or 'Regency Meadows'. Each of us wanted different futures. I worked in a printing plant, where my basic duty was to count Montreal telephone directories coming off the press. Not much of a challenge, but with a decent salary. I was unhappy.

'Come on, don't just sit there,' said my energetic wife. 'Do something.'

'Like what?'

'What would make you happy?'

'I don't really know, but I do know that my future in telephone books has its limits.'

'So, why don't you try something else?' she suggested.

'It would upset our plans.'

'What plans? Right now we haven't got any.'

Her family was in plastics, with a house and a car and a bank account. She was the typical product of a business environment that only recognized success. She realized that in order to give our home life a chance, I shouldn't sit around, frustrated.

With our meagre resources we could just about afford a night at the cinema. I don't know what it was, but I was irresistibly drawn to the silver screen, Hollywood, and the glamour. I took a daring decision: I would make my career in the film business.

Film-making in those days was only possible if your father owned the bank which put up finance for a production, or your uncle was secretary of the local branch of the union of film technicians. Otherwise there was hardly any chance of getting into a celluloid factory. You most certainly didn't take a stab at it if your background was that of an immigrant college student. This was the Stone Age of television, and technical courses for camerawork or film direction did not exist. But, even worse, there was hardly any film industry at all in Canada: only four relatively minor companies, spread across a vast continent. I wrote to all four.

Two replied; so, armed with boundless confidence and an 8mm epic on the Indianapolis motor speedway, produced with my father-in-law's camera, I went to see the first one in Montreal. Just to make sure that they would screen my story, I brought along my small projector. The producer who was supposed to look at my screen art was interrupted by constant phone calls, and hardly ever glanced up. He ended with the statement: 'You'll never make it, kid. Film is not your line.' I was disappointed, but far from discouraged.

The other letter that came was from an Ottawa company, Crawley Films Limited. This time they didn't even want to look at my mini-classic.

'You want a job?' asked Tom Glynn, head of productions. 'You can start in the camera department as an assistant, your pay is thirty-five dollars per week. What do you say?'

I wanted that job so badly, I even forgot to ask what they expected me to do.

The boss was Budge Crawley. With his wife Judy, and using his family's wealth, he had started a small production unit which supplied training and propaganda films for the Canadian war effort. It was one of the many cottage industries which got off the ground simply by being near the seat of government during a time of crisis. After the war they bought an abandoned church on the outskirts of Ottawa and transformed it into a film studio. Their technical equipment was not state-of-the-art, but it was film-making just the same, coupled with a dose of daring, and that was what counted most. Before the war, all products on the Canadian screen had originated south of the border on the sunny shores of California. That, incidentally, was true not only for films, but for Canada generally. The country had become a market outlet for the United States. Canada reacted, brought in new blood, and thus began an industrial boom. Crawley Films was caught in the movement, and rapidly expanded.

Stanley Brede was the chief cameraman. A talented Canadian, who knew little about technique but possessed a great feeling for what was pictorial, he could create a mood on the screen which said it all. He was the artist.

Frank Stokes, number two cameraman, had worked in Ufa – the film studios of Goebbels' propaganda machine – in Berlin before the war. Frank was the technician.

Norman Allen was the product of union battles at Lime Grove Studio in London. He was the survivor.

For the next few months I cleaned, I carried, I watched – and I learned. From Stokes I picked up technique, and from Brede the approach. My fights with Allen taught me to survive. Our productions were exclusively in documentaries, low-budget films for private sponsors as well as government contracts. Some of the subject-matter was not wildly exciting – how can one possibly make a chocolate cake-mix which refuses to rise glamorous? Or the efficiency training of a production controller in a steel mill sexy? But I learned a lot. I found out that even a boring story, given enough care and talent, can be made to look acceptable.

Eight months after my initiation came my break. We were covering the Canadian Open Golf Championships. My job was to drive a camera car and load magazines. The tournament was over, so everybody thought: the front runner had an unassailable lead. Then he triple-bogeyed the last hole, and it was all up for grabs. The outcome was to be a sudden death playoff. Crawley had three crews, and all three were inside the clubhouse, guzzling champagne. When I saw the crowd streaming away from the clubhouse towards the first tee, I grabbed a springwound camera, and for the following fifteen minutes I hopped and skipped and jumped to capture the drama. The tournament was over, a new winner was declared, and our producer was facing a disaster until I handed him my camera with a simple: 'It's all in the can.'

My reaction had saved the producer, the company and our sponsor. My images were only as good as could be expected from a novice with a Mickey Mouse camera, but they were the only pictures available. Perhaps it was a minor incident, but for me it was important, since it pointed me towards my future role, a cameraman who responds quickly to any given situation.

It was a personal triumph, but a professional disaster. In the boardroom, I looked good and the producer looked lousy. A few weeks later we were on a shoot where everything possible had gone wrong. The script was lousy, the actors quarrelled, the cameraman had an infected toe and couldn't walk – it was a mess. I should have known better than to suggest an improvement to a particular scene. The producer stayed on, and I was fired.

Years before, my ski coach had given me a piece of advice: 'Once you start, there is only one way to win, and that is to cross the finishing line.' This time there was no finishing line in sight, but I made calls and knocked on doors, and finally discovered Hollywood.

My first stab at the glamour factory was not with what could be described as a 'big picture': as a matter of fact, it was a downright cheapie. The film's scenario was based on the hope of getting the last foot of film out of a seven-year contract with an actor who had badly aged, due to his love affair with the old devil alcohol. He was tall, gaunt, and grey-haired. The tough face that had once launched a thousand Indians in hot pursuit and brought swooning maidens' dollars to the box offices was now a disaster area. Wrinkled, bleary, with large pouches under his eyes – it was the face of a tired old man the viewing public would never be allowed to see. There was one additional problem: he sincerely believed that he was endowed with unlimited talent.

This swashbuckling daredevil of the silver screen could hardly hang on to a horse. After his early morning glass of gin, followed by his mid-morning double vodka, he just about found enough strength to ride the prairie in search of his lunchtime triple martini. The director was frustrated, the crew was restless and the producer was tearing on his remaining tuft of hair.

The production team from Sunset Boulevard had invaded a prairie province to add yet another immortal cowboy saga to the never-ending money-spinners about the bloody conquest of the Far West. In keeping with the high standards of the industry, they had hired me as a third camera assistant. I checked into the local motel, which served as production headquarters, the star's accommodation and general feeding and watering trough for the crew. This place was miles from nowhere, and the production staff were forced to live together in perpetual discord. By the time I made my triumphant entry an atmosphere had developed which is best described as a mutual loathing. The crew hated the actors, the actors hated each other, the director was not on speaking terms with the producer, and the motel manager threatened to stop providing meals unless his overdue bill was settled, and pronto.

I knocked on the director's door, and a gruff voice from the inside asked, 'What is it?'

'I am the new camera assistant.'

'Come back in an hour.'

An hour later he granted me an audience. 'Go and see the chief gaffer, he'll give you something to do.'

It seems that I was hired not for my talents, but because a union boss had threatened a strike unless a third camera assistant was added to the picture, as specified by the union rules. I went in search of the chief gaffer, whom I found taping up his ankle. He had stepped into a gopher hole.

'Take paper leaves and staple them to telegraph poles, we've got to hide them for the next scene.'

I had come in search of glamour, and found a stapler. I told myself it could only improve, as I created forests in an otherwise treeless prairie. In the evening I was presented to the director of photography, a nice elderly gentleman.

'I want you to bring me coffee in the morning,' was his command, and for the next week I carried coffee in paper cups. My training as a competent cameraman was thus assured.

When the script called for an attack by wild Indians – on foot, since the production couldn't afford ponies – I was sent to corral some Ukrainians in a nearby settlement of Doukhobors. I leaned them against a wall and sprayed them a reddish colour with the help of a paint-gun. That mob became our fierce tribe of Apaches. Their lines were relatively simple to memorize:

'Ulululululululululululululululululululu.'

I was promoted to director of synchronization, Hollywood hype for clapper-boy. At least I got on film: 'Scene forty-five, take fifteen.' I was quite good at that.

The only pretty lady on the set was the make-up girl. She was a strawberry blonde, about twenty-six, with an ample body and always a kind word. It was said that she got the job because she slept with the producer, the director and the star – not too difficult a task, since all three were way past their prime. The only problem I could see was for her to arrange her schedule so that something was left for me.

'What are you up to? Still stapling leaves?'

'Nope,' I had adopted a Western drawl to match the rest of the gang, 'I have moved up in the world. By the way, are you free tonight?'

'What's today?'

'Tuesday.'

We had stopped counting days. In the lonesome prairie this mattered only to the producer who had to shell out the cash.

'All right, I'll come to see you after I've had dinner with Charlie.'

I had the feeling that Charlie would be short-changed tonight.

At this moment our star staggered towards us and brought our scheming to an abrupt halt. This was Charlie. He collapsed in a folding chair, the kind made of canvas with the name of the star stencilled on its back. She produced creams and powders, and proceeded to hide his wrinkles behind a mask of greasepaint. I couldn't help comparing her work to that of an undertaker trying to beautify a corpse.

'Scene forty-seven, take one.' Bang! Down came the candy-striped stick on my clapperboard, and I raced off to the side, to clear the camera's field and to get out of harm's way from the onrushing steed.

'Action.'

On the first pass Charlie and his horse missed by about thirty feet. They kept on going and disappeared in a cloud of dust.

The second take was an improvement: he was only fifteen feet off his mark.

On the third go the horse ran down the camera, and the camera crew.

'Scene forty-seven, take fifteen.' This was it, take fifteen would be the good one. When I saw the horse racing towards me, and Charlie desperately clutching the mane of his steed, I dived over a light case and went into hiding.

'Cut,' yelled the director, 'Print,' yelled his assistant and, 'Get off that fucking horse before it kicks the camera,' yelled the producer.

It was around scene sixty-five when the production ran into financial difficulties, and the union boss agreed to staff cuts. I was the first victim. In any case, the episode had taught me a valuable lesson: Hollywood was not for me. When I kissed my blonde make-up artist goodbye, she murmured in my ear: 'Will I see you on our next picture?'

'Not likely,' was my exit line.

I returned to Ottawa, where my former production boss asked how I had made out on the prairies. After a few laughs he came forward with a suggestion: 'You are really good at action. Drop all that stage nonsense and go for the fire.'

'That's a great idea, but I hardly have the means to freelance.'

'What it takes is guts, and an old camera. There's an old Bell & Howell stashed away somewhere. If you can find it, it's yours.' I found it, rusty and chipped. As I oiled it and checked the single lens, I imagined all the events its Cyclops eye had captured – a parade long gone by. The mechanism was beautifully machined, handcrafted magic, and it still produced crisp images.

Newsreel was now the logical direction for me. The few companies still in operation by 1955 were located in New York, headed by Fox Movietone and Hearst Metrotone. I gathered my courage to conquer the big city. I was instantly impressed by its sheer size, by the way that business was conducted in a no-nonsense manner, and by the furious competitive spirit in the community. All this gave me a tremendous lift, a desire to succeed.

I went straight for the famous company whose newsreels I had so much admired for their daring exploits. They had sent forth crews in rickety cars into the deserts of Abyssinia to report on the war which pitched Haile Selassie's barefoot soldiers against the tanks of Mussolini. Crews had gone to interview flood victims in the Mississippi Valley. Their most spectacular scoop was certainly the explosion of the dirigible *Hindenburg* in Lakehurst, New Jersey – the balloon bursting into flames as passengers raced to safety, or perished in the blaze. The headquarters of this company was hidden away in a garbage-filled street on New York's West Side. A small sign near the front entrance read: Metrotone News. The outside walls were a flaky grey, and inside the plaster was falling from the ceiling into long corridors painted in the familiar dark yellow of police stations.

Looking out on a rusty fire escape, behind a desk covered with film cans, cigarette stubs and paper cups with stale coffee, the news editor decided what people would talk about during the coming week from Indiana to India. If the office wasn't impressive, Casey Davidson, the boss, was. He looked me over: 'So, kid, you want to get into the news business. What do you have to show?'

'Not much, but I really want it.' I gave him a brief résumé of my career so far, and he chuckled when it came to my Hollywood escapades.

'You know, there's not much glitz in newsreel. It's hard work and you'll get no thanks for it.'

'I'm aware of that.'

'You've got your camera with you?'

'Yes.'

'Let me have a look. My God, I had one of those in, let me think, it was in the dustbowl, must have been '33 or '34. These are good machines if you know what to do with them.' He reached into a drawer and came up with two short rolls of film. 'All right, here you go. Shoot me a test.'

'What subject?' I asked.

'Pick one, but make sure it moves.'

'Thank you very much. By the way, how much do you pay?'

'If we take it, thirty bucks a shot, and we'll give you the film stock. That okay?'

'That's fine.' It wasn't, but I had little alternative. As I was about to leave, he offered me the greatest piece of advice anybody can ever give in the news business:

'When I send you out to cover a fire, I don't want ashes, I want flames. I don't give a shit how you manage it, and neither does my audience, just get me flames.'

Armed with two rolls of film, I returned to Ottawa and covered a meeting between the Canadian Foreign Minister and his American counterpart, John Foster Dulles. I did everything wrong, but was saved by the two negotiators who chose to stop in a corner where they thought themselves unobserved, which happened to be in front of me. I passed my test, the piece was used, and I earned thirty dollars.

Unfortunately, Metrotone folded after three months – not, I hope, due to my inadequate contribution. I had used my time well, learning the basics of action coverage: speed, and a quick eye. The important things were to get to the event on time, and preferably before the competition, to pick out the truly significant aspect and to stay with it. The newsreel company had fallen victim to a new technology, the instant transmission of news, and it didn't take a crystal ball to see that the future was in television. The news editor at CBOT – the local television station in Ottawa – accepted me in a freelance capacity.

I traded my 35mm antique for an equally aged 16mm springwound piece. Tom Earle, who doubled as local as well as national reporter, offered me thirty-five dollars per item. Since stories were not assigned frequently to freelancers, I was lucky to receive one call per week. I went out looking for my own stories. It was amazing how many cars crashed and how many houses burned, and how many majors shook hands and cut ribbons. There were school festivals, and ladies' cook-outs presided over by political party bosses, and open debates on

whether or not dogs should be permitted to pee on public lawns. I
offered my stories to the station and my finances improved, as did my
experience.

The pioneer days of Canadian television were vigorous and full of
new discoveries. We committed blunders, such as my interview with
Canada's Prime Minister. There was no microphone stand, and so I
slung the cable over the chandelier. In walked the private secretary,
who stumbled over the wire. Down came the chandelier.

Sound was exceptional, and the news was mostly covered by silent
cameras. The band of the Coldstream Guards provided pompous
background music, while a serious voice might be announcing the new
bumper crop of apples in the Niagara peninsula. Each item was
presented with the solemnity of an opening shot in World War Three.
The control room kept getting the wrong picture on background
projection. For instance, the familiar picture of His Holiness the Pope
might appear on the screen while the newsman, or newswoman in the
case of the beautiful Joyce Davidson, read an item about a hockey
game. The weather man used simple chalk on a blackboard to warn of
a forthcoming hurricane.

We cameramen had our own particular problems. Our film had to
make its way from crash site to airport, from airport to laboratory, and
from there to the newsroom. All too often, the screen went blank, the
broadcast being interrupted with a familiar slide: 'Please do not adjust
your set.'

Everything had a new and great complexity which nobody really
understood. Television was run by a kind of 1950s Yuppie generation:
eager young men and women, falling over cables, doing jobs they
were not hired to do, just so that the show would get on the air. The
fierce competition of present-day media, the constant alertness for
some investigative scoop, the aggressive interviewing style, all that
was yet to come. Journalists who came from print, whom the public
did not know by name or reputation, normally got the news but didn't
know how to talk in front of a camera: their trademark was to look
into the wrong lens and away from the rapt audience. So someone
who had a good voice and the right hairdo was employed to read what
others wrote. These stars of the pioneer period even took the same
elevator with the rest of us, because there was only one elevator that
worked.

My marriage was on the rocks – I had forsaken a personal relationship for professional advancement, something not uncommon in today's media. My wife and I met from time to time between a bridge opening and a train crash. When I had a night off, she spent the evening with her choral society. Even worse, we didn't try to find our way back to each other. When local news items were getting too limited for my ambitions I started to look further afield. Recognition wasn't coming my way; either I wasn't good enough, something that my ego would not let me admit, or I was in the wrong place, too far removed from television's seat of power and decision-making. Whatever it was, I had to go after bigger fish, which meant the international scene.

4
FIDEL CASTRO

(SIERRA MAESTRE, SEPTEMBER–DECEMBER 1958)

'Speech was given to man to disguise his thoughts.'

Talleyrand, 1754–1838

'Libertad o Muerte!'

Give me liberty or give me death! Often drummed out as a revolutionary slogan, only this time another phrase was added: *'Viva Cuba Libre! Libertad o Muerte!'*

He was tall and powerful. He wore soft leather boots caked with reddish mud, olive army fatigues, washed, pressed, and wet with sweat. An insignia on his collar, black and red, with a white star. A commandant with a strong face, framed by a scraggly beard. His eyes captivated me with their penetrating stare. Above his head he brandished a hunting rifle with telescopic sights. He fired into the air, and cried at the top of his voice:

'Viva Cuba Libre! Libertad o Muerte!'

Fidel Castro, 32 years old, revolutionary extraordinary, had opened his one-man show for my camera. From this moment on, I knew that my career was assured.

I had come a long way. The first dollar I was paid for a television story I put in a frame. I still have it. I had saved up enough to purchase a second-hand sound camera. One of my Ottawa valley featurettes caught the attention of a producer, Patrick Watson, who had helped to create a new national magazine programme, *CBC Close-Up*.

'If you come up with something of interest to us, call me, here's my card.' I searched, and found nothing. In the summer of '58, when Ottawa was hot and full of black flies, I stumbled on an article by Herbert Matthews in the *New York Times*. It concerned a bearded rebel in the mountains of Cuba, Fidel Castro. Rebels, beards and coconuts ... it sounded like a good adventure story. I invested in a long-distance phone call, and was put in touch with a Hungarian-born photographer, Andrew St George. (Years later I read that he had been an agent for the CIA.) He asked me to meet him in New York. That set everything in motion. Watson in Toronto was neither hot nor cold. He was a pro and could see the pitfalls.

'Go ahead. If you want to go to Cuba and if you get to meet Castro, and if he talks to you in English, and if the pictures are fine, then call me and I'll look at them.'

Not much of a guarantee, but at least a promise. With youthful exuberance and unbounded selfconfidence, I plunged into the venture. What little money I could scrape together I invested in film stock. I left Canada with 40 minutes of film to make a half-hour television programme. In a field, where a fifteen-to-one ratio is thought of as outstanding, I was planning to shoot one-to-one.

One of the conditions set by St George was that I did not reveal our final destination. In two days and two nights we drove my old car to Key West, and crossed on the ferry to Havana.

We checked into a house which called itself a hotel, but was actually a bordello-by-the-sea. Señora Lola seemed to be on friendly terms with Andrew. He, however, had little time for the lady and announced that he must visit 'friends'. With that he left me in the midst of fleshy señoritas with steel teeth and very tight sweaters. I asked politely where one might find some special entertainment. Lola smiled: 'Ah, señor, at the Shanghai you will find much joy.'

The place turned out to be a small cinema in a side street off the harbour district. The auditorium was so smoky that it took a large fan to blow a hole through the cloud for the audience to see the screen. The night's main feature was a motion picture about a famous Hollywood star entertaining a varsity squad in her bed, all fifteen, to raise their morale for a football game. The print had seen better days and was so scratched that some of the juicier scenes looked as if they had been filmed through prison bars. Not many of the patrons were following the action on the silver screen. They were generating their own entertainment with the numerous available girls, all versions of what I had tried to avoid at my hotel. Steel teeth were definitely in vogue, and these girls didn't bother to wear tight sweaters, just skin. A beer was three dollars and a lady for ten minutes another three.

The lights dimmed, the spotlight came on, and the 'queen of the night', a woman with unreal tits, walked on stage. She started an auction with herself as the prize. The lucky winner, a sailor from New Orleans, performed to general amusement right on the stage, for which act of bravery he received a howling ovation. I threaded my way past drunks and whores back to my hotel. Suddenly, in the night, there was banging and shouting, people rushing around in the hallway and girls screaming. I opened my door to a scene from a Marx Brothers movie. Policemen were climbing up the stairs as bare-arsed men tried to disappear out of windows and down fire ladders. It took twenty minutes to quieten down – the time it took the cops to disappear with the girls into their warm beds. Confused by all the brouhaha, but utterly serene, was an elderly American couple who had been packaged into this 'two-star hotel' by their local travel agent in St Louis, Missouri. I was worried that the authorities were after rebel contact men and that we would be flushed out. In fact, the madam had not paid her monthly protection money to the local police chief, so a raid was ordered to remind her of the back payments.

In the early hours Andrew returned and after a hug from Lola, who whispered 'Kiss Fidel for me', we set off along the carretera central in the direction of Santiago de Cuba. After a day's drive we arrived at Bayamo, where there was a police checkpoint. I produced my blue passport and my cover story: 'We are visiting an American army friend at the US naval base at Guantanamo.' We were passed through. From there on we encountered no more traffic on the road. Once in a while the charred remains of a truck, a bus or a private car partly blocked the way, or a cross beside the road bore witness that someone had met with sudden death. We came upon the scene of a recent ambush, a burnt-out truck with roasted cows overturned in the ditch. The grass was still smouldering and a group of Indios were chopping into the roast beef with their machetes. Glass was every-where, planted expressly to shred a car's tyres. That we would be sitting ducks in case of a blow-out never crossed my mind. All I could see was what was at the end of the road. After three hours of weaving through fallen trees and broken bottles, we arrived at an army checkpoint on the outskirts of Santiago.

We moved into a motel, and for the next three days I watched the coconuts grow. On the morning of the fourth day, I found that a mysterious caller had slid a message under our door:

'Return to la Bodega in Bayamo and ask for Pepe.' Nothing else to say that our arrival had been signalled to rebel headquarters or whether our visit was welcome. Slowly it dawned on me that I had staked my future on something quite insubstantial. Patience has never been one of my great virtues, and now I was being sorely tried.

Our return slalom through burnt-out vehicles and broken glass should have been little different, except that we ran into a gang of bearded rebels, my first contact with Castro's men.

One stuck a .45 through my open window. Next to him was a bearded child clutching a bottle with a wick and a match. They were about to burn my car, my film, my camera and my dreams!

'*Yo soy periodista canadiense.*' I hoped that he was sufficiently impressed at being face to face with a Canadian reporter. He wasn't, until Andrew produced a magic piece of paper which changed his mind. They gave me a kiss, and waved after us. The bodega was located in a narrow street littered with bottles, rusty cans and banana skins. In front of the door two naked boys were peeing into a puddle. We entered Bayamo's finest wine dispensary. The man behind the counter was fat and wore a torn sweatshirt.

'*Donde está Pepe? Yo soy Erik.*'

He fired off a joyous welcome in staccato Spanish, then gave me a bear hug and a wet kiss. He placed a bottle of Indio beer in front of each of us, we clinked bottles and with a zestful '*Viva el revolución!*' downed the brew. After the fourth bottle he took us into the back, showed us to a small, cool room and told us to bunk down for the night.

I had imagined that our contact would be established on a moonless night with the passing of a secret handshake. Instead, our arrival was openly celebrated in the only bodega of a village crawling with Batista's secret police. The following morning, we piled into my car and drove on a dirt road which led us away from the main highway towards a thicket of trees.

'Hide your *máquina* in there.'

I smeared red mud over the glaring paint. We were half a mile from the sleeping quarters of the *regulares*. Any well-organized attack could have wreaked havoc on this lackadaisical army garrison. The country road had come alive, Indios carrying bundles and ox-carts loaded with sugar-cane.

I prepared myself mentally for the most difficult step in our journey, the cross-over from the territory held by troops loyal to the president, to that of the rebels in the hills. I steeled myself to rush across waterfilled trenches, from palm tree to palm tree, facing instant extinction by enemy machine-guns in the typical no man's land of war. I had seen too many movies. We did not have to dash and crawl and jump. We flagged down a tractor. From his ripped pocket Pepe pulled out a red handkerchief from which he produced a six-shooter. He shoved it into his trouserband, thus creating an indent in his bulging belly. He had asserted his authority. Flinging my bag with the fragile camera gear on to the flatbed, he began to tell one and all that I was a '*muy famoso periodista*' who had come to talk to their '*muy glorioso líder*', and that he, gun and all, was here for our protection. I couldn't help wondering what shock effect this fat man with his rusty weapon would have on an army patrol. Would they laugh first and then shoot us, or would they just shoot us?

We were welcomed with lots of backslapping and kissing. In my week in Cuba it had become clear that Castro's revolution was very popular. Not only could he count on the support from his own class, the rich planters, the university intelligentsia and middle-class urban society, but, more vital to his uprising, he had the unconditional support of the peasantry. If Mao Tse-tung's dictum: 'Revolution can only succeed if supported by the masses,' was to be believed, then Fidel Castro was on the road to victory.

Our tractor came to a halt by a river bank. '*Vamos!*' said Pepe, which freely translated means: 'From here on we walk.' Walk we did, for two solid weeks, sometimes day and night.

Eventually we waded across a river and were welcomed by a group of bearded men in fatigues, all with red and black armbands bearing the inscription '*26 de Julio*'. This was Castro's vanguard. I was offered my first cup (of a thousand?) of rebel coffee, a sticky black glue, always piping hot and served in thimbles. During the next month my guides and I never walked further than thirty minutes without stopping off at some Indio hut for a coffee. The cups changed. I was given glasses with cracks, bully beef tins with handles, home-made earthenware jars, and even a Wedgwood cup, its characteristic blue showing through a black crust of coffee grounds. But the coffee, no matter how it was served, always tasted the same.

The first night we camped out in the open: I clamped my hammock between two handy palms and dozed off. Bang! Bang! Startled, I toppled from my suspended bed and found myself surrounded by grinning faces and a smoking gun. The joke was on me. It was their way to frighten the gringo.

It became clear to me much later that those who joined Castro in the *maquis* came from a cross-section of Cuban society – students, car mechanics, lawyers, typists, sugar-cane cutters, a few disgruntled soldiers – but that this was a revolution started and run by young intellectuals. These were the leaders of a new era, with their particular brand of political inspirations and ideologies. I listened and searched for signs of communism, but couldn't find a trace. They talked revolution, but it was neither left nor right, it was strictly Cuban. The reasons which had brought them to join the rebel forces varied as much as the people themselves. Some came for the purest of nationalistic reasons, others joined up to relieve the boredom of ordinary city life. Some were the jobless adventurers one tends to find in every armed struggle. The peasants joined to escape their slave existence and to rid themselves from oppression by the big land-owners. There were also those with less noble aspirations, whose main purpose was to be well placed when future positions would be distributed. And yet this ill-matched crowd was formed into a coherent force by one man.

Most of them never saw action: it wasn't that kind of war. Sometimes I wondered if it was a war at all. In the beginning, Batista, residing in his presidential palace in Havana, had tried to flush out Castro. The mountains were too rugged and the government troops too lazy, or it was too hot. Whatever the reason, Castro used the time wisely to fortify his position. When I reached the island in the autumn of 1958, Batista's soldiers were content to hold the towns, and leave Castro his mountains. The rebels had control of the central highway, but couldn't move into the urban areas. There was a fifth column in the cities, and those were the ones who suffered the highest casualties – betrayed, tortured and executed.

Our way wound steadily uphill, à narrow path in the broiling sun. *El grande líder*'s hide-out was a closely-kept secret, at least from me. During these travelling days, the hardest thing to come by was a straight answer. Our group leader was a young gaucho with a bandolero of brass cartridges slung across his chest. His name was Ramón, and it was rumoured that he had joined the rebels to escape the wrath of a sugar planter whose daughter found herself pregnant after a nocturnal visit by dreamy-eyed Ramón. Then there was Orlando, a radio repairman from Havana, a nice man in his early forties, with an electric blue shirt and a toolbox. Rebel headquarters had called for him to fix the frequent breakdowns of the voice of the revolution, Radio Rebelde. He was like a recording – when he wasn't talking to me he talked to himself.

Our other two companions never uttered a syllable; they compensated for their silence by devouring everything within reach, like warrior ants, and their conversation was restricted to belching and grunting. I named them Castor and Pollux.

The sun and the rough trails were taking their toll. Ramón, as officer in charge, rode a mule. The others walked. I suffered from heat, thirst, and a prickly rash. At every shack along the jungle path we stopped for coffee followed by endless discussions about the advances made by *el revolución glorioso*. We were proceeding at a snail's pace, which was very tiring and did not help my growing impatience. Every evening I was given the firm assurance that *mañana* we would finally get there and every morning a light plane disturbed our promenade, buzzing high over the jungle and trying out its machine guns on the vegetation.

Ramón killed a vulture munching peacefully on a dead dog. One evening we played billiards. The table was standard British, Something and Sons, London 1872. The baize wasn't very green and the moths had used it for their lunch. The gringo had to be given a lesson, and I found myself playing the local snooker champion. He knew the lay of the green, the holes in the baize, and the slant of the hillside. He buried me and I had to buy the rum. We didn't move forward, we seemed to move sideways and soon I had given up all hope of ever reaching Castro's Camelot. 'When will we get there?'

'*Mañana.*'

It was just another steep hill on another hot day. We stepped out of the jungle and I saw the huts. Could this be it? At this point in our travels I was too weary to care. I took stock of myself: my eyes were puffed up, my tongue was swollen, my arms were infected from mosquito bites and thorn scratches and my feet were one large blister. In other words, I was a mess. I sank down next to a hut and drifted into sleep.

His shadow woke me. I recognized him by the beard. Who says that Latins are short and dark-haired? Here was a blond giant towering over me, the soggy cigar clamped between his teeth. With a grin he pulled me up and pumped my hand: 'Welcome to *El Cuba Libre*! Anyone who joins our struggle is welcome. Take a rest now, we will talk tonight.' With that he disappeared.

I was billeted in the bamboo hut which housed the 'editing and printing offices' of the newspaper *Gramma*, named after the boat which had brought Castro to Cuba. An antiquated duplicating machine stood lost in a corner surrounded by bundled-up paper and sleeping bags. I strung my hammock between the walls, and fell asleep in the editorial office. The sun had slid behind the mountains when Orlando came to wake me.

'*El Jefe* wants to talk to you.'

For a moment I didn't know where I was, or who wished to talk to me. Then it all came back, I was on top of the Sierra Maestre, and about to talk to the modern-day Robin Hood, Fidel Castro. He was sitting in front of his hut. There were two other persons with him, a tough looking woman in her late thirties, and an elderly studious type who didn't quite fit the scene. Castro got up and grabbed me around the shoulder: '*Buenas tardes, periodista*, this is Celia Sanchez, and this is my English professor. Have some coffee. Who do you work for? What brought you to us?' He fired the questions at me.

'I am a Canadian, 28 years old, I work as a cameraman for the Canadian Broadcasting Company and I want to interview you.' There was no reason for me to pretend that I was some reporter of great renown. I simply told him about a dream, the conditions I had been saddled with, and that he, *El Jefe*, was the first personality I had ever confronted on my own. He smiled: 'We all have to start somewhere.'

I had never given this much thought. Now, faced by this green giant
with his piercing eyes and shoulders like a line-backer from a football
squad, I had to admit that the basic reason for my visit was not to
publicize Castro's political aims, but to further my own career. Castro
nodded: 'I like you – you like béisbol?'

'I prefer football.'

'I play lot of béisbol. Boom, I like hitting.' I had an image of Fidel
slamming a home run through Batista's window. 'Okay, we will make
good interview. You will have to take much time. *No rapido*, but I must
learn. Must be good.' He had already decided that his message would
come down from the mountain, and that I was the chosen one to tell
the world. He forgot to tell me.

'I like los norteamericanos, but Cuba is a long cow, with its head
grazing on the island, and its teats being milked in the USA.' He was
not far off the truth. When Castro was a student, the country's
economy was divided between sugar interests and the American
Mafia, running a lucrative string of casinos and brothels along
Havana's fashionable Malacon ocean front. Famous film stars and
whores alike congregated for their cocktail at Sloppy Joe's, before
engaging in their nightly fun. At the Copacabana a rapt audience
cheered live performances of 'Superman's' amazing feats of virility.
The marinas were the rendezvous for a Who's Who of Jane's pleasure
crafts, and gentlemen in white tuxedos had their shoes polished by the
dregs of the gutter. Dream creatures in low décolletés displayed their
baubles, but the couples didn't have the married look. Havana was not
the sort of place to take one's own wife: 'You know, darling, it's hot and
dirty, and in any case I'll be in meetings … ' It was a place to get laid –
and charge it to expenses. To the proud Cuban, that was an appalling
state of affairs and he started his revolution, which found instant
appeal across the country. Within twelve months, Castro's rebellion
had become a threat, taken extremely seriously by the government.

The man who sat in front of his hut sipping coffee, his eyes
consumed by a holy fire, had charisma. His manner of speech was
direct, but for a man of his size he possessed a high-pitched voice. His
way to obtain attention was with a wave of the hand as if to say 'Be
quiet' or 'Shoot that man', and then he would stab a finger at his chest
to make certain that no one misunderstood, that it was he, Fidel, who
had given the order. His beard was a reminder of the day he had taken

a vow to stop shaving until he had achieved the liberation of his country. At least, that was the myth. A more rational explanation for his trademark was that when their little band was chased up into the dry mountain regions, they had just enough water to drink but not to shave, and their stubbles grew into beards.

He had named his movement '*26 de Julio*' in memory of an earlier uprising. In the early hours of 26 July 1953, Fidel and a band of followers attacked the army garrison at Santiago de Cuba. They sneaked past a sleepy guard into the local barracks and stormed into the headquarters building. A soldier spotted them, shots rang out, officers tumbled from their beds and raised the alarm. Soon it became obvious that the danger came from a group of rank amateurs who had trapped themselves conveniently inside a building with only one exit, the front door. By noon it was all over, a valiant but futile gesture. Thus ended Castro's first attempt to seize power.

Fidel learned his lesson, as he jokingly told me. 'First time we are too young, now we are much much older.' His second attempt was the good one, and by now he was well entrenched with his troops. He wore the shoulder badge of a *comandante*, or major, a white star on a black-and-red leaf. However, it hardly needed any insignia to recognize Fidel, he was so much taller than the rest. His regional commanders were also *comandantes*, mostly selected from the original *Gramma* twelve. His aides were *capitánes* and *tenientes*. His ministers were under thirty, his field commanders students in their late teens. He enforced strict abstinence from alcohol and women. To make his point, he had an offender tied to a tree and shot.

The key to Fidel was Celia Sanchez, the only rebel in camp without a beard. She was Fidel's confidante, secretary and, according to some, his mistress. Everything had to pass by her to reach the ears of the *líder*. She was present at all council meetings, she passed Fidel's orders, issued safe-conduct papers, and made coffee. Celia was the heart of the matter, she was the regimental sergeant major looking after the cookie jar. Although Fidel certainly took all decisions of a military nature, he was susceptible to advice on matters which were not of imminent importance, but which would have farreaching effects. Her main task was to point out unsound suggestions, or eliminate orders not directly in line with their revolutionary zeal.

When the sun went down, both would sit on the bench in front of

Fidel's *casa*, 'la comandancia', four wooden poles supporting a thatch of palm leaves, and nobody dared to interrupt them. From a safe distance I watched them argue, Fidel often in a heated voice, Celia always soothing, calmly filling up another cup of coffee. During daily operations, when something went contrary to his wishes, Fidel would show fierce impatience; whenever an order was dealt with in *mañana* fashion he stormed around, absolutely furious. I once saw him reduce a commander to quivering jelly because a mule train with badly needed supplies had not arrived on time. It was during such moments that Celia appeared on the scene to provide the calming female touch. Long before Fidel, she had understood that leadership and diplomacy were the art of the possible.

She shared his hut, but I never observed anything more between them than a strong bond of comradeship during a dangerous time. Over the days I got to know Celia quite well. One day, while pouring me a cup of coffee, she asked if ever there had been a woman in American politics who had helped her president husband. I was stunned: 'Certainly. In the case of Eleanor Roosevelt she practically ran the country.' It was the only time I saw a smile on her haggard, tired-looking face. (The baggy fatigues she wore did not enhance her sex appeal.)

Celia wore no badge of rank: she didn't have to – everybody knew her and feared her. When I requested Fidel to give the interview in English, he appointed Celia to look after it. She located a high-school professor whose task it became to translate a sheaf of Fidel's notes into coherent English. (Today it would be unthinkable to supply questions in advance, but no such restrictions existed in those days.) In the early '80s Celia Sanchez died under mysterious circumstances following a meeting of Castro's inner council. The cause of death was given as cancer following a long illness.

While my questions were pondered by Fidel, Celia and the professor, I strolled around the camp. My movements were not restricted: quite the contrary – I could hardly move ten feet without receiving the obligatory invitation to coffee. The camp was built on a heavily wooded hilltop, called La Plata. Like a vulture's head the peak was bald, with a gnarled hanging tree on the summit. Many times I sat in the shade of this tree, staring at the Caribbean like a lake of molten silver in the distance. The encampment was made up of about fifty huts, administration, propaganda, and living quarters. The most important hut was given to Radio Rebelde, 'The Voice of Free Cuba.' It was protected by some wooden beams, on to which rocks had been piled as protection against the event of aerial attacks. When I thought of Vienna and what a well-aimed bomb could do, I had to admire their confidence. The miracle was inside: an obsolete US Coast Guard short-wave transmitter, held together by tape, hairgrips and hope. My travelling companion, Orlando Payret, the radio specialist, was very proud: 'We have killed many mules to transport this radio to the top. They all died for our final victory.'

As we talked, he kept caressing some rusty dials, coaxing a spark to strike the transmitter tube.

'Tonight, Fidel will give a speech to the nation.' The importance of these transmissions cannot be stressed enough. Castro's revolution became a living event, and people across the island tuned into his nightly broadcasts. His rhetoric improved, and his attacks on corruption secured him the base from which he was to launch his long march on Havana. During these days Fidel learned the basics of exhorting the massive crowds which, in years to come, he would whip into frenzy in the public arenas.

I watched him on several occasions as he sat in a rickety chair in front of a microphone without prepared notes. He spoke in simple language everyone on the island could understand. The country was hungry for news; these clandestine broadcasts engendered a public response comparable with the messages carried by the BBC to occupied Europe. The radio became the final nail in Batista's coffin. Napoleon had remarked: 'I'd rather face a thousand bayonets than three unfriendly newspapers.' The value of propaganda can only be measured by its success. For the first time, a Latin American revolution had progressed from the proverbial Mexican shoot-them-up into an example of modern intellectual intercourse, bent on capturing the mind of its population by means of electronic impulses.

Sometimes Castro would ask me to have coffee in his *casa*. He pumped me for information about the Yankee baseball series, about the FBI and John Foster Dulles. There was little I could tell that he wasn't aware of. He justified his unavoidable showdown with

American power politics with platitudes such as: 'I know that the American people will support my just fight.'

When he was called away I stayed on, and browsed around. The interior of the hut was dark and humid and a favourite meeting place for mosquitoes. The floor was made of hard-packed mud, and the only furniture was a table and two benches. This was where the future of Cuba was decided in bi-weekly council meetings. In one corner a makeshift bookshelf, with works by Clausewitz, Rommel and Skorzeny, but definitely no Marx or Mao. His fascination with German military thinkers actually suggested more of a right-wing influence than a communist connection. His favourite reading was war novels, and there was a great supply of these in paperback. The table was covered by bits of paper, orders awaiting his signature, three-week-old newspapers, and a few cups of stale coffee. His sleeping quarters were in the adjoining room, separated by a blanket nailed to the ceiling. It contained a simple bunk bed, and, on a nail above it, the hunting rifle which he had saved from the sinking *Gramma*. (He was never without a 9mm Browning automatic, carried on the hip in a brown leather holster.) Outside the hut was a metal washbasin on a wooden bench. At least he had water, something I rarely managed to scrounge. When I took on a rather ripe smell, a Samaritan supplied me with enough water to shave, probably on Celia's orders. My prickly heat rash had healed and the old mosquito bites were covered by new ones.

'Celia wants to see you.' I found her and the professor in deep discussion with Fidel. They were actually planning the strategy of my interview! It had been decided to give it in the morning. It was high time – I had run out of fingernails to chew. Fidel chomped on his cigar, looked over our shoulders, and leafed through his notes while the professor explained. A few times he interrupted with a question, shook his head, and the two made an improvement to the tone of the answer. I only interfered to change their Latino brand of English. The interview would provide the flavour of Castro, the rebel-with-a-cause not only for his native Cuba, but all the way down the Cordilleras de los Andes and up into the Caribbean. Carefully the professor read out sentence after sentence. Fidel picked up the text phonetically without repetition. They went from answer to answer with a speed which drove me to despair. My whole future depended on a man who spoke almost no English, and who had decided to address North Americans in their own tongue. I could not wipe from my mind the final warning from the producers in Toronto: 'Unless the man speaks a known language, forget it.'

It was 9 November 1958. I had passed a tormented night. The future of one man was in the balance – mine. When the first ray of sunlight announced a new beginning I knew that everything would go fine. As my outdoor studio I had picked the bald hilltop, from where a vastness stretched across the battered island. The dead tree which had provided soothing shade during my contemplation extended its branches into a leaden sky, and just touching the horizon was a faint glimmer, the sea separating me from America and my future.

I set up the camera, quite a primitive machine – a small motor-driven unit with a built-in optical sound unit. Its purchase had used up all my life's savings: a necessary gamble if I wanted to get ahead in life. I checked lens and filters and batteries and the sound cable. From a branch I improvised a microphone boom. One of the bearded rebels was railroaded into holding it aloft, so that the mike was placed just above the leader's head. I was ready. Now the stage was set, it was no longer a matter of technique. Mentally exhausted, I sat down and counted flies. An eternity later I saw his familiar head coming out into the open.

'Today will be a good day, full of strong sun, a good start for us.' He lifted his rifle with the sniperscope. 'Make sure the world hears what I have to say. *Vamos!*'

A shot, a shout: '*Viva Cuba Libre! Libertad o Muerte!*' The show was on.

He was in great form, jovial and joking, puffing on a cigar. Fidel was a born showman: he knew exactly where to look, when to change facial expression, how to stress a violent emotion. He had an uncanny talent for visual effect and was able to mesmerize his audience – in this case, me. I was relatively new to the game, and if I did miss a few things it was a permissible error. I was spellbound by his personality. Castro had memorized every word. It took us two hours to get through the interview, with me looking through the eyepiece as I fired off questions from behind the camera. The technical means were by no means sophisticated, but this piece of film provides the only historical glimpse of an outlaw who was to become one of the controversial figures of our time.

At the outset he launched into an attack on Cuba's president, Batista:

'He is a very bad one, personally I feel no special hate for him or any other man. Batista is a vain and ambitious man. Would you call a democratic man of Hitler, or Mussolini? Well, Batista is like a pocket Hitler.'

'On what do you base your belief in the final success of your revolution?'

'We have had two years of fighting. At the beginning we had not control of the country. We were continually persecuted, but fighting hard against Batista's forces, after about six months we got control of the mountains and kept them out. Now we have a big part of the plains too. Really, the only outlaw since the beginning was Batista.'

During recent skirmishes in Havana there had been heavy civilian casualties. I tried him on that. 'Your movement has been accused of indiscriminate killing of innocent bystanders.'

'Almost everybody has been killed in these riots. Our men are much too carefully with civilian people. On the other side, Batista's men have killed many thousand of innocent citizens. Our conscience is completely in peace, because we give our lives for saving our people.'

No one had yet tried to come up with an estimate of the number his movement encompassed. Castro's revolution was solid enough in his mountain redoubt, but what about the rest of the country? 'You don't seem to have enough people to combat or defeat a regular force such as the one at the disposal of the president of Cuba.'

'You are mistaken. You are mistaken. Who has had little success in defeating us was Batista. Always the people who fight for freedom get victory, sooner or later, facts have proven our faith. I can only tell you with how many men we began this fight. We were only twelve men. Now we are too much more. The terrible fact for Batista is not how many men we have now, but that we grow every day.'

'Do you claim the full support of the majority of people across Cuba?'

'When we begin, we were too small a group and Batista's army was very strong. In spite of that we continued to fight and we have won many victories against him, and his forces are now being defeated in all parts. You see, about ninety per cent of the people of Cuba are with us, without that it is impossible at all to fight such a war. Is that not enough reason for hoping in the victory?' That was a straight reference to Mao's principle of successful guerrilla warfare. However, it would be another five years before I was to read the book by the Chinese leader.

'Is your fight a struggle for power?'

'We are not fighting for power. We are fighting for finishing tyranny and then our movement will fight power by free elections. We don't want power by force.

'I am leading a revolution because the legal government of my country was overthrown by the army led by Batista, eighty-two days before a general election in which the people of Cuba were to elect its own government, and instead of that, General Batista established a bloody tyranny. For finishing that tyranny, and for establishing a legal government in my country, we are fighting now.'

'You are accused of being influenced by communist ideology. Are you, or are any of your followers communists?'

He was ready for that one. Nevertheless the good showman clenched his teeth and bit into his cigar. Then he took the stump out of his mouth, brandished it at the camera, and shook his head vehemently.

'*There is no communism or marxism in our idea!*' His brows narrowed and his eyes became furious slits, angry that anyone would dare to accuse him of such a vile possibility. Fidel stabbed his cigar at the camera as he continued his phrase: 'Our political philosophy is representative democracy and social justice in a well-planned economy.'

He had made his point, the tension was gone, and Fidel continued in a calmer tone: 'Now there is lack of freedom and justice, and after that a lower standard of living, hundreds of thousands of young men without jobs. Cuba is a rich country with a wonderful future if we only have good government.'

'So what will your personal role be in this new government? Do you plan to be president?'

'I don't think of being president. I am not fighting for that nor for any other public charge. I cannot answer you about myself because I don't think about that. Our provisional government will be an honest judge, Dr Manuel Urrutia, and after him the president who ought to be elected by the people of Cuba in free elections, in the most short time possible after the finish of the revolution.' A smile crossed his face, 'I hope to improve my English to explain it to you better next time.'

'There are fears in the United States that you will expropriate American interests.'

'We will not seize any land from anybody. What we will do is buy those lands out of production to give them to poor countrymen. We don't think to establish a special measure for foreign holdings than for national ones.'

'What then do you expect of the United States?'

'What we want from the United States is sympathy to the Cuban people for their fight for freedom, and we are very grateful to them. In the United States some believe that a strong man is good for their aims in Latin America. I think this is a mistake for the credit of the United States as a democratic nation, and we hope that such politics will be changed.'

As future events were to prove, he was absolutely right – only it was not Batista who was the strong man, it was Castro himself, and this was to create endless problems for American influence in the hemisphere, climaxing in the missile crisis of '62. I felt that he was winding down, the sun was getting so unbearable that even the flies had fled into the shade. I posed my final question: 'When will I see you in Havana?'

'I cannot tell you exactly when, I can only tell you that Batista will be overthrown and very soon.' His prophecy was to come true within a few weeks.

He extended his hand to me, and said: 'I hope to shake hands with you again in free Cuba, not too late that you become an old man.' That was his parting phrase. One final time we shook hands, then I was alone, standing on top of a mountain in Cuba, looking at green hills, and into a distant future. I was so impatient to get the film to Canada that I decided to leave right away. I said my farewell to Celia, who handed me a safe-conduct.

'That'll get you through our lines, it will not help you beyond the mountains. You must leave your camera here, it is much too dangerous to take it along.'

'But that's all I have ... '

'Is it worth your life? If the butchers of Batista catch you with it, they'll shoot you for sure.'

I unloaded the film from the camera, taped the film cans and packed them into a metal box. Then I stared at the camera, my only possession. The footage counter read 756 ... 756 exposed feet between me and fortune? That was the least of my worries. First I had to get the film back. Should I take a chance with the camera?

The decision was taken from me. Faustino Perez, head of the Administración Civil del Territorio Libre, and number two man in the camp, had come to say goodbye. 'Fidel says you must leave the camera.' I put it into the shack of Radio Rebelde.

'Please, take good care of it ... one day I'll come back for it.'

From the camp it took me a week to reach my hidden car. When my rebel guide bid me a backslapping '*Hasta luego*' by the side of the road he didn't bother to warn me that mine would be the first vehicle to drive on the country's carretera central in more than three weeks. From Bayamo, the town nestling on the mountains, the road led through sugar-fields away from the mountains. It was twenty kilometres to Cauto Cristo. On the rusty bridge across the muddy river, that's where they jumped me, the ragtag remainders of Batista's army. To them, I represented a ready victim for a highway robbery, and a gringo symbol on which to vent their hatred. Not having the camera probably made the final difference.

'Don't shoot the *yanqui!*'

It was not until the following year that I finally learned the true circumstances of my miraculous escape: five weeks before the incident which almost cost me my life, a Cuban army patrol had pulled an American citizen out of a car and shot him dead. It was cold-blooded murder, and the senseless brutality stirred an uproar in the American press. The US State Department had called in the Cuban ambassador to Washington, and voiced 'indignation'. Faced by increasing pressure, President Batista had had the officer of the killer squad summarily executed on a public square. Bingo, equalizing justice! Looking back at the incident, the man who came running to save me from being blown away was most likely as scared as the one staring down the barrels.

On 11 November 1958, Fidel Castro left the Sierra Maestre. In the first week of December he marched on Santiago de Cuba. On 28 December Che Guevara took Santa Clara, and the road to Havana was open. On New Year's Eve 1958, Fulgencio Batista fled Cuba. Fidel made his triumphant entry into Havana on 8 January 1959.

With growing panic, I followed the hourly news flashes as I gunned the old engine through Florida, Georgia, New Jersey and New York. Was I already too late? I reached Canada on the night of 29 December 1958. I found my home like the Canadian winter – cold, with a note from my wife informing me that she had found happiness with someone else and had left with him: for Cuba. Then the phone rang, and never stopped ringing for a week. Every newspaper in the country wanted to hear about the bearded Cuban ...

The sudden ascent into the limelight was a heady feeling which replaced all other emotions. Overnight I became a television celebrity, the 'man who had been the only eyewitness to the Cuban revolution' ... but real recognition came the day when a child stepped up to me in some airport and asked for my autograph. I was dined by the Lions and the Kiwanis. I was placed on the rostrum next to the head lion, invariably the president of a bank or insurance company, looked from my heights down at mere mortals, who were fed shrimp cocktail and peach melba, and waited for the applause to subside before resuming my speech. People who had never noticed that I had lived next door now patted me on the shoulder, and the producer who told me that I was not destined for a career in films sent a note: 'I always knew you'd make it!'

These days of limelight reached their climax on a celebrity-studded gala evening, when a star of the silent screen announced to a hushed audience: ' ... and the winner ... ' hushed pregnant pause while she slit open the envelope ... 'Erik Durschmied, for "Castro" ... ' The rest was drowned in applause and somebody pushed me on to the stage. With the award came recognition and cheques – all of a sudden I had a bank account with something in it. I was riding the crest. Flashbulbs and sudden fame obscured the realities.

'Hurrrryeh ... hurryeh ... hurry ... jump on the merry-go-round, come on, Erik, you've made it, travel the globe, see oriental palaces and meet important personalities ... '

Now television producers would ask me, the cameraman: 'What would you like to do next?' Not: if you get there and if you come back ... but actually, where would I like to go? I jumped on the roller-coaster, and within twelve months I was to meet Khrushchev in

Moscow, Chiang Kai-shek in Formosa, witness a public execution in
Ankara and a bloody uprising in Iraq. I was shelled on Little
Quemoy, the Chinese offshore islands, shook hands with President
Nasser in Cairo, and visited the Lion of Israel, Ben-Gurion. To me
there seemed no limit and I kept on pushing.

Once more I tried to talk to Castro, but the Cuban system had
changed. The revolutionary comradeship which had been the cement
of his movement was replaced by *Realpolitik*. His friends from the
Sierra Maestre were exiled to the provinces. Several had even been
sent before a firing squad, while those with close connections to party
hardliners were installed in key positions, which they used to build a
fence around Castro. For three frustrating weeks I parked myself in
the Havana Hilton which had become the 'Havana Libre'. I tried and
called and cajoled and waited. Then I left.

5

JAMES MOSSMAN

'He's been in Vietnam again. You should read
the papers sometimes,' he told her.
'Poor old Dan. I wonder what he'll do when there
are no more wars to go to.'

Lifelines, James Mossman, 1971

'Erik, how would you like to go to Paris for us? Cover the war in Algeria?'

The call from Radio Canada's *Premier Plan* had come rather unexpectedly, but the offer was not without its merits. My marriage had recently ended in a Cuban divorce, and my Ottawa apartment was at best a place of convenience, just a table, a bed and a TV set. The CBC's English service had nothing precise to offer and no contract to sign. What finally decided me on Paris was the one-eternal-love I met at a bash. She was vivacious, exuding sex, and for a boy with cold feet she was Delilah and Marilyn Monroe in one. She was also very French and I had never met anyone like her. I fell, not in love but in passion, and when she promised she would be mine forever, I packed up and joined her in Paris. Our love lasted two passion-and-fight-packed weeks. Then she moved out, and I stayed on.

After the frosty climate of Ottawa, Paris was aflame with vibrancy and merriment. No matter that the telephones didn't work and the plumbing was lousy. The two facets of the city which had intrigued so many of the great writers, the futuristic atmosphere striving towards the 21st century, and the reminder of the Middle Ages when citizens used to bump each other off for unrequited love, I found extremely attractive. Paris became the place where I kept polo shirts for the spring and heavy sweaters for the autumn. The beginning was difficult because I spoke no French. I moved into a small hotel off the Champs-Elysées which rented rooms by the hour. When it became apparent that I kept my room for days at a time, and thus disturbed the brisk business of '*cinq-à-sept*' – the time between five and seven, when married men are supposed to be returning home by Métro but prefer to visit their *maîtresses* – I was asked by the manager to find alternative quarters.

I ended up in a sixth-floor studio in Montmartre. Parked permanently in my doorway were two *dames de la rue*, one quite young and pretty, the other older than the first one's mother. Her name was Jeanette, and she was as wide as she was tall and had enormous boobs, which she displayed freely under a vinyl coat. Both had their regular clientele, which they took to the small hotel across the street. To my utter amazement, I found that one of their peak periods was just after breakfast: before the men went to work, they had a *quick coffee with Jeanette*. On rainy days, when no business could be found, or when their customers had to return home to take care of the family which had gone down with the 'flu, the ladies came up to my flat and made coffee, and we talked. Scout's honour, that's all we ever did. They were real pros and free gifts weren't on their agenda. And that was my only experience with *Jeanette la Douce*.

In 1960, while filming the Algerian civil war, I received an invitation from the BBC to visit the editor of a newly created programme, *Panorama*. A London taxi brought me to a crumbling building site, which turned out to be the famous Lime Grove Studios. Was this the mighty BBC? The editor was closeted in a tiny room with a barred window. He was a large man for such a small office. His name was Paul Fox. 'How would you like to join the programme?'

'Doing what?'

'Taking pictures, what else?'

'I have an arrangement with Canadian television.'

'I know, the choice is yours.'

I liked Paul from the moment that we met. I joined *Panorama* because of his charisma and certainly not because of the opulence of Lime Grove Studios, a place which had never really recovered from the blitz. Their reporters were first class and widely respected. Perhaps, I thought, some of this would eventually rub off on me. A few days later I was to join one of them.

He was sitting on a battered blue fibre suitcase, when I first spotted him in the lounge at Rome airport. Paul Fox had assigned me to a story about Chinese refugees flooding into Hong Kong. I had come from Geneva, he from London.

'You must be Jim Mossman?' I said as he looked up at me.

'Yes, and who are you?' A public school accent, not very friendly. It was not a good start.

'I am Erik, and I am supposed to fly with you to the Far East.' I was equally frosty; I saw no reason for special courtesy. At worst, I had to bear him a few days, and then, if heaven and editor were kind, would never have to set eyes on him again.

'I see.' With that he put his head down and returned to his book.

'Flight Air India ... will the passengers please proceed to gate ... '

He got up and went to the check-in counter. He was very tall, six foot six or seven, and had a funny way of walking as if making certain to place the right foot in front of the left. He put his ticket on the counter. He barely gave the check-in girl a glance when she asked politely:

'Smoker or non-smoker?'

'Doesn't matter, just give me a corner where I can be on my own.' Definitely not a good start.

My first impression of Mossman was of a cold human being. As I was to discover, this was his shield against unwanted intruders into what he called 'my sacred privacy'. He never bothered to be friendly to people he didn't know, or didn't like. Many times thereafter I watched him cut down the pretentious statesman or the overbearing industrialist with one short phrase. He had a formidable weapon, a tongue like a Damascene sword. I watched him play mongoose and cobra. But this was still the opening stage of our encounter, and I felt that we had to settle our differences before we got off the plane. He had found his place in a corner, reading and ignoring me. Encouraged by misguided self-importance from my precious few achievements, I went over to the attack: 'If you don't want to work with me, find somebody else, I don't need you.'

He looked up from his novel, and with an icy smile he said: 'Let us finish what we've come to do, then you may return to your usual company.'

I should have left it at that, but I was boiling. How dared he? I had proved my worth in the jungles of Cuba, I had survived the street battles of Algiers – that snotty, stuck-up son of a bitch, I'd cut him down to size.

I never did find a way. Our problem was settled on the second night after our arrival in the Far East. We had taken the ferry to Macao, and were walking back from the Vice-Governor's office. The streets were dark and covered with a slippery film of dirt and fishgut; the rattle of mah-jong stones came from the open windows. A smell of garlic and fried duck prevailed. The place had the air of a mid-Thirties Hollywood sound stage, except that the actors were real people. What set off our argument I can no longer remember, perhaps it was the stifling heat or the spicy food, perhaps it was that Jim walked fast, and always two steps ahead of me. In any case, I screamed at him, he screamed back, and we split. He turned left, I turned right. A bad mistake in night-time Macao.

I did not see them. All of a sudden I was on the ground, with several thugs on top of me, holding me down, tearing through my pockets. I tried to turn, and was struck on the side of my head. Suddenly their weight came off me, first one, then another, and then two were running down the cobbled street and one was lying face down in the gutter. Mossman was standing over me, helping me to my feet. 'You ought to be more careful,' is all he said. He took me to the hotel, washed the blood from my face, and put me to bed. I fell asleep knowing he was there. The following morning I came down for coffee covered with Band-aid. Jim never mentioned the episode.

He and I became inseparable. If ever there has been a single person who influenced my philosophy, my outlook on life, what's right and what's wrong, the professional and the personal approach to any given situation, it was Mossman. He was light years ahead of his time. I was quick to recognize his qualities. He was a friend to be trusted. During the night in Macao the 'Jim and Erik' act was born. The credit must go to Paul Fox, our boss; it was he who first discovered the benefits of a roving team, not tied by standard conventions or any particular theatre of operation, combining the investigative brain, the sharp word, and the roving eye.

***

Jim always gave the impression of a tall scarecrow, thin and bony. His upper body was hunched slightly forward, dragged down by the weight of his jacket and the burden of television. The rest fitted together like disjointed entities, each with a mind of its own. This was due to his gangly walk, and a pair of desert boots, size 13. His most remarkable feature was his face, lean and handsome, and a mouth twisted into a grin of cynicism and, perhaps, contempt.

'Why do you always grin?'

'I don't grin, it's what my mouth does when I have to listen to stories.' He was always in control of the space he occupied, and quite frequently that of his neighbour as well. He didn't seek friendship, and he was slow about offering it. But once he had committed himself, he was a faithful companion. His trademark on the screen was a blue blazer and an expensive tie. The portion not shown by the camera was more relaxed; a worn-out, not to say threadbare, pair of corduroy jeans. He actually possessed two pairs of trousers, both similar in age and colour.

Once, when he had received a last-minute request to change a script line, and I had installed my camera along a Tel Aviv beachfront, he quickly changed into his blue shirt, tie and blazer.

He opened: 'The war, which is now in its third day … ' I couldn't help it, I simply had to tilt my lens to his lower section. It made the BBC's New Year funny reel: covering his feet was a pair of oversized rubber flippers.

He had long, slim fingers, like those of a concert pianist. It was hard to imagine how such fine hands could ever hold a gun, yet I saw those very hands point a .45 into the jungles of Vietnam in a manner which promised no good to a lurking enemy, and which showed that he had handled weapons before. Mossman was born in 1926, when the rich were roaring and the average had to struggle for a living. His widowed mother had two little boys to look after. Both boys showed early promise, and were offered scholarships into some of the better public schools. Jim went to St Paul's in London. In the late 1940s he was called up for national service in the army and became a sergeant.

'Mossman, you must apply for a commission.' His colonel was firm about that.

'Sir, I don't want a commission,' replied Jim.

'But Mossman, you owe it to your class.'

Jim Mossman owed nothing to his class, nor to anyone else either. He could have been a general or a banker, but he wanted to read books and look at the world. After two years in His Majesty's forces, most of which he spent contemplating Greek temples and Mesopotamian art, he entered St John's College, Cambridge. He received a Commonwealth grant, and studied for two years at Princeton and Columbia. He became a writer and journalist. His texts were brilliant, cutting, and to the point.

We were in Addis Ababa during the opening of the first Pan-African Congress. The princes, presidents and sundry heads of state had been entertained during an endless series of luncheons and we had nothing to talk about. No statement, no declaration, no decision, just plain nothing. We went to the game park and looked at lions. On our return a reprimand from London awaited us: 'WHY YOU NOT COVER AFRICAN CONFERENCE? VITAL YOU EXPEDITE PICTURES AND TEXT BY WEEKEND. PANORAMA.'

'I suppose we have to give them something. Any ideas?' When Jim was bored with a story he was really bored, and showed it.

'Why don't we stand outside the palace gate and ask them what they had for lunch?' I suggested.

'Good idea, go there, I'll join you later,' he replied, which meant that he had a new book to catch up on.

I lugged my camera to the entrance of His Imperial Majesty Haile Selassie's palace, sat down, peeled an orange, and waited. The gate was guarded by two soldiers in resplendent uniforms out of *Ben Hur*, shiny breastplates and lances and helmets with red horsehair down the middle. I counted changes of the guard and I counted the palm trees and I counted the clouds. By now Jim, back at the hotel, must have reached page 327. It was a long luncheon, a very long luncheon. Finally there was feverish activity. I started my camera. The dignitaries descended the grand staircase, uniformly in protocol black. Missing were their top hats. These were not long in coming. The problem which suddenly arose was too many dignitaries and not enough flunkeys. Dressed in their Louis XV attire, these rushed hither and yon, precariously balancing a giant black stack of presidents' top hats.

It started a ballet. One servant held a stack of hats, and the dignitaries grabbed the first to come off the pile. I couldn't control the camera from shaking, it was so hilarious. There was a giant of a president, who had a tiny hat perched on his bald head, like a sparrow on a branch, and next to him a very small gentleman, whose only saving grace was that all the hats he tried came to a stop on his nose and his extended ears. Some hats were already on the floor, and a servant, in his eagerness to pick them up, bent over while his own stack of chapeaux collapsed and rolled across the imperial courtyard. This was most confusing to the two giant breastplated guards, who seemed at a loss. Were they supposed to spear the hats, or offer their own headpieces? Finally, the dignitaries disappeared into the cavernous interiors of a fleet of ancient Rolls Royces, and calm returned. The only remaining trace of the battle for the hats, was one forlorn topper trampled into the dust at the feet of the Imperial Guard.

When I returned to the hotel, Jim was on page 414.

'Shall we order tea?' Not, what have you got, or was it interesting, just: let's have tea. Since he hadn't been an eyewitness, he let his imagination play out the scene.

'How about *Eine kleine Nachtmusik*? Does that fit?' What a fabulous idea.

'Yes,' I readily agreed, 'to go with your commentary.'

'I wasn't planning on one.'

That was the way we sent it to London and how it was transmitted. My pictures were accompanied by the airs of Herr Mozart's violins. The item created a diplomatic row.

6

THE HEAD CUTTERS

(YEMEN 1962)

Here comes a candle to light you to bed,
Here comes a chopper to chop off your head ...

Children's rhyme

URGENT

DURSCHMIED SHEPHEARDS HOTEL CAIRO

YOUR CABLE AGREE YOUR PROPOSALS YOU GO YEMENWARDS AND
UPLINK MOSSMAN LATER STOP REPEAT CABLE SENT YOU YESTERDAY
THESE INSTRUCTIONS QUOTE SUGGEST YOU ONPRESS YEMEN WITH
BRITISH DELEGATION SECURING BEST POSSIBLE PICTURES REPUBLI-
CAN REGIME AND EGYPTIAN HELP STOP DONT CONCENTRATE ON
PICTURES DELEGATION BUT ATMOSPHERE

YEMEN EFFECTIVENESS REPUBLICAN REGIME EGYPTIAN ASSISTANCE
STOP SUGGEST MAXIMUM THREE DAYS FILMING IN YEMEN THEN JOIN
MOSSMAN ROCK HOTEL ADEN STOP PLEASE ADVISE BROADCASTS
LONDON/W1 REGARDS

FOX

The Imam was an old man who liked to cut off heads. So when his soul
passed on to Allah, his subjects decided to rob his son of the
opportunity to continue the tradition. That started a revolution. A
certain Sallal, the local – but not loyal – commander of His Majesty's
armed forces, ordered the only two tanks in the kingdom to shoot up
the royal mud castle. He failed to kill the young Imam, a bad mistake,

since this one managed to slip out by the back door and make for the hills. There he gathered the tribes, loyal through ancient bloodlines, and started a civil war in a country whose only income derived from a leaf named *qhat*, a narcotic stimulant. This biblical land had one road, built initially with Graeco-Roman labour, and repaired some two millennia later with Russian money. King Solomon ventured there to court his lady love, the Queen of Sheba. It is now the Socialist People's Republic, formerly Kingdom, of Yemen.

At the time of our visit its capital, San'a, was a conglomeration of clay skyscrapers. Its population lived in these lofty structures when Manhattan was a collection of buffalo-hide wigwams. The country had only one car, a gift from the Soviet Union to the old Imam. For the ruler, a paralysed drug addict, the automobile featured such extras as an elevator to hoist the shrivelled creature into his seat. The old man was a cruel despot. His favourite pastime was to watch his enemies' heads being chopped off, and then to display them on a crippled olive tree outside the city gate. When the rebels took charge, they lopped off a few of the royal retainers' heads and gave the old tree a new crop of skulls.

We were ferried in by the only plane that would venture to land near the 'camp of the camels'. When we overflew the meadow, to chase some peacefully grazing animals from the primitive landing strip, the disturbed herd beat a hasty retreat. That got them as far as the bedouin tents, which collapsed on screaming tribesmen. At the town gate, in the shade of the tree with the skulls, we were met by the chief of police and local customs controller, whose office was a canvas-covered date stand. Passing customs was simple: any passport containing a five-dollar bill did the trick. The bribe was in line with the importance of the country and the socialist revolution had not changed ancient customs. To the police chief we proudly presented our visas, which had been issued in Aden by the local grocer with a stamp marked

ABDEL'S FRUITERIE
PAID.

He looked at us, and we looked at him: we were two, so another five-dollar bill changed hands. We had successfully entered the forbidden Yemen. The assistant foreign minister came to greet us. We were led to the guest house, a dark and dingy hovel, which was part of the city wall and had been a medieval dungeon. From a hole appeared a young man who presented himself as the US consular agent. Next to him was a gruff character who turned out to be his Soviet counterpart. Now we had been introduced to the CIA and the KGB in probably the only country where prevailing circumstances had forced them to live in harmony.

Lunch was served on a long wooden table in the musty dungeon. The seating arrangement was simple. The rice dish stood in front of the Russian, who passed the plates through a neutral zone – a French nurse and a Dutch schoolmaster – to the West. Total silence reigned throughout the meal.

We took a stroll, expecting the man from Nazareth to appear around any corner and visit punishment on the moneylenders – nothing had changed in two thousand years. Buildings, some as high as twelve storeys, had biblical air-conditioning, funnels which caught the breeze from the nearby mountains. Through dark lanes, made claustrophobic by the looming height of the buildings, women glided along the walls, covered from hair to toenail by black shrouds. Their faces were hidden behind a knitted mesh. To take pictures of these mummified creatures would have meant instant trouble, possibly even death. I could picture the headlines in the *Daily Mirror* – BBC CREW CRUCIFIED – GOVERNMENT DENIES RESPONSIBILITY.

Petitioners were lined up outside the Imam's palace. They may have heard that a change had taken place, but old customs die slowly, and as far as they were concerned, the new ruler was only today's version of yesterday's king. A scribe, coughing and spitting, perched crosslegged on a mud heap and distributed scraps of paper. Whoever was not amongst those lucky enough to hear their name called had to come back the next day, and the next, and the next … *Inshallah* … God's will be done.

At supper I advanced coexistence by sitting down next to a newcomer, a chilly Russian.

'A radio technician', explained the Dutch schoolmaster. The Soviet radioman did not utter a syllable. He sat there, brooding and frosty. I could feel for him. This was not swinging Moscow, this wasn't even swinging Ulan Bator. I decided to bring some colour into his drab existence. By sheer good fortune and foresight I had come prepared for a medical emergency, and had smuggled a bottle of vodka into this country of the faithful. Quietly, I lifted Vassili's glass and filled it up – out of view of our Koranic hosts – with the prized liquid. I placed it in front of his nose. It looked like water. He sniffed and a grin split his face.

'*Kharasho!* Very good!' With that remark he gulped it down in one go.

Three glasses later we had become friends. His name was not Vassili but Grigori, and his English was good. We opened our evening's discussion by exchanging names of brothels in Jakarta where he and I had experienced certain pleasures. Then all the lights went out. Grigori broke into laughter.

'Come, I fix.' With that he dragged me into a cubby-hole where wires were sprouting in a gay bouquet. 'I fix yesterday with big nail, make fuse. One day, boom, all San'a kaput, I go back to Moscow ... hahaha ... ' he doubled over, as he shoved another iron nail into the fusebox. I can't remember what happened next; all I know is that the following morning I woke up on the floor. And the Russian was gone. Some time during our raucous night he had confided to us that he was actually a major in the Soviet air force.

A public rally was laid on to impress the first visitors from the world's press, Jim and me. Just looking at this screaming ocean of tribal humanity, armed with flintlocks of dubious vintage, made me pray that they were short of ammunition and not too high on *qhat*. A young revolutionary leader, just back from his oratory training in Cairo, brought the crowd to fever pitch. He pointed at us frequently. The hate in the eyes of the mob needed no translation – whatever was being said about us wasn't friendly. The speaker's assistant, who had studied English in an Aden high school, whispered a translation to us:

'The evil Queen of England gives rifles to the tribes in the mountains, they will come and behead you and rape your wives. The *Inglesi* are the real trouble makers, the despicable dog of an Imam Badr is only a puppet in the hands of these imperialistic colonialists. We must fight imperialism. We must fight the rebel tribes and kill them all. These people here are representatives of England, they will make pictures and show them to their queen, so let us show them that we do not like the *Inglesi* and their imperialistic, capitalistic, neo-colonial politics ... '

We were surrounded by the mob. Faces, distorted by hate, smeared across the viewfinder of my camera. Wielding their wickedly curved knives, the crowd hovered on a thin line between hysteria and heroics.

Had the British Foreign Office made some statement to support the young Imam, without realizing that two BBC men were inside revolutionary Yemen? Would the frenzied mob do away with us? Could the sheer mastery of the speaker's tongue restrain the mob from cutting our throats as they did to their sheep?

We lived through a hectic ten minutes, but the resulting pictures were certainly worth the fright. It was a unique glimpse into AD 633. Early next morning, when we felt that we had grossly overstayed our welcome, Jim made a statement of the obvious: 'I think it is high time to bid this place farewell.'

The old Imam's car drove us to the airstrip, where we were unceremoniously dumped into the small plane which had brought us in. The pilot was more than happy to see us. He had spent a sleepless night in the cockpit, afraid that some weirdo would put a curved knife through a tyre. To get a replacement would have taken about two and a half months by mule or camel. However, luckily for all of us, the tribesmen had left him alone, they just wanted to inspect that curious silver bird, touch its metal skin, and stroke it gently. Then they parked themselves nearby, lit a fire and slaughtered a sheep. They were still there when he started the engine, then they fled for their lives, followed by hobbled camels.

The reason for the hatred to which we had been subjected was to be found in the British presence in Aden. From their air base, the Royal Air Force controlled the countryside. Whenever one tribe got it into their heads to shoot up another tribe, an expedient way to bring a quick end to the fighting was to fly a jet-fighter low over the tribe's herds and turn on the afterburners. The earsplitting roar panicked the herds over mountains and valleys, and kept the tribesmen busy for ages rounding up their dispersed goats. This way their energy was funnelled into less destructive activity than a brawl with their neighbours, or the British.

When Jim and I returned to Aden we realized that we had only half of the story. In order to present a clearer picture of what was taking place in this strange land which was indicated on any map of the world by a white blob and the words *uncharted territory*, we had to find out what the other side was up to – the mountain tribes camped around their religious chieftain, the young Imam Badr. The RAF flew us to Beihan, where the local emir put a Land Rover at our disposal, and, even more vital, put us under his personal protection. That meant that anybody tampering with our good health would lose his head.

Three hours over a rough track and we arrived at a cleft in the chain of black rocks which until this point had formed a natural barrier to our left. It was the gateway to the centuries-old spice route from the Orient. This narrow gap had been crossed by the legions of Muhammad on their way to the holy places of Islam, by slave traders with their ebony cargo and by spice caravans for the rich burghers in the lands of the sinking sun. A lookout tower marked our return into the kingdom of Yemen. Before our eyes opened a breathtaking vista of sand – an endless expanse of desert as far as the eye could see. Dunes of dizzying heights, deep valleys. Formations, sculpted by the winds, gently sloping on one side, cresting into a sheer drop, which threatened to break and bury the traveller under tons of sand. The scene was strangely fearsome in its beauty. It was quiet, and yet filled with strange sounds. This desert was the fruit of an unholy marriage of wind and stone. Heat-fragmented rock, stones chafed by the wind, ground into infinitesimal grains, millions, trillions, zillions of little atoms, all chasing each other through the process of nature's sand mills. Every one sought a place to settle. The wind blew them across another crest, pushed them into another valley, with a noise mightier than the angry sea. In the late afternoon light the desert took shape. Shadows of deep blue formed endless waves on the deadliest of all deserts known to mankind, the Rub-al-Khali, better known as 'The Empty Quarter'.

We skirted closely round the highest dunes, and within two hours found ourselves staring down at Harib, a hamlet protected by two mountain ranges. There was a castle, bleached and polished by the winds into glaring white, and a meagre crop of thistles for the ever-hungry goats. Some twenty huts, shelters against sun and drifting sands, encircled the central waterhole. The local dignitary was a small hunchback with a large Mauser .98 rifle. We were offered his hospitality in the cool interior, seated on homespun carpets made of brightly coloured goat's wool, where we were served sweet tea. The emir of Harib was surrounded by his advisers, the cast from a Frankenstein movie. He tried to prove his good will towards a peaceful solution of the present struggle by producing a few Egyptian soldiers, his own crop of POWs, whom he kept in a cage like monkeys. They were better treated than the local convicts we had seen crouching in the pitiless sun, legs shackled by chains to the castle wall. Our bedouin driver acted as interpreter. He explained that the law of the Koran was applied. Thieves had their hands cut off, adulteresses were buried in the sand and stoned to death, but these were honourable fighting men, although misguided, and had to be treated with respect. This respect was not reflected in the eyes of the Egyptians, who were clearly terrified by the ever-present curved knives. After ten cups of tea and some polite grunts from the hunchback, the sherif provided our driver with a scrap of paper for the nearest outpost of the Imam's fighters, which he said was 'Somewhere out there,' as he pointed in the direction of the sands.

The track from Harib to Marib, the abandoned capital of the once mighty realm of Sheba, is an endlessness without life. There are not even sandbeetles. In biblical days, so we were told, a dam irrigated wide tracts of land, making this a fertile paradise. But, as the Bible goes on to tell us, the people sinned, the dam broke and the land was repossessed by the sands. The only landmarks which allow navigation in this sea of sand are ragged blue rocks, distant beacons to aim for. At one point we had to traverse a formation which resembled a dinosaur's back. That was where our trouble began.

Our driver had graduated from camel to rally driver without bothering to find out about the delicate mechanisms of the internal combustion engine and the gearbox. Even on the steepest incline he obstinately refused to shift into low gear. He laboured the poor vehicle until something snapped. Undisturbed, he overcame this handicap by gunning the engine a bit harder, and triumphantly made it over the top to start the descent, a perilous piece of driving even for a real champion. With him it turned into a game of chicken. On the loose gravel of the rock face the Land Rover lost its tracking, and several times we came dangerously close to the precipice, a drop of several hundred feet to the desert floor. On each occasion, Allah protected us

– such was certainly the belief of our jeep-jockey. When we reached
the sliding sands, matters rapidly moved from bad to worse: by now
the sun was fully up and the jeep's water temperature warning light
was bright red. We finally ground to a halt. I slid underneath to
inspect the damage.

'Jim, I am afraid we have a problem.'

'Only one? Make me happy and tell me what.'

'The four-wheel drive is gone, the connecting driveshaft to the front
wheels has snapped, and the oilpan has a hole.' It was beyond
emergency repairs: slivers of steel had jammed the linkage. One such
piece of metal had punctured the gearbox, and oil was leaking. As
nourishment we had brought sweet dates, and now I asked Jim and
the driver to chew some of them. With the paste made from this sticky
substance I managed to plug the hole. At least it would keep us going.
Without four-wheel traction we got stuck in the soft sands every few
hundred yards, and had to shove and dig. Towards water there was
only one direction: forward.

On the horizon appeared the ruins of Marib that had fallen victim
to the moving sands. We passed a sign of life, a herd of camels nibbling
on a desert delicacy, a thorn bush. A few miles further on we happened
on the carcass of a burnt-out Egyptian helicopter. This, our driver
informed us, was brought down by rifle fire, when the pilot mistook
the ruins for an Egyptian fort and came in for a landing. Then we came
upon the remains of an Egyptian relief column sent to rescue the pilot.
They had been stopped by the terrain and by the fierce royalists.
Cartridges by the thousand gleamed in the slanting rays of the evening
sun. We found several skeletons. Those killed outright were more
fortunate than the ones left wounded to die of thirst, with vultures
picking on them. All that was left were bits of green uniform on
bleached bones.

'My God.' Jim was stunned by the spectacle. 'This must have been
quite horrible.'

'Many Egyptian dead,' smiled our guide. 'First car we blow up,
throw bomb from up here, boom! They get stuck in rocks, we kill them
all. The one who run we kill in desert. Come airplane, come
parachute, we shoot them. All dead, out there.' He pointed into the
distance.

'How many were you?'

'Oh many, many hundred.'

The Egyptians had been a mere fifty, although protected by armour. The tribesmen had set their trap between the outcrops. The armoured cars had to pass through the defile, where the tribesmen dropped flaming petrol into the open vehicles, burning and shooting the soldiers. Then the Egyptians had tried to send more relief by air, but the paratroopers were picked off still dangling in midair. 'How long ago?'

'Ten days, fifteen days ago.' In another ten to fifteen days, this grim reminder would be hidden for ever by the drifting sands.

They appeared from behind rocks and rose from the sands – royalists, a band of about fifty wild warriors. There was a lot of screaming, laughing and hugging. We were kissed and passed around for more kisses. What was it that the revolutionary leader had shouted at the crowd back in San'a? 'We have the whole country under our control … ' We were a mere twenty miles from San'a. The situation was quite simple: the revolutionaries and their Egyptian allies were confined to their fortified cities, and the royalists didn't have the heavy weapons to get in. The warriors of the Imam told our driver to park his vehicle near a cliff, and led us across a steep slope into a narrow confine between two outcrops of volcanic rock. It was like the smuggler's camp in *Carmen*, with several hundred wild and screaming warriors. They were clinging to the sides of the gully like a flock of tan-clad birds. On our approach they let out a war-cry to curdle anyone's blood. At the headman's cave we were confronted by an assembly of bearded gentlemen with dangerous gleams in their eyes. They would give no pardon, and expected none. *An eye for an eye.*

They rose as we entered, and the dignitary in the centre put his hand over his heart. The prescribed forms of politeness were observed:

'*Al Salam Alekum* …' he said.

'*Ahlan Wasalhan* …' I replied.

'*Kayfa Halakoum* … how is your life?' he enquired.

'*Al Hamdulilah* … Thank God, it is good,' came my answer.

'*Kayfa hal Al Aela* … how is your family?' I didn't have one, but it was not polite to mention this, so I countered:

'*Kulahum fe saha jaydah* … all of them are fine.'

'*Ma hya akhbarakum* … how is the news?'

'*Aall baekhair* ... the news is good.' Like a game of tennis, with the ball bounced back and forth. After we had all found out that our families were fine and the news was excellent we could sit down and drink coffee, very strong and very black. The rest of the afternoon was passed in silence around a hookah. We finally got up, bowed ourselves out of the cave and gave the leaders a chance to plan their next war strategy.

The sun had disappeared behind the dunes and it was getting chilly. We had one thin groundsheet between us, and we rolled it around ourselves like a crêpe Suzette. I fell into an exhausted sleep.

My nightmare revolved around a nursery rhyme:

> *... here comes a candle to light you to bed,*
> *here comes a chopper to chop off your head ...*

My dream didn't last. I woke up, freezing. Following the immense heat of the day, the rocks had cooled rapidly and the temperature had dropped by thirty-five degrees Centigrade in a matter of hours. That change caught us by surprise. It was to be the coldest night of my life. Jim was already up. Tired as we were, we had to move in order to keep warm – there was no other solution. Fires were not permitted: we were too close to the Egyptian artillery for such luxury. The sand was as cold as snow and in the blue light of the moon it looked like a winter land-scape. We looked at the stars, and I could understand the great fasci-nation that astrology held for Arab scholars. It was the perfect night sky. We were at 8,000 feet and there was no industrial smog, no diesel exhaust fumes, not even water condensation, just clear, cold sky. I watched Orion and the Great Bear and the North Star wander across the firmament. And I dreamt of the caravans of bygone years, which found their way, guided by these very stars, across the Empty Quarter.

It was a night of purity, of confessions, of dreams. We walked and we talked. That night was a revelation. Jim talked about subjects that had been taboo – his philosophy, his family, his disappointments and his future hopes. I told him about my father and my years in the terrible war. We talked about music and poetry. The stage-set was grandiose, two human pebbles in a vast universe, observed only by the gods and the stars. It was a night of pure magic, a moment of eternity in man's short lifespan.

The first rays of the rising sun broke the spell. The royalists were making their appearance, and we were recalled back to earthly realities. Kneeling on the sand, the tribesmen prayed to their Allah, their heads bowed in the direction of Mecca, their faces raised towards the heavens, palms humbly extended to the One God. They covered their faces with their hands, and asked for His forgiveness. Our driver informed us that we were expected in the chieftain's cave. The ceremony of *Salams* was repeated, and a samovar produced. For this morning they decided to have 'a little fun' with an Egyptian fort guarding the approach to San'a. The tribal chief was keen to tell us about his loathing of the Egyptian foe.

'They are not men. They have no hair, you cannot get a good grip on their heads.'

His explanation was accompanied by a circular movement with his wicked dagger. The word went out and in no time a hysterically howling mob surrounded us, rifle in one hand, wicked blade in the other. This unruly band set off at a trot through the sand. It was getting hot, stifling hot. It was not surprising that our group of noisy, undisciplined joggers was discovered by a spotter plane, and soon a series of heavy shells came whistling our way, passing with the roar of a runaway locomotive above our heads. The projectiles exploded several hundred yards behind us in a rockface. Their bangs echoed across the desert.

We had reached 12,000 feet. The heat, together with the altitude, made breathing an effort. We climbed up to the lip of a gigantic bowl about four miles in diameter. The walls of the crater, formed by glazed, ragged cliffs, were shimmering blue, floating on waves of intense heat. The bottom of the bowl sizzled like a giant frying pan, the superheated air sending up gusts of turbulence towards our nest on the outer rim. Our eyes smarted from the glare and the sun's fire. In the centre of this lunar circle below was a fortress built of crater rock. A squat beetle crept across the sand, spitting fire in our direction. To prove their courage, our valiant warriors let go with a few rounds from their ancient Mausers and Lee Enfields at the heavy tank. The only noticeable effect of this rather futile exercise was that it brought our location to the attention of a cannon placed on the wall of the fort. Its rapid-fire bullets zipped like angry bees past us. I watched as the turret of the tank turned towards our position.

'I think this is sheer lunacy, we might even get hurt in this pisspot battle,' was Jim's way of assessing the situation. 'Let's go and have lunch.' We descended from the eagle's lair just about the moment when a shell struck and sent rock fragments zinging through the air. One of these splinters struck a tribesman and broke his arm. He screamed and crashed from the cliff to the sands below. There he lay, quite still. He had broken his neck. Some of the gang walked over to him, and used their rifle butts to cover the inert body with sand.

'The sheikh asks you to lunch,' said the guide. A sheep was driven to the middle of the gully and its throat slit. Blood spurted on to the white sand. The head was severed, and the beast skinned. Then they put it on a long pole and stuck it across the flames. A kilim, a handwoven tribal rug, was produced and placed near the cliff in the little shade there was to be found in this Arabian broiler. We were invited to sit down, but first we removed our shoes. It was a pleasure to shake the sand out of them and let fresh air pass between my fried toes. 'What now?' asked Jim.

'What now what?' I shrugged my shoulders and waited. I soon found out, when we were offered the delicacy of the day – the sheep's eyes, raw! To refuse the gift would have been the paramount insult, probably punishable by death. We swallowed and retched, and calmed our rebellious stomachs with a can of fruit salad which Jim had liberated in a cave. The roasted sheep was brought and a grab-with-your-right-hand started. The chief ripped a large morsel, and, breaking it in half, presented both Jim and me with the meat. It was very fatty. This was followed by a ball of rice. I couldn't help thinking of the eyes and the body with the broken neck.

Time came to say farewell, and with the usual '*Shoukran*, we thank thee' we slid down the slope towards our Land Rover. After several miles of fine sand the engine started to knock and the gearbox to boil. We had reached the scene of the ambush of the Egyptian armoured convoy. Our car rolled in amongst the carcasses of the vehicles and then died. Water gushed from the radiator. I was taking a few shots, when Jim all of a sudden pointed at the sky, and yelled: 'Erik! run!'

I knew Jim wouldn't panic without good reason. I ran until I could hear behind me the noise of an engine, and the high whistle of the diving brakes from an aircraft. We were heading in the direction of some rocks, but we never made it.

'Down,' screamed Jim, while two shadows zoomed over us. They were observing – probably they had spotted our dust trail from high above and had come down to inspect. It was only luck that they hadn't seen us running across the sands, or spreadeagled on the ground.

'Jim, up there, the rocks,' I called out, already scrambling up a dune. Some two hundred feet from us there was an outcrop. I turned briefly to see the planes come in for the kill. We had to get to the rocks or find some other shelter. They had spotted our driver, because one went down to have a look at him. That gave us a few more precious seconds. I was there first and threw myself behind a rock, Jim came down on top of me. He jammed my arm into a sharp rock. I was cut, but that was nothing compared to the danger that the two sharply banking planes represented.

Vrrrroooom – vrrrrooom – they passed over us, and winged away into the blue. I had only two explanations: one, they were out of bombs and bullets, or two, they took us for dead. If they were out of bullets they would have radioed our present position, and we could count on more company. We simply had to get away from the open sands. A hundred yards from our position I noticed a wall, probably remains from the long-forgotten civilization. Frankly, at that point I wasn't interested in archaeology, my main impulse was to get there, and fast. We had hardly reached its relative safety when two more planes started to dive in. I clutched the camera in my bleeding hand, but by now I was out of film. All the spare rolls were in the jeep, parked on the site of the ambush. The first plane came swooping low over the dunes. There was a sharp crack, followed by a dull boom, and a cloud of dust rose to the sky. They must have decided that we were hiding underneath the trucks. We kept our heads down. A thought came to my mind: if they hit the car, how would we ever escape from the Empty Quarter?

By a miracle we found our vehicle in working order with only the windscreen shattered. The bomb had struck the lead truck from the old ambush. The water in our radiator had cooled sufficiently to start up, and we circumvented the crater of the explosion. Our driver's mind was blown by the blast and he raced across the sands in sheer panic. Regardless of terrain, he kept his foot jammed on the accelerator. We rode a rollercoaster, until we hit patches of soft sand. And then a giant dune loomed. The way up was the gentle rise, which meant that the other side was bound to be the sheer drop. I was worried about the soft sand and the state of our vehicle.

'Ahmed,' I said to our driver, 'please wait here. Jim and I will go up and see if we can get over the top. Under no circumstances drive before we come back.' Still shell-shocked, he stared at us and nodded. We had hardly reached half-way up the dune, when Ahmed the Mad passed us in high gear, whining up the incline, until his tail lights suddenly disappeared. Our jeep had jumped over the edge.

Ahmed's life was saved: he had landed in a patch of quicksand, a hundred feet down. The car was gone, with no hope of recovery. The sand was already up to the dashboard, with Ahmed clutching the steering wheel. More sand poured in by the second, dragging him deeper and deeper. 'Ahmed, get out!' He moved slowly, dazed.

'The water, Jim get the water.' He raced to the back while I was tearing at my bag with the film. Jim got hold of the watercan and our bag of 'Fat Ladies', the Maria Theresa thalers, the only accepted currency.

From the way in I recalled a mountain ridge somewhere in the blue distance. If we could reach the life-saving shade of the rocks before sunrise we stood a slight hope of survival. Jim started the hike with a significant gesture. He reached into the bag of Fat Ladies and strewed the surrounding sands with them. What good was silver, what could it buy in the desert? Its weight would drag us down, and we needed to conserve our strength to carry the essentials, water and film. Jim took the tape recorder, I took my camera and Ahmed took his Mauser. A last glance at our vehicle, which had settled with only its top showing above the moving sands, and we set off.

There really is no good way to climb a steep sand dune. For every two steps forward I slid one back. The sand got into the top of my boots, my ankles turned into chafed skin and sand got between my sweaty thighs. Our immediate prospect was a series of three-hundred-foot dunes in front, and the threat of the sun on our backs within a few hours. Our choice was extremely limited. We kept moving, two steps forward, one step back, two forward, one back ... how many times during the next five hours did I consider dumping the film and the camera?

We slogged on, we dragged on, we stumbled on. To make things worse, our guide had taken a nasty bang on his head when he went over the cliff. His glassy eyes stared at nothing. Sometimes Jim dragged him, and sometimes pushed him up a dune, to let him tumble down the other side. On we crawled, miserable beetles in a vast nothing. Sand in the shoes, sand in the crutch, grinding onwards, upwards, downhill. We couldn't talk because of the sand between our teeth – only a grating noise came from our mouths. Our faces were masks of sand stuck to sweat. Up another dune, up, up, then we sat and slid down, got more sand up our raw thighs, reached the bottom and the climb began again. Wait, where was Ahmed? There – no, that was Jim, where the heck was Ahmed? Oh, there – falling down over the top, rolling towards us. We were on the devil's rollercoaster. It was too dark to make out the distant rocks. Would we ever get closer? To stay on course we kept to a series of tyre marks. How much longer before that ball of fire rose? Ahmed was finished, kaput. How long would Jim last? I was weakening with every dune crossed, and my forward motion had become a mechanical movement without thought.

A mirage? A fata morgana? Had the fatigue doped my senses, or was I losing my marbles? I thought I'd better not tell the others, but I was certain I had seen lights, a flash in the sky. That could mean only one thing, another vehicle, people, somewhere out there. Then I stumbled towards Jim, clutched his arm and spun him around: 'Look … '

Through eyelids heavy with sand, Jim stared at me with an amazed expression: 'Saved … ' It was more of a question than a statement.

'Not yet.'

'Must … stop … them.'

Like a man possessed, I gathered my last reserves of strength, dragged myself to Ahmed, ripped the rifle from his shoulder and stumbled along the crest of the dune in the direction of the approaching lights. I focused on two headlights, a great distance away, and pumped a bullet into the chamber. I didn't dare to think. If they did not stop, I would have no choice. Such is the law of the desert. Water plus transport equals survival. We had to have transport. I started to tremble.

The lights came closer and closer. If they did not stop, I would kill them. Faintly I could hear the approaching engine. I tried to scream, but nothing escaped my throat but a hoarse whisper. I pulled up the

Above: Hitler's arrival on the Heldenplatz, Vienna, 1938

Right: Erik Durschmied in 1943

Below: Durschmied's classmates surrendering to the Allies, 1945

Left: Bomb damage to the Albertina, Vienna, 1945

Centre: Erik Durschmied at Crawley Films, Canada, 1955

Foot: Fidel Castro's guerrillas in action, 1958 (frame from Durschmied's 16mm film)

Second Section

City Car

CASTRO (LEFT)

Brings Pri
From Guer

By Phyllis Wilson
Citizen Staff Writer

Erik A. Durschmied of 203 Cameron Avenue, 28-year-old freelance cameraman, was lucky to escape from Cuba a week ago with his life and priceless footage of a filmed interview with Fidel Castro.

Mr. Durschmied spent six weeks in the mountains with the Cuban rebels, two of them with Castro at his headquarters. It would probably be an understatement to say his Cuban sojourn was exciting.

On an assignment for the CBC, Mr. Durschmied arrived in Havana about Oct. 20 with his camera well hidden in his car, set out for Santiago and Bayamo. He was held up on the way by rebels who were burning every car they saw at the time. He was allowed to go, though he had a tough time saving his car which he eventually hid in the jungle.

It took Mr. Durschmied 12 days

divorced and young son. F

In
Emphasizin
friend of nei
the governme
said he had
pressed with
sonality.

"He is a
so he is not
is not a Com
much an idea
did not war
would not ru
is very cleve
Whether he v
man behind
don't know."
was Castro's
dent.

Mr. Dursch
evidence of
that he heade
he saw him
cause had st
Buil

He also ne
built schools
Sierra Mae

Right: Pass supplied by the Cuban rebels

Below: Newspaper cutting showing (left) Durschmied with Fidel Castro in the Sierra Maestre, 1958, and (below) his famous picture of Fidel Castro

..... de Sierra Maestra .....

El Sr.(a.) Mr. Erick Durschmied

esta autorizado (a) a transitar por el Territorio Libre hasta:

La Habana .... por asuntos: propios ......

El portador _si_ lleva carga.

Jefe de Estacion

NOTA: En caso de llevar carga se debera realizar al dorso una declaracion detallada de la misma.

Este pase debera ser presentado ante cualquier autoridad que lo exija en cualquier momento, y debera ser devuelto antes de salir del Territorio Libre en la Estacion Local.

Cualquier ciudadano que no resida en el Territorio L y no este provisto del presente pase, sera detenido y ducido ante la autoridad correspondiente.

La carta, papel o documento que el portador presenta en la Estacion Local para proveerse de este pase debera adjuntarse.

En caso de ir armado el portador debera estar provisto de una autorizacion del coordinador o responsable del Movim miento de donde proceda, de lo contrario debera entregarsela al guia que lo conduzca, hasta que le sea ordenada su devolucion.

THE OTTAWA CITIZEN

OTTAWA, CANADA, FRIDAY, JANUARY 2, 1959

Pages 21 to 38

...man Faced Cuban Firing Squad

...CHMIED   *A CUBAN REBEL*   *THE WOMEN MEAN BUSINESS*

...s Film Camp

...d by the wrongs done his ...try rather than by any per-...l feeling.

...took Mr. Durschmied six ...s to get out of the mountains. ...unwhile because of the presi-...ial elections Castro had ...red his guerillas to stop all ...ic on the roads. Mr. Dursch-...l retrieved his car, not know-...it was the first seen on the ...way in three weeks.

...Cauto Christo he was ...ed by a government armor-...atrol, dragged out of his car ...stood up against a wall be-...a firing squad. The ser-...t in charge was loading his ...hine gun when an officer ...across the courtyard yelling, ...n't shoot the American."

"Uncomfortable"

...was very uncomfortable." ...Mr. Durschmied. Finally ...patrol told him to get going. ...unately his camera was not ...n. Because of just such ...t, Castro's people kept the ex-... film at headquarters,

THE GUERRILLA CHIEFTAIN

Castro Always Sure He Would Topple Batista

By Larry Allen
Associated Press Staff Writer

HAVANA, Cuba—Husky six-foot two Fidel Castro voiced confidence from the start that his ragged guerrilla force would eventually topple the dictatorship of Fulgencio Batista.

The 32-year-old, bearded rebel leader has never wavered in this belief since he and 81 armed companions landed one dawn a little more than two years ago on a beach in eastern Oriente province and melted into the nearby hills. For Castro, it was a return home from years of exile.

Despite repeated reverses, the lawyer son of well-to-do planter parents plugged ahead, burning plantations, shattering communications lines, kidnapping, striking where and how he could. His strength, in men and arms, slowly grew.

Used Guerrilla Tactics

From the thick woods of eastern Cuba's sierra maestra, the bespectacled revolutionary waged a relentless guerrilla war until he finally had brought down the once powerful Batista machine. From exile, Batista said it was the Cuban army was not trained.

Montrealer Agent For Rebel Chief

Left: Durschmied interviewing Colonel Otto Skorzeny, Madrid, 1959

Below: With Jim Mossman, desperately waiting for a non-arriving plane, Mogadishu, early 1960s

Above: Mossman drinking tea with the British Army, Aden, early 1960s

Right: Royalist tribesmen on the lookout, Yemen, early 1960s

gun, fired into the air, once, twice. The beams turned towards the shots, I was blinded by the sudden light, I waved the rifle. The car came to a stop two metres from me. I was too exhausted, I could only point in the direction of Jim and Ahmed, then somebody hauled me into the back. Someone lifted a goatskin and poured glorious water over my head and into my shirt.

I opened my eyes to find myself on the floor of a house, wrapped in blankets, surrounded by other sleeping bodies. I recognized Jim by his bleeding ankles: he was too long to be fully covered and his feet stuck out from the blanket. I shifted position, causing another figure to grunt: 'Whatsa time?' Definitely not Arab. My guess was New York.

What was this? Where were we?

Other bodies stirred, voices beneath blankets like:

'Morning, Dick, sleep well?'

'So so, Dana.'

'You sure made a lotta noise coming in last night. Who are the wanderers you picked up?' That had to be us. Jim unrolled from his cover and stared in disbelief. He said, 'We are from the BBC.' Now it was the others' turn to stare at us.

'Well, I'll be darned! Hi, I'm Dana Schmitt from the *New York Times*. And this here is Dick Conde, an American turned native.' Richard Conde had become Abdul Rachman Conde and was acting as public relations man for the deposed Imam. He kept a generally watchful eye on the developing situation in the Arabian sands. They had been returning from a different band of royalists near San'a.

'I picked up your car tracks, and when I found your vehicle buried and figured what had happened, I followed your tracks in the sand. The clincher was your shots.'

'What can I say?' I asked.

'Nothing, this is the desert. But tell me, what would you have done if I hadn't stopped?'

I looked away, and then said, 'Honestly, I don't want to think about it.'

'Well, don't worry, I had a gun on you. I woulda shot you first.'

We were in the guesthouse in Harib. I was washing the sand from my teeth with strong coffee. A brouhaha was building up outside our lodgings. Our friend the hunchback of Harib had organized a royalist demonstration in our honour. The only part which bore any resemblance to what we had witnessed in San'a's revolutionary square was the knotted beards and wicked blades. The massed warriors were armed with flintlocks, Mausers, Enfields and even blunderbusses. Enough *qhat* had been passed around to ensure a festive mood. From a trumpet emanated piercing noises. In their midst I noticed a few terrified prisoners. Occasionally someone pulled a trigger, and the powder-flash would shake the narrow confines of the town square. High above the excited crowd fluttered the banner of Islam and the Prophet. Silver swords on green. Religion, Saudi gold, and a loathing contempt for the Egyptians united these savages in a *jihad*, a holy war.

The procession moved off into the desert, into the sands which had almost cost us our lives. Once a terrible scream drifted across, and I saw knives flashing around something on the ground. Then even the blood-curdling wail faded away ...

There is little else to report, except that the film won an award, mostly on account of the brilliant commentary Jim composed. He took a well-deserved recuperation period, which he used to write a novel. As for myself, I forgot the warriors of the Yemen over a stuffed Christmas goose.

7

THE JIM AND ERIK SHOW

'A reporter? Fantastic!
I wish I had time to read ... '

*Prime Minister William Tubman of Liberia
to Jim Mossman, 1963*

On a different occasion, we were in Aden to cover the uprising against British colonial authority. It was high season for the dismemberment of the British Empire, a time when the United Nations became overcrowded with newly independent republics. Because of our position in *Panorama*, we became the BBC's eyewitness envoys to all the death-pains in what had once been Her Majesty's Commonwealth of Nations. This time, HM Government had decided to break off relations with Somalia. We got the invariable cable:

'PROCEED TO SOMALIA TO COVER DIPLOMATIC CRISIS.'

'Erik, Somalia is hot and humid and the food is terrible, I don't think the Royal Navy will bombard the shores, and in any case we won't get a visa. Let's give it a miss.'

'But we have to try. London would be simply furious, if they found us on the golf course.'

'Yes, I suppose so.'

We went into Aden's Crater, a desolate city centre in a landscape which can be best described as the dark side of the moon. Other than cheap transistor radios, and goats devouring garbage, Aden has nothing to recommend it. In a small street we found a barred and shuttered house.

A plaque on the clay wall announced that this was the Consulate of the Republic of Somalia. A sigh of relief from both Jim and myself, it seemed very shut indeed. Foolishly I rang the bell. An unshaven face appeared behind a crack in a window shutter. 'So sorree, mister, we are closed.'

'Thank you, we just wanted to make certain you don't issue any visas. Never mind, we'll cable the office in London.' Me and my big mouth ...

'Oh mister, you are from London?'

'Yes, from the BBC.'

'Oh, my goodness me,' the door was flung wide open, 'please do come in, come in gentlemen, the BeeBeeCeeeee? I am honoured.'

He was small and had a fuzzy hairdo. An Indian who, for tax reasons, had purchased the right to be the honorary consul of the Republic of Somalia. He grabbed Jim by the hand and pulled him through the door. I followed into a dark room, piled high with cardboard boxes tied together with string and electrical wire. There were revolutionary pictures of their great leader on the floor, and discoloured spots on the walls where the pictures had been removed. A naked lightbulb on a wire was held up by a combination of hope and cobwebs. In a corner was a cat nursing a litter. The place smelt of curry and cat's piss.

'Please gentlemen, make yourself comfortable, I'll make some tea.'

With this he used his sleeve to dust two boxes and asked us to install ourselves. Soon he returned with Indian tea in tall waterglasses, made with concentrated milk and undrinkably sweet.

'Every morning I listen to the BBC cricket score. Middlesex isn't doing so well in 'Pindi. Are they bringing Freddie Truman to Calcutta?' Neither Jim nor myself were cricket fans, and the query was beyond our competence.

'I really don't know. Now, what about our visas?'

'Oh yes, visas, of course, forgive me gentlemen, I almost forgot. It is so nice to talk to gentlemen ... ' and with that he moved into a corner to untie the string from a box. Out came a weird collection of newspapers, books, and some pots. Triumphantly he looked at us.

'I have found the stamp,' he announced proudly. 'Can I please have your passports?'

The stamp was dry. Now, where was the ink pad? He rummaged in the box, and when the first yielded nothing, he opened a second, a third, and finally found the pad on the bottom of the fourth.

We received the stamp and with it the unavoidable duty to proceed towards what Jim had described as a hot and humid climate.

'How much do we owe you?' it is always courteous to ask.

'Oh please, my privilege to be helpful to the BBC. A great honour to my country to have you gentlemen come and visit us.' My country? He wasn't Somalian, he was from Madras or Bangalore. 'By the way, I also distribute Rolex watches, would you like one?'

I wasn't in the market as I had just received a new Rolex, the type of watch that will tell you one hundred feet under water which way Berlin is, or what the temperature is in Moscow. Jim showed some peripheral interest, which was enough for our Indian watch distributor to start unpacking. He unearthed a gorgeous watch, circa 1933, gold, with roman numerals. A black leather strap, really beautiful. 'Eighty pounds for you my friend.' It was worth at least one hundred and fifty.

'That much?' answered Jim, as if surprised by the demanded price.

'Sixty?'

'No, I'm afraid I don't have that much on me,' said Jim.

'How much have you got?'

Jim took out a wad of notes, mostly singles, and counted to thirty-eight. He waved these in the air. 'Thirty-eight?' a very disappointed Indian said, 'All right, done.' With that he grabbed the money, while Jim strapped the watch on his wrist. The Indian was not aware that Jim had at least another two hundred in the other pocket.

'So what do we do now? You've got a watch and we've got visas.'

'How unfortunate, now we will have to proceed to that dreadful place.'

He had been absolutely right, it was hot – hot and humid. On our first night in Mogadishu, the concrete flower on the horn of Africa, we tried to escape into the airconditioned comfort of the best eatery in town. I had fried chicken and rice, and Jim tried the local goulash, a dreadful error, which turned into a drama. All night I sat there, pouring water into him and leading him to the outhouse to make sure he would vomit the poison. It didn't take long to discover the cause of the food poisoning, an acute fuel shortage resulting in an electricity cut every six hours. Jim's goulash had been defrosted and refrozen several times over. Jim struggled for two days, aided by an Italian doctor who was an admirer of Mussolini, and who pumped endless injections and pills into him, to get back on his feet. I half-carried him on to the plane, and deposited him at his mews house in Kensington. If nothing else, Somalia had been a memorable feast.

Speaking of food, we both liked a good meal. Once we were on an extended trip to the Middle East and found a superb two-star restaurant which catered to oil money, not quite within our daily allowance. Jim found the solution, a fictitious commandant Bonvoisin of military intelligence. Twice a week we sampled the delicious *mezze*, washed down with a bottle of claret, and twice a week the BBC accountants received our expense claims with the remark: ' ... for confidential debriefing by commandant Bonvoisin.' That went on for a month, until the home office cabled: CHECKED WITH PARIS BUREAU, NO COMMANDANT BONVOISIN ON LIST OF INTELLIGENCE AGENCY, OR EVEN ARMY. PLEASE EXPLAIN. PANORAMA.

To this insinuation of expense fiddling Jim replied: ALWAYS HAD DOUBTS ABOUT BONVOISIN. WILL STRIKE HIM FROM MY INVITATION LIST. MOSSMAN.

By now we had become very close. Each year we shared over two hundred days living the same existence, forced upon each other. And yet, I knew precious little about Jim the man. He was discreet. Professionally, we were certainly one of the more successful combinations, constantly in search of yet another pisspot war or revolution 'by popular demand'. It wasn't at all unusual to find us one week in the Argentine, and the next week in the Congo. The wide world, and no place in particular, had become our permanent home. Slowly Jim started to confide. On these nights in tents, caravanserais or favelas he would tell me stories about his past. One day in Cairo when we were sitting in the Mena House with the overpowering nearness of five millennia of glorious past, he told me about an event during his time in the services.

'I was here before, it just seems so long ago, almost in a different life.' Strange, Jim wasn't melancholy or moody, but something bothered him that night, something he wanted to share.

'I was here during my service days. I was military but I never wore a uniform.'

'How did you manage to do that?'

'I was in a special service. Actually, I was in military intelligence.'

There followed a moment of silence, as if he was wondering whether to burden me with his past. He glanced up at the pyramid. 'I was ordered to deliver a suitcase to an Egyptian officer. It was at the height of the Suez crisis, the roads were blocked and controlled, and here I was, driving this ridiculous little car all over Cairo in search of a man I had never seen before. I ended up inside an Egyptian army camp. I was immediately surrounded – I don't know who was more confused, them or me. So I told them that I had lost my way, and, believe me, they were only to pleased to get rid of me. They even helped me push my car back on the road. I had had a scare and returned to the flat the service had provided for me. I dragged up the suitcase and opened it. It was stuffed with pound notes!' He indicated piles and piles. 'A lot. Fifty, sixty thousand at least.'

'I hope you kept it.'

'Of course not. Next morning, I started off again, and this time I found the man and gave him the money.'

'What's it like?'

'What's what like?' Now he was playing dumb.

'The intelligence business.'

'It's like the game we all played as children, you show me yours, and I'll show you mine. With variations, but it's all a silly game. It's spies spying on spies. There are few secrets, and both sides know bloody well what the other is up to.'

'What about patriotic motivation?'

'You mean strange notions like *Vaterland?* That went out of style with Mata Hari, and she was a Dutch belly dancer who gave it away for the Kaiser. Spooks are grey people in grey suits with rolled-up umbrellas. They sit in small offices, and when they aren't worrying about their children's school fees and their progress up the social ladder, they study wheat futures for the Ukraine, so that HM government can speculate in gold futures, and make up for their budget deficit. Some get it right, but others miss, and burn up.'

'There must be more to it.' Jim remained noncommittal. 'Are you still in it?' I had to know: some day it might make a great difference to me.

'Don't be silly, I got out of it when I left the service.'

'Does one ever really get out of it?' I asked, perhaps rather timidly.

'Don't worry, it's over.'

For Jim, the subject was closed. What puzzled me was that he was much too intelligent to join the spooks, nor had he ever shown the slightest interest in money. So what was it that made him do it? Jim never did anything without a valid motive. A touch of daring? The old school tie? I should have pushed him, but I left it at that. It did not end there. A few months later Jim wanted to go to Beirut, and we stayed as usual at the Hotel St Georges. Jim was fidgety. 'I'll go down to the bar.' 'Go ahead,' I shouted from under my hot shower, 'I'll join you when I'm dry and perfumed.' What I didn't mention was that I had run into a friendly Air India hostess on stopover, and we had only forty minutes before her departure for Bombay. The dear girl had lamented that she expected to run into a spell of chastity, and that she simply ached to rid herself of frustrations.

An hour later, when I finally entered the bar, I spotted Jim and a fiftyish-looking man who hadn't shaved in a week sitting in a dark corner. They were deep in discussion and did not notice me. Somewhat startled, the man looked up when he saw me hovering near them. He wore a wrinkled linen suit and looked as though he had been living on a diet of double whiskies for a very long time. He was probably much younger than he appeared. 'Oh, there you are,' Jim looked at me, then turned to the man. 'I would like you to meet Erik.' The man glanced at me, stretched out a hand, and mumbled something. Jim turned to me: 'Erik, this is a colleague, Kim Philby.'

A few days later, the 'colleague' disappeared and a month after that his voice could be picked up on the wavelengths of Radio Moscow. British intelligence and the CIA had red faces. For years, Philby had been the number two man in British Intelligence as well as the most valuable agent the Soviet Union had in Europe. When his escape became known, Jim voiced a dry comment: 'Glad that's over.'

I had not forgotten our meeting with Philby. 'What's over?'

'Philby. They finally found out who the third man really was.' He never said who he had referred to as 'they'.

'What do you mean, third man?'

'Remember the Burgess–Maclean affair in the late fifties?' He was referring to the spy scandal which had shaken the United States and Great Britain. They had been tipped off and fled.

'You see, for a long time I was a prime suspect!' This struck like a bomb, and yet somehow it fitted. Most of their group expressed an equal dislike for female companionship, and they had, at one time or another, all been members of the same 'club', an intellectual Cambridge fraternity of homosexuals. Somewhere in this nebulous past a master spinner took fragile threads of loyalties and wove them into an old-boy spy network. That loyalty became synonymous with betrayal seemed to matter only to outsiders.

'Real Boy Scouts, those MI Sixers. The only ones they hate more than the GRU are MI5. Philby did MI6 harm, and they hate MI5 for not finding out, or, what is even worse, not telling them. Insane jealousy between two outfits over who gets more money to waste. Don't ever get involved in this business. They never let you go.'

I have no idea what was really running through Jim's mind that day. I have met a number of recruiters, a lot of whom were quite blatant about it. Some were clumsy, some tried to hire me for their cause, for conviction, or for money. I was never interested, not even for an all-paid vacation for two to Wonsan plage. For all those who ever suspected me of having supplied information for someone's *Vaterland*, let me make it quite plain: I never have. What worried me was that we had probably been among the last Westerners to be seen in the company of Philby. It didn't take long before it became clear that this could have consequences, but Jim didn't seem bothered.

The more inseparable Jim and I became, the more he became irritated with my amorous adventures. Not jealous, just irritated. It was a kind of possessiveness born from a close relationship over a long period of time. An interview with the Austrian chancellor had been pre-arranged, and we were expected in Vienna. Because of bad weather the plane was diverted to Zurich, and our solution was the overnight train. We stood on the platform of Zurich's Hauptbahnhof, quite lost – globetrotters, who jumped from one plane on to another without a moment's hesitation but had no idea how to board a train. As I was pondering the problem, I noticed a splendid figure behind a pile of Louis Vuitton suitcases. She was a slender symphony of Dior and *Harper's Bazaar*. About thirty-five, with a face that says: I know what I want, and how to get it. I asked her if this was the right *perron* for the night express to Vienna. She smiled.

'Do you have a reservation?' Hungarian? In any case, a pleasant accent, probably finishing school in Lausanne. 'Compartments are hard to come by.' I could imagine. The roads across the Alps were blocked by heavy snow, and the planes weren't flying. 'How many are you? Two? Let me see what I can do.'

'*Guten Abend, Madame*,' said the trainman as the row of blue sleeping cars pulled into the station. I noticed some notes change hands, and then he turned to me:

'*Kompartement Nummer 16 für die gnädigen Herren.*'

'Thank you,' and to her, with my best smile, I said, 'I trust that you will find time to join us for dinner.'

'That will be fine, I am in fifteen.' Right next door, what luck.

'Jim, we've got a compartment.' He flashed a forced smile towards our travelling companion. 'How simply marvellous.' Jim took the upper bunk, I took the lower. 'I asked her for supper.'

'Did you?' Not surprised, but definitely annoyed. The train had crossed the Austrian border, and dinner was being served. I knocked on her door. A melodious voice from behind the closed door answered. 'I'll join you in the dining car.'

We took a table and before long she appeared, very lovely. She had changed from Dior into Gucci. Jim made an effort to be friendly. 'How nice of you to help, we have to be in Vienna in the morning.'

'So do I. Are you on business?'

'In a way; we have to speak with the Austrian Chancellor.' Very dry.

'You must be reporters.'

'Quite so.' That about ended Jim's effort at conversation, leaving it to me to entertain the lady. After the meal, she briefly turned to me and said: 'Come and see me later.'

Jim brushed his teeth and climbed into his bunk. He wasn't communicative, he was upset.

I was expected, so I said: 'I'll see you later.'

'Going for a stroll in the moonlight?' Typical Jim.

'Yeah, sort of.'

I knocked on her door. 'It is open.' She wore a flimsy negligée, and before I could even say a word, she threw herself on me and whispered: 'Don't talk, just fuck me.' With that she opened the robe, and installed herself on the bunk, with her back to the wall and her legs wide. She was an exciting woman, something from a mystery novel, the kind one expects to meet on a train, the kind one hardly ever meets in real life, and I needed very little encouragement. She moaned and then she screamed and I thought of Jim on the other side of the thin wall. Unless he was dead he couldn't help but hear. The train raced on through the night ... I was about to reach the clouds, when she noticed my hesitation, pulled me deep inside and in a hoarse voice whispered: 'Stay in me, please stay, I want your child.' Before bidding her a pleasant dream, I promised to pick her up for breakfast just before our scheduled arrival in Vienna.

'Yes, I'd love that.' she smiled.

I entered our cabin where Jim pretended to be fast asleep. I fell on my bunk and dozed off. The following morning I knocked on her door. There was no answer. I knocked again, this time a bit more insistent. The conductor appeared: 'Madame left the train at Salzburg.'

I never did discover the identity of my beautiful stranger on the train. For a week Jim carried a grudge, and our conversation was restricted to professional remarks. Furthermore, he had lost his interest in the Austrian *Bundeskanzler*. I hated to see Jim upset. I managed to scrounge tickets for the Vienna opera. We were seated in the back row of a box, with a couple from the American midwest in front of us, friendly people with a big farm in Kansas. Brief smiles and introduction, and 'we are on our first trip to Europe, we have four children, our older daughter studies ... ' and the curtain went up. The performance was excellent, and when the second act came to an end, and Tosca had stabbed Scarpia and everyone on stage tried to out-sing each other, the nice couple turned around and invited us to join them for dinner. 'Why, aren't you staying for the next act?' asked Jim. 'Is there more? But they're all dead.'

Mossman was not easily impressed by the cult of personality. He avoided the formal 'Mr Prime Minister' or 'Your Excellency' – it was 'Mr Nehru' or, if the situation required a certain diplomatic protocol, simply 'Sir'. Politicians are actors, their tricks of gesture, their tilt of the head, their smile: 'I know all about this' and 'I will immediately look into that', are all part of their basic stage art. On rare occasions, the cameraman manages to tighten the shot in such a way that hands are not visible, but a camera cannot erase a facial expression.

Leaders from the socialist bloc had all been passed through the same mould. Somewhere deep in the Soviet Union there must be a training centre specializing in the art of waving hands, and exhorting crowds. I have watched them closely, from North Korea, Romania, Afghanistan, or the local Communist Party. The gestures invariably resembled each other. On many occasions, Jim broke through their stage veneer, or their rehearsed answers. He could be tough to the point of being insulting. During an interview with the British Prime Minister, Mossman asked a pertinent question. The country's leader flinched, and was saved by a timely intervention from the programme's moderator: 'I don't believe that this is a question for the Prime Minister.'

'And why not?' Jim snapped back, 'I believe that the country has a right to know, and I insist that the Prime Minister answers my question.' But these were exceptions. Normally, if he suspected dishonesty, he would simply allow the interviewee to get tangled up in an obvious lie in front of millions of voters.

Take a notorious arms merchant, whose advertising slogan for an 81mm mortar was: 'The ultimate tube for the smooth-bore fanatic.' Our task was to find out if his guns found their way to terrorists.

'I only sell to legitimate governments,' said the dealer. 'For instance, I have just sold some 200,000 hunting rifles to Albania.' Jim made a point of telling the audience the size of the hunting population of Albania, by showing the discrepancy between a recent population count and our arms merchant's delivery quota.

Jim was very fond of India and its people, and he was on friendly terms with Pandit Nehru. On quite a few occasions the Prime Minister invited us to his residence in New Delhi. He would ask Jim questions about the state of the world, and Jim gave his unbiased opinions of what he, the journalist, thought of certain political decisions, or how these could affect the outcome of talks, bargaining sessions, even peace negotiations. Nehru listened to Jim's assessment of America's Vietnam policies, or socialist reforms in the United Kingdom. Jim's subtlety as an observer of world affairs came to the fore. However, when it came to discussing Indian affairs, Nehru would not give, and accused us of superficiality. I must admit, he wasn't far off the mark. India is too vast in size, and too varied in population, for us to understand.

One of Nehru's principal interests was to explore the foreign support which India hoped to gain during renewed aggression by Chinese troops across the Himalayan mountain passes. Nehru felt that the West was letting him down, and said so. He threatened closer co-operation with the Soviet Union. The West wouldn't listen, nobody took his warning seriously, including us. It ended with a subtle but well-founded rebuke by Nehru:

'You people always come for just long enough to completely misunderstand us.' An undeniable truth.

Take the day in Calcutta. It was an exceedingly humid afternoon. The town clerk wore a white suit – well, almost white. There were large sweaty patches under his armpits and on his back, upon which the red dust from the sports field had encrusted magic patterns. He was rotund, as wide as he was tall, and the sweat ran in driblets from his nose. Standing on his soapbox didn't make him any taller, or more impressive. He sported the moustache of a British Guards officer: the sweat made the scraggly whiskers stick to his cheeks. The suit was his status symbol to impress the lower employees of City Hall, the smile was for our camera.

He was addressing a large crowd (Indian crowds come in two sizes: large or massive) of town hall employees on a field in the centre of Calcutta. Our hotel, the Oberoi Grand, was only a few steps away, and we were in considerably better shape than the rest of the crowd, who had had to march for many a hot mile before they reached the sports ground. The man was about to open the yearly sports competition of the city's employees, a colourful collection ranging from pale, hollow-cheeked desk clerks to the deep brown of the muscled sanitation workers. His opening address was an obituary.

'The Corporation of Calcutta has always encouraged this annual function for a great variety of reasons. It promotes friendship and understanding between our good workers in the City of Calcutta ... '
A few haughty words in Bengali were heard, a disturbance had started at the back.

' ... it gives you joy and delight which all of you need ... ' The Bengali background comments became distinctly haughtier.
' ... Gentlemen, this year the flag must fly at half-mast. This is due to a melancholy event which happened last night. Last night, one of our members, *Sri ... Sri ...* '

He turned enquiringly towards one of the lower echelons near him.

' ...*Sri* ... ', and then followed the murmur of meaningless sounds which is so typical when the speaker forgets the name he is about to introduce, ' ... committed suicide. I believe from his colleagues that he has been long suffering from melancholia and ultimately he fell victim to it! Last night he jumped from the Howrah Bridge and drowned.'

The background scene to this dignified eulogy had turned definitely sour, a glorious free-for-all had started between the 'joyful workers' and the 'delighted workers'. Everybody joined in the punch-up, with the noted exception of our town clerk, who made a neat exit from his elevated stand. He was last seen at a safe distance carrying the cashbox which contained the voluntary donations by the city workers to the good cause. Rising above a cloud of red dust I noticed a splendidly white-robed gentleman with a terrified look on his face and holding out his hands like a praying mantis. He immediately fell victim to a punch into his belly delivered by a small brown-faced man in shorts, and disappeared from view into a mass of heaving limbs. The little man's victory pose over his fallen foe lasted only a few moments, before he was felled by a cricket bat.

I pushed to the centre of the fray, using my camera as a battering ram, and ended up in front of a bald, sweaty giant in ripped pyjamas who was occupied in throttling one of the dignified hollow-cheeked clerks. When he saw the camera, he dropped his victim, who collapsed breathless at my feet, and turned to the camera, all smiles.

'The trouble is, that down there ... during the long distance race ... '

His explanation doesn't stop him from kicking a pale man in the shins. 'They have played malicious tricks ... '

'They've played what?'

'Malicious tricks, foul tricks ... ' as he staves in another attacker's nose, still smiling for the benefit of my camera. He really enjoys the fight and at the same time basks in the glory of being the star of television. Somebody is trying to tackle his legs, he deals out a mule-kick – scratch another member of the opposition.

'What did they do?'

'Our champion runner is in front, abundantly, he is first and ... '

More defensive action drops another town hall clerk. I weave with the battling forces. A cricket bat flashes past me, and our giant gets it right on the head. It doesn't seem to affect his smile for the camera.

'They pull down our running champion ... ' Kick, followed by another kick, another clerk is hoisted across the crowd, dropped in the red dust beyond the centre of the mayhem. Jim's head towers above the punch-up, undisturbed, aloof, a referee in a rugby game.

'So, what happens now?'

'We demand that the authority let the race start again, this is our demand. Our runner was first, so the other group, they see this, they jump on the track and they pull him down, so that their runner wins the race, and now the second runner is first, and we demand justice. Now we want to race again.' I nod as if I had understood him, and our good man continues:

'If the authority now announces to have the race again, we stop demanding.' With which he probably means that he and his buddies would cease demolishing the clerks of City Hall.

I shake my head, disbelievingly, 'So, why don't they do just that?'

'The authorities, they say, see the track judge. So we speak with him and we say, someone has played a malicious trick ... '

'A what?'

'A malicious trick, a bad trick, and you know what the judge replied? He simply said "*Cho Patahai*", yes, he said "*Cho Patahai*",' and with that he nods sadly.

'So what does *Cho Patahai* mean?'

'Ah, it means: it is natural, it has happened!'

Of course, what simple logic; or, as the Indian Prime Minister said, we're just long enough in any country to misunderstand the local population.

Some of the encounters we had to face were not quite as amusing. A Ku Klux Klan meeting took place in a field outside a small town in Alabama. Very effectively the show began in front of a flaming cross with a speech by the Imperial Wizard.

'This here is our Jimmy. He helped rid this world of three creatures bent on the destruction of the white race. I say, let's give Jimmy a big hand. Let me hear it!' And the crowd, hiding behind white masks, roared their approval. The story had it that, one dark night, Jimmy and a bunch of armed cohorts had been riding around in their pickup truck and had rolled up alongside three senior reserve officers in the US army. One of them happened to be black, and Jimmy had stuck a shotgun out the window and killed him. A jury had found him not guilty. Now he was the local hero.

Sickened by the scene, I said something like, 'Jesus!' and in no time I had a scrawny kid in front of me screaming, 'Whatsa matter with ya, ya nigger lover?' The shout brought me to the attention of a few Klansmen.

'Well, do you really think killing people is right?' I asked. Perhaps it was foolish to argue back in such an environment of hate, but I couldn't help myself. I was outraged by their complacency towards murder.

'Hey, we've got ourselves a nigger lover here.' Scrawny got more attention than the main speaker. A crowd had gathered around us, all beefy men with beer bellies. 'You gonna spy on us with your fuckin' camera?' He got himself all worked up.

'Oh, do be quiet,' interjected Jim with his superior air. 'The judgement of life or death is not a matter for idle discussion. It is God who gives, and takes, and to make this final judgement is not the right of a youngster with a gun.'

'You sons o' bitches! You lousy fuckin' nigger lovers!'

I realized we were in for trouble, and I pulled Jim into our car. An axe-handle caved in the windscreen, and the doors were torn open. I was dragged out and thrown to the ground. Feet smashed into me, I could taste blood in my mouth. I could only see the axe-handle. Women in the crowd joined the excitement and screamed:

'Kill them sons o' bitches.'

The crowd parted and a husky state trooper appeared on the scene. He pulled me up by the neck, and half-dragged, half-pushed me into his patrol car. 'In there!' He punctuated this with a final shove. Jim was already in there, blood on his torn shirt.

'Who do ya guys think y' are, comin' down here and startin' a riot?'

'We didn't start a riot, we were just doing our job. The crowd attacked us.'

'Your job is to stay away from here, that's that. Jake, read them their rights.' Jake, his partner, took out a card and pronounced our civic rights. We were allowed to make one phone call. He punched the button of his siren and slowly drove us through an alley of hostile stares from behind black slits in white masks. At the police station they booked us for inciting a riot. We were fingerprinted, and Jim was allowed his one call, which he made to the BBC office in Washington. After a night in the hole with the local drunks, the wife beaters and a black kid suspected of rape, the door opened to the sugary smile of a Southern gentleman. He explained that he was the local attorney, that we had been released and that all charges had been dropped. Somebody in Washington had a lot of clout which reached all the way to the sweet South. We left the hospitable hamlet minus a camera and covered in Band-aid.

Jim held to strict professional morals:

'Never try to manipulate a person to your line of thinking and force him to surrender his own ideas. Never attack any man personally, or you will make him your enemy for the rest of his life.' One time, when I talked about a girl who had taken her own life, he said: 'Life isn't given to you to take it.' I was to have occasion to recall that phrase.

Whenever we returned to London, which was infrequently, Jim locked himself into his mews house in Kensington, where he stored the memorabilia he had collected on his travels. There was a cannonball from a fort in St Kitts, a Buddha's head from Katmandu and a clay fertility god with a small head and a large penis. The house was run by an elderly charwoman. When she picked up the brittle sculpture, Jim said, 'Be careful, don't drop it.'

'Oh, Mr Jim, I've never dropped a thing like this in all my life,' she replied with a mischievous giggle.

Jim's only permanent companion was a visiting cat. He had wall-to-wall books and a kettle that bubbled constantly. He would sit and read and drink endless cups of tea, avoiding the BBC studios whenever possible. He didn't fraternize with the programme's technical or editorial staff. For all practical purposes, he didn't look for companionship. His happiness began the moment he left London. He craved escape from the cosmopolitan rumble. We lived our strange lives in all the assorted pisspots. One night, in some unspeakably horrid place, he confided: 'We don't have to compete, we have different likes and tastes, and yet we are very much alike. In any case, with you I don't have to pretend. That's why it works.' This was a great compliment from a silent man like Mossman.

PART TWO

A LONG, SAD WAR
VIETNAM 1961–1980

'We are not about to send American boys
away from home to do what Asians
ought to be doing for themselves.'

President Lyndon B. Johnson, 1964

1

THE NEW BUSH-WAR

'Time is on our side, time is our
best strategist if we are
determined to pursue our
resistance to the end.'

*Truong Chinh, General Secretary of the
Communist Party of Vietnam, 1947.*

'Vietnam is a prescription for chaos. If not stopped soon, it will turn into Asia's worst problem since the last war.' This was Jim Mossman at his most pessimistic. I was amazed – to me Vietnam was just another one of the many bush countries with a minor problem we had reported on. I was not to know that this country would become a global battleground, and that our very lives would be intricately entangled with Vietnam's tragedy. We were only in 1962, and I felt Jim was overdoing it a bit.

'I don't really think it's as bad as you make it sound,' was my reaction when I read his script. 'This place is not half as bloody as the Congo.'

'The Congo? You fool, what's the Congo got to do with Asia? In Africa a few European mining interests are vying for mineral rights. A few assorted nasties rape French nurses and it makes headlines, but it isn't political. Vietnam is. This is the Americans versus the Soviets, who have interposed their satellite battalions in a power struggle. At stake is predominance in Asia. The Vietnamese may follow the Russian line, but they aren't easy prey for anybody. Look at the Chinese – for centuries they have tried to subdue the Vietnamese, and look where they are today. Next came the French, colonial might with cannons fighting little people armed with bamboo poles. Or so they thought until they too were crushed. This isn't a simple bush-war. This is big! ... and will turn most unpleasant.' It was a long speech for Jim.

I couldn't see it. In the past few years, I had witnessed so many jungle wars that I had grown immune to their pretensions of global importance. But what proved to me that Jim had fallen into an unjustified panic was Saigon itself. The city was pleasant. It had all the flavour of a quaint French provincial town, with the gaiety and vice needed for the enjoyment of the good life. Granted, a war had scoured the countryside for years. The French suffered defeat at Dien Bien Phu and the North had been separated from the South along a line drawn at a conference table in Geneva, and turned into a socialist republic. But the shooting had never reached Saigon, nor its restaurants, or residents.

A cable from London had found Jim and me 'somewhere east of Suez', this time with a Gurkha unit fighting communist rebels in the jungles of Borneo.

'PROCEED TO SAIGON AND PRODUCE FIFTEEN MINUTER ON NEW BUSHWAR.'

I was tired of Malaya, with its mosquitoes and its foul food, so the 'new bushwar' suited me fine. With a meal of crispy duck we bade farewell to Singapore and headed for Saigon. On our arrival at Tan Son Nhut airport we found little evidence that there was anything unusual. On the contrary, customs officials remained as efficient as they had been taught by their former French colonial administrators.

'*Avez-vous quelque chose à declarer?*'

No, we didn't have anything to declare, just my camera and a few rolls of film. Jim had a bottle of tax-free whisky and I had my new Rolex. It had been presented to me as a farewell present by a Swiss maiden, with the tearful wish that I would never forget our brief but emotional encounter. Her name was Heidi and my memories of her lingered on for all of two weeks. It was a nice watch.

'No, we have nothing to declare.'

At passport control we were handed *un questionnaire à remplir pour l'immigration*.

1. What is the purpose of your visit?

2. Are you a member of, or have you ever been a member of, any communist movement?

3. Have you visited any communist country in the past three years?

Under number one I put: cameraman, to cover present events. What these present events were, they could best decide for themselves. There was no reason to refer to a war. Officially it might well be described as a minor internal disturbance.

Item number two was easy enough to answer: No. On number three I simply lied. Why bother the poor immigration man with the tale of Mira, who had recently shared my bed at the Ukraina Hotel in Moscow, and whose portrait, together with mine, was now on file in some dusty KGB basement.

We were waved through customs. A row of rickety Renault 4s was lined up outside the terminal.

'*Monsieur, taxi?*' ... 'Monsieur, me good car, me good driver ... ' and so on. The bargaining started in English. When I broke into French, the driver stopped haggling and we quickly agreed on the regular, non-tourist rate to the Hotel Caravelle. The taxi was small, Jim's legs were long, and I ended up sitting on my camera case. The Caravelle, one of Air France's terminus hotels, was fairly new, the service *très français* and clean, the food excellent. It was built in the centre of town, facing the Hotel Continental (of *The Quiet American* fame) and the national theatre.

The palm-lined square in front was in constant motion, an anthill of stinking, honking motor scooters. Each corner was taken up by a pushcart vendor. If the cigarettes were real Lucky Strike, Camel, and Gauloises, their price was not. The street vendors' source of supplies was cartons which had fallen off the back of a lorry, and the smokes cost a fraction of those sold on the official market. Actually, everything in Saigon seemed to fall off a lorry. Even the motorcycles had seen earlier lives in Hong Kong or Singapore. They had been stolen, hidden in fishing vessels and finally offered by the boatload at Saigon's quayside. The parade of young wild ones could buy these for a thief's price and then stink up the town circling aimlessly around the square to impress their girlfriends, who were hanging precariously on to the package carrier. The boys were skinny copies of James Dean, blue jeans and checked shirts, the girls were uniformly pretty, with large conical straw hats and long silk dresses.

Jim and I were given rooms on the third floor with a splendid view of this nocturnal scene. The terrace of the Hotel Continental was crowded to capacity by French couples, the men in white linen suits and their wives, or mistresses, in the latest fashions from Paris. Bistro tables were laid with *pastis* and green olives, or Cinzano vermouth. The square was framed by a palette of flowers, bougainvillaea in lilac and deep purple and flaming crimson trees. Little children in tatters were doing a brisk business shining shoes. Once in a while a uniformed Vietnamese would stroll past, but that was about the extent of visible war activity.

The Caravelle's dining room was on the top floor, with a fabulous view across the city. The food was exquisite, *lapin à la moutarde, poularde farcie, salmis de palombe.*

'Perhaps Monsieur would like a salad.'

'What wine would Monsieur like with his main dish?'

'Tonight we serve cracked crab, just arrived. Would Monsieur like to try?'

And with the wine and the crab and the coffee and the strawberry sherbert came a reasonable bill. We spoke French – *alors*, Monsieur was not a tourist – and we were treated with the reverence reserved for all the French rubber planters. The night was spent in great comfort, and I couldn't understand what the rush was all about to send us to Vietnam and do a 'fifteen minuter on the war'. As a matter of fact, this was the kind of place I would pick any time for a relaxing holiday.

Next morning, after a *grande crème* and croissants, we sauntered to the Vietnamese army press office, which was located on the second floor of a dilapidated mansion near the main square. If the outside was unattractive, the interior was even worse: a black cubicle where a bored young lieutenant, leafing through a French pornographic magazine, hardly offered us a glance as he handed us a set of forms. He asked us the same questions as on arrival: whether we were members of the Party and so on.

'How many journalists are there here?' Jim wanted to know.

'Actually, you are the only ones.'

'We are from the BBC.' That did not impress him. Perhaps we should have said we were the Voice of America or Radio France International.

'We would like to go out into the field and accompany a troop on active duty.'

The lieutenant seemed annoyed. He put down his girlie magazine, duly took notes and then looked up. 'We will arrange a programme for you.'

'Where is the US military advisers group?' This was the obscure title that everybody had agreed upon to explain away the American presence, in a feeble attempt to camouflage who was really running the war. Americans were 'military advisers', and in this summer of 1962 their number was quite limited. 'They are down the road, in the cinema.'

'Thank you. Please let us know when everything is arranged, we are at the Caravelle.' The lieutenant plunged back into the girlie pages and we wandered to the cinema. A smart US marine stopped us at the door. He asked politely for our passports, picked up a wallphone and then we were asked to step up to the second floor. Our reception here was different. We were ushered into the presence of a major in a trim uniform with creases in his trousers which, as with all American uniform trousers, did not quite reach the ankle, a pair of black patent leather shoes, combat eagles on his chest and a thunderbolt on the peak of his cap. I had to admit that it was all very impressive, that is, if you were eleven years old. On his desk was a plaque with his name engraved – on tortoise shell! Behind him was the star-spangled banner, and on the wall a map of the Republic of South Vietnam.

'Welcome to US military advisers group Vietnam. My name is Major Laupenheim, I am the press co-ordination officer.'

'How many press are here at the moment, major?'

'Well, we have a photographer from *National Geographic* magazine who is doing a picture survey on the montagnards in the highlands. Then there is a feature writer from the *San Francisco Chronicle*, he is up in Hue, doing a colour piece on the imperial city, I believe.'

'Well, major, we would like to have a look at the war.'

'Ha ha, the war, yes, I guess you would.'

'Yes, we would very much like to join a group in the field. We have already made our number with your Vietnamese counterpart.'

'That's just great.'

'The Vietnamese officer has promised to contact us.'

'Well, he won't, but I will. Where are you folks staying?'

'At the Caravelle.'

'Fine, I'll get on to Danang, let them know you folks are around, and see what we can come up with. I'll drop by this evening and liaise with you.'

That ended our morning's official activity, and we headed in the general direction of the harbour. Saigon was amazing – there was simply nothing which couldn't be procured at cut price. Since we had to be outfitted for our combat outing and fine military equipment was available at better than moderate rates, we went on a buying spree. There were waterbottles from the French army and US army jungle boots. There were cans and tins and stuff. By stuff I mean anything that hadn't been nailed down by a previous occupation force. And there was Mr Ho of Tudo Street, who tailored overnight the most incredible fantasy uniforms. It was during our second fitting that afternoon that we found out that it wasn't actually Mr Ho who stitched the clothes, but four bearded Sikhs in a back room, chained to their chairs by needles and thread. Mr Ho just smiled, held out his hand, and collected the cash. And speaking of money, since the local Dong wasn't renowned for its stability, Mr Ho offered to exchange our dollars at a considerably friendlier rate than Vietnam's central bank. He eventually became a very wealthy banker to journalists.

Burdened with our treasures we arrived back in our rooms like a pair of Santas whose reindeers had landed on earth six months too soon. My phone rang. It was the American major. 'Mind if I drop over?'

He had changed into a civilian outfit. His trousers were still too short and the shirt was now too loud, but his crewcut made him stand apart from the rest of the colourfully dressed tourists.

'I've got you an action in the North. Tomorrow, you've got to take the Air Vietnam flight at o-nine-hundred to Danang. There will be someone to meet you at the airstrip.' He then proceeded to hand us our accreditation and stayed for dinner.

The following morning we left for Danang. To obtain a seat on the plane we had to grease the greedy palm of a local ticket agent. After we had boarded our flight we noticed many empty seats ... otherwise the trip was uneventful. Waiting for us alongside the tarmac in Danang was a tough-looking soldier with a leathery face. He wore jungle combat fatigues and a holstered .45.

'I'm Major Dwyer, and I have been assigned to look after you people.' Assigned, not volunteered. I noted the distinction. He was probably wondering: why don't they let us get on with running a war, and stop asking me to babysit for damn reporters? But he was too well trained to express his feelings, at least to us.

In 1962 Danang was a sleepy fishing town with a baby airstrip, a few small aircraft and about twenty clapped-out helicopters with ARVN markings. The US military advisory group numbered two hundred, camped in an abandoned Catholic school along the river. The major took us to the camp and gave us a choice between staying off base or on base. We made a mistake – we chose off base.

That evening, the major collected us from the Hotel Moderne and took us to the base theatre, where we watched *Auntie Mame*. The cinema was in a converted church hall, and the only draught was provided by slowly rotating fans attached to the ceiling, which gave the impression that the church hall was about to be carried off by a fleet of helicopters.

The Hotel Moderne was not quite what its name promised, lacking all modern comforts. It had hot and cold water – dripping down the walls. Our room was like an oven, and my bed was a battleground for fleas, lice and spiders. We survived the itchy night.

In those pre-historic days of the Vietnam conflict, the only action to be found was concentrated in the central highlands, west of the port city of Danang. The total strength of the enemy throughout the country was estimated at between 5,000 and 8,000, poorly armed, but certainly fanatical. Their hit-and-run guerrilla raids weren't as yet cause for military concern. The political decision which was to turn this containable rebellion into a global nightmare was still years off. Establishing contact with the enemy – something we wouldn't have to worry about in later years – was difficult; the armed bands would rather fade into the jungle than stand and shoot it out against a well-armed, but not highly motivated troop. On the rare occasions when the Vietnamese army pounced on them from the air and cornered them, they had no alternative but to fight. In history books, the enemy would be written

up as Viet Cong; it didn't take long for the Americans to dub them
Victor Charlies, or VeeCees. Until that day of our arrival in Danang,
American war casualties had numbered two killed.

Major Dwyer informed us that we were to go along on a battalion-
size engagement. There had been rumours of VC presence: native
tribesmen, who had fled the dense jungle of the central mountain
range, reported a large band of intruders in black pyjamas forcing
villagers to give them rice. When the villagers refused, they had shot
two village headmen. The Vietnamese ranger battalion planned to
jump this group, annihilate them and then sweep through the highlands. A detachment of ten American advisers was to accompany the
action, both to study and to teach jungle warfare. That was the plan.

Our escort had organized an artillery spotter aircraft, which would
bring us ahead of the main armada of helicopters to the jumping-off
place for the operation. That would give us time to film the arrival of
the task force, and furthermore keep the three of us together rather
than parcelling us out amongst various aged choppers. To crank them
up, mechanics had to inject an explosive device into the start chamber.
With a loud crash, the first engine roared into life. This procedure was
repeated eighteen times, and the scream of eighteen non-synchronized
aircraft engines was stunning.

The heavily-armed Vietnamese climbed into the first seventeen, the
Americans were assigned to the last in line, number eighteen, and we
hopped into our spotterplane. The mighty fleet took off. Twenty
minutes later, we passed them overhead, visible only by their painted
rotor blades which designed a strobe pattern on the green jungle roof.
Then they dived into a cloud and we lost sight of them. We landed on a
dirt strip forty miles from Danang. We had been on the ground for
about twenty minutes, when the first tiny specks appeared on the
horizon. My first Vietnam war footage. How could I have known on
that afternoon in the central highlands that my next ten years would
be a never-ending series of horror films from Vietnam, and that this
conflict was to change my life.

The specks were gaining in size, one, two, three, four, five ... fifteen,
sixteen, seventeen.

'How many have you got, Jim?' asked the major.

'Seventeen.'

'That's funny, so have I.'

'But there's supposed to be eighteen,' I added.

'Don't I know it,' said the major.

We counted, then recounted, it was still only seventeen. Where was number eighteen? Number seventeen's pilot was a Yank. Our major strutted over to the landed helicopter, dwarfing the gesticulating Vietnamese battalion commander already there. The pilot leaned out of the cockpit: 'That's strange, when we headed into the cloud bank he was right behind me … '

'This is Delta Bravo, calling Delta Papa, over … This is Delta Bravo, calling … ' The call was followed by complete silence.

The Yank from number seventeen, his engine still running, screamed down: 'Hop in, I'm going back.' The Vietnamese ranger commander loaded up three more choppers for security, and we lifted off. The cloudbank was above us and a slight drizzle soaked my pants which were hanging out of the door. The helicopter raced at thirty feet above the leafy roof, towards a steep hill. Just before we reached the hill – and I mumbled a silent prayer: 'Lift, bird, please lift up' – the helicopter made a steep bank and then rose sharply. I clutched for a hold, since I didn't wish to dive head-first into the bushes. Just as we crested the hill, Major Dwyer pointed ahead. He grabbed the mike next to him and spoke into it. I couldn't hear the words, but his expression had changed and he looked worried. Then I spotted it, a thin column of black smoke, rising above the jungle. The pilot pulled back on the stick, bringing our helicopter up, to allow us a better look. He slowed as we approached. Below us was a twisted metal structure engulfed by an inferno, a pyre of rubber, gasoline, and human bodies. This was the American advisory group's helicopter. Eight men had been aboard it.

Two hundred yards from the crash site our pilot made an approach into a clearing. He was unable to set the machine down for fear of getting stuck in the mud, so we jumped from the hovering machine. Forty Vietnamese rangers and a few Americans headed for the fire. Pretty soon we could feel the heat. The stench of burning rubber and kerosene was nauseating. Then we noticed a clearing through the dense layer of leaves, slashed into the jungle by the rotor blades of the dying helicopter. There was little for us to do. It was impossible to get near the fire. There was nothing to be saved.

A shout came from nearby underbrush – a ranger had discovered two bodies, thrown clear when the machine exploded. Both were breathing. Fire victims never fail to give me a queasy feeling – I shall never be able to get used to the sight of charred flesh. These two were no different: no hair, no eyebrows, and their uniforms had burned off their bodies. They were in deep coma, but alive. Ever so gently we lifted them up and put them on stretchers. The Vietnamese carried them through the brush to our landing site and loaded the wounded on the hovering helicopters.

An American medical team had been flown in and was waiting on the airstrip. The military operation was postponed until the following day. One of the two casualties died during the night. Only the pilot survived. Seven were dead: America's most serious war casualty since Korea. These Americans died before they had ever heard a shot fired or faced an enemy. They perished before they reached the war.

The chance of a surprise attack was lost. The Vietnamese battalion commander, advised by Major Dwyer, ordered camp to be pitched alongside the airstrip. We tied our groundsheets together, and put up a four-man tent. During the night, a downpour sent floods into our sleeping quarters. I could feel a cold rivulet running down my back. Changing position didn't help, as the tents were too confined. We were under orders for a total blackout. The monotonous drumming of the rain on the tent stirred in me a desire for relief. Slowly, so as not to disturb the sleep of my comrades-in-arms, I rose, opened the tent flap, and stole towards the nearby bushes. I was about to commence, when I heard an unmistakable sound: the click of a safety catch. Then I felt warm breath on my neck, and a voice whispered something in my ear. I didn't need to be fluent in Vietnamese to get the general idea. I pointed at my urgent need, and proceeded to satisfy it. The soldier and his gun never wavered from my side.

Steam rose from the soggy ground when the three of us crawled outside for a first glimpse of the red ball of sun emerging over the green canopy of jungle. True to the old army motto: Hurry up, and wait, the compound burst into hectic activity. Jim looked at me with a grin: 'Did we almost lose you during the night?'

'How would you know? You were asleep.'

'Dwyer woke me, he was ready to intervene. He wasn't worried about the Vietnamese with the gun, but about the trip wires around the camp. He said the soldier only wanted to stop you from getting blown up by our own mines.'

Ever since then I have taken great care never to venture away from a tent at night. And I have learned to look for places of relief in front of or behind the vehicle, but never alongside in a bush. Better to be seen than to be blown up.

At three in the afternoon it was finally decided to press ahead with the attack. Jim, Major Dwyer and myself were split into three separate helicopters. Our smoke-belching battlewagons roared off to an uncertain future. The carefully laid 'surprise plans' were now thirty hours behind schedule. We approached a series of hills, bare of trees. The helicopters zoomed downwards, the pilot gave a thumbs-up, I switched on my camera, and we piled out from the hovering craft. The moment I hit the ground I felt a piercing pain in my left leg and my posterior. I had landed in a bloody bamboo bush. The young, sharp thorns spiked me, and there I was, like a porcupine with needles protruding from its behind. I kept on filming the cavalcade of choppers disgorging a ranger company. But no Jim, or Major Dwyer.

In no time I was surrounded by Vietnamese soldiers. They chattered like copulating ducks. It appeared that they thought of me as their American adviser, and were seeking guidance. As it turned out, they had neither an officer, a map of the region nor any idea of our intended target. The gentle contours of the hills which the commander had pointed out to us on his battleplan were nowhere in sight. It had become clear to everyone involved in this operation that we had been put down on the wrong hill, perhaps even in the wrong valley. Using Jim's expression: to put no finer point on it, we were lost.

However such was not my immediate preoccupation: what concerned me was the pain in my leg. I could feel the blood soaking into the sock and into the boot. There was an acute danger of infection, and not just a minor one, but tetanus.

I pulled down my trousers, and the damage became quite visible. One of the bamboo spikes had pierced the calf muscle and lacerated the blood vessels. Like a broken arrow, the ends stuck out from both sides of my leg. A Vietnamese medic inspected the gash, and with a swift movement, pulled on one side. I screamed, as only half of the

spike came out. The rest had broken off inside. Fucking wonderful!
The medic pushed a stick between my teeth, as two soldiers held me
down. Then he pulled on the other end. I almost passed out. My
Florence Nightingale poured disinfectant powder on the wound and
covered the bloody mess with an absorbent bandage. This didn't quiet
the hurt, but it stopped the bleeding. That still left me with a spiked
arse.

Through painclouded eyes I spotted figures crawling up the hill
towards us, not in a skirmish line, but one behind the other, without
the slightest attempt to hide their approach. They had to be pretty
certain that there was nothing to be afraid of. I recognized our tall
American major leading a line of small Vietnamese, and right in the
rear, strutted gangling big Jim. When they reached me, Jim could not
hide his amusement. There I stood, bare-arsed, in the midst of
kneeling Vietnamese, all busily removing thorns from my bleeding
posterior.

'You are ready for the purple star,' remarked Dwyer.

And Jim added: 'Can you walk, my porcupine?'

I pointed to my leg. 'I will, if you carry me.'

'Let's have a look at your leg,' said Dwyer, and once more I pulled
down my pants. 'That doesn't look too good, we better get you an
anti-tetanus shot.' He jabbed a needle into my rear, and I could feel
the antidote flowing into my muscle. 'You have to stop walking for a
while.'

The major decided that it was impractical to go into battle with one
hobbling cameraman; besides, we were now forty-eight hours behind
schedule, and any real chance of catching the enemy unawares had
evaporated. 'By now the Victor Charlies have faded all the way into
Laos, at least, that's what I would've done,' said Jim, as Dwyer
signalled base HQ that we would pitch camp on the hill. Just to
remind us that he didn't agree with Jim's assessment, and that we
were still facing danger, the good major cheered us up with the
remark: 'I believe the Charlies are still inside our perimeter.'

Frankly, at this moment I didn't care who was where.

To our great relief the night passed without interruption. Next
morning I could not get up, my leg was stiff, blue and badly swollen.
Jim helped me up, and I tried a few steps. Standing on it improved
matters, and pretty soon I was able to hobble around. Jim removed

the bloodsoaked pad, and bandaged the leg. The exit holes did not look infected but I had to be careful not to walk through swamps. An explosion shattered my thoughts. It was our own artillery providing fire support.

'Damn,' announced our highly decorated major. 'If this is a friendly shell then this is about as close as I ever want to be to one.'

Unrattled, he produced from his tunic a battery-operated razor and started shaving. A Vietnamese corporal brought us hot water in a steel helmet, a useful cooking pot when hung by its strap over an open fire. The major poured some into the palm of his hand to brush his teeth, and Jim used the remainder for instant coffee and whipped up breakfast. It consisted of salt crackers, apricot jam, and Jim's brewed concoction. Fortunately, Jim pulled magic from his bag of tricks, a flask with an all-purpose medicinal juice which had a definite resemblance to forbidden cognac. Dwyer didn't protest. The spiked coffee tasted wonderful and lit a fire in my tired and aching muscles. From the nearby valley came the sound of small-arms fire. This had to be the nearby Ranger company, engaging in some kind of action.

'They're probably shooting their lunch,' said Dwyer. 'Might as well enjoy the coffee and the morning breeze. It's gonna be broiling soon enough.'

Nobody seemed in any particular rush to confront the foe. The major finally issued an order to move out. Our stroll – there was no other way to describe the line of soldiers strung out like an African safari – trundled across rice paddies towards a row of bamboo huts with thatched roofs. Man-size clay jars contained all the village's rice supply until the coming harvest.

There wasn't a soul in sight. The montagnards had been frightened into hiding by the roar of the monster birds reaching down for them from the sky. The village was abandoned – even the animals had disappeared. The punishment for being frightened into hiding I found unnecessarily severe. An order was issued to level the village. The military logic behind the decision was to remove shelter from the enemy. A soldier ripped a bundle of straw thatching from a hut, lit it with a match, then threw it on the roof. A small flame at first, licking upwards. Fanned by a light breeze, the hut literally exploded, the dry bamboo cracking like pistol shots, the fire spread to the next hut, and before long the whole village was enveloped by fire. A dense cloud of white smoke rose above the jungle. For good measure, a grenade was dropped into each rice jar and a year's food supply erupted into a shower of kernels.

Just in case the enemy was deaf, or had failed to hear the clamour of our troop of geese strutting through the rice paddies, the smoke signalled to anyone within a twenty-mile radius our present position.

'We'd better get away from here before they hit us with mortars,' said Dwyer. The troop moved off. I lingered behind, took a last picture of the burning houses.

'Hey, Erik, move yer ass, you might get hurt.'

The prospect of being slaughtered, if not by the enemy then surely by the returning montagnards for incinerating their livelihood, induced me to limp after the disappearing soldiers. Then Jim suddenly remembered that he had left his rucksack with all our film on the edge of the village. The major muttered to himself, probably something about civilians. He unbuckled his Colt, and chased after Jim. 'Come on, let's go.' Finally we all joined the rest.

Our company had reached a wide open expanse of paddy, fresh green shoots of rice emerging from three inches of water. To the military mind this was not food, but an ideal helicopter landing zone. The soldiers spread a plastic orange marker in the sign of a cross. Dwyer called in a supply drop, which was to bring in light artillery and more troops.

'We might as well call it quits, our noisy friends here have made sure that Victor Charlie knows where we are. They could have ambushed us anywhere along the track. This is going to be a futile exercise in slugging it out through the mud, and Erik's leg won't hold. Let's get on the next chopper.' I was certainly not one to argue with such brilliant logic. A few moments thereafter a hand reached down and pulled me into the belly of the whale.

My first encounter with the Vietnam conflict came to an inglorious finish. When we arrived back in Danang the American base doctor had a look at my wound, took a scalpel, and made a deep incision into my leg. He then pulled out several shreds of bamboo. I still carry the scar.

'You wouldn't have walked very long on that one,' was his judgement. 'What you need is some R and R.' Rest and Recreation was my ticket, and I promised I wouldn't miss it. Saigon was just the place for a little of both. An old Indochina buff had once advised me that the best way to forget the mosquitoes and the jungles and the swamps and the war, and everything else for that matter, was to go to the Hotel Continental, a yellow stucco building, early French colonial vintage. It offered superbly large bedrooms with carved mahogany four-poster beds covered by dreamy mosquito nets, no air conditioning, but wonderful, big-bladed ceiling fans, latticed windows, large balconies with an abundance of flowers, and bathrooms with white tiles and huge bathtubs the size of ping-pong tables. Most important, it offered discretion. It was a paradise for planters from the far-flung provinces, that army of white-suited gentlemen from the Michelin plantation, the spice dealers from Hue and the French colonial officials from Vientiane. The French administration was gone, but the hotel maintained its impeccable standard. The place was owned by Corsicans with suspect connections – wonderful, warmhearted people with a foot in the opium trade.

But the real ruler was Mr Loy the concierge, who could procure everything, from grass to girls, from gambling to information. He was 'the source', expensive, but certainly worth his price. He possessed a wealth of contacts, to provide the well-paying guest with everything from information about the place of a forthcoming VC attack to the date when the husband of a certain lady would be out of town. Nobody passed his desk without Mr Loy taking notice. He kept the room keys hidden from view, so that no one could tell who was in, and who was not. Discretion was paramount.

Rumour had it that many moons ago a gang of local thugs had somehow managed to slip past him and had burgled the room of a rich couple. While doing so they had raped the lady. The following morning, the story continued, the entire gang of thieves had been found, with their throats slit and their balls cut off, lining the river bank. Yes, Mr Loy had connections, and it was wise to become his 'dear guest'. The price depended on the requirements and on the nationality. It was most helpful to be fluent in *français*.

French was not only important in my contact with Loy – it was the introduction to the most widely played game in Saigon. It all started on the dreamlike terrace of the Continental. Thick bougainvillaea trees, blood-red blossoms and deep purple stars, clinging to wrought-iron arches, provided a fragrance of the Orient. The tables were white iron, the chairs of lattice design. For more discreet comfort clients could retire into the semi-darkness of the lobby bar. There, hidden from inspection, was a row of wickerwork planters' chairs with cushions. It was here that some of the more profitable deals were concluded.

However, it wasn't to conclude a fabulous deal that I came down to the bar. It was to join in the ancient French colonial game of *apéro*. This was short for apéritif pick-up, the favourite pastime at about five in the afternoon. It always started with a drink, and sometimes ended upstairs. The rules of the game were laid down by age-old conventions. It had variations, but it was invariably played with elegance and finesse. Nothing crude or vulgar. The ladies, in their floral Parisian dresses and beautifully coiffed – they had passed the morning at their favourite Jacques or Georges or whoever their hairdresser was – would gracefully slide on to a bench behind a table, just about visible in the intriguing shadow of the bougainvillaea. This gave them a distinct advantage: to observe from their obscurity the unfolding scene on the terrace, or out on the square, to pick out a suitor, or notice the approach of the husband. In the latter case, they had ample time to steal silently away past the ever-observant Mr Loy. For such an emergency a special exit was provided out the back.

The opening gambit of *apéro* was subtle. The gentleman would sit down at a table next to the lady's and order a pastis. He then found a reason to turn his head, or bend over the back of the chair; a friendly smile and, if there was a smile in return, a conversation could be started, but not one about the war or other equally banal themes. Vital interests were discussed, such as the latest fashion or the love life of a chic film star. At the same time it was quite imperative to display a room key in such a manner that the lady could take note of the number.

Mr Loy thrived on intrigue, he was the orchestrator of seduction. If an emergency arose – such as the sudden appearance of a husband, or the obvious failure of the engaged affair – and he felt that interference was called for, he would approach the table and interrupt with a polite: 'Monsieur is demanded on the telephone.'

This allowed the gentleman a graceful exit from a compromising situation. The rest was simply what the Americans referred to as R and R, with the major accent on the mutuality of recreation. The gentleman would say his public *au revoir* to the lady, perhaps go so far as to kiss her hand, and then retire to his lodgings. If the lady so desired, a knock on the door a few minutes later would indicate acceptance, or if the right vibrations had not been established the lady could decline the invitation. It very seldom happened that the same partners met twice; an unspoken agreement had it that such affairs were not to become permanent and create unnecessary problems, or even scenes of jealousy. In either case, Mr Loy always came out ahead, and in proportion to rendezvous concluded, his bank balance grew. There was only one way upstairs, past his box. Discretion was of value, and expensive.

It was to this Saigon that the injured warrior returned, and I passed the next week recuperating from my wounds in gentle company – *le repos du guerrier*. It also gave my chiefs back in 'the real world' time to decide where they wanted me to head from Vietnam. I was never much surprised by their geographic choice of subjects. The boss on our programme had a pocket diary with a miniature atlas, a useful tool for any foreign editor travelling on a crowded underground. Beneath the streets of London he would read the latest edition of the *Guardian*, the *Observer*, and the *Daily Mail*, and then decide where the next major story would break. Sometimes he missed, very often he hit it right on. He looked it up on his map, scale five million to one, then cabled:

ONPROCEED SPEEDIEST YEMENWARDS. AFTER ALL, YOU ARE HALFWAY THERE. EDITOR. PANORAMA.

2

THE MILLS OF THE GODS

(VIETNAM 1965)

Though the mills of God grind slowly,
yet they grind exceeding small;
Though with patience He stands waiting,
with exactness grinds He all.

Henry Wadsworth Longfellow, 1807–1882

Many times while travelling in the Vietnamese countryside I noticed children. I had the strange impression of a world being built by children because their parents were no longer interested in taking care of survival, working the fields, feeding their families. So the children took over.

I saw children playing soldiers, perhaps because their father was a soldier, or perhaps because he had been killed by a soldier and now the child was practising an imaginary revenge. Always the war, wherever one glanced, always the war, and the misery that followed in its footsteps.

The whole future of a country depended on these youngsters, but they had no future, just as they had no past. Thirty long years of bloodshed – these children had only known war. From their very first step they had been forced to conduct their lives as responsible adults. Too soon they were confronted by incredible suffering. They grew up to distrust their own local brand of new nationalist liberators, but with an equal loathing for all foreigners. The first kind stole their buffaloes, the second bombed them. It wasn't much of a choice. Many times I had to face the stares of these children, accusing and judging me at the same time. For them, I was just another one of the devils striking from the sky …

Looking back, everything has a significance, but some events stand out more than others. Vietnam left me with a series of impressions. I find it difficult not to remember certain actors in the drama, because they brought significance to a particular event, and with that, a moment in my life.

Phone calls tend to catch me sitting in a bathtub, or dead asleep at around two o'clock in the morning. The phone rings. I look at my luminous timepiece before turning on the light. One forty-five! 1.45 a.m.

'Hello?'

A nasty growl at the other end. 'Where's our drinks? I ordered them an hour ago.'

'I don't serve drinks at this time of the night.'

'Whaddya mean, night?' I can't tell if he's angry or puzzled.

'Well, night, dear sir, is night, and I'm tired.'

'But it's noon.'

Slowly I think I am going crazy or my watch is wrong. 'Where are you?'

'You bloody well know where I am, this is room 2246 at the Sheraton.'

There is no Sheraton in Saigon.

'What town?'

'What town?' He must be talking to his drunken friends, I hear something like, 'Hey I got a real live wire, he wants to know which town', and then to me, 'New York, wise guy.'

'Well, my dear sir, I am a guest at the Continental Hotel in Saigon, and it is now two o'clock in the morning and I wish you good luck with your drinks.' And I put the phone down.

I do not make a point of complaining to Mr Loy. Long distance calls have become very difficult in this fifth year of war, and the poor old guardian of little flickering lights on the night switchboard who had patched me through to the thirsty party back in the 'real world' had only been doing his job. It was a mistake, and it was over.

Ring! It feels as though the bell is going off in my head. I am not very fresh, some of which has to do with my previous night's performance. A group of the Saigon-based press clowns had gathered around local beer and imported booze to perform Shakespeare's immortal drama.

'Hamlet, and his Yiddisher mamma'. I was the *shikse*, Ophelia. Oh my God, my head, will that telephone never stop? Please! I reach for it and curse the person on the other end. It's the Canadian Broadcasting Corporation, head office Toronto, where I started all my adventures in television broadcasting. I recognize the voice of a friend who helped me when it was hard for me to get a start. Perhaps I don't owe him all that much, because had it not been for him I'd be married, father of four kids, with a suburban bungalow, a ten-year mortgage, and a 'regular' job, instead of lounging out my life in creepy hotels.

'Erik, have you got time to help us out with a documentary?'

'What do you have in mind?'

'You know the place, what can we get?' Oh, it's going to be one of these 'you pick for us' productions.

'There are no Canadians getting shot up, if that's what you're after.'

'No no, it's the bigger picture.' Now I've got it; *the bigger picture*, that's what they're after.

He carries on. 'I have this young producer woman working for my show, her name is Beryl Fox, she'll join you in Saigon. She'll bring the film stock.' That's just great. I am about to say no, when he continues, 'Erik, you owe me one.'

From the hometown grapevine I have been given to understand that he is about to marry the lady, but first he wants to make her famous. That's how *The Mills of the Gods* got its start. It was a good film. Beryl had talent, she put it together. I only went out and got her the material.

The end product turned into a kaleidoscopic impression of a war which was going from nowhere to nowhere. The highlight of the film was an occurrence in the skies over the Mekong Delta near a place called Can Tho. Its central character was a jet-jockey from Texas. It all began at six o'clock in the morning on the airfield of Southern strike command.

His name is Tom, and he is right out of Central Casting for a character role in a shoot-them-up Western: ten gallon hat, fancy boots, a holster. All he needs is a horse, but instead he rides a plane, an evil-looking contraption, with a propeller in front and a lot of bombs hanging under the wings. All these bombs, ordnance he calls them, have 20-inch pieces of pipe sticking out of their snouts.

'Them are daisy-cutters. When the pipe hits the ground, it shoves in the impact fuse, and the ordnance explodes just above the ground. That gives a lot of fine shrapnel and takes everything down.'

We are now in the autumn of 1965, and he is going to take me to the Mekong Delta. They give me a flight suit and a parachute and a helmet and good advice about what to do in case I should end up in a rice paddy surrounded by people in black pyjamas.

His aircraft is an A1E Skyraider, rather an antique flying machine in our high-tech jet age, but very useful, because it can deliver a lot of bombs very accurately. The only problem I can see is that it doesn't fly faster than a tennis ball, and will make a beautiful target once the duck season starts.

A ground crew busies itself around the plane, checks the bombs, checks the fuel for dirt or air bubbles or whatever and then stuffs me into the cockpit. I will have the privilege of sitting not behind the pilot but next to him. It's like a '39 Nash Rambler with bucket seats, quite comfortable. A mechanic plugs my tape machine into an internal socket, I test it, it works fine. I can now record the whole action.

Tom climbs in, and shows me a yellow lever with red stripes.

'In case we have to ditch, and you have to jump, pull this, it'll blow off the canopy.' I think I would rather crash than jump. I still have a backache from my last attempt at floating to earth.

We have to wait for the rest of the group to get their act together. This gives me an opportunity to find out who I am flying with.

'I have flown ninety, that is nine-zero combat missions. It's a lark. You'll see, nothing to it. It's a nice day, you'll see everything and be able to take some number one shots from the cockpit. I'll fly you low over the target.'

He raises his hand and signals the mechanic.

'Today we have some front-line targets, our flight number is six-one, and my call is one-one. We've got two additional craft with us, one-three and one-four.' I daren't ask what happened to one-two. 'Our forward air-controller will be Beaver two-three, and our ground control is Bullburst.' Where does the army find such names?

The mechanic on the ground gives a thumbs up, and with a bang and a blue cloud of smoke the engine roars into life. The propeller whines. Tom releases the parking brake and we start rolling forward. I see two more aircraft falling in behind.

'A great morning for flying,' says the captain. He pulls the cockpit's perspex shut – we're now sealed in. Tally-ho!

Static on my head set cuts into our conversation. It's the tower with final instructions, wind direction, speed and temperature.

'Flight six-one, you're cleared for immediate take-off.'

Tom checks his gauges and sets the throttle. 'Okay, here we go.' I switch on my tape recorder, from now on we're live, and all of the following dialogue is as it was actually recorded, word for spoken word.

We pass over endless rice paddies. Sometimes a lonely palm sticks out like a beacon in an ocean of pale green. In the distance we can see the majestic Mekong river meandering its way to the sea. A little behind us are the other two aircraft. Their shiny aluminium skin reflects the sun. It is warm and I wish I could open a window. I am wet under my flight suit: not sure if it is the heat, or fear.

Many times I've flown in helicopters, and I've been in jets before, but cruising towards a well-armed enemy in this slow-flying bathtub is a truly new experience. My cowboy must know what he's doing: he's done it ninety times before and he's still around to brag about it.

'Okay, we're in front to the target now, we are down in Fourth Corps. We'll be approximately 45 miles south of Can Tho in the Southern peninsula. We're going to make a strike with four Sky-raiders.' Four? I only saw three, maybe we picked one up along the way. He looks around, checks if his red-eyed herd is still around. 'I'm forced to look away occasionally. The Skyraider is an outstanding aircraft. We use it within the six-oh-second Air Command Bomber Squadron because it carries so much ordnance. It's an aircraft that carries normally 6,000 pounds, and it's absolutely outstanding. Today you will see bombs and napalm, so it should be fairly exciting. We should see a little ground fire and a lot of napalm burning. Maybe we'll see a few Victor Charlies. This aircraft is slow, but that is real flying, we dip down right amongst them, you just can't do that with jets.'

A call comes through from the forward controller. 'Beaver two-three … '

It allows me to look at Tom, or in the military jargon, check him out. He is a lean, tough character, and he exudes a morbid fascination.

I have misjudged the man; underneath his cowboy veneer is a professional, no-nonsense flyer, and that's what has made him survive. He rides his machine like a bronco at the local rodeo. I am trying to convince myself that he will bring us back in one piece from today's raid. I look ahead through the perspex – light reflects on the flashing blade. We have dropped altitude and are approaching a river.

'This is forward control, I want to report to you that the area is clear of helicopters, over.'

'Roger that, out.' He glances sideways, at his flock.

'This is one-one – six-one flight check in.'

A moment of silence, then once more. 'One-three and one-four, check in.'

I stare through my glass cupola at the two aircraft, their bellies bulging with bombs and napalm canisters. I point them out to Tom, he nods. He adjusts his sights and sets the release counter.

'We're now waiting for the forward air controller to check in. He will describe the target for us, and we'll tell him what our ordnance is and so forth.'

I have a foreboding, a pressure where my gut is. Here we are, the deliverers of certain death, the bird of the Apocalypse, to rain fire from the skies. Vienna 1945 – that's how I felt, looking up at the metal monsters in the sky. It all comes back in a flash. Once these planes make their final run, nobody down there has the slightest chance. We are still miles from the actual target and already the people down there are doomed.

Unlike the battles of an age gone by, when the history of the world was decided on a field about double the size of a football pitch, modern wars are carried on over endless distances. Wellington's cannons were a mere fifty yards from the French squares when they fired point-blank into the massed soldiers on a field which would become a synonym for defeat: Waterloo. And here we are, flying endless miles to a target which we will never see.

Those people down there have no names, they are only reference points on the map grid of some forward air controller. We will annihilate a group of humans whose existence or death is unimportant to the final outcome of the war. This is not some kind of chivalrous cavalry charge. Our aim is to drop napalm canisters on some poor sods huddling in a hole.

The voice of the controller startles me from my dreams. 'Okay, I have you in sight over the target area now.'

Tom puts his plane at a slight angle to obtain a better view.

A high-pitched Texan voice comes over the radio. 'Six-one flight check in ... '

Tom, sotto voce: 'Beaver two-three, wait. This is flight leader. This morning we have two aircraft with hard bombs, eight five-hundred-pound general purpose bombs apiece, we have two aircraft with napalm.' He doesn't know the exact load of the fire bombs, he checks with his wingman. 'One-four, say your load.'

One-four comes on the line. 'Roger, we have four seven-fifty napalm and twelve two-fifty napalm ... '

That should be sufficient to burn down Schenectady, NY.

We hear the ground controller's voice, he is with an infantry unit about two miles from our initial target. They're down there some-where in one of the rice paddies, most likely camouflaged in the mud up to their ears. 'Beaver two-three, this is Bullburst, I'll be with you in a minute.'

Tom has ordered his flight to circle above the target area. It is a small river, one side paddies and swamps, the other bank, which he now points out, wooded, with some large palm trees towering above the undergrowth.

'One of our field units tried to cross the river yesterday, and was ambushed from that brush down there. We know that they're dug in, probably too deep for bombs, so we've got to burn them out, bring them out into the open, then we can strafe them.'

'Alpha-one-echo.' That must be the call sign of a ground unit. The airwaves are alive with confused radio traffic.

'Beaver two-three, this is Bullburst, over.'

'Go ahead, Bullburst.'

'All right, we've had some reconnaissance by fighting down there. Now we're asking them to go back in and mark specific positions, and lines of positions. They've encountered some bunkers about forty metres south of the river at various places. We'll try to give you smoke and tell you where it is. Over.'

Tom is fidgety, looking down, adjusting his sights. Beneath his calm shell I can see the tension building. 'Boy, we've got a good target today. As soon as they mark it and they'll explain what they want done, we just go in.' With these simple words he has sealed the fate of whoever is down below.

Those human beings down there, do they have fathers, mothers, wives? Are they tough enemy soldiers, are they just villagers hiding out in fear, caught in a madness which has begun to sweep throughout the entire country. Who are they? When Tom and his roughriders are finished with them, will there be enough left for a decent burial? Will we ever know?

'This is Bullburst. The positions have been identified, they are located in the heavy mangrove just south of the river. Be sure to concentrate on that strip with all your strikes. Over.'

Tom to his flight: 'Affirmative. You copy that flight six-one?'

There are three brief positive replies. The flight is now ready. The fireworks will start.

Tom tilts the plane. Now I can make out the mangrove quite clearly – it is about 200 yards long, just above the river bank. I can see some entrenchments, some earth bunkers. I see also something else, a herd of peacefully grazing water buffaloes right in front of the trenches, and a few hundred yards further up there are five or six faces staring up into the sky. Two wear the conical straw hat so typical of Vietnamese women, the rest are children.

'This is flight leader. One-three go for a run. I'll cover.'

The aircraft on our left wing tilts forward, Tom brings our plane into a parallel position, and the pair race towards the ground. Seconds before I see the long cylindrical object detaching itself from the wing of the other aircraft, our plane is shaken by a violent vibration. I jerk round, terrified, and then look straight at our wing guns, spitting fire into the trees below. Tom is strafing. As we flash overhead, I can see something move. Could be people running, I can't be sure. My sight is blurred by the speed and the forces of gravity.

The forward air controller has fired smoke rockets to mark a new target. 'Okay, you see where my rockets hit?'

'Right in that southern treeline near the mangrove?'

'That's affirm, I'd like you to lay a couple in there.'

One-two goes in for a dive, there is a flash, our aircraft shakes slightly, and then we race towards this cloud of red dirt, pass through it, pull up. My stomach is left behind, I can feel the tail-rudder whip up as our own bomb explodes right behind us. My camera is in my lap and I can't raise my arms – there is too much gravity pull for me to be operational.

'Lead, your bomb exploded about twenty metres south of the treeline. The wind may be from the north-north-west instead of due west.'

'Now he tells us,' remarks Tom, like saying, sorry that we've wasted that one. And to the air controller: 'All right, we'll send in another run.' He points out of the window, in my direction.

'Okay, watch one-two, he'll be just about ready to roll in now ... there he goes ... there he goes.' My camera follows the dive. What I had looked upon as a flying bathtub is now a diving falcon. I am struck by its deadly beauty as it heads straight for the trees.

'Okay, follow his run ... his bombs should hit noooow ... there they go!'

A milli-second whiteness, a bright yellow flash, and a slowly rising red cloud. There is one thing I'm missing: the herd of water buffaloes. They're gone.

Tom points upwards, into the sky above the cockpit. 'Hey look up there, we've got buddies.'

'Attention, there are flights all over this area, flight six-one, go to eight thousand feet and hold. You should be all right up there.'

A new voice comes in on the airwaves. 'This is nine-five, we're due south. We can see the strike in front of us. Whaddya want us to do?'

'Roger nine-five, I'd like some napalm. Let's cover the treeline with one run.'

'That's okay, we'll make two passes with napalm.'

The tone of this conversation is clinical; it sounds like asking your wife to remember the popcorn for the movie. These are pros. They look upon the people down there in the trees as 'target', and at the inferno they are creating as 'strike'. The run goes in – another flash, another strike.

'Six-one, I want one napalm a little bit short of his last pass.'

'Roger.'

Tom looks at me, takes the gun-safety off. 'We're gonna give him cover, hang on.' We are at 8,000 feet, the plane falls over the right wing, we have commenced our dive. The engine howls, earbursting whine, the plane starts pitching. Tom is on the radio.

'I'm over it right now.' Gunfire shakes the frame. 'Look out, Erik, look out to your right,' he screams at me over the noise of the engine, 'look out, get it with your camera.' I can hardly move my arms, they are pinned to the side of the perspex. 'Right down there now, okay, shoot, shoot! ... there it goes ... oh, look at it BURN!!!'

Flame all over the jungle, a snake of red flame races through the trees, a black greasy cloud of smoke: napalm, the terror weapon of Korea. Our plane pulls up, I see sky and a racing propeller.

'BABY ... THAT'S NUMBER ONE!!'

We have gained altitude again. This is unreal. I feel as if I am watching a film, completely removed from what is going on down there. Perhaps it is only a movie, perhaps it is only my imagination that makes me believe that this evil red snake of fire with its blinking yellow eyes and its black tail is real. Down there it means annihilation. When I worked in feature films, we used drums of out-dated gasoline to simulate the heroic stand of a group of marines surrounded by hordes of enemies. Neither the hordes nor the marines were likely to suffer casualties. But this is real. Napalm fries the skin and sucks the oxygen from the lungs. What a horrible way to go.

'Okay, get your camera ready, see him go in, look to your right, to your right, start shooting your picture, start taking ... yeaaah, okay right, down there ... attaboy!!!' Another red snake appears in the trees below.

'All flights. I've had a couple airburst there. Just near the treeline.'

Tom looks at me. 'Those bastards are shooting back.' It seems to surprise him that people try to put up a defence.

'One-one, you got any strafe left?'

'Roger, I can make two strafing passes for you.'

'Okay, right on that damned treeline, please, pronto.'

'Roger, will do.'

Now that I know they will be shooting at us, it changes my position from unconcerned spectator to active combatant.

'Erik, tie down, we're going after those bastards. Okay, we're gonna strafe NOW!!' And with that he pulls his stick. We are going in.

A radio message: 'One-one, are you in yet? It is fucking hairy down there!'

'That's one-one going now ... '

Then I see it, it is unreal. Thin threads are hanging in the air, all pointing at my very centre. Like carnival streamers, they drift lazily into the sky, past my canopy. The engine howls, I am crushed into the seat by the force of the acceleration, I cannot move, cannot escape, I stare in horrid fascination at the white laundry lines into the heavens … our cannons roar, the plane recoils violently, pitches, rolls. Tom has his hands on the button, depressing, trying to steady the bucking ride … a leaden weight punches in my stomach, presses all the air out of my lungs.

Then I see only sky – blue, clear sky. I cannot breathe, the gravity pull is too strong, my camera is pressed against my belly. This isn't Coney Island, this isn't the Big Dipper, this is the roller coaster of death.

Tom screams: 'We pull up, up.'

The forward air controller comes over the air. 'Good hit, good hit – real fine – real fine!'

Desperately trying to pump air into my deflated lungs, I hover between suffocation and vomit. I stare out at the white threads now torn apart by our propeller's wash, at death that didn't get me. But it isn't over yet, we are going in once more.

'Okay, Erik, hang on, here we go.'

The plane tilts forward, the same ride into oblivion has begun. This time I know what to expect. It doesn't make it simpler, it just changes everything into a kind of slow motion, the action, the attack, the thoughts. The noise abates, I can see, I can hear everything that goes on.

'There is ground fire from the first one we hit … '

'Okay … good hit … '

'Here we go, shooting.'

Tom has done this ninety times before, looked ninety times at tracers flying at him. Others would have cracked up long before. Or perhaps he's been so busy doing his job that he has never noticed what was coming at him. He sits there, steady, pointing his aircraft from ten thousand feet down, a ride into hell. What if something gives and he can't pull back?

I see his hands on the controls, his thumb punches the red button … our plane shudders, all cannons fire at once. Flashes, stabs of fire from the wings, empty cartridges are ejected, clanking down into the void. In slow motion I watch, fascinated by the nearness of sudden death, my sensors are everywhere. The firing, Tom's hands, white, frozen at the controls, and the tracers flying at us. I sit there, I am not in control of anything. The eyepiece of the camera presses into my face, I cannot move it. My nose bleeds. Enjoy the ride, he had said. Some ride, some fun. He is crazy, I am crazy!

Tom screams over all the static and the engine howl. He has got a terrifying gleam in his eyes, moist with excitement. This is the way he gets his thrill.

I must admit, it's a bizarre, sexual feeling, flying into hell. We are in the coffin with a splendid view of the grave.

'See the target down there … keep the camera running … attaboy … keep running … I'm going very low now … very low … to avoid the ground fire … now I pull up … see the treeline?' The trees are racing at us – damn it, pull up.

'Now we pull, there we are … ' We've cleared the trees by what seems to me inches. The wings have clipped a palm leaf. 'WOW! WE'VE GOT THEM!'

'I'm out of film.' My remark sounds banal after what we have just gone through. That last run was too much and I cradle my camera like a baby. It feels nice and safe.

The forward air controller gives his assessment: 'Real fine, real fine!!' and then he turns straight to another flight, 'calling whisky-romeo-three-five-six … ' More napalm from the sky.

I don't look so good. Tom laughs. 'Okay, we're through.'

'Can I open the canopy a little bit?' This isn't a jet, it should be possible – I've seen Tyrone Power do it in the movies.

'Okay, we're through. Oh, open the slide? You sure can!' A grinning hillbilly, my Tom. He's mocking my misery. Over the earphones I can hear instructions for another drop to another flight with another number. It doesn't concern us any longer, we're headed for a cold shower and lunch. Oh, my God, lunch, the mere thought of food makes me want to throw up. I am drenched in sweat, I think I'm sitting in a puddle of fear and excitement. Excitement that I lived through it. A great feeling, now it's over. I'm still convinced this isn't real. The radio reminds me that it is. 'Okay, flight three-five, you can start where that heavy smoke is coming out … '

Tom takes a piece of chocolate, offers it to me and I shake my head. He takes a bite.

'As you can see, they forced us into a non-standard tactic on this one. Okay, now this was an outstanding target, when we bombed first of all, we could see the people running everywhere. It was fantastic! It is very seldom that we see Victor Charlie run like hell. When we do, we know we've got him! If we can keep them on the run, we know we're gonna really hose them down ... ' A quick burst of laughter, perhaps a nervous reaction to the horror. 'We were receiving heavy ground fire. You could see the tracer bullets coming past us. Fantastic!' So he did see them after all, and thought of it as fantastic!

'Do you think you've got them?'

'Oh, didn't we get them! Couldn't you see them run down there?' I couldn't be sure what I saw, everything happened so fast, I had a camera pressed to my eye, and my vision isn't used to the speed at which we were skimming the trees.

'Man, I know we got them. Because I got four twenty-millimetre cannons you can see out here and we really hosed them down. And by Joe, that's great fun, I really like doing that!'

This is the first time since this morning that Tom has let himself go and shown emotion, he is all worked up now, joking, laughing. The words flow from his lips with great passion, almost a sexual high. Killing is sensual. I am also excited, but for a different reason. For me it's the fact that I am still around to tell my story.

He points at the rice paddies way down below. We are now at fifteen thousand feet, a safe distance from anything that the VC might be able to throw at us. The countryside looks lovely – endless fields of rice. There is no sign of violence, and the wounds we inflicted upon this fertile ground only a few moments ago are way behind us. Tom looks up, there are beads of sweat on his face. We have the sun directly overhead and even with the air intakes right on our faces, it is stifling hot. A flight of jets sweeps over us, silver bellies in an azure sky. I can see the bombs on their wings, fat green cigars.

'When you press right down into them they cannot get a target on you. Now, if I pull up immediately then I am a number one target and they're gonna shoot my ass off – and yours too, for that matter ... ' he laughs, ' ... so we don't like to do that. I press right down into their muzzles and that way I can concentrate my fire, that way, if they shoot at me, they don't only shoot at me but into each other. But man, we were low!!! I'll bet you never have been that fast that close to the ground before.'

He wins, hands down. Not only was I close and fast, I felt like I was dragging my behind on the rice. And that is too close.

'I think you got some outstanding film. Did you get the bombs falling off the airplane? And the cans hitting in the trees? Outstanding!'

I am sure he is right, the pictures are certainly unique. Whether they are outstanding is another matter. 'How many enemies do you think you did get?'

'Oh, I don't know. We probably got about seventy-five or one hundred. The army will go in this afternoon. They will probably have to fight their way in, because you can never get them all out of their bunkers. So it should be fairly exciting. I really wish I could go in on a search-and-clear immediately after one of our airstrikes, just to see, you know, how effective we are. The army really praises us for our big bombs and the napalm. They really like it. The ones that napalm hasn't burnt up, why, the Victor Charlies are just addled because of our big bombs, it breaks their eardrums, and makes them kind of senseless, I guess. I would be too.'

We approach the airstrip, an uneventful landing, I shake Tom's hand, he grins, pumps my hand, offers lunch, which I really don't need right now. Perhaps I'll be in the mood for dinner, but not lunch.

'Well, so long, pardner ... ' and Tom strolls off.

At 3 p.m. the operation against the targets of our air raid will be launched. I join the troops of an airborne division. Most of them are boys who may have heard of the night drops at Ste Mère-Eglise in '44, but are too young to know where the place is. But they are not too young to have tasted fire, and only the day before two of their buddies had been killed while crossing a supposedly friendly village.

They are learning fast never to suppose.

During a briefing my group is ordered to protect the left flank of a three-company movement on an S-and-D mission. S-and-D means search and destroy, or to put it in a subtler, more military way: flush 'em, waste 'em and cut off their balls. We line up alongside a large heliport. Silence, interrupted by a chirping of crickets. The grunts are immersed in their individual thoughts. Some check and recheck their rifles, some fiddle with their belt buckles. Most smoke and stare ahead, their minds already out there, in the swamps.

They carry a veritable arsenal. Automatic rifles, grenade throwers, bazookas, rockets tied to long bamboo poles, colourful signal flares, blood plasma. All have covered their name and rank badges with black shoe polish. The wristwatches and the beltbuckles have been turned inside to avoid reflection.

The air comes alive, first a faint hum. Like a swarm of flying scorpions our helicopters appear out of the noon haze. Activity explodes all across the field. Sergeants get their flocks into shape. 'C'mon ya guys, lift yer asses, get goin'.' We are in the second wave. Our riding shotgunner, hunched over his LMG, tells us that the first wave has taken casualties. As we approach the target, the rice paddies and the river I had seen only a few hours back from the Skyraider, I can see some Vietnamese rangers with their brightly-coloured helmets firing into a swamp. The helicopter sleds come down hard.

I start the camera and take the precaution of locking the button so that it will not stop by accident. I stay glued behind the sergeant, a giant from a sandhole somewhere in Texas. We rush through ankle-deep water. We are completely in the open, running targets in a flat landscape. Fifty yards ahead is the rim of a bomb crater, probably a bomb from the very plane I was sitting in. As I reach the hole, out of breath, I jump over the edge just as the last of my film grinds through the camera. I land in water. Only now do I notice all the geysers spouting up all around us. We have come under machine-gun fire.

'That's Charlie! Heads down.' The sergeant barks out his orders. 'Shoot covering fire!' He turns to me: 'That's a fuckin' ambush.'

I can see two Skyraiders diving towards a group of palms at the water's edge. The ground shakes as the bombs strike. A black cloud is all that is left of the trees. Helicopters race towards that cloud, their gatling guns blazing away. Hastily I change the film. After the dull thump of the heavy bombs I can make out the noise of small-arms fire. Ours? Theirs? You cannot see a bullet, you only hear it when it has gone past – a sharp snap. I make certain to stay a few feet behind the sergeant. His platoon is spread out around us, half-submerged in the rice paddy, taking cover behind water walls.

'THERE!!!'

Bang – bang – ratatatatatataaaa, bang, ratatatataaaa ...

'What is it, sarge?' I haven't seen a thing. What are they shooting at?

'A couple of black pyjamas. I think we got them sons o' bitches.'

A soldier, mudcovered, rifle raised, zigzags towards us, his head bent low for cover. 'They're over there,' he points to a set of trees, 'about three hundred feet to your right.' He tries to catch his breath. 'They don't move any more ... they got in right between Bravo company and us ... I think we zapped them from all sides.'

'Okay, get on the horn and tell Curly to get his ass over here and set up cover. I'm going to take a look.'

'Check.' The soldier jumps up, doubles back to his position. A few moments later I can see the machine-gunner giving a signal. He is ready for our dash. Yes, it has to be 'our' dash, because I need to get what I came for, a few pictures. Ah, what the hell, let's hope they're dead.

The sergeant turns to me: 'I hope the bastard knows what he is doing. Let's go!' He jumps up, and we hurtle low through the paddies, towards a black object, half-submerged in the muddy water, like an inflated inner tube. The air has been trapped inside the clothing.

A rifle sticks out of the mud. A hand frozen on the trigger. The body lies face down. The sergeant points his gun at the slumped body – Texas Jack has learned not to take chances. With his giant fist he grabs hold of the soggy black hair, pulls the head from the water. It is an ugly sight, the bullet has struck between the eyes, forcing them out of their sockets. The front is a mess of water and red. He looks about eighteen. The sergeant lets go, and the body flops back into the mud.

Three soldiers come running towards us, they take a quick look at what a few moments ago was a man. 'He shouldn't have run,' says one, blowing a balloon of bubblegum, which explodes like a gunshot and sticks to his lips.

'Sarge,' says the radio man, 'Bravo company is moving out, we're to cover their left and move alongside.'

'Anyone got hurt?'

'Yeah, Burt is down.'

'How bad?'

'He's alive, they're waiting for the medivac.'

I notice a group of men huddled around their fallen buddy.

'All right, snap out of it, ya guys, let's move it.' He turns to a soldier.
'Take this Charlie's gun, the rest of you guys follow me.'

We slosh through water, the shooting has stopped. It's less than five
minutes since we jumped from the helicopter. Bravo company has
lost five men, we have lost one. The Vietcong had been lying in
ambush, and we landed right in the middle of them. Now it is over.
Near the clump of trees we find four dead VCs and a Chinese machine
gun.

After half an hour's walk we come to the site of this morning's
bombing. It is a mess, the earth has been churned into impassable
mud, trees are tangled and broken, the bleeding carcass of a water
buffalo hangs impaled on the shards of a smashed palm. A black
smear where napalm hit. Some charred forms which could have been
human beings.

We circle around the scene, and within another half-hour come
upon a hamlet. It is abandoned. A soldier discovers a hole in the
ground. He hollers down. Nothing. He climbs into it, gun at the ready.
A few moments later the wrinkled face of terror appears. It is an old
woman with a child hanging on to her trouser-leg. A GI takes a
chewing gum and offers it to the bawling bundle of misery. The old
woman simply stares at us. She has never seen Americans before.

'Sarge, there's a man in here.'

Inside a hut we find the body of an old man. He has bled to death.
Misery all around us.

A commotion in a hut further on. They have discovered a middle-
aged man hiding in a hole behind the fireplace. It must be presumed
that he is connected to the Viet Cong. He is dragged out of the hut,
carrying a child on his arm. The sergeant walks over, points at a
woman who has materialized from the hut, and says to the man: 'Give
the baby to mama-san, come on, give the baby to mama-san.'

A soldier tries to take the screaming bundle. The tiny tot hangs on
to the man with its stubby little arms and yells. The sergeant forcibly
grabs the infant, hands it to the woman. 'Okay, there you are
mama-san, we'll bring back papa-san.'

The woman falls to the ground, hangs on to the sergeant's trousers,
looks up, her face a mask of tears. The sergeant tries to move off, but
she won't let go and he drags her along on the ground. Two soldiers
step up, tear her away, and carry her back into the hut. They tie a tag

around the man's neck – place of capture, time, etc. The baby lies on the ground, wailing. What shit.

'Corporal Priller, red smoke.' A helicopter comes in. I jump on.

I make out a pair of boots beneath a blanket. Dead GI. Facing me is a village boy, about fifteen. He is guarded by a soldier who has pushed his gun into the boy's stomach. The eyes of the youngster are pools of fear. His hands are tied behind his back. Next to him is a piece of wood with a metal tube attached to it by wire, a home-made shotgun. Most likely the boy has been told by his VC commander that the Americans will kill him.

'What happened back there?' The pilot asks me over the intercom.

I give him a brief account. I ask, 'Who's the kid?'

'Well, when we skimmed the Charlies the lieutenant told us to go down and take a look. There were just too many gooks for each water buffalo. When we came in, most of them tried to run, but two shot at us and got my rear gunner. We took care of the rest. This one we're bringing in for interrogation. He didn't run, he was either too scared, or really a cowboy. Who gives a shit anyway ... '

The surviving gunner has spotted a target and opens up, the helicopter comes in for a tight turn, and we are thrown against the side. From beneath the bodysheet, covering the dead American GI, an arm plops out. I stare at its whiteness, dead fingers reaching out for me. There is something obscene about it. At first I cannot tell what it is, I can only feel it. My mind is befuddled by too many skydives and too many explosions: I keep staring at this object, until it comes into focus. A red second hand turning. The mechanism continues where life has ended. The watch ticks on a dead man's wrist.

We land near a tarmac road, soldiers grab the boy and pull him out. Slowly our helicopter lifts off. At this moment an old woman comes along the road, all her worldly goods piled on an oxcart. The whine of the blades unnerves the animals. The woman tries to hold them back, but the rope is torn from her frail hands. The animals stampede across the field. The cart bounces crazily over the dry rice paddy, pots and bedding fall off, a bag of rice tears open, and a rivulet of white cascades to the ground, marking a trail of panic.

We are back in the air, the pilot, the body and I. Beneath us, the boy prisoner is marched along the road, the woman runs after her cart, the scene gets smaller and smaller, and finally disappears from view.

On the dead soldier's watch it is now seven o'clock.

For me it has been a very long day.

Saigon had changed. The war had finally reached the city. In a raid which was wasteful, but spectacular and highly publicized, the Viet Cong had attacked the core of the American political presence in Vietnam, the US embassy in Saigon. They had launched raids into Cholon, and their fifth column within the city was recruiting more volunteers every day. The streets became battlegrounds. There was rape and murder, opium dens and gambling dens. Venereal diseases were out of control. Gone were the quaint little restaurants. The few remaining French *colons* had retreated to the bar of the Cercle Sportif, and only the diehards ventured in the evenings to the Guillaume Tell, the last of the feeding places that still served cracked crab and decent *vin blanc*.

The planters and export managers had put their bored wives on the first plane out, and were now enjoying an equally boring freedom. Their dainty Vietnamese mistresses had forsaken them for the mighty American dollar. The rubber plantations had been defoliated or burned, or both, and their splendid mansions were now in the hands of black-pyjamad Viet Cong.

The biggest visible change was in the streets of the city: a multitude of American uniforms. The Yanks were everywhere, on the docks, in the market, in the coffee shops, and in the bars. The whores had been quick to adjust to the new situation and had learned a special brand of pidgin English, enough to establish contact. 'Hey boy, want fucky-fucky?'

The bar girls ranged in age from fourteen to forty. Almost all of them had clap, a disease they shared lavishly with the American fighting forces. The prices for a tender moment with a barflower were steadily on the rise, keeping in step with the rampant inflation, and the time permitted in the sack with the lady of passion was getting shorter. The girls were in demand. Tudo Street had blossomed into a half-mile long bordello, an avenue of carnal pleasures catering exclusively to American GIs. Arcade after arcade of gaudy bars, neon lights, girls with blue-black hair and slit skirts, seducing soldiers into rooms. It was an often-repeated procedure: walk into the bar, have your drink, 'Five dollar please'. Enter one of the dark and smelly booths in the back, 'Ten dollar please'. A few faked moans later, and the madame-owner-cash-collector pulled back the flimsy curtain to inform the soldier that his time was up and that there was a line-up in front of his stall. Soldiers didn't mind, they were pimple-faced kids with money to burn. They would move into the next bar with identical cubicles, peel off a few more dollars, and repeat their performance.

Finding forgetfulness was getting expensive. Whores are something every army has to contend with, and, in general, armies manage quite well. However, the Vietnam war brought a new phenomenon, much more vicious and dangerous: drugs. South-East Asia supplies practically the whole world with heroin. It was easy to procure and it was easy to find oblivion. Marijuana was sold on every street corner, from Acapulco Gold to Saigon Shit. I remember participating on a scout patrol deep into enemy controlled territory, and as we bunked down for the night in a log-covered trench, somebody produced a hand-carved pipe, filled with the finest grass. It turned into a session which put all the fighting men to sleep. To drift from soft drugs to the real killer, Big H, was an easy step. Heroin is a short-cut to death. I have seen what it can do.

One afternoon I had arranged to visit a contact at the Royal Hotel, when I ran into two drunk Americans coming down the stairs. The black soldier was doubling up with laughter.

'Heyabuddy, Betty Boobs is chugging a train, a big train, a real biggie!'

'And where is that?'

'Third floor, just follow the moans.'

The Royal was a sleazy fleabag run by a Frenchman who didn't care what was going on in or around Saigon, since he had found permanent nirvana in the bowl of his opium pipe. His lodgers were all those who couldn't afford the plusher places, or needed a room by the hour.

The place of action could not be mistaken, there were hoots and laughter and moans and blaring country music. The door to room 32 was ajar, and provided a vista of drunkenness, and raw sex. A tangle of naked limbs and hairy torsos was sprawled over a fleshy blonde, plunging into every available orifice. Her shrieks were a mixture of pain and pleasure: 'Nooh ... nooh ... stop ... oh, please stop ... nooh, don't stop, ooow ... '

'Hey, Betty Boobs wants more,' roared one of the participants.

Slouched around the rumpled bed, were another four naked men, alternating between a bottle and sucking the girl's distended nipples.

'C'mon ya guys, give us a break, you've been on her long enough.' There was a general repositioning, the girl was lifted up and turned around, as the partners exchanged places. For a brief moment I caught a glimpse of her face, flushed with the satiation of hard sex, but quite attractive in a robust way. Once more she was enveloped by arms and legs and flesh pumping into her, all moving and groaning in unison.

Several days after I had witnessed this scene someone knocked on my door. It was the blonde from the Royal, quite changed, almost demure, although even her plain dress could not hide the ample flesh which had given her the nickname.

'Please excuse me if I am bothering you, but I have been told that you have just been North. Did you by any chance visit Anloc? It's a strategic hamlet twenty miles southwest of Danang.'

'I know the place, but I wasn't there this time.'

'Have you been there?'

'Yes, about a month or so back.'

'Well, did you by any chance meet a tall American in the perimeter telephone exchange, his name is Billy Joe? He is my husband.' Desperation showed in her voice.

'No, sorry, that rings no bell.' She started to cry. I opened the door, 'Please do come in. Can I offer you a drink?'

'Only a soft drink, if you have one, please.' I had an icebox full of the stuff.

'I am so worried, I haven't heard from him in well over a month.' She had an attractive accent, a Southern drawl with a German R.

'There hasn't been any major action in that region – I'm sure he's all right. Why don't you fly up and join him?'

'The military won't allow it. They say it is in a combat zone, and they will not permit civilians into the region.'

'So, you find yourself parked in Saigon, and waiting?'

'Yes, it's horrible, I have these dreams that something has happened to him.' She took a sip and wiped away a tear. 'I just sit, and wait, and hope he'll come back soon.'

I didn't mention that I had already watched her sitting and waiting. And yet there was something strangely fragile and warm about the big girl with the pale blue eyes and the blond mane. A frightened child, crying out for someone to take notice.

'How did you ever end up here?' I asked.

'I am from Würzburg. I met my husband when he was stationed in Germany with the Third Infantry. He is no longer in the army, he is working on a civilian project.'

We talked until late into the night. She told me about her youth in her native Bavaria. She got so frustrated by her family's insistence that she should marry the farmer next door that she left home and took a job as a salesgirl in Würzburg. There she met her husband, and he took her to South Carolina. She told me how they had shipped out to Saigon on the promise of a big salary, and when Billy Joe had found out what the job was really all about, and had refused it, everything went sour. They had no money to return, and he had found a job for a communications organization. They had sent him North. She didn't know anybody in Saigon, and so, out of sheer boredom she had taken a lover. To further his perverse tastes, he had introduced her to hard drugs, and now her only escape was to give herself to anybody who wanted her.

'Please, I can't go back to my place, they are waiting there, please can I stay, I am so scared.' She took the bed and I bunked down on the couch. It may sound corny, but that's the way it happened.

She made breakfast and livened the place up with flowers, and I tried to help her chase away her dragons. Sometimes she would wake up screaming, then come to me and clutch me in a furious embrace, only to fall back into an exhausted sleep. Sometimes she would get up during the night and sit naked in front of the air conditioner, staring out the window, probably towards a place south-west of Danang.

'Please don't leave me all alone,' she would plead every morning, and 'I'll try to be back tonight,' was my standard reply.

I realized only too well that she was still shooting up, the needlemarks on her arms were fresh. However she never did it at my place, nor did I know where she got the means for her expensive habit. She never told me, although I could guess. Proof came a few months

later, after she had gone. A civilian pilot was arrested for trans-
porting drugs to the United States. He talked, and implicated the
leader of a Chinese tong in Cholon. The Military Police apprehended
the sexagenarian, and when they searched his place for drugs, stumbled on photographs. I was called in to identify some of these
pictures.

The Polaroids were a gallery of voyeurism, involving men, women,
and animals. Betty was always the star. For her performance the old
man had compensated her with drug-induced relief. The Chinese
was sentenced, and then quietly released on a swap, and today he
lives a comfortable life somewhere in the South of France, perhaps
remembering Betty and his dogs, but not her dragons.

Our friendship lasted a month, until the day her husband returned
– in a metal box. The Viet Cong had overrun the hamlet and executed everybody, from local headman to American engineer. When
she was given the news, I was in the field. That evening, when I
returned to the Continental, Mr Loy just said: 'There has been a sad
event and madame has returned to the Royal.'

Still mudcaked from the trip, I rushed to the Royal. A soldier was
just leaving, and grinned when he saw me rushing in. 'There's no
hurry, there's plenty left upstairs.' I didn't bother to go up; I knew
what I would find.

I tried to call her, I left messages which she didn't answer, or
didn't receive. I heard about her wild parties. Then, about a week
later, I received a call: 'Mr Durschmied, this is the Military Police.
Could you please come right away to the Royal.'

'What happened?'

'There has been an accident.'

It hadn't been an accident. She had injected herself with an overdose, and was now stretched out on a rumpled bed. Clutched in her
hand was a tortoise-shell frame with the photograph of a happily
smiling couple – her wedding picture.

'Can you identify her?' a young lieutenant with an efficient voice.

I took a look. 'Yes, I can.'

An MP covered her with the sheet. The officer handed me a letter.
'We found this. It is addressed to you.'

The message was in German, and scribbled in a child-like hand on
a piece of paper torn from a notebook. It was as simple as it was sad.

'Do you mind telling us what it says? We need it for the inquest,' he said politely but firmly.

'It's in German, I will translate it: *Mein lieber Erik, bitte hilfe mir ...* please help me. My husband has been the only one who has ever been decent to me. Please ask them to bury me next to him ... '

There followed a moment of silence, I stared out the window, down on the stinking Hondas and the cigarette hawkers, but I didn't see them. Please ask them to bury me next to him ... drugs, corruption, war, Saigon, all so hopeless, so rotten, so final.

The officer broke into my thoughts: 'Did you know her well?'

Did I really know her at all? 'No, I didn't. We were just two people who met in a horrible place.'

The lieutenant nodded, he had heard it all before. 'All right, we'll take care of that', he motioned towards the body under the sheet. 'I'll see to it that her wishes are passed on.'

'Thank you,' I said, and walked out into a street of stinking motorbikes and black marketeers.

By now the press corps had swelled into the hundreds. There was hardly a newspaper or television station which at one time or another did not send a 'special envoy' or 'war correspondent' or simply 'our man in Saigon' to cover the daily events. Most were from the 'hometown media', and these reports focused on their local boys. It was through some of these contacts that soldiers in the field were told what was going on back home, and how everybody was worrying about their wellbeing. Some stories were definitely exaggerated, others were killed in the editing room, or simply ignored when the publication ran out of space, or the newscast ran out of airtime.

The Caravelle had been taken over by the three major American television networks. Each occupied an entire floor. Day and night the halls reverberated to the rhythmic rattle of telexes. Bathrooms were converted into projection booths; sleeping quarters doubled as camera storage, and the fridge was filled with cold, imported beer. The folks back home were eager to be informed about their fighting boys, and each day television crews ventured into battle to bring back material for next day's newscast. At times there must have been as many men shooting film as shooting at the Viet Cong.

This was the 'television war'. For the first time in history, people across America could actually watch – via satellite – a firefight which had taken place at a town called Quang Tri or Hue or Khe Sanh almost as soon as the shots were fired.

The dining room of the Caravelle had become a disaster area. The food matched the cracked mirrors over the bar. The drinks served were now bourbon, with or without Pepsi, rum and coke, and Bloody Marys. The waiters ferried these from behind a busy counter in prodigious loads. The choice of evening fare was chop suey, steak or hamburgers. All tables had to be booked in advance, each press corps had its special corner, each network had private tables paid for by a healthy expense account, and those left were snapped up by the slightly less well-paid officers on R and R, and their companions. The waiters had stopped addressing their clientele in French. Nowadays, tips were considerably better. The Caravelle terrace still provided the same lovely view, only now it featured nightly fireworks of exploding rockets and shell flashes across the Saigon river. The small roof garden was the place to meet and to discuss the day's events, to plan the next move, and to catch up on the latest baseball scores.

At any time of the day or night, the Caravelle bar was crowded with media representatives from every publication imaginable, from small-town paper to prestigious national weekly, all in identical war corres-pondents' uniforms from Mr Ho of Tudo Street. Combat jackets came in three colours, grey, tan and dark green. All were provided with a stitched-on pocket for pencils. The ballpoint had become the badge of rank. Correspondents were all after the 'big war story'. Thus the Cara-velle bar was the centre of gossip, rumours, and sometimes next day's news headlines. It was here that some great careers were launched.

It happened on one of these evenings, in a bar overflowing with PR personnel and reporters, all eager to recount to no one in particular their latest feat of journalistic enterprise. Most stories I had heard before, in another country, during another frazzle. Journalists' stories seldom vary. The stock tales of horror and glory had been adapted to fit the Vietnam scenery. I had found a secluded table behind a potted palm, peaceably nursing a '33', the local beer. This in itself set me apart from the Schlitz-and-Budweiser gang. I was not looking for entertainment, I was craving quiet without being holed up in my damp hotel room. A shadow fell across my table.

I looked up to discover a soldier-like figure in camouflaged battle-dress, clutching a tall glass of clinking ice cubes and pale liquid, a vodka something. He flashed a grin. 'Hi, mind if I sit down?'

'Feel free.'

He was tall, gaunt, with silver leaves. The fact that his leaves were shiny established him for me in the non-combatant category. At this stage of jungle fighting, the real war boys were using everything from oven paint to shoe polish to hide their rank behind a thick layer of black. The second give-away that he hadn't seen much of sunny Vietnam was his complexion, best described as Pentagon-pale. His job was definitely chairbound. He stared at me challengingly. I could hardly keep my eyes open, and did little to hide my fatigue. He fired the first shot: 'You a war correspondent?'

'No, just a cameraman.'

'Oh, then you're one of them guys taking pictures of us up-country.' I noticed how he had managed to slip the 'us' into his query.

'Yes, I am one of them guys. I've just returned from Danang.'

'Danang? Not in my sector.' No, it wouldn't be. 'Whaddya think of the war?'

What did I think of the war? I took a sip of my '33' and thought of something clever to answer. I could think of nothing. 'You don't really want to know what I think of the war.'

'Are you one of those who believe we ought to let the commies walk all the way to San Francisco?'

'That would be a great feat, better than the one performed by Moses.'

'Moses?' He was obviously not versed in the Bible.

'He was the one who parted the waters of the Red Sea.'

'That's real funny.' He stopped one of the ever-present, white-coated Vietnamese waiters to ask for another vodka. 'And bring us some olives.'

'Please?'

'Olives,' he said again in a drawn-out drawl.

'Yes Sir, ooh-leeves.' A steel-toothy smile from the waiter.

'They can't even talk English.'

'Why don't you try him in French?'

He rubbed his chin, wondering what to say next. It was up to me to ask a pertinent question: 'What do you think we should do?'

'Well, we certainly cannot pull out. This is part of the communist conspiracy to control all of Asia, all the surrounding countries – Laos, Cambodia, Thailand, Indonesia, Malaya – they would all go down the drain, all become stooges of the Russians. Our allies, like Japan and Korea – they would be outflanked, and the road to California would be open.'

He continued with his military logic. 'The real reason we're not going anywhere is because we are running this show as a limited operation.'

'You mean, a limited war? Do you think anybody has bothered to inform Hanoi?'

'What do you mean? Why should we let them know how we run the war?'

'Because a limited war is only such if both sides agree to limit it, and then you have to clearly define its limitations. But if you drop endless tons of explosives on to a place, then this is hardly a limited war.'

'Well, in any case, we're going to lick Charlie, we're gonna shove him back into the Stone Age.'

'There is little doubt about the military might of the United States.'

'Defeatists, the whole bunch of you.' With that he grabbed his thunderbolted cap and walked out of my life.

We, the group we called 'the Saigon regulars', we simply took it for granted that we would survive. That wasn't always true. Yesterday a character with his Leica had us in stitches when he played Hamlet's Yiddisher mama, and today they buried him somewhere in a swamp. The reporter who could drink a beer doing a handstand failed to return from Cambodia. We weren't looking for compassion, we were colleagues in a difficult environment, and as professionals we had to compete with each other. It was hard to strike up a permanent friendship, especially with those who were known for taking risks.

Larry Burrows was a quiet, courteous Englishman, in a profession that has more than its share of prima donnas. When asked about a bloody battle, he would say, 'Quite lively.' Destiny, and our bosses, had thrown us together, during daylight hours in combat helicopters, and during the long nights in army camps. We slugged through the bush and pulled each other out of the mud. And yet I did not get to know him well. One day he did not return. They never found his body:

he is still somewhere inside Laos. A short while ago, his grandchildren inaugurated a monument for fallen war correspondents.

Saigon saw some of the very best, who got their information from direct observation of the fighting. They used to sit quietly in a corner of the bar, and kept their opinions and observations to themselves, only to be shared with their readers. Some had become legends in their own time. John was an old-timer from the toughest newspaper pavement in the world, London's Fleet Street. He worked for a tabloid with a mass circulation, and once I suggested to him: 'John, with your contacts, and your talent, why don't you work for a prestigious paper, like *The Times*?'

To this he replied in typical Fleet Street fashion: 'The one I work for pays more and has a bigger circulation.'

John was famous throughout the Far East for his varied exploits and scoops. He had been present during the rape of Nanking by the Japanese, he was captured at the fall of Singapore. The Japanese had tied him by his thumbs to a beam in the ceiling, and let him hang there, trying to extract information: they were convinced that he worked for British military intelligence. But John escaped, to join Wingate and his Chindits in Burma. There he picked up the fever. After the war he covered the French Indochina conflict, and walked with General Giap into Dien Bien Phu. When it came to Chinese thinking and Vietnamese cunning, John was a living dictionary. Probably he did work for some intelligence agency, although it was difficult to say for which side, since he possessed contacts, and information, most of us could only dream of. Recently he had been evacuated to Hong Kong with a recurrence of his Burmese fever. Now I had heard that he was back in town, and I was about to run into him.

After dark Saigon was no longer safe. Gangs of kids roamed the streets, peddling dope and robbing pedestrians. One night while headed home across the square in front of the Majestic, across from the harbour, I witnessed such an attack. Two teenage boys, fourteen at most, rode past a peacefully strolling couple, when the driver suddenly braked his Honda, and the boy on the pillion grabbed for the woman's wrist. The girl let out a scream of anguish and fury. A jerk, the wristwatch came off, and the scooter raced away.

The girl's companion spun around, and in a swift motion brought up his arm. I saw something golden in his fist. A flash split the darkness, followed by thunder. The two boys, like in a slow-motion film, tumbled from their motorbike, clutching each other in a lover's embrace. The scooter sent up sparks as it skidded to a halt, with the engine roaring and the back wheel spinning. The two forms on the ground were quite still, then one jerked a leg and finally even that stopped and both were united in death.

The man who had fired the shot held the girl who continued shrieking. Nobody seemed to take the slightest notice of the drama. A few passers-by glanced in the direction of the bodies, but then hurried to disappear in the darkness. I ran towards the two. She was pretty and young. He was in his forties, with a hard, lean Asian face.

'Can I help?'

'No, thank you.' A clipped voice. At that moment a military jeep braked to a halt. A young Vietnamese officer jumped off, and, seeing the man, came to attention. By the conversation I could see that the MP showed great respect. His driver had walked up to the churning motorcycle, and silenced it with a tremendous kick. He then picked it up and threw it into the back of the jeep. He signalled two men on a boat, and with their help dragged the two bodies across the street, leaving a dark smear on the asphalt. Unceremoniously they dumped the corpses on top of the scooter in the back of the vehicle. Once more, the officer saluted, jumped into his jeep, and drove off. The man led the hysterically sobbing girl across the square and disappeared into the hotel.

Within minutes all was back to quiet, as if nothing had taken place. On the brightly lit patio of the Majestic I discovered a familiar figure – John, the Fleet Street legend. He had aged, and quite badly, since I had last seen him. His face had become cratered by malaria and whisky. He waved me over, and in a voice hoarse from too many cigarettes said, 'Hallo, my boy, join me for a drink?'

'John, love to. Good to see you.'

'Cut the crap.' He motioned to a waiter. 'What will you have?' he asked.

'A beer for the thirst and a shot for the emotion.'

'Bring this man a Bao-Ba and a Dimple Haig, and me another double.' He turned to me: 'Been upcountry lately?'

'Yes, last week, in the highlands.'

'How is it there?' I am sure he knew the situation better than

I, although he very seldom had to leave Saigon to get his information.

'Bad, lots of rain, lots of Charlies, and lots of casualties, ours.'

'The Yanks should stop this silly nonsense, they haven't seen the end of it. Jungle wars can be bloody unpleasant, nobody ever returns victorious.'

He knew that the fever was slowly killing him, but he wouldn't leave the jungle. That was his beat, the Far East his only faithful mistress. He had nowhere else to go, nobody was waiting for him at the end of his line. So he stayed on and reported. His caustic columns often gave an insight into jungle warfare in a manner no other writer had ever managed to convey. Once, when his editor asked John for a thousand words on the probability of a forthcoming enemy offensive, he had simply cabled back: MY BALLS ARE UNMADE CRYSTAL. J.R.

'How's Jim?' he inquired.

'He is back in London nursing a cold.'

'Poor Jim, how he must miss the rainy season out here.'

'Not much, judging by his last letter: he's found a new friend.'

'Boy or girl?'

'He didn't say.'

We were sitting talking banalities, when only ten minutes before a drama had played out, sudden death on the sidewalk. But such was Saigon; one hardly ever talked about dying. Still, I wondered why the police had done nothing about the man with the gun.

'Did you see that cowboy stuff?' I asked. How could he have missed it, thirty feet away?

'Yes, spot of excitement. Tough luck on the kids, they picked on the wrong man.'

'How so?'

'He's the colonel of a crack ARVN unit. His trademark is unconventional warfare and a gold-plated .45.' Which explained the golden flash just before the shot. 'He just blew one very large hole through two waferthin Charlies.'

I was curious: 'What will they do with the bodies?'

'Dump them in the river, I suppose,' and with that he took a long sip, and sighed. 'Scratch two from their valiant war effort.'

'You sound rather disappointed in America's allies.'

'Let's stop pretending, my boy. The only ones who could have any punch are the Yanks, and they aren't getting anywhere.'

'Why is that?'

'They are fighting phantoms in a jungle without a road sign. They are going around in circles and shooting at shadows. A thousand soldiers in a hundred helicopters trying to encircle one pyjama-boy with a flintlock. It's the proverbial jar of candyfloss. The deeper you stick your hand into it, the more you get covered with sugar.'

'Can you see a solution?'

'Sure, an easy one. The Americans have to apply the principle of hopeless warfare: send in troops, make a splash, achieve nothing, declare victory and go home!'

On my way to my hotel I mused over John's prophecies. Was he a visionary? A few months later John passed away, victim of too many cigarettes and too much liquor, too much fever and too many jungle wars. They buried a legend with him.

John's final words kept haunting me: *declare victory and pull out*. There was a strange logic to it.

The United States armed forces are second to none when it comes to fighting. They are brave and resourceful. But most important of all, until now they had been invincible. This wasn't a war, this was Vietnam, a country on the coast of nowhere, with no castle to storm, no final flag to hoist. There was no everlasting glory to be gathered. Never before had the morale of American troops been so low. The breakdown in fighting spirit stemmed from one major factor: lack of purpose.

This was not a fight to save humanity from the spectre of some global conquest by an evil force. At the end of the long road there was no Berlin, there wasn't even Hanoi, there was nothing. An army of aimless battalions, going up the hill and down the hill and back up again.

The propaganda unit of the US Military Advisory Group–Vietnam cranked out information at high speed. For them, we were winning. Every afternoon a religious procession of the international press corps wandered to the cinema across the square to attend the '5 o'clock follies'. At that time the chief of public information, US MAG–V, a civilian by the name of Barry Zorthian, gave a briefing about the latest from the war front. In general the news was positive.

'Everything is under control,' was the phrase most often pronounced. For the last two weeks I had not been out in the field, recuperating in Saigon from an 'everything-is-under-control' adventure which had cost the lives of six marines. I had to start earning my salary and find the war. That wasn't difficult, it was everywhere. This time I decided to go to the Central Highlands.

To reach the front wasn't much of a problem. We could simply proceed to any military airfield, and with our MAG–V press card, a green plastic affair which gave our name, affiliation and purpose (and for the more senior reporters even a make-believe rank to give them priority on the aircraft) we could board any plane or helicopter to the destination of our choice. The only restriction was the availability of space and the willingness of the pilot. If there were no seats in the aircraft, one could always ride on a crate of fragmentation grenades or a load of Hawaian pineapple juice.

Recently I had been joined by Sepp. I had met him on a pair of skis. Nowadays I had to be careful: any injury would have cramped my journalistic ambitions. That didn't stop me from enjoying a fast run down any mountain. My problem was that I could never find someone to ski with me. One day I noticed a little boy racing down a slope. I followed him, and joined him on his return ride up the ski lift.

'You ski very well.'

'Thank you,' he replied in a shy voice, but with a warm friendly smile.

'Let's ski together.'

Sitting there, feet dangling above the ground, steadily moving uphill, neither he nor I realized how I was to change his life. By the time he reached eighteen he had made the Austrian ski squad. A series of training accidents sidelined him, and by the time he was back in shape and tried to make a comeback, it was all over for him.

He had turned into a handsome devil – blond curly hair, a nose like an eagle and a shy grin – the kind of person women love to baby and girls love to kiss. I asked him to accompany me on one of my field trips: he jumped at the opportunity and showed his willingness to be helpful by carrying my suitcases. Since I could hardly justify the expense of a personal bag-carrier, I taught him the principles of sound recording. He loved the idea, caught on with amazing speed and from then on became someone I could depend on as my permanent sound engineer. Together we had travelled the world – he was thrilled to see the

wonders of the High North and the Deep South and the Far East.
When in the field, life can be monotonous, and it is vital that one's
partner is witty, funny and shares some of the same interests. A
two-man team is a professional marriage, forced to share a daily diet of
joys and fights. Once I was driving with Sepp and the rest of our team
was in the car behind us. I had an argument over some minor issue.
He got out of our car and stopped the others.

'Why don't you want to ride with Erik?' they asked, somewhat
baffled.

'I'm punishing Erik.'

'Why are you punishing him?'

'There's always a reason to punish Erik,' was his reply.

This was the young man who joined me in Vietnam on an autumn
day in 1967.

Early one morning in November we went to Tan Son Nhut air base
and hitched a ride north towards Pleiku, the big military supply base
in the Central Highlands. The ride was uneventful but freezing cold.
Our transport had two side-mounted machine guns and no doors. For
safety reasons we flew at high altitude. Sitting in an icy draught, we
huddled in our thin ponchos.

The giant blades of the rotor cut a swathe through the morning mist
as we came in for a landing. The countryside was placid: water
buffaloes neckdeep in water, little boys with long sticks driving a flock
of ducks, slender-necked women with heavy baskets balancing on
bamboo poles, trotting barefoot along the small ridges separating the
rice paddies. The sun was reflected in the stagnant water of the fields.
There was no sign of war, or impending danger. All was calm, and
peaceful.

Music drifted across the field. It was the song of the day – Nancy
Sinatra's 'These boots are made for walking … '

The airfield was protected by four watchtowers, from which
machine guns pointed at the water buffaloes. There were two guards
to each tower, conscripts from Georgia or Indiana, huddled in their
olive-green parkas to escape the morning chill. After having spent a
whole night in the frosty open, they displayed little enthusiasm to the
world in general. A half-asleep soldier carried a metal tray towards a
tower, the morning's food ration. Bread in brown sauce, better

known as shit-on-a-shingle.

A bugle sounded somewhere, the US flag was raised. The airfield was slowly coming awake. Sleepy grunts got up and stood at attention. An old woman, hunchbacked over a broom, swept in front of a radio hut. Sour-faced gunners were stuffing helicopter gunships with bullets and rockets for this morning's action. On one side of the field I discovered the notorious flying battleship nicknamed 'Puff, the magic dragon'. It had acquired its reputation from its deadly cargo of multiple gatling guns, which could rain a stream of fire from the skies, killing everything in the dragon's path. The name derived from the title of a popular song by an American folk group, but rumour had it that 'Puff' referred to marijuana, and not to the plane's dragon teeth. Puff had been out on a night foray, and was now quietly grazing next to a score of sleepy giant helicopters.

We ducked under the whirling blades of our transport and made for the nearest watering hole, a Quonset hut on the edge of the field. A sleepy conscript from the deep South asked, 'Want some coffee?' and proceeded to pour transparent liquid into paper cups. It tasted like army coffee the world over, thin. But it was hot.

In no time a major strolled over to our small group and introduced himself: 'I'm the battalion PSYWAR specialist.' I'd heard many abbreviations, but this one was new to me.

'What precisely is PSYWAR?'

'Psychological warfare. We fly over the jungle with two very potent loudhailers attached to the underbelly of a helicopter and we broadcast a message to Victor Charlie.'

'And what sort of message do you give them?'

'We tell them, if they come out peacefully and surrender, nothing will happen to them.'

For a moment I was stunned, and I could not believe that I had heard right! How could anybody be so naïve as to believe that a Viet Cong, who had chosen to disappear into the jungle to fight, would now simply come back out and surrender? In my book the VCs had only two choices: to come out either dead or as victors. To think that the enemy would even listen to such a message was a sad joke. There had to be something more to it. Perhaps this was the justification for a forthcoming action, a sort of ecclesiastical approval for the deed about to be performed.

'What happens if they don't come out?'

'Then we send in the battalion and splap them.'

'Splap?'

'Have you ever heard an M16 going off in the jungle? It goes splap.'

'You mean you kill them.'

'That's right.'

So much for psychological warfare.

After this highly informative briefing on inducing a reluctant foe to surrender, he took us into a hut where a large map of the military region was taped to the wall. It was covered by a sheet of transparent plastic, and had arrows in red and blue pointing in all directions. It became evident that military intelligence was not a precise art.

'Where do you think we should go to?' I asked.

'If I were you, I would go up there, to Dak To.' And with a swift motion of his hand-carved bamboo pointer, he found a place almost off the edge of the map. As far as I could make out, there was a Dak To all right, and next to it was nothing. A few isolated American infantry battalions, but no red arrows to indicate the presence of bad guys. I wasn't quite certain whether the good major simply wanted to rid himself of our bothersome group by designating a fairly safe place to minimize the risk of losing a few journalists in a well-publicized ambush, or if he really had a notion that we would find some action there.

The next supply chopper for Dak To left around noon – a flying banana, two rotors, front and aft, and extremely noisy, like riding inside a concrete-mixer. We stuffed toilet paper into our ears.

The helicopter surged skywards, as far up into the blue as the rarefied air would permit the whirling blades to take their banana. Just to make sure that we arrived at our final destination with all our parts still intact, I took my helmet and sat on it. Better to be prepared than to be sorry for the rest of my children-producing life: that was my policy. Sepp and Hubert knew me, and both followed suit. (Hubert, a well-known stills photographer, was in his early thirties. He knew Vietnam and its people. We had met in Algiers during the French colonial war. Since then we had shared adventures and mistresses, and it was only natural for me to ask him to join me in Vietnam.) Sitting on a round piece of steel in a vibrator isn't comfortable, and we were pounded like schnitzel. The noise made me drowsy and I dozed off.

If war is great glory, getting there isn't. Thousands of war correspondents, cameramen and sound engineers have bribed, cajoled, forced or simply begged their way on to any form of available transport. Anything beats walking. We were no exception. We jumped from the cabin, and on the way to the headquarters tent along the airstrip we passed a small helicopter, ready to lift off.

'Whereabouts are you headed for?' I screamed over the noise of the engine.

'Bringing mail up to a firebase.' Up must mean one of the surrounding hills. If action was to be found, it wouldn't be down here around the main base, at least not at the outset. My choice was not difficult.

'Got room?' To make sure he understood over the din, I used sign language.

He pointed towards the cabin: 'Sure, jump in.'

I had not reported to the local commander, but he'd find out soon enough that a few journalists were in his region, by which time we would be with a field unit.

We climbed aboard, and roared towards the green jungle. This time I wore the helmet and sat on my flak jacket. This item had been handed to me at division headquarters as a must-wear-at-all-times. Somebody had stencilled across the chest: Press. It looked like 'Plague, beware of infection'.

I was wearing tropical fatigues and had a rucksack filled with film and spare socks, a week's supply of K-rations, a watercan made of inflatable plastic, and a heavy battery belt around my waist. A tetanus jab in a sealed container, just in case, and the vital diarrhoea pills. A roll of toilet paper, to clean camera lenses and for other use. A pair of army-issue jungle boots made of green canvas with black leather tops and a steel inlay sole, in case of pungy spikes – booby-traps made of a rusty nail dipped in excrement and planted on jungle paths, which had a nasty habit of penetrating the rubber sole and going right up through the foot. This led to infection and amputation, and I was rather fond of my feet. Better to stumble on with blisters.

Sepp was burdened by the paraphernalia of a combat sound engineer. He had bottles clanking from his belt, and a heavy bag with spare batteries, spare cables, spare tapes, food, water, pills, bandages and his own roll of toilet paper. The tape recorder was slung over his shoulder. Hubert completed our trio. He acted as back-up cameraman.

Vietnam was now in its seventh year of American presence. What had begun as a small advisory commitment had mushroomed into half a million troops drafted from across the United States, all with an equal dislike of Vietnam and their military duty. To some, war was a profitable chore – fighting the battles of Saigon's black market – but the less lucky ones got the regular combat treatment. The drop in morale which infected the rearguard had not as yet reached the forward units, led by tough, battle-hardened officers, veterans of Guadalcanal and Korea. It was into such a unit that we were dropped by our helicopter.

The 119 men of Alpha company were spread out over several hundred yards along a jungle path. I made contact with their commander, a wiry bundle of dynamite by the name of Captain Foyt. I am not sure if he was surprised, annoyed or both to have us around his neck. A tired-looking soldier had just finished his report to the captain. Foyt turned to him: 'Sergeant Coons, look after these television people.'

It wasn't surprising to find field commanders who had had unpleasant encounters with television crews; after all, this was a television war, and little remained uncovered by the various television networks. I was trying to present a different image of myself and our crew, but at first sight in a humid jungle, who cared?

Sergeant Harry Charles Joseph Coons, from Georgia, was twenty-nine, a professional soldier, with a wife he absolutely adored and who had given him two children. He was of medium height, never without a smile. He even smiled when he fired his machine gun. He was in charge of a heavy weapon squad. He was a farm boy of the sort one finds on country roads in a half-ton pickup, going for groceries to the little town nearby. He had the look of a preacher man, and talked with the Southern drawl of the Bible teacher who spreads the Good Word from the back of his mobile altar. Inscribed on his helmet was the name by which everybody called him: JC.

Private First Class (PFC) Jim Buchner was one of his gunners. Jim was twenty-six, well built with soft brown hair and gentle eyes that were searching for something in the distance. Perhaps he was dreaming of his native Derby, New York, where he was expected to run his father's restaurant following his tour in Vietnam. He had passed through a disastrous marriage to a childhood sweetheart who had grown up faster than he did. He was handsome all right, and in contrast to Coons talked slowly and thoughtfully: with an accent from upstate New York.

Jim was a cheerful type, and whenever his buddies fell into a morose mood he was ready with a funny story. More than any other soldier in the group, he was a thinker, who tried to figure out the underlying reason why they had been sent to Vietnam. He thought he had found the reason, but wasn't quite sure.

And then there was Bruce Black, the hippie from California, a bronzed muscle builder and college dropout. His hangout had been Haight-Ashbury. He had come to the conclusion that it would be healthier to give Vietnam a miss and go on an extended vacation to Canada. Something or somebody changed his mind, and he ended up in Alpha company. Within six months he had been promoted to sergeant.

In their four months in battle, the trio had become inseparable. The men of Alpha company called them the Three Musketeers. By a quirk of fate, and because a certain JC was standing near his company commander when our helicopter touched down, they became the lead characters in a television documentary which became famous as *Hill 943.*

3
HILL 943

(VIETNAM 1967)

The noble Duke of York
He had ten thousand men
He marched them up to the top o' the hill,
And he marched them down again.

Popular, 18th century

During the French colonial period, Paris had sent out surveyors to map the highland wilderness of Cochin China, near the border junction of Laos, Cambodia and Vietnam. For these surveyors, suffering from malaria and snakebites, the jungle was too dense to penetrate, and so the maps were mainly recorded from a central point. The simple way to identify all these hills was with a number. The French, using their metric system, marked their maps with *Hill 875, 762,* or *697* according to their height. One of these many hills in the wilderness measured 943 metres, and was thus named Hill 943.

Jumping from the helicopter, we saw just another muddy, damp hill, full of snakes and booby-traps. Since we had been assured by the press information office of the US forces in Saigon, that 'all was quiet and under control', there was little reason to expect any major enemy engagement.

The hill was about five miles from the Cambodian border, as the crow flies, that is. There are not many crows in the jungle, and on foot, averaging one mile per day, Hill 943 was five days' march from the Ho Chi Minh trail. It was six days' march from Dak To.

The battalion had taken up a position on one of the hills surrounding Dak To, assisting the three companies operating in the field with ground fire. The US Air Force kept up sporadic harassment, dropping bombs at random on the approaches to Dak To. Alpha company had been slugging their way through the humid jungle for eight days, going blindly from nowhere to nowhere. They had engaged in no hostile contact, there was not the slightest indication of enemy presence. There were only strange sounds in the jungle, such as the screeching of monkeys and birds, disturbed by the crashing of shells, as the American artillery kept up sporadic fire on the surrounding jungle.

Alpha company is tired and dirty. They are besieged by leeches and lice and attacked by swarms of mosquitoes. They suffer from diarrhoea and body rash. Their battle dress is torn by the knifelike bamboo, their skin infected by sweat and dirt. Rivulets of salty sweat sting their eyes and run down their unshaven, flybitten faces. Their shoulders are hunched down by heavy burdens of grenades, machineguns, light mortar tubes, self-propelled rockets, bullet belts, flare guns, claymore mines, radio-telephones, food, water, rifles and spades. The ground is covered by rotting leaves, a treacherous carpet hiding booby-traps. Each path has to be cut through dense tropical forest, each step carved out of the red mud which covers the slopes of the steep hills.

My first question must sound quite silly to them, but it is enlightening to the viewers back home: 'What's the worst thing about this war?'

Sergeant Williams, the platoon commander: 'The hills, climbing those hills, the jungle, beating your way through it, being sniped at. Not knowing where it comes from, shooting at shadows.' The heat is so stifling he almost runs out of breath. 'Our own artillery going in around us – that's hairy, never knowing when the shrapnel is coming down on you.'

Buchner, leaning on a tree, grins: 'Sarge, what you gonna do when you get to the top? Come down, and then climb another bloody hill. That's all.'

'No, it ain't. If the gooks are up ahead what I'm looking for is a pistol, a Russian type. I hope we find an officer up there.'

'What makes you think that you're the one to get to the top?' says Buchner.

An ugly grin on Williams' face, 'Ha ha, wise guy, put you on ambush, next ten days straight.' He turns back to me. 'Just hope it goes faster than this ... the days gone by all right, but not as fast as I want them to go.'

A shell whistles in and we dive headlong into the mud. In the dense undergrowth there is no way of telling how close the missile strikes, or how far the deadly shrapnel will fly. Williams gets up, brushes mud from his face. 'I'm looking forward to getting out of here, that's the main thing.'

Most of the men are fresh from basic training. This is the most dangerous period in any soldier's existence. 'Survive the first month and you're a helluva lot closer to the freedom bird home,' was the drill instructor's advice. In their camps in the United States they had been fed on a diet of military protein and off-base hamburgers. They learned how to march forward, sideways, and backwards, how to salute officers, take abuse from the sergeants, clean the latrines, stand guard duty and peel potatoes. They were told to address their superiors as 'Sir', and their comrades as 'buddies'. They were given an issue of combat fatigues, combat boots, a helmet, an M16 automatic rifle, a few blank rounds to fire, a blanket, a poncho, and a lot of good advice. They received injections against smallpox, yellow fever, cholera, tetanus, typhoid, and a lesson on how to avoid getting the clap. Over the weekends they were issued prophylactics and then they headed for the nearest Dairy Queen to spend their military pay on milk shakes, and get laid. One thing nobody told them: what Vietnam was going to look like – that there were no roads to march on, no hamburgers and no Dairy Queens.

The day they walked off the plane, or the troopship, they just kept on marching until they were confronted by a situation they hadn't been prepared for and had to handle as best they could. Being all-American kids, and having learned from early youth to fight their individual combats in Brooklyn and Watts and Little Rock and Butte, most managed to survive when the 'shit hit the fan'.

Alpha company was no different. Half were black and half were white, half were from Dixie and half were Yankees, half were city kids, and half came from the farm. They all had fathers and mothers, sweethearts and wives, and they kept writing to their families that they had just spent another lousy month in the jungle, wandering aimlessly from hill X to hill Y crossing river Z on the way. And how they missed the Giants and Jackie Gleason and root beer and even a lousy job like parking limos in back of Mr Meyer's restaurant. And how everything would be different as soon as they were back home again, and 'Betty, please wait for me, as soon as I get back we'll be married, I just plain forgot to ask you before I left.'

A supply helicopter comes in, and Hubert gets on it, going to retrieve a battery we abandoned at the firebase. As he lands in the main camp, the battalion commander, Lieutenant Colonel Jamie Hendrix, codenamed Grizzly, orders this chopper to take him on an inspection tour over his battalion's advance companies. Soon they are skimming the jungle at treetop level. Grizzly is attached to his seat by a seatbelt, his map on a clipboard across his knees.

Bolted to the side of the helicopter is a shortwave radio. Grizzly checks the terrain and calls in a stream of artillery observations to his headquarters. 'Pilot, I wanna take a look at 943, it's the one at ten o'clock.' A hill looms up in front of them, and the pilot makes a sharp bank to his left.

Suddenly an explosion rocks the helicopter and a mass of red smoke fills the cabin. Grizzly throws his hand to his face – the aircraft has been hit. There is confusion, the red smoke blinds the pilot who ejects his door to let the draught clear the view. The smoke is blown into the passenger compartment through the open doors. The colonel bleeds, Hubert coughs, and the gunners loose off a stream of bullets into the jungle.

There is a nasty tear in the aluminium where a heavy round has ripped through the floor. The bullet has gone through the radio and exploded a red smoke grenade attached to the set. Fragments have struck Grizzly in the face: blood flows unchecked down his cheeks. Despite the explosion the pilot has kept control of the machine. We, on the ground, can hear it roaring overhead. We hear the machine guns and once more dive into the mud. The tree cover is too dense to see what is going on. The noise trails off.

The helicopter makes it back to the firebase. Hubert jumps off and helps Grizzly down. The sidegunner finds the smashed bullet stuck in a hydraulic pipe. Another minute, and the rear rotor would have failed, sending the aircraft spinning to its death somewhere in the jungle. They were lucky.

The gunner hands Grizzly his clipboard. There is a neat, round hole through the middle.

'That's as close as I ever want to get,' says the colonel in a dry Texan drawl. 'Now we know where they are.' And with that he moves to the wall map and points at a marker. 'This is Grizzly, I want you to fire a 15-minute preparation on point nine-four-three.'

'That is a 15-minute preparation on point nine-four-three, Sir,' comes the answerback over a crackling loudspeaker.

'That is affirmative.'

The first rounds leave the barrels of the 105mm howitzers. Their destination is a tree-covered hill a few miles to the west.

'Spider one-two, this is Grizzly, over.'

'This is Spider one-two, over.' The voice of Captain Foyt.

'Spider one-two. We've just had enemy contact on Hill 943. I want you to get your men there and check it out. How far are you from there?'

'One moment, let me check,' and after a few moments of silence, Foyt's voice is back, 'Hill nine-four-three, that is, Sir, we can probably make it in twenty-four hours.'

'That's real fine. Be careful on the approach, they're there all right but we don't know what they've got up.'

The company has dug in for the night, the claymore mines have been set, and the wiretraps are strung. Buchner stops me from a harmless walk, adds with a smile: 'Hey Erik, don't go piss, you might hit the express to heaven.'

It reminds me of another camp in Vietnam, when I was less careful. I fill up an empty tin with my bodily fluids, and then pour it carefully behind the nearest tree. We crawl into our self-made mudholes and roll into our ponchos. There isn't one soldier in Alpha company who is still unaware that Grizzly has been wounded, or that we have been ordered to head towards a suspected enemy stronghold. That night, sleep does not come easy to the boys from Alpha company, nor to the television crew with them. The last thing I can hear is a whisper from JC's direction: 'Please, O Lord ... ' I believe JC is praying.

Early next morning Alpha company moves out. We have to cross a gully. It is a slow process, handing down people and equipment. The gradient is steep and the ground slippery. One soldier slides, and comes to a violent halt against a tree trunk. He has sprained his ankle. There is no time to remove his shoe, the medic straps a bandage over

Right: Early days in Vietnam – Erik Durschmied and Jim Mossman in Danang, 1961

Below: Mossman in tent in Vietnam, early 1960s

Above: Mossman in helicopter over the Mekong Delta, early 1960s

Left: Durschmied and Mossman in helicopter over the Mekong Delta, early 1960s

Left: Durschmied filming street fighting

Below: Buddhist uprising and street fighting in Danang, 1965 – typical pictures of Vietnamese women and children running for cover. The army attacks – the wounded and the dead – a Buddhist prayer covers a dead man's face (frames from Durschmied's 16mm film)

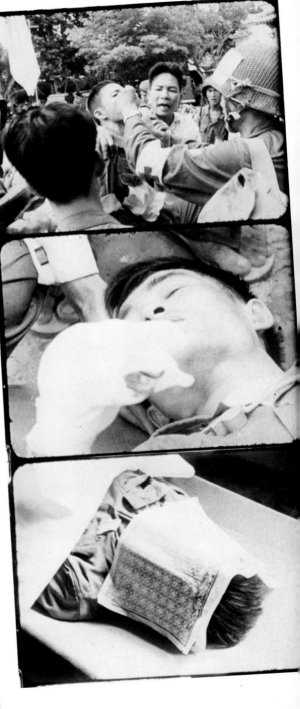

Above: Hill 943: Erik Durschmied and Sepp Thoma interviewing Sergeant Joseph Coons, 1967

Left: Hill 943: Durschmied (with camera) and JC tending to Sepp Thoma after he is wounded

Below: Hill 943: Erik Durschmied and Colonel Jim 'Grizzly' Hendrix, Vietnam, 1967

Opposite above: Hill 943: into the jungle, Vietnam, 1967

Opposite below: Hill 943: the last cigarette

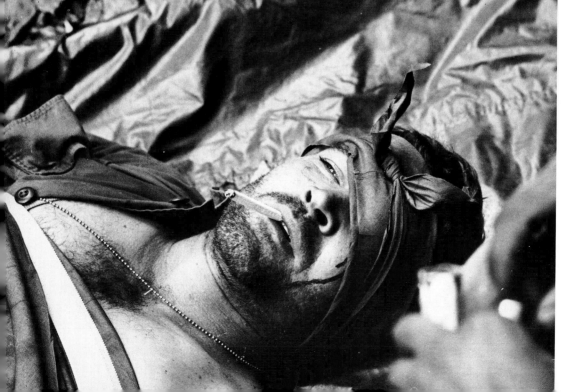

Hill 943: Durschmied filming the attack

Hill 943: the storming of the hill, Alpha Company advancing behind a curtain of fire through sharp, splintered bamboo – the last few metres were a running attack uphill (frames from Durschmied's 16mm film)

Left and below: Hill 943: Alpha Company suffer casualties as they take the hill (frames from Durschmied's 16mm film)

Opposite: After the battle of Hill 943

Left: Bruce Black

Below left: Joseph Coons

Below: Jim Buchner

the outside of his wet junglepants and tapes it over his boot. In no time the white has changed into a camouflage brown. Through the bottom of the gully flows a creek, its banks soft mud. I am stuck, grab a rifle, pull up, move my knees, get stuck again, pull once more and fall flat on my face into the stream. It's nice and cool; if it wasn't so muddy the water would taste good. Like a soldier protecting his weapon I have kept the arm with the camera above the water, but my feet are still anchored in the mud. Sepp gets hold of my backpack and pulls me up. We wade across, the water fills our boots and squishes between our toes, then runs out through the holes in the canvas. It is a nice feeling, water through the toes: it feels cold and clean, not like mud and leeches. We take a minute's rest to fill up our watercans. We are careful to add water-purification pills: the result tastes awful, like swimming pool water. But that's jungle warfare: first it hurts, then it squirts, and then the body gets numb and the mind refuses to obey. It happened to me more than once.

The climb up the bank is equally treacherous. Buchner has hoisted himself to the top of the lip and now reaches down the barrel of his machine gun. I grab it and he pulls me up. Now the real sweat starts. It takes five hours to advance four hundred yards and reach a relatively level place.

We don't spot it at first and almost stumble past. But then JC lifts his finger to his mouth and points in the direction of a bush like all the others. It is a dugout, covered by jungle weeds: our first evidence of the enemy. JC and Buchner point their guns and release the safety catches. Black crawls to it. He takes a grenade from his belt, pulls the pin, throws it into the hole. When he tries to jump back, his foot catches in a root. There is a bang, and smoke comes out of the hole.

Black is all right. 'Hey Brucie, got to dig it out of your sole?'

'Hell no, but the smoke almost choked me. Got to wait a few minutes, then we climb down and check it out.'

We follow him in: the acrid smoke of the grenade lingers. The bunker seems empty. Black is ahead, a flashlight in his teeth, his M16 cocked and ready. There is a dark tunnel ahead. Black doesn't take a chance, he fires a couple of rounds into the gloom. We dive for the ground, we can't see, we can only hear bangs.

'It's okay, you guys, just being careful, that's all. Have a look at this.' With his light he points at his discovery. An aluminium mess kit, a heap of bloodied bandages, a syringe and a bamboo helmet.

'What the hell is that?' I ask naïvely.

'That, my friend, is a helmet straight from Hanoi.'

His statement sends a shiver down my spine: we are no longer facing Viet Cong, but the regular army of North Vietnam.

Captain Foyt crawls into the hole to assess the danger. He gets on the radio to advise firebase of our discovery. The company is ordered to dig in. Despite the acute danger, there is a general sigh of relief as everybody drops their backpacks from aching shoulders. Someone starts an argument and the voice of the company sergeant booms across the jungle: 'Do-what-I-say-and-shut-the-hell-up.'

A wave of laughter is the only reward for the poor GI who dared to stand up to the sergeant and it puts an end to the quarrel over who would dig tonight's hole. The company needs supplies and has to make a helicopter landing zone. Sergeant Williams picks the only level spot, heavily wooded with several big trees. He has a simple way to cut them down: a white sausage of plastic explosive is tied to the trunk, a fuse is inserted, and – boom. One of the trees splinters, and a chunk hits a soldier on the head. He is knocked cold. The medic revives him – groggily he opens his eyes, moans.

Buchner reaches for the boy's hand, white hand on black, a symbol of camaraderie among fighting men. That also is Vietnam. 'What's wrong with him, doc?'

The wounded man lolls his head, his fluttering eyes showing the white. 'Could be shock.'

'What's his pulse?'

'One-twenty.'

'Okay, get him bandaged and let's move him out.' Captain Foyt has taken the decision.

The medivac helicopter reaches the treetops, its pilot feeling his way down through the narrow gap. A rotor blade chops off a branch. The ship sets down and boxes come off, followed by Hubert who is carrying a mailbag which he hands to Sergeant Williams.

Buchner and Black drag the stunned soldier into the chopper. Helping hands reach down and pull him into the belly. The whole operation has taken less than thirty seconds, then the machine lifts off. For an instant it hovers like an angry dragonfly, then it tilts forward and is lost from view. JC plus his little group are perched like vultures around the mailbag.

'Rawlings ... Buchner ... Hyman ... Coons ... and again Coons. That's all.'

The lucky ones with mail clutch their letters and sit down under trees.

Black walks up: 'Where's my mail?'

The sergeant throws him a dark look: 'There ain't none, so pipe down.'

Buchner tears open the envelope. He turns to me. 'Some of these letters, they sure make you homesick. Can't wait until I get back. Next August, boy, I'm gonna have a big party when I get back. I sure miss the good times and all the people. When I was back there working I really didn't like it all that much, working for your family, but now, when you're away from it ... '

JC has got two letters from his wife. They contain mostly smalltalk about the babies, the grocery bills, everyday life in Smalltown, Georgia, USA. But for JC it is headline news, for it smells of home. 'Today's her birthday, she says she's old, thirty years old. She's only a young chick.'

'Get in the hole!! Dammit, get in the hole!!'

Jets roar overhead, I see one on its back for a final target inspection. Then it rolls over for the dive. A bomb whistles down, towards the hill nearby. Another jet lines up on the approach, dives, releases the bomb, pulls up. The ground shakes. We have all scrambled into our freshly dug holes. JC ignores the shakes and the bangs, he remains planted under his tree reading his wife's letters, over and over again.

'JC, get in here, come on – scramble, you gonna get hit.'

There is a sudden shriek as shrapnel from the thousand-pounders shreds everything in its path. Leaves float on JC's letter. He looks up, finally realizes that he is sitting in an airstrike, and quickly slides into the hole. In here it is too dark to read, so I help him with my Zippo lighter and, as if nothing else is going on around him and there are no bombs and bangs and airstrikes, JC continues to read his precious mail. Finally, he carefully folds it, and puts it into his tunic pocket. 'Still a young chick.' He smiles proudly to no one in particular.

***

Shortly before midnight I am startled by an infernal scream, followed by a crash and a roar that sounds like a locomotive in a tunnel. I notice Black, his pants around his ankles, peering over the edge of our shelter.

'What is it, Brucie?'

'Take a load of that.' A terrifying sight, as a stream of fire pours down from the night sky.

'Puff, the magic dragon' sings Black to the well-known melody. 'I only hope there's not gonna be anything left when we get there. But the gooks dig down deep! Forty feet or more, you only get them out by putting a grenade up their ass.' He points at the nearby hill, looming dark above us. 'Let's just hope they hose them good. We've got to take that bitch, that's for sure.'

None of us can find sleep, and for the rest of the night I kill mosquitoes.

At 8 a.m. a reconnaissance patrol stumbles across the enemy's command post, a mere fifty yards from our bivouac. The Vietnamese have pulled out during the night. They were close enough to lob grenades into our camp but have chosen to fade away, luckily for us. Foyt gets on the radio and gives the news to Grizzly at firebase. An hour later, the commander's chopper comes to the landing zone. Grizzly wears a dressing on his cheek.

'That's what we found, Sir.' Foyt hands over the bamboo helmet. Buchner has found several 50-calibre cartridges next to a ladder of creeping vine, dangling from a tall tree. 'Sir, have a look at this.'

The place from where the shots on his helicopter were fired.

'Got a man on top of this thing?'

'Yes, Sir, we've got one up there, more for security.'

'Can he see anything?'

'Yes, our own firebase.' The North Vietnamese have been looking right down into Grizzly's cooking pots for God knows how long!

'Okay, get him down and have this thing destroyed. Get your recon patrol ready to go.'

'Yessir. Okay, Sarge, get a patrol ready.'

The final climb up Hill 943 is about to start. Buchner looks at Black who looks at JC. There is a moment of silence, as they all pull the straps from the sides of their helmets and tighten them under their chins. I follow their example. Every soldier has two magazines taped to his automatic rifle, back to back, to be ready.

'Hyman, you take the point. JC you give them cover. Move out.'

The patrol moves into the jungle. Sepp and I have spaced ourselves between JC and Buchner. I feel exposed and can't help feeling that we are being watched. We have hardly moved eighty yards when the first bullets zip right over us. We drop to the ground. The firing continues sporadically for about a minute. Neither JC, nor anyone in our group has responded, we can't see a damn thing. It's the enemy's bullets that are whizzing all around us.

We cling to the ground. I roll to Buchner. He doesn't even notice when I film him. He looks at me and whispers: 'Any of you guys know what happened?'

We all look to each other for information and assurances. I have none to give. I also would like to know what's up ahead, who is shooting at us, who got hit and if a man with a bamboo helmet has his gun lined up on my back. We are tense. There is a rustling to our left. Buchner lifts his rifle.

JC's face appears between leaves. In a hoarse voice he whispers, 'Hey Jim, tell them to be real careful. At least one guy got hit.'

'You guys hear how bad he's hit?'

Black, who was slightly ahead, comes crawling down on his belly: 'A couple of guys just ahead got it.'

'How bad?'

'Don't know, I got down in time.'

'Hey Jim, tell them not only to watch in the trees, but for spiderholes and shit like that ... spiderholes,' he mumbles as an afterthought.

'Jim, be real careful, watch out, real careful.' JC is worried. He is not the only one. We all are, but not paralysed.

Sepp points his microphone and I operate the camera and ask the questions. To Buchner: 'You scared?' What a silly thing to ask, but right now I cannot think of anything else, I only transmit my own thoughts, I want to be reassured that I am not the only one scared.

'A little,' with an unconvincing grin. 'Well, when those shots first go off you get real scared. Now that you're down on the ground, under cover, you start thinking about it ... but I'm sure glad I'm not up in lead.'

'Where would you like to be right now?' Another stupid question, but then, whenever people shoot at me I'm not wildly bright. The next time he answers a bit more calmly, with a sad smile, 'Back home on a beach with a cold six-pack, chasing girls.'

'What do you think of this war?'

'Well, I don't know, I don't believe we should sit back and pull out the way everybody is talking. I think we should be here, and stop it, stop communism. From some of the things I've seen, I wouldn't want anything like this going on in my country. So, it's better to fight in somebody else's country and have everything messed up.'

Another volley whistles overhead. We cling to our wet leaves. JC crawls over to us. 'Makes it so bad over here, you can't even see the people shooting at you. You just hear the sound, that's it. You can't see them. The only time you see them is when they're dead, that's about the best time to see them.' He looks up at the trees. I follow his stare, but can't see a thing. Just some distant birds, singing – a strange vocal backdrop, considering our situation. 'Any war is bad when there's death going on; war is war ... '

There is movement up ahead: JC and Buchner raise their guns. I roll to the side and break a twig. It snaps with a loud crack. They whip their heads around, look at me. There is rustling beyond the bush. What next, a grenade lobbed through the branches? Relief, it's an American voice whispering from behind the leaves. 'Hey guys, hold it for fuck's sake. It's us, we're bringing down our guys.'

Crawling and dragging, they appear, pale faces first, then the rest of the muddy, bleeding ghosts. Two soldiers drag one with a makeshift bandage around his head. He isn't moving. 'Dead?' One shakes his head, points a finger and pulls an imaginary trigger.

'It was bad, we just walked into it. They let us have it up the ass.' His buddy has a severe head wound. A black soldier crawls on his knees, his left hand hangs lifeless by his side and blood is spurting from a wound in his abdomen. He is held up by another GI with a bandage on his arm. Black, Buchner and JC slide over, grab them and drag them into the shelter of a large tree. Then they cut a couple of sturdy branches and make a stretcher with a poncho. They load the most serious casualty on to it. JC takes the lead, followed by five others. A sad caravan, tired, frightened, bleeding. Only twenty minutes ago healthy American kids walked up this path.

High up in some tree, the bird keeps on singing. After a few minutes we have reached an abandoned enemy position. By now company has been informed of the encounter and of the casualties. Captain Foyt has called battalion HQ with a request for an immediate air strike. The message that jets are on their way is relayed to us by radio. There is no need to tell us to get as far as possible from the hill, to hurry under cover and to crawl into the deepest hole in Vietnam. We are slowed up by the wounded. Sepp and I drag one of the boys towards a trench dug by the Viet Cong. It is not deep, but any port will provide some cover in a storm. We stagger towards it and dive down as the first jet roars overhead. We are much too close to his target.

'Get your heads down and stay down,' screams JC. His gunbelt feeder, a boy from New Mexico, almost disappears into the ground. Buchner is right next to me. Sepp is down and like a fool I sit on the lip of the trench, filming. By now, everybody is completely oblivious to the camera; to them, its single eye has become an extension of me.

A scream, a whistle and a bang! The tops of the trees come down on us. The bomb is close, really close, and the shrapnel scythes through the jungle. I fly over the lip and into the trench. Fuck filming!

Buchner has his head between his shoulders, now he looks up at me. 'Makes you nervous too. Even the air force up there. Bombs coming in, I don't like that. They very seldom make mistakes, but there's always a first time … '

Another howl, and a burst.

'I hope they bomb it really heavy before we try to take it. We'll have to go up, we'll have to take it now … ' another crash pulls the words from his mouth, Jim pulls his head between his shoulders, ' … as long as you're over here you never get used to that bombing.'

With a shriek, a jet passes overhead. There is a tremendous crash and more branches come down on us.

'That's what I mean, I don't like that stuff. I'm glad they're on our side.'

After an eternity of banshee shrieks and airbursts a strange quiet returns to the jungle. We climb out of the trench, load up our casualties and start down the hill. We do not get very far – a headless American body blocks the path. He must have been running for cover when shrapnel from one of our own bombs hit him in the head. I take my poncho and hand it to a soldier, who covers the body. We radio to company, and Foyt promises to dispatch a squad to give us a hand. For the time being there is nothing we can do. We need help, and need it desperately. We collapse where we stand.

Buchner stares into the distance and talks, but mostly to himself. 'There's one boy who went up the hill, we started talking just before he went up there, he said he just had a few days left. Joking like, about 'Nam. Well, he said, boy, this is the last hill I have to take. Got up there and got killed.'

Black sighs, he's heard the story before. JC has wedged his back against a tree, he shakes badly, puts a hand on my arm.

'I've seen a lot of boys getting wounded and I've seen a lot of boys getting killed too. When you see one of your boys lying right there, it hits you really bad. When I see a dead VC it bothers me no bit. Walk up, walk by and keep right on going. But I see a dead GI and it stirs me up, it stirs me all to pieces, and you really start thinking, God's looking over me.'

A squad arrives. From now on they will take care of the injured.

'All together now, we don't want to hurt him.' The wounded soldier has opened his eyes and grimaces in pain. Blood seeps from his head bandage.

A rescuer has lit a cigarette and shoves it into the boy's mouth. 'Take a drag.' A cough, but a smile of thanks.

'Think of all the pretty nurses you're going to see, lucky you.' And for him it may be luck. For him the war is over, he will never see action again, and he may still be alive to talk about it.

A helicopter comes in, the two wounded are hoisted aboard. Another helicopter is brought in. Whenever possible, Americans do not put wounded and dead on the same ship. The body is still wrapped in my poncho, only his boots are sticking out. JC gives a thumbs-up signal to the pilot, the ship lifts upwards, out of our sight but not out of our thoughts. So far we haven't been anywhere near the top of the hill and the company has already suffered four casualties: three wounded and one dead.

As night falls, we know that in the morning we will have to go up the hill, and we think about the enemy waiting for us up on that ridge. In the hole I share my space with Buchner. He twists and turns. I can smell fear, not only his. He turns his head towards me. 'You sleeping?' he whispers.

'No.' I cannot find sleep, my thoughts are on the nearby hill and on tomorrow. I have a bad feeling something is going to go wrong.

Buchner puts it all in a nutshell. 'Who gives a fuck if we go up there, storm this bloody hill, and die? What will it change? Nothing, fuck all.' He has come up with his own answers.

But why am I here? What is my motivation? What is this hill to me? A story? Glory on tomorrow night's broadcast? Financial reward? Nobody can pay me enough to commit suicide. The same goes for glory. My motivation is buried in my past, in memories of the horrors of war, my recurring nightmare. I want to portray war as it really is, ugly. Tomorrow I will climb the hill as a witness to this madness that has possessed humanity since the outset. When men lose their ability to converse with one another, they pick up axes and kill each other. I am part of the madness: the recording historian. Sleep, all I want is sleep, trying to forget my youth …

All throughout the night the artillery pounds the hill.

During the night somebody has decorated a tree, Christmas balls and all. Buchner has put up his patent stove, and more plastic is burned to give us a little heat. I sit next to Sepp.

A blinding flash! A noise so loud I never hear it. A blow so hard I cannot really feel it. Something has struck my bulletproof jacket and I am lifted up to crash into the foxhole. I see bodies flying, a scream, a surge of heat and a smell of evil. I feel my body, my bones, it all seems still to be in one piece. And then Sepp's voice, strangely remote: 'Erik, I've been hit.'

Sepp is two metres from me, lying on his belly. There is a large red spot on his back, just below the flak jacket. I jump from my hole and dive towards him.

There is confusion all over the camp. Was it enemy mortar? They must have discovered our position. 'Get in the hole, get under cover!' I grab Sepp by his flak jacket and drag him into the trench. Then I feel his back. A large piece of metal sticks out of a wound. It isn't funny, but I can't help remembering a joke about a guy who was hit in the arse. Sepp's wound is deep, bleeding profusely. Black throws me a bandage. I tape it on. Buchner has rushed over to cradle Sepp in his arms. My hands are covered with blood, I wipe them on my jacket. Somebody else, I can't remember who, slaps on another bandage. Blood starts to seep through the white gauze. Gently we turn Sepp over and it is then that I discover he's also covered with blood in front. He's alive, and that is all that counts. What has saved him from being torn apart is his bulletproof vest, literally ripped to shreds by shrapnel. We remove the jacket. Nothing seems to have penetrated into his vital parts.

When the shell hit, Sepp must have been positioned between the impact and me, because he has absorbed most of the blast. All of a sudden, Vietnam is real. I look at him and it strikes me that this is not some disconnected image I see through my viewfinder. There must be something positive I can do for him, but I can't think of anything.

I kneel down next to him, take his hand, blabber whatever comes to my mind. 'Does it hurt?' To him, it must sound like: do you want a banana?

'A little, but it's okay.' He winces. He forces a valiant smile, although I can see pain. Our roles are reversed, now it is he who tries to maintain our spirits. Perhaps he has already arrived at the logical conclusion that there is nothing we can do to help him, and that he is on his own. Before too long the same thought occurs to me. He will be evacuated and we will have to go up the hill. JC and Buchner heave him on to a stretcher, Black wrapping him in a blanket to protect him from cold shock. They have placed the sound recorder next to him, his bloodied hand reaches over and strokes it.

JC takes a yellow tag, writes Sepp's name on it, and for rank puts civilian, television sound engineer. With a piece of wire he pins it on to Sepp's battledress. Only then do I notice that we are surrounded by bleeding, moaning casualties. The shell hit the centre of the company's position.

'What the fuck was that?'

'Sounded like artillery.'

And then reality strikes: 'It was one of our own fucking 105s, a short round.'

'Oh, Jesus.'

One soldier has lost his leg. A medic kneels next to him and, while two of his buddies hold down the injured man, administers a shot of morphine. The horror is followed by muted numbness, a silence broken by soft moans.

Buchner breaks the ice, smiles at Sepp: 'You'll be all right, the medivacs will be here any moment, they'll take you to division hospital. While they fly you there, we gonna walk up that fucking hill. Say hello to the world.' As if to assure Sepp that he is better off than we are, that he doesn't have to go up that hill and get blown away, a distinct possibility for us a few minutes from now. Sepp's face is a white mask with a painful grin. My mind is functioning again. Rationality is called for, panic will not help any of us. Shall I go with him, make sure that they take good care of him in the hospital, or shall I stay and go through with the attack?

Question: What can I do for him in the operating theatre?

Answer: Nothing. The surgical staff will be much too busy taking care of his wounds, and all the other torn limbs and ribs, to answer my worried enquiries.

The decision is taken out of my hands. Sepp wasn't the only casualty, but we hadn't realized how bad it really was. Altogether thirteen have been hit. Two choppers roar in, we carry Sepp to the clearing. The medivac team is professional, efficient and want us out of their way. JC, Hubert and I lift Sepp up ever so gently and carry him to the helicopter. The scene on the helipad looks like *The Raft of the Medusa*, the lifeboats of the Samaritans are overflowing with bleeding, suffering men. There is no space for tourists. I stay behind.

The rotors howl into maximum revolutions. I have just enough time to yell a request to the co-pilot: 'Please, tell them at the hospital to contact Erik at Alpha company.'

He nods, the helicopter lifts off. I haven't been without Sepp for almost three years, there is an empty feeling in my gut, staring at the underbelly of a helicopter which takes away my friend.

Hubert has grabbed the sound recorder. 'I'll take the sound, what do I have to turn on?'

In a minute I teach him the simplest way to work the machine. 'Flick it on automatic and point the microphone like a rifle, that's all', and I add, as an afterthought: 'Never mind the quality. Get noises. Let the technicians back home do the rest.' If he doesn't get it right, at least he shouldn't feel guilty about it.

The incident has delayed the attack on Hill 943. Now that the wounded have been taken care of, the real business can commence. The American artillery opens up, more furious than ever. It is the first time I have been in such a bombardment, my initiation to taking the

high ground. I see history in the red and yellow flashes. This is what
the thousands of grey soldiers must have felt a hundred years ago at
Gettysburg when they were ordered to fix their bayonets for Pickett's
charge, listening to their artillery pounding the hills above them,
knowing there was only one way to go: up!

We scream to communicate. 'Hubert, don't do anything silly. Just
take sound – don't take chances.' I am sure that thought has already
occurred to him. I load a new roll into the camera, and jam a few more
into my various pockets. All of a sudden, the pressure is off, I am no
longer nervous or excited. I no longer have control over my destiny. I
have become a camera, invulnerable, looking, pointing, executing, as
if answering to a higher command. I know that I will be all right. I will
watch the action in black and white, I will see flashes in slow motion, I
will see soldiers race, run, shoot and fall. And I will reach that cursed
top!

The metallic voice of the company sergeant interrupts my thoughts
as he issues the order for the impending attack. 'Get ready to move.
Tom, you ready to move? JC, you ready to move? All right, move them
people out over there, clear them out.'

'Five-two Charlie over.'

'Five-two Charlie, this is five-two Bravo, over.'

'Hell, I've lost my cigarettes.'

'Okay, stay low and keep pushing right as you go, we've got to move
north, keep them low.'

'Five-two Charlie ... '

A machine gun opens up somewhere on our left flank. There is the
pop of grenade launchers and the crump of mortars. Artillery shells
explode up on the crest of the hill. Shrapnel is flying all around us.

'Hold it there.'

The firing has increased in intensity. Mostly small arms, a continuous hammering of a heavy machine gun, staccato bursts from
automatic rifles. A platoon advances on our flank. JC and his machine
gun fire burst after burst, to provide cover. The last two days of
shelling and bombing have ploughed up the hill. Splintered bamboo
sticks out, sharp lances to spear the careless. Tree trunks block the
advance, unexploded shells are a hazard. A giant's fist has crushed the
hill. It has robbed us of cover, we are in the open and vulnerable.
There are two deep craters ahead of me. I crouch down next to

Buchner. He fires a burst across the rim of one of the craters. I see Hubert with his Leica and my recorder. I motion for him to turn it on.

One of the soldiers gets up, points a grenade thrower over the lip, fires.

'That's good, Mack. Throw another at them.'

Another grenade explodes. JC is behind us – his machine gun has jammed, the barrel has overheated. He swears, rips open the breech, slams in another round. He looks like the man from the mountain, with a rag around the forearm to protect him from burns. He leans against a tree trunk, the only erect figure in the boiling madness, like the fearless sheriff at the OK Corral. The Mexican kid hands him another belt. He opens the breech and slams in a round.

Bang! One round goes out. Bang! Another jam. He opens the breech and slams in another round. Ratatatatat, fire erupts, a salvo leaves the barrel. Bang! near us.

'What the hell is that?'

'Incoming?'

'Shit no, that's one of ours.'

'That's a seventy-niner?' A soldier has fired his grenade launcher at an invisible target. The grenade has hit a branch in JC's tree.

'Hell, that's our own guys over there, what the fucking hell!'

'Hold it, we've got people on top.'

Another burst belches from JC's gun.

'I've got people up there.' A voice from our right.

Black shouts, 'Hold it, they've got people up there.'

JC is about to deliver the *coup de grâce*, instead he lowers the barrel.

'Hold it all, there are our guys ahead of us.'

Confusion. I am crouching behind a large tree trunk, about thirty yards from Captain Foyt. Hubert is next to me. We dash over to the company commander. He yells into his radio: 'Who's on top?'

The reply is garbled.

'You've got what?'

The automatic fire continues, especially on our left flank. I roll towards the cover of a bamboo thicket. I feel a sharp pain in my left leg, and when I reach down, my hand comes up covered in blood. Have I been hit? I look and discover blood seeping through my green combat trousers, and a large rip. It's nothing more serious than bamboo. In my pocket is a first-aid bandage, I rip it open and slap the disinfectant pad on the bleeding wound. That should stop the bleeding and any infection unless the bamboo was poisoned, and then I'm headed for a tetanus shock. Let's hope not.

'All right, five-three is almost up there. We need to push them down, about 200, and then we come right back.' Foyt has now ordered the right flank to pull back, or they will risk getting caught in the crossfire from the two platoons below them.

A soldier with a blank look strays across the battlefield, stops at JC. 'Do you need more ammo? I got it.'

JC shakes his head and the soldier continues his stroll, a young man wandering aimlessly across a madhouse.

Foyt signals JC to sweep around the right of the crater, and to position his machine gun near the top, so that he can provide covering fire for the leap-frogging frontal attack by the company.

I ask him: 'JC, where are they?'

He points with his barrel. 'Up there, I hope – I hope not!' he adds, with a crooked smile.

Slowly we move towards the edge of the crater, where we come upon a caved-in bunker. And behind it another, which looks intact. JC sends one of his squad down. There is a moment's hesitation. JC yells at him, 'So check the damn thing out, it won't bite you.'

The soldier is scared and tired, but each position has to be checked out. Imagine if we bypass it and a suicidal Vietnamese pops up and lets us have it in the back. JC gently guides the boy down and in. 'All right, walk in it. Move back about four feet, like a grown-up.'

The bunker is empty, but the ground fire renews in intensity. The kid has found his personal hole and stays down in the bunker: for him there are enough heroes up on top. Bullets fly all over the scenery, and no one can tell where they are coming from, where they are going to or who is shooting at what. Death is just a loud, sharp bang from somewhere.

Time to change film. I jump into the same hole. The kid sits there, back pressed against the red mud wall, rifle clutched between his knees. Slowly he raises his head: 'Brother, that's a bad movie ... '

Hubert and myself have now joined up with Buchner, who ducks behind the cover of a trunk. I recognize him by his good luck charm, the wooden elephant stuck in his helmet. Buchner looks like he can use a bit of good luck, he is worried. But so are we all. He sees me.

'Have you heard how Sepp is?' To my shame, I must admit I have been so busy that I haven't had time to think about my friend on an operating table. But the radio traffic is devoted to the ongoing battle and we will not receive personal messages until Alpha company gets its present priorities over and done with. Word is being passed along the line of soldiers, hiding out behind tree stumps and in artillery craters, that there will be a charge. We are now about fifty yards from the top of the hill and the fury of the small-arms fire hasn't abated a bit.

A cloud of smoke from an air strike on the nearby hill obscures the sun. The smoke drifts across to our position, acrid dust particles which stick to the back of our throats and make us cough.

Hubert looks questioningly at me. I motion to the recorder and mouth over the crescendo: 'Take sound, keep running as long as you've got a tape.' He nods. It has been a long time since we've stopped being a coherent team linked by the famous umbilical cord. Synchronous sound? What a silly technical notion: in the heat of the battle, the main thing is to record something.

I crawl over to him and scream: 'When we get back to Saigon, you can pick the juiciest mama-san on Tudo Street – it's on the house.' He grins. Why shouldn't we make it? It's only fifty metres, and still no sign of the enemy. Perhaps they're all dead.

I have always had a secure feeling that nothing evil could possibly befall me. The man next to me, certainly, but myself, never. The thought of getting hurt or killed had never crossed my mind. Sitting down after a battle and thinking it all through, it was a different matter but during the fight I never thought that somewhere up there was a bullet with my name on it.

I am standing up – since I cannot take pictures lying down – oblivious of the danger, a mechanical man, a picture-taking robot.

Buchner gets up, waves his hand, shouts. 'Pull out! Pull out! Up!'

And a line of ghosts appears from behind bamboo shoots and tree stumps and shell holes, a yell goes up and we rush uphill. I see JC, firing from the hip. Black gets up, then stumbles, and falls! I watch him disappear slowly, like a drunk going down ... then, he rises again, gives me the thumbs up and points to his ankle as he hobbles uphill. Twenty yards, ten yards, we jump across a splintered tree and we're on top.

***

There is nothing up there. No trees, no stumps, no Viet Cong, no dead officers with Russian pistols, nothing. We've captured an empty hill. The enemy has withdrawn, taking with them their wounded and dead. I look at Buchner who shakes his head. 'Tell the world hello.'

JC unravels a rebel flag, ties it to a stick, and plants it in the ground. The South has carried the day, the flag of Dixie flutters over a smashed, crushed, zapped hill in Vietnam.

'When the first contact started, I got scared,' he says. 'I got real scared, that big fear inside me. But I moved. And then I said, there is nothing up there. JC, don't be scared no more, and I moved.'

There are no cheers, no congratulations. This is not the end of some football match. The soldiers are battle fatigued, deaf from the continuous din, their faces black from powder and sweat, their eyes bloodshot from the cordite, tears run down their cheeks. I stand on top of Hill 943, in the midst of tired men, and record their 'victory' for posterity. For the first time I notice the blood on my flak vest, Sepp's blood. Foyt comes with good news: 'I've just heard from base, Sepp is going to be all right, they've already operated on him. He's being flown to the hospital at Pleiku.'

'Thank you' is about all I can say. Emotion, tiredness or a mixture of both.

JC, Black and Buchner are hovering around. Black slaps me on the back. 'Well, lucky Sepp, that is one hill he missed.' And Buchner adds, 'I'm glad he's all right.'

I am very tired. I am drenched in sweat. I am overcome by a void, an emptiness. Automatically I unload the camera. Hubert hands me the recorder: I remove the tape, put it in its box, write on it: the attack. I mustn't let tiredness overcome me – if I lie down I will sleep for days. Danger is a thing of the past, now fear has its place. I'm alive. Why do I participate in this madness, why do I record wars? Does anybody care what I am doing, and do I care if anybody does? Why do I do it? Because it has purpose. Life must have a purpose. War is evil, people perish, the guilty and the innocent. In war no one stands a chance. A bullet does not have an address, it strikes from far away. A shell rips and tears, a bomb blasts, and when it is over we all retreat into our caves, because that's all that remains. Nobody wins. I look down from this hill and my thoughts go back to the distant day when my father took me up a mountain of eternal snow, and introduced me to the beauty of this wonderful world. And when my poor country ran out of time, my home lay in ruins, my family's blood was spilled and I thought that my life was finished, I realized then that life is never finished. Life ends when you give up hope, abandon the will to live. When you sit down and say to yourself: why bother? When you let it be over and done with, and you ride your avalanche into oblivion. Only then is it truly over.

This is not the moment. This is now and I am alive. It matters little that no one shot at me those last few yards as I was stumbling uphill. For me the danger was real: everybody was shooting at everybody, death was imminent until I reached the top. Now I am standing on a hill that means nothing to anybody but the ninety-six survivors who have taken it. It will not be written up in any history books as the decisive battle of Vietnam. There will be no handing out of medals, there was no spectacular sacrifice. The whole troop was equally heroic. These men were under enemy fire, they were frightened and went through hell. On our side, nobody has been killed. What happened to the enemy we would never find out. The intensity of the artillery barrage has obliterated any trace of whatever the enemy left behind. Those who survived the deluge of shells, bombs and bullets have vanished with their wounded and dead into the jungle, or left them buried in the rubble beneath our feet. We will not waste our efforts digging up the fallen foe just to provide another useless statistic of enemies killed, so aptly called the 'bodycount'. (Military procedure specifies touching a corpse and announcing, 'I count one enemy body.') The dead would remain buried, and the rest had disappeared. It was just as well.

There was however one strong reason why this particular hill might be remembered. Not only was it stormed by the soldiers of Alpha company, but they were accompanied, first by three and then by two men who recorded the moment, the struggle and the men. Millions would be able to see it and share in the battle's emotion. Of that I would make certain. To ensure that this film was seen would be my next goal.

The battalion commander's helicopter lands. Captain Foyt reports: 'Sir, we didn't find any enemy.'

'All right, I want you to check out this location ... ' Grizzly says nothing about the recent fight and is eager to discuss the next one. 'I'll see to it that you'll get more ammo, what do you need?'

'Well, sir, we just about need everything.'

'Okay, I'll make sure you'll get it. I'll send some warm food and the mail.' I have been recording this conversation, now Grizzly looks at me, smiles. 'How are you holding out? I hear one of your boys got hurt.'

'It was our own artillery, as you may know.'

'Yeah, well accidents do happen in war.' I don't want to get into a long argument. Of course he is right, and as far as he is concerned we shouldn't have been here in the first place.

'Can you please radio the hospital and get a message to Sepp that we are all thinking of him. Tell him we are all right.'

'I promise.' With that he salutes, gets into his helicopter and disappears, ready to lead men into battle on another hill with another number.

4

THE BATTALIONS OF
THE NOBLE DUKE

(VIETNAM, CHRISTMAS 1967)

'Tell the world hello!'

PFC Jim Buchner

The hill is quiet. Our heroes have started to dig in for the night. One is sitting there, not digging, but writing down his account of the recent fight. The usual argument ensues.

'How do you rate that. We've got ambush, and we're digging your hole.'

Buchner and Black are leaning on a tree stump. Buchner contemplates his wooden elephant and says, 'If it wasn't for this ... '

Black has a similar lucky piece, a star. The trouble is that it is a puzzle called 'Instant Insanity' and is now in ten separate pieces. The trick is to fit all the pieces back together again. That will take time, which they have plenty of now that it is all over. 'I had it together when we were in the bunker during the air strikes.'

'So why didn't you leave it together?'

'The stupid thing fell apart,' says Black. 'I bet you my folks would be surprised how aggravated we get over that.'

Black fiddles with the pieces, he is a picture of total concentration. Meanwhile, in the background, they have started to blast a new supply landing zone. There is a bang.

Buchner fidgets, then laughs. 'That sort of steadies your nerves.'

Black says, 'I think I've got it, if I can only get that one thing in.'

'Fire in the hole.' It seems they are serious about that blasting, and want everyone to go into their shelters.

'Jesus, a big blast. If I ruin this now.' We scramble into our dugouts, with the noted exception of Black, who searches the ground near him desperately. 'I'm missing a piece. I'm missing a piece. Don't anybody move, I've lost a piece.'

'Watch out, Black!'

Black looks up – a tree is coming straight down on us. Black dives to one side and the tree crashes down, ends up across a trench. Williams comes running. 'Anybody in there?'

'I don't know.'

Frantic activity as everybody pitches in to pull branches from the cover.

'No, nobody there, just their equipment.'

'Lucky sods, first you climb the fucking hill and then to get a branch up your ass wouldn't be very romantic.'

Two supply helicopters are hovering in. Water, food, ammo boxes and a couple of mailbags.

As the sergeant distributes the mail, everyone stands around in hopeful expectation. 'Webb, Law, Gary ... ' Letters are handed out, ripped open. 'Gavit, Gavit, Coons, Perrerio, and Perrerio ... '

'Damn, I ain't got a letter today.' Disappointment shows on Black's face. He is very friendly with this California blonde, but she doesn't write a lot. 'Tough shit.'

JC has gone into hiding with his letter. Today he is not going to share it with the company.

Buchner installs his patent cooker. We heat pork and beans and tea, all in the same can.

'Hey Buchner, what the hell is that?'

'Don't talk to me while I'm dining.' It'll go into the same belly in any case and coming from a field ration package it all tastes alike. Sawdust with horse piss.

Now is the time when we finally take stock of the way we look. Everybody is mudstained and haggard, with ripped uniforms and bandages. I look a mess: my trousers are torn, I have a clean bandage over the cut in my thigh, but the rest of me is covered in dust and mud. On my flak jacket are dark brown stains from Sepp's dried blood and my sweat. We are dirty, unshaven, and we stink. The jungle stinks, a blend of heat, mouldering leaves, rotten vegetation and cordite. If only a breeze would get up, take away that smell and give us one gulp of clean, fresh air, that would cheer us up. A few of the boys have wandered into the nearby bushes. Each carries his shovel.

'John,' shouts Williams, 'I've got you down for a buck. Didn't take your shovel. Get the hell back out there and bury your shit.'

JC and Black have gone to plant claymore mines around the company's perimeter, to protect us from night marauders. Most of the time it isn't the enemy trying to intrude, but herds of hungry monkeys who can smell our leftover rations. They sneak across, trip the wires, the mines explode and we jump up, sleepy and bleary-eyed. We stay alert for the rest of the night, and next morning we find a family of dead baboons.

The night passes relatively calmly and without other interruptions. Or we are too tired to notice. Next morning, Grizzly countermands his orders for the Search-and-Destroy mission and battalion decides to lift out the company. We blast a big landing zone, burn all the garbage and wait for the airlift. At about eleven, a fleet of helicopters appears over the jungle: a welcome sight to the soldiers, and to me, I must admit. I am worn out – the attack, and the worry about Sepp have taken their toll.

JC and his squad pull rear guard duty; they have formed a defensive perimeter around the evacuation zone. The rest of the company jumps on the ships. Over the noise of the blades, I shout to Black: 'Which one?'

'Next one, next one after this one.'

When the next chopper comes down, we duck under the blades and pile on. I get a seat near the rear gunner, JC next to me.

'How does it feel, JC?'

'Feels pretty good, going back to firebase. That's about the only time it feels good, though.'

We lift up. Our hill offers a spectacle of utter devastation. Nothing remains standing, a jumble of twisted, broken, mutilated trees. Once the war stops all will be healed, but the two giant bomb craters will remain, a memorial to the day when fire rained from the heavens. (I returned there in 1980, and the jungle had regained the upper hand.)

We fly away and Hill 943 fades into the distance. We cross other hills with different numbers. Could these be tomorrow's battlefields?

In the distance an airstrike is pounding a hill. At its foot are probably some more JCs and Buchners and Sepps, all waiting to climb it.

At the firebase, the guns have interrupted their continuous fire to allow the helicopters to land.

One of the earlier evacuees comes up to us. 'Welcome home.' He taps Black on the shoulder. 'My hero!'

Black's knees are protruding from his torn jungle pants and one shoe is cut open to allow a bandage to fit around the ankle he sprained during the final rush up the hill.

'Step into some dogshit?'

'Fuck you,' is the laconic reply from a tired Black.

The guns open up, this time on a different hill with a different number. Sergeant Williams appears with a hefty mailbag containing all the parcels they couldn't get while out in the field.

'Line up, guys, here comes Santa.'

Heads appear from holes, and in no time Santa Williams is submerged in a mass of men.

Is it already Christmas? Of course, it is only two weeks away. What is Christmas like at home? Clean snow, a warm fire, and the family. Everybody talks a mile a minute, about loved ones, about marsh-mallows and their wives. I don't have a family, I don't even have a dog. Nevertheless, it is still Christmas. The group hovers like hungry vultures around the mailbag, starved for news from home, hungry for the small gift which tells them that they are not forgotten.

'That's mine, that's mine,' yells JC.

'What is it, JC?'

He lifts the long parcel to his mouth, laughs. 'Juice, oh man, juice. What kind?'

'Well, open it, and find out.'

Black clutches a parcel, rips it open. 'Oh boy, Hickory Farm's white wine jelly … ' he smacks his lips.

There is a tiny tape recorder in JC's parcel. He switches it on, it's a cowboy's lament: ' … *a special way of saying how our little home is blessed* … ' The voice warbles on, punctuated by the crash of 105mm howitzers. The hit parade of fighting Vietnam.

Black passes his small bottle of bourbon along the line, it goes from man to thirsty man, everyone allowed one gulp. I taste it, it burns beautifully. I always hated bourbon, but this one is special. It's good.

Buchner appears on the scene, a big cigar clenched between his teeth. He has liberated it in a bunker. Now he towers over us, a big grin on his face. 'It's from Gallagher, that's my buddy, it's his last one. That's why I'm really going to enjoy it. He's probably down there in the bunker swearing at me.' He takes a deep puff. 'Tastes beautiful – it's fresh too.'

Black throws his wrapping paper over his shoulder. 'I'd hate to dirty everything up.' That has them in stitches.

One of the soldiers has received a fold-up Christmas tree, the kind made of wire and green crêpe paper. Everybody sits around it and helps to decorate it with glass balls. Black shoves a slice of salami into his mouth. JC has retired under a tree as usual to read the letter from his wife.

Buchner keeps puffing on his cigar, daintily brushes off some ashes, looks at it with great admiration. 'Uptight!'

Every war coins its phrase, and Vietnam has *'Uptight'*. The word stands for everything and nothing. *Uptight*, when you liberate a cigar that tastes good. *Uptight*, when you are lucky and get assigned to a base camp job. *Double uptight*, when you get your papers to ship out. Just 'Uptight.'

Night falls, a song drifts across the camp, a Christmas song:

> *Jingle bells, mortar shells, Charlie in the grass,*
> *you can take your bloody Christmas, stuff it up*

Peals of laughter drown the rest. The spirit is there, but I guess it wasn't a Christmas song after all.

We've had white wine jelly and bourbon and salami and a lot of laughs, and now we are pleasantly full and tired, and have crawled into the damp and humid bunkers to bed down in the airless heat of the night. There is more space in the base camp's underground dugouts than in those miserable ratholes we had called homes for weeks. Whatever you call it, it is still a hole, but this is a relaxed place, with no dark hill looming nearby. Outside the hole is the paper Christmas tree, and inside a bottle of forbidden 'juice' wanders from hand to hand through the darkness. The mood is festive. Everybody tries to tell his favourite joke, or reveals his special dream. JC has dreams of a pizza.

'Pizza, man, pizza pepperoni, spaghetti and meatballs. You know, back in the States, me and my wife, mostly on the weekends, we go to this pizza place that specializes in pizza … '

Buchner plays the wise guy. 'Most pizza places don't serve hot dogs.'

This remark is greeted by howling, JC ignores the ribbing and carries on with his story of the pizza. 'Can you imagine a good 48-inch pizza, not 24, but 48! … and if this continues, it's gonna be 64 inches … '

I strike on a touchy subject. 'Now, men, whaddya think of women?'

'Oh, that thought never crossed our minds … '

'How long has it been since you've seen your last woman?'

'Say it a little better. We see them all right when we're in camp in Pleiku – but a chance to get at them … '

'The last time I've had a chance to get at them was in August,' the voice sounds like Black's but I cannot be sure since everybody starts his own fairytale and the dark shelter reverberates in a babble of hoots, ribald jokes, and tales of backstreet adventures.

I continue my in-depth investigation into the number one subject of any soldier. 'So what's the first thing you're going to do when you get back to the States?'

Buchner answers what they all think. 'What do you mean the States? As soon as I get on that airplane, I'm gonna grab myself the hostess in the back of the plane … '

And with that dream of an airborne love bout we fall asleep.

When Hubert and I climbed on to the helicopter that would finally take us away from the boys of Alpha company, they all gathered to wave us goodbye. We stopped over in Pleiku and paid a visit to Sepp. We found him in a large, sterile hospital room, together with many other casualties. He was in relatively good spirits. We were not allowed to stay. The doctors assured us that his wounds were not critical and that he could expect to recover within three months. We told Sepp that we would make arrangements to evacuate him to his native Alps as soon as he was fit to travel.

Back in Saigon, one of my first priorities was to call Sepp's family and to assure them that, although wounded, he was fine and should be back with them before the New Year. The family had friends on the local newspaper, and one evening they mentioned that their son had been wounded in Vietnam. The next day I received a phone call from the *Salzburger Nachrichten* to interview me about his condition. The Austrian headlines were different from the realities in the Far East. Sepp's story was more important even than the latest results of the national ski team. Austria had its first real-life Vietnam war hero.

I kept my promise to Hubert and, as soon as we checked into the Continental in Saigon, I asked Mr Loy, our friendly concierge, to provide us with the juiciest mama-san on his inventory. With that we went upstairs to take our first shower in weeks. Then we crashed into bed.

Somebody tried to wake me. Through my sleep-drugged eyes I vaguely made out a smiling Vietnamese girl with her tits hanging out next to my bed. It was my promised survival present to Hubert. I looked at him on the bed near me: he was dead to the world. If one thing was certain, it was that no girl could stir him to sexual prowess for at least another forty-eight hours. What had seemed so important in the heat of the battle, to prove that we were in one piece and still capable of making love to a woman, lost its significance after the battle. Fatigue took over and sex became secondary. I handed the girl some notes to pay for her spoiled afternoon and sent her off in search of fresher clients. Then I promptly fell asleep.

Forty-eight hours later, we had our first meal in the roof restaurant of the Caravelle. The press was still there. People said, 'I hear you've been north,' and 'How is it up north?' and 'What goes on?' But the questions were not too inquisitive, just polite murmurs to indicate that they knew where we had been, and to make sure they hadn't missed a decisive encounter. Come to think of it, our encounter was not that big. Let us not exaggerate, let us put it into its right perspective. It was really nothing: a few men got killed and a few men got wounded, and nothing had been achieved.

Saigon was different from the city we had left. It was some time before I realized that it wasn't Saigon that had changed, but me. I was getting tired of Vietnam. I had to get away. After a few days there was a knock on our door and Sepp stood on the doorstep, leaning on a stick. Against the advice of his doctors, he had simply walked out of the field hospital. He had but one wish, to go home. That same night, I booked us on an Air France flight to Paris.

Sepp arrived in his snow-covered village the day before Christmas 1967. He had come home.

In the first days of the New Year, Sepp received an invitation.

At home he had become a legend. He had been fêted and inter-viewed at length by the popular press about his exploits in Vietnam. Sepp was a shy person, and the continuous barrage of photo-reporters invading his mountain privacy upset not only him, but also his family. Sepp's mother put a stop to it. When the doorbell rang, she was about to slam the door into the face of the young man standing there. 'Sepp doesn't want to see any reporters,' she said firmly.

'I'm not a reporter, I am from the army.'

'The army?'

'Yes, the Austrian army.' He handed over an envelope, 'This is his call-up. In two weeks he is to report to the infantry barracks in St Johann.'

Poor Sepp – he had been away from his native land for years and had neglected to ask for a deferment. Now the celebrated war hero had been brought to the attention of the local commander, who had passed his name on to the Ministry of Defence in Vienna. They simply drafted him, since the country needed young heroes like Sepp. He spent his next year defending the fatherland from an invasion of German tourists with an abundance of Deutschmarks. And whenever the company commander ran out of ideas about mountain warfare, he would turn to his recruits and say: 'Go and ask Private Sepp, he can tell you all about that ... '

That should be a fitting ending to my story. But it isn't. A few weeks after I waved goodbye from my open helicopter door to Coons and Black and Buchner, they went back up Hill 943. This time the enemy didn't run.

Harry Charles Joseph Coons, better known as JC, was caught in the crossfire of the enemy's guns and badly wounded. He was one of two people in his platoon who survived.

Bruce Black was wounded while trying to pull another soldier to safety. He was evacuated and lives now in California.

And Jim Buchner, the boy with his good-luck elephant, whose dream it was to return home, chase girls and lie on the beach with a cold six-pack – Jim Buchner was killed.

Nobody was awarded a medal, and the action isn't mentioned in the history books of the Vietnam war. The only way that the younger generation can perhaps visualize life and death in the jungles of a faraway place called Vietnam is to visit Washington. There is a monument in a park, known as the Wall. Among the fifty thousand names inscribed on it is this one: Buchner, James Irving, US Infantry, +1968.

A few days after this last battle fought by Coons, Black, Buchner and all the other men from Alpha Company, the Viet Cong started their Tet offensive, and thousands more were killed, mostly enemies. As the Americans were to realize, the regular North Vietnamese army had been massed all this time on their doorstep, ready to launch the biggest offensive of the whole war. Our encounter, though accidental, should have told military planners something.

When all the bodies had been counted, the outcome of the Tet offensive was proclaimed a great American military victory. What US generals and political leaders did not recognize went far beyond military considerations. It was the beginning of the end of the American predominance in Asia. The war was to drag on another seven painful years. I was not there to watch its end.

Hill 943 was shown first by the CBS television network, and then watched by many millions around the world. I do not think that it influenced in any way the outcome of the war, or the eventual decision to withdraw American forces from the Vietnamese quagmire. I only know that in the brief span of a few days, 119 men of Alpha company went up a hill and then down a hill. And when they came down there weren't as many as when they went up.

There is a hill in Vietnam, a nameless, uninhabited hill, known only by a number, 943, which was assaulted twice, taken twice, and abandoned twice by Americans, and today, Hill 943 is again controlled by the North Vietnamese.
Epilogue to *Hill 943*, spoken by CBS news correspondent John Lawrence on 8 June 1968

5

A CONFEDERACY
OF VILLAINS

Rule number one:
'Thou shalt not get caught'.

Jim Mossman and I had spent many adventures together. Finally, in the late sixties, we both became tired of our repeat performances. The big passenger jets had shrunk the globe. Places 'practically nowhere' were harder and harder to find. The age of electronic wizardry had revolutionized communications. Wars, just like international sport events, could now be transmitted live by satellite.

As our partnership had begun, it ended abruptly at an airport. 'Erik, the time has come to quit,' said Jim.

The partisan passion for the things he had believed in had abandoned the great reporter. To him, television had taken on a different quality. It broadcast new conflicts, such as fighting on the soccer stadiums of Britain, with its racist songs and violent partisanship, which had gradually devalued the importance of his reports about the volatile relationship between East and West, or the ecological damage done to our planet. More 'explicit' programming now offered tabloid television shows, which specialized in sensationalized accounts of violence and sex. Jim couldn't adjust to this. Was it personal fastidiousness? I don't believe so. It must have taken him a long time before he had the courage to say it out loud.

'Is television going to become what it has already turned into for millions, a mere spectacle of marginal violence?'

I looked at him for a long time, thinking about the fact that Jim and I were going to split up. 'It's hard just the same.'

Jim smiled sadly. 'You shouldn't have a problem. For me, it's different. I cannot go on.'

'What will you do when you pick up your morning paper and read that a war has started in the Sudan? Or that 10,000 people have marched through Jerusalem, shouting "Shalom achshav" [Peace now]?'

'Let somebody else go there. I simply must get out of it.'

Something had been bothering Jim for quite a while, but he never talked about it. At the time I put it down to a bout of mid-life crisis. He was now forty-three.

'It's been a great time. Thank you for everything.' With that he extended his hand and I looked into eyes clouded by sadness. I was not feeling so good myself, but I knew he was right. He turned round, and strolled towards the exit. I looked after the disappearing figure, and remembered all the adventures we had shared. They had been a wonderful eight years, but now they were over. Jim left *Panorama* to join an arts programme, and I left the BBC to produce my own films. We were to join forces just once more. Paul Fox had been appointed head of BBC1, and asked the 'Jim and Erik act' to produce a prestige three-part series, *Democracy on Trial*. The first two programmes dealt with California and West Germany. The third was to be about Great Britain.

Jim had met a young Canadian sculptor, Louis Hansson, and together they had moved into a larger house on the Fulham Road. When Jim and I started on the final part of the trilogy, I rented a small studio so as not to intrude on their menage. We usually had coffee at their house before I set off with Jim on the day's shooting. It was on one of my morning visits that I first noticed the blue Ford Cortina parked opposite their house. The man in it was reading a newspaper. The next day, the car was still there but its occupant had a different face. Strange. There were other small indications that either Jim or Louis was being followed. It wasn't just my fertile brain imagining secret agents, it was quite real. I had to mention it to Jim.

'You know there's a car parked outside your door with a guy in it? It's been there for the last two days. It's the blue Cortina over there.'

Jim went to the window, and came back looking pale. He shrugged it off. 'Probably a jealous husband.'

I was sure it wasn't a husband trying to catch Jim or Louis *in flagrante*, I was certain it had to do with Jim, and I was equally certain that he was aware of it. 'Jim, remember the night in Beirut – Philby. What went on between the two of you?'

'Nothing, nothing of importance.'

'Did you know that he was about to go to the other side?'

'Of course I didn't know!' he snapped.

'Jim, for God's sake, you were almost the last one to see him. Don't you think this has something to do with it? They think you warned him off. Was there somebody else involved?'

'Nonsense.'

'It isn't, and you know it! They – and only you know who they are – they are still out there! They will put two and two together, and come up with five … '

'Oh, stop it, will you, *just stop it*!' He was more upset than I had ever seen him before, and that was the end of our conversation. At that moment Louis stormed into the room and threw a jealous tantrum. I fled.

When I stepped out into the street, the car had disappeared.

A few days later when he had calmed down, Jim talked about that evening in Beirut. 'He told me something, and I treated it as his cynical brand of fun.'

'Let me guess: he said you weren't clean.'

'Not quite like that. We would sometimes swap yarns. Journalists' talk, that kind of thing. Of course, that night he was quite drunk, and he told it as if it was a joke he'd invented.'

'But he hadn't, had he?'

'I don't know. In any case, when he jumped fence I was relieved.'

'What did he tell you?'

'Nothing much. "James, my dear friend, sweet auntie will bury you beneath her fallen battlements. Don't wait, take a shufti … " Something like that. Absurd. He sounded like a drunk fortune-teller.'

It took me some time to figure it out. We always referred to the venerated BBC as 'auntie' – but that wasn't what Philby had meant. I was certain that Jim had also reached that conclusion. 'Does Louis know?' I wondered how Jim's boyfriend would take it.

'Why tell him? He'd only be jealous.'

***

One morning I received a hysterical call. The caretaker had found Louis, dead from an overdose of sleeping pills. I rushed over and tried to comfort Jim. He was sitting on his living-room couch, staring at some distant point beyond the mantelpiece. Why had Louis taken his life? Or had he? I had a nagging feeling something was terribly wrong, but I couldn't tell what. Our film was cancelled, and I returned to Paris. For Jim the world had collapsed. His new arts programme lacked the Mossman wit, and he left the show. He buried himself in his country house, and locked the door on the world. I didn't see him for months. He didn't answer the phone. He didn't reply to my notes.

One day I got through. I really wanted to see him, find out if he had kicked the nightmare. 'Jim, I'll be in London tomorrow.'

He sounded fine. 'That's nice, why don't we have dinner?'

'What have you been up to?'

'I have just finished another novel, I'll tell you all about it. I'll cancel my evening with myself.' A happy, excited voice, just the Jim I used to know in the desert and jungle days. We met in a small Italian restaurant near the Kensington Odeon. He walked into the place as if he owned the town, or had just won the pools. He grabbed my hand and shook it, all smiles. 'It's really good to see you.'

And then we talked, and had spaghetti, and talked. 'Remember the Pope who wouldn't see us?' and, 'I've heard Dana Schmitt was in a car crash,' and 'This spaghetti beats the goulash in Mogadishu.'

Jim produced from his pocket an early copy of his latest novel, *Lifelines*. 'It's mostly about us, what we did and what we wanted to do. The places should look familiar. I am sure you'll recognize your film star Heidi and a few others of your females.' With that he took out a pen and signed it: *To Erik, love Jim*. And he added the date: *15 March 1971*.

'Jim, I have a great idea. I'm going to my chalet in Chamonix tomorrow, why don't you come along? It's a change from the London rain.' He had visited my place many times and loved the chalet atmosphere and the *fondue Savoyarde*.

'I'd love to. I have to get out of this town before ... ' he suddenly stopped, took a sip from his glass, then added: 'Tell you what, I'll call you tomorrow around four and let you know which flight I'll come on. You will pick me up in Geneva?'

'Of course.' I replied.

I went to Chamonix, put on my skis and forgot about films and revolutions. When I came down from the mountain I expected to find Jim's message. There was none. Typical Jim, he had probably changed his mind, or else he would call later. There was no message the next day either. On Monday I received a call from Paul Fox: 'Erik, Jim is dead.'

I was too stunned to react. It couldn't be right: only three days before he had been Jim reborn. He had found a new lease on life and his trauma had passed, he had told me so himself. It simply couldn't be. 'Paul, for God's sake, what happened?'

'He went to his cottage and took sleeping pills. He was buried this morning.' I gave myself time to think. I tried to relive all our moments, all our conversations. I gave him an old Citroën and he gave me a tie. I gave him a pink cuckoo clock and he gave me a gilt Eiffel Tower with a thermometer. He cut my hair and I cut his. We had shared so much. I refused to accept it. Something was wrong. I could feel it, Jim would never have taken his life. I remembered how he had once said to me, 'Life isn't yours to take.'

I called London. 'Was there an inquest?'

'There was. The coroner's verdict is an overdose of barbiturates.'

'That is not true.'

'The inquest is closed.'

Jim left a final note: 'It is getting stronger every day. I don't know what it is, but I cannot take it any more.'

Years have gone by and Jim is a dear memory. The ancient Greeks believed in retribution, he had once told me. 'Those whom the Gods love, die young ... '

I have never publicly voiced my suspicion, but I am sure that there was more to Jim's death than was explained. The final scenario is wrong, something doesn't fit. Or, as Jim would have phrased it: 'To put no finer point on it ... '

By the time my shock had turned into frustration and I reached London, Jim had been buried and there was no way to trace what had led to the drama. He was in the prime of life, healthy, with a bright future. So why? ... *Any man's death diminishes me; because I am involved in mankind* ... Jim repeated the immortal phrases in the jungles of

Vietnam ... *therefore never send to know for whom the bell tolls* ...

'Our time hasn't come yet.' These were his very words when all hope seemed lost in the desert of Yemen ... and now, the bell had tolled for him. Why? Nobody had an answer. And those who had, kept quiet. Everyone seemed sad – poor Jim this, and poor Jim that – and how he never got over the death of his friend. I knew this wasn't so.

Jim's death affected me deeply. I ran away from memories and stumbled over ghosts, always the face of Jim, calling out to me to join him, to help, to come to the rescue. In a rice field surrounded by black pyjamas. I was tied to a tree, Jim was on the ground, and the dark figures were picking at his eyes. Jim screamed, pleaded: 'Pity! Pity!' And a voice answered 'What colour is pity?' Hiding behind a bush was a tall white man, at least he looked like one, he had an umbrella but he didn't have a face. He gave the orders to proceed with the unmanning. Jim died, then they came at me. I screamed ...

'*Qu'est-ce que t'as, tu n'as pas envie?*' The voice, the searching fingers and the body belonged to a girl I had met the night before in a bar off the Avenue de l'Opéra. I had gone there because I couldn't stand it any longer waiting for the call to another assignment. I had to get away, Chile, the Congo, I didn't care.

Mossman's death was an enigma. Sure, they had found the note (which I never saw) and a bottle of sleeping pills, but there were too many questions left unanswered. Our conversation about the right to take one's life. On that issue he had been strict. He had reaffirmed it after Louis' suicide. And there was the deep mystery: had he been a spy right to the end? And if so, where had he slipped? Had the stress been too much, had he shown signs of endangering others? Which side had put him away? There is no distinction between the good guys and the bad guys, they do not wear different coloured jerseys. There are grey men with rolled umbrellas and school ties. Faceless people. Jim had a face. He didn't belong to the club of grey shadows in striped business suits and briefcases.

I had many reasons to remember him. It was somewhere East of Suez, and we were sitting in some steamy bar by a steamy ocean, attacked by clouds of mosquitoes. 'Why, Jim?'

'Why what?' he answered, without really listening.

'Why did you ever get involved?'

Jim knew what I was referring to, and he looked beyond the horizon, at a cottage surrounded by springtime foliage, half a world away. 'Does it matter?'

I stared at the melting ice cubes in my lemon drink. A fly had drowned in it and was now floating on the surface. After a while, Jim looked at me and said: 'If the phone rings, don't answer it. If someone offers you a visa, or a woman, don't accept it, the gift is poisoned. If they catch you in bed with someone's wife, or someone's houseboy, scream and tell the world. Then they cannot get to you.' The flies were getting unbearable, and we climbed under our mosquito nets. Next morning the conversation had become a thing of the past, drowned in silence, but not forgotten by me.

'*Puis-je parler avec Monsieur Erik, s'il vous plaît.*' A voice along a wire, hooked to another telephone somewhere in the city. A voice with a foreign accent. A soft voice.

'*Un instant, je vous passe Monsieur Han.*' The next voice was metallic, with the same accent.

'Hallo, this is Han. I would like to meet you.'

'What for?'

'About your visa application.' In my life I have applied for so many visas, I tend to forget which country I want to visit, unless a positive reply comes within a few days.

'Do you want me to come to the embassy?'

'No, that won't be necessary. My friend Kim and I will come to your place, if that's all right.'

Why not? They came, Han and Kim, or Kim and Han, same height, same clothes cut along strict socialist fashion, both with nylon ties and stickpins bearing the face of their great leader.

'Mr Erik, I am Han, this is my colleague Kim.' Then they offered me a visa, a very rare visa indeed, which would allow me a glimpse of their socialist dreamland. Then followed the hook. 'We understand that you have easy access to the South ... ' that meant south of their disputed border. 'We would like you to make a similar film there, and we are particularly interested in harbours and airports.'

I heard a bell go off, and I remembered Jim and our night beside the steamy ocean. 'Gentlemen, thank you for your offer, but I am not in the market.' Sixteen years later I was given a visa, this time without strings attached. Their attempt had been blatant and clumsy. There are, however, more subtle ways to entrap.

I was covering a visit by a Western prime minister to the Soviet Union. My government guides never let me out of their sight. The chance of any serious film coverage of the conference was negligible. I found myself with lots of free time.

'Would you like to go shopping, Mr Durschmied?'

'That might be a pleasant change.' I wanted to add: from doing nothing.

They drove me to Red Square, where they dumped me in front of the doors of a giant greystone building with cavernous hallways: Moscow's one and only department store, GUM. The drably dressed crowd parted as the Westerner made his triumphant entry. I followed the sign in English, Visitor's Store, to be confronted by an assortment of cuckoo clocks from Bulgaria and cigars from Cuba. I don't smoke. The only item of interest for a foreigner with hard money was Beluga caviare. Grey pearls of excellent quality, and reasonably priced.

I thought I stumbled on Mira by accident. She was a strategically placed caviare salesgirl, a Tartar beauty imported from the steppes of Azerbaijan. High cheekbones, slim waist and a slender neck. Her eyes had a dewy quality, distant and dreamlike. From the bevy of dumpy buxom women in the streets of the Russian capital, she stood out. When I looked around for my trusted guides to translate, they had miraculously disappeared. What luck that the girl spoke English. I smiled, she smiled back, and after the usual 'How much for the caviare?' and 'Are you free tonight for dinner?', I paid ten roubles and received 'Yes' for an answer. I liked to think that my charm and winning personality made her accept my invitation.

She suggested six o'clock at a restaurant reserved for foreigners who paid in hard cash, with balalaika music and all the shish kebab trimmings. Six seemed early to dine for a working girl, but I didn't press the point. When my car brought me to the Moscava she was already installed at a table in a discreet corner, away from a noisy trade union delegation from Glasgow. The food was all right, the bill not outrageous, and her conversation a delightful change from the propaganda mill of my guides. At the end of the meal she produced a surprise.

'I have tickets for Prokofiev's *Romeo and Juliet* at the Bolshoi.'

How she had managed these items, which were on every foreign visitor's most wanted list, and for which I had vainly offered endless black-market dollars, was beyond me. This should have been my first clue – a sign as big as the Bolshoi, which I missed. But here she was, lovely Mira, with the priceless tickets. The Bolshoi Theatre, with its red velvet curtains, gilded balconies, and a select audience from the highest echelons of Soviet society, was in itself worth the visit. The performance by the stars of classical ballet was breathtaking.

During the interval we sampled Crimean champagne. After the performance the actors received their due applause and I suggested my hotel. She accepted. I did not know what to expect at the Gastinitsa Ukraina, the compound for visiting journalists. Each and every floor was securely guarded by a husky woman, who handed out the room keys. We passed this hurdle without trouble – the second clue I missed. Mira was all I could hope for, a savage from the Russian steppes, although I wonder whether her idea of throwing back our bedcovers at the sublime moment was solely prompted by her physical pleasure, because suddenly my door was thrown open and a flashbulb went off. I became aware of two characters in heavy overcoats. One was holding a big black box with a flashbulb attachment, and displayed a keen desire to portray my naked posterior. He kept licking the flashbulbs, to provide better electrical contact, and snapping away, as his second barred the door against any attempts to escape. The only thing missing from a Hollywood period flick was press passes in their fedoras.

My 'Get the hell out of here!' was answered with a steel-toothed grin by guard number two. That Mira was in my bed was now public knowledge.

What my avid, flashbulb-exploding audience did not know was that, although still married, my American wife and I had tried for quite a while to reach an amicable divorce. The following morning, I took the bull by the proverbial horns, and confronted my guide from Intourist: 'Remember the girl from the department store? Well, we ended up in bed in my hotel room, and while we were making love somebody took our photographs. Could you please find out who these people were, and perhaps ask them to be so kind and let me have a few enlargements. I'd like to keep them as a souvenir.'

I never did hear another word about my amorous escapades in Moscow, nor did anyone approach me with a 'we've got you on picture' smile.

The most dangerous spy category is the government official who has been turned because of his political or social convictions. These are no ordinary men, they are generally high calibre civil servants, deeply motivated, with access to classified material. A number of such outstanding men, who eventually rose to prominent positions, were recruited by Soviet agents during the late thirties on the Rugby fields and in the hallowed halls of Cambridge, the university Jim Mossman graduated from. The most notorious spy trio was that of Burgess, Maclean and Philby.

Donald Maclean and Guy Burgess held key positions in the British embassy in Washington and as such had direct access to confidential communications between the heads of the British and United States governments. They diligently copied a number of classified reports, and passed these on to their Soviet resident contact, or to a third man, whose identity remained undiscovered for a very long time.

Through a series of minor mistakes, such as a speeding ticket issued by a Maryland highway cop to Guy Burgess, who wasn't where he was supposed to be, their disloyalty was suspected. At the last minute they were tipped off that American and British counter-intelligence were on to them. Only a man in the top echelon of counter-espionage could have known that their cover was blown. The third man finally turned out to be the number two in British Intelligence, Kim Philby. He was the deepest and most efficient mole the Russians had ever planted.

Burgess and Maclean took a boat train from London to Paris, where they vanished to resurface in Kubishev, 500 miles from Moscow. The Soviet Union had scored a major coup, and the duo were fêted with great pomp and publicity as heroes of socialism. Their period of infamous glory lasted for three months. Once squeezed dry, their new masters relegated them to the oubliettes.

Both were given jobs translating technical literature, and they disappeared from view. Like everyone who reads newspapers, I knew about them, but never did I expect to locate these super-spies. During a reception at the British embassy in Moscow in January 1959, I found myself standing next to a junior diplomat.

'Any idea how to get hold of Maclean or Burgess?' I asked, not really expecting an answer.

'Call them,' he said. Just: call them!

'Where?'

'I don't know about Maclean – in any case, he's a crashing bore – but here is Guy's number,' which he scribbled on the back of my cocktail invitation.

Next morning I gave it a try. After a few rings, the phone was answered by a Russian: '*Da.*'

'May I speak to Mr Burgess, please.'

'Moment.'

'Hallo, this is Guy Burgess.'

'Good morning, my name is Erik Durschmied, I'm a Canadian reporter, and I wonder if it would be all right to meet you.'

'Are you one of the recent bunch at the Ukraina?'

'Yes I am, room 1013.' There was no reason to play it coy, all phones were tapped. We knew that for a fact, and they knew that we knew. By now 'they' had already recorded what I was up to. The entire thirteenth floor of our hotel was reserved for one specific purpose, an electronic listening centre to bug their guests' conversations with the world.

'And you say your name is Erik – what was the other name?'

Nobody has ever been able to spell my name – even Austrians get it wrong – so I spelled it for him. 'It is D, like David, U like … ' That also permitted the other members of our party line to produce the correct file for a read-out on one Erik Durschmied, Canadian, born in Vienna, Austria …

'Right, I'll call you back.' With that our line was cut, and I expected never to hear from him again. Ten minutes later my phone rang. 'Mr Durschmied, this is Guy Burgess. If you are free this afternoon, why don't you drop in for a drink?'

He must have been issued with his instructions.

'I'd be delighted, can you tell me how to get there?' He gave me a long explanation which I wrote down.

'Oh, and Mr –, can I call you Erik?'

'Of course you can.'

'Yes, Erik, I have nothing to offer you to drink. Think you could manage a bottle of Scotch?'

'I'll see what I can do.'

'All right, see you then at three.'

Was the invitation genuine? Was I being set up? How could they set me up? All these were thoughts crossing my mind. I had nothing to hide, it was a simple meeting between a journalist and a *retired* spy.

Armed with two bottles of tax-free whisky, I hired a hotel taxi to take me to the address. I don't believe I was followed: there was no point to it, they knew where my appointment was. We ended up in a fairly run down neighbourhood – a row of matchbox buildings of socialist construction and style which had already taken on the patina of a destitute slum. He had only provided me with a number and it was hard to locate. He did not live in a street, he lived at block number, house number, stair number, and door number. The man was not a person, he was a zipcode. Dark steps led to a door on the fourth floor. I rang, the door opened, and there stood Guy Burgess.

There was nothing sinister or evil about him. A tired-looking man, run down like the building he lived in. He was not what I had imagined a super-spy to look like. On hunched shoulders he carried a worn-out tweed jacket over a good quality white shirt, which had endured too many washings with Russian detergent. A bow tie, baggy pants and a pair of Church's brogues, worn down on the heels, completed his outfit. His face was blotchy and his teeth stained by tobacco. But his eyes were something else: there was such deep sadness in them. Pools of despair. A man who had given up hope.

'Come in, I am so glad to see you.' I could see that he really meant it. He was an abandoned commodity, a man whose usefulness had waned, a liability the Soviets could not get rid of. So they had just parked him in this building, provided him with a houseboy – actually an electrician who went by the name of Tolya, who doubled as boyfriend-lover-informer – and kept him on ice. Maclean had somehow managed to build a new life along established socialist lines, Burgess had not found the strength to start anew. He could never be anything else but a product of Eton and Cambridge and Washington cocktail parties. In Moscow, he was slowly dying of boredom drowned in alcohol.

On a rickety table in the living-room, like two soldiers expecting the arrival of a king, were two crystal glasses. I handed him the bottles, and he immediately poured some very stiff drinks. The first sip was slow, appreciative, 'There's nothing like good malt.' While we talked, he kept refilling his glass. I nursed mine.

Hovering in the background was the houseboy, ostensibly dusting framed reproductions from the English hunting scene.

Burgess showed me his prize possession, a first edition of one of Churchill's *Collected Works – Arms and the Covenant*, with a signed fly-leaf: 'To Guy Burgess, Winston'. These valuable volumes were stashed on a home-made brick-and-board bookshelf, together with a few books about racing cars and – of all things – a yearbook of English roses. There were no flowers in the place, and the only view from his window was a row of identical flats.

'Do you have a car?'

'No, you see, I can't drive here, I've no licence. In any case, I don't need a motor.'

'Don't you miss it? Didn't you have a Packard while you were in Washington?'

'Yes, that was a nice car,' he said with a sad smile. 'Of course, I loved high speeds.'

Yes, I know, that's how they caught on to you, I wanted to add.

'Look here, Erik, perhaps you could send me a few sports car magazines, you know, something to leaf through. Have you seen the new Jaguar?'

'Yes, I filmed last year's Le Mans, Hawthorne was driving one, it's quite fabulous.'

'What kind of engine have they put in? A straight six, or a V-eight?' It was pathetic, here he was, a sports car nut, and he knew that he would never again get his hands on a steering wheel, unless his new friends allowed him to test-drive a Volga truck.

'You know, I have never done anything wrong, it was all circum-stantial. Nothing was ever proved in court.'

Of course, nothing had ever been proved, and nothing would be proved. The Western intelligence community had not emerged smell-ing of roses from the affair, there was egg on everyone's face, from Whitehall to Washington.

An embarrassment, to say the least. How nicely it could have ended if Maclean and Burgess had only jumped from a high building. They didn't oblige: they defected, and, worse, they talked. Most un-British.

'Do you care to talk about it?'

'About what?'

'The reason why you did it?'

'You know, it may sound strange, but I am not really guilty. I stand accused of treachery, and all I did was run away. In retrospect, a serious misjudgement on my part.'

'But even that ... why?'

'Why? Today I wonder ... ' he kept pouring himself another shot ... 'Loyalty to friends, love ... ' his voice faded, and he found solace in the yellow liquid.

'What about Maclean?'

He smiled. 'Poor Donald. He panicked when he got caught in something he couldn't handle. I held his hand, that's all.'

'Do you see him?'

'Sometimes.'

'What is life like?'

'Life?' There was a long silence. He stared through the window and focused on a point in time and space, some three thousand miles from Moscow and several years ago. 'My life ended when I left London.' His gulps of whisky were getting longer. 'I still have a mother in the United Kingdom, and I would very much like to go back and see her. Do you think you could enquire for me with the British government if that would be feasible?'

He couldn't be that naïve? He was just desperate, beyond caring. It was most dangerous for such talk inside the Russia of Khrushchev, and to a foreign journalist at that. It was an admission, a confession. Of course, I would convey the message, but he knew the reply. 'I will pass on your request, but what good will it do? The Russians will never let you out, and they'll put you in jail in England.'

'Yes, of course, there is too much to protect ... ' What did he mean by that? But before I could think about his answer, he continued. 'Oh, I wouldn't mind going to jail ... ' and with that, tears came to his eyes. I had my final answer: he was desperate beyond caring. A soul dumped on the big human trashpile. No hope, no future, just death at the end of the tunnel.

He was hastening his demise with an overdose of alcohol. During the hour I had been with him, he had gone through the first bottle. It didn't even show.

'I would like to interview you, will you do it?'

'Why not?' And with that, he accepted the serious consequences such a televised interview might carry for him. 'I say, let's go to this nice place where I often take walks – it's tranquil and gives ample vistas to contemplate the future.'

I did not know what to expect, but I accompanied him to the outskirts of Moscow, and there, in the snow-covered graveyard of an abandoned monastery, I interviewed the spymaster whose perfidy had shaken the Western alliance, and who had been retired by both sides.

A man who was out in the cold for good.

The interview, although not quite as outspoken as our talk in his flat, was as pathetic as the man who gave it. He tried to justify his actions with his own brand of logic, he begged to be allowed to return to an English jail, and pleaded to be buried on English soil. Snow had started to fall; the white flakes settled on his drab Russian coat with the grey fur collar, and on my stylish Canadian winter jacket. My small sound camera was on a tripod, fixed so that it captured the image of two men sitting on a bench in a Russian cemetery, speaking one language but with an unbridgeable gulf separating them. Burgess poured his heart out. The past had finally caught up with him, and he was paying for his betrayal. His parting words to me, and to an unresponding British government were: 'Goodbye, and I hope to see you when I come to England.'

I returned to my hotel with its tax-free whiskies and glitzy caviare girls, and Guy Burgess went back to his flat, his cheap vodka and his Russian boyfriend. When I returned to the West, and delivered his request, nobody in an official capacity wished to hear what he had asked me to pass on. They probably knew. Protect, he had said. But what, or who? It only earned me some icy stares, and a polite: 'Thank you for coming to see us, Mr Durschmied.' He had become a non-person. A few years later he died. The man who shook the West did not make *The Times* obituary column. He was lamented by no one, except perhaps his mother.

The names of other spies may come more readily to mind, but Guy Burgess, the super-mole, will remain a black mark on Western counter-intelligence for a long time to come. He was not caught. And yet he was not in league with the real James Bonds, who are men out in

the open, for the whole world to see, and to fear. Those are not
ordinary men, they are the ones who have the power to start things
happening. They are certainly more efficient than any fictional
character will ever be. Some look gentle and carry umbrellas, others
have a certain look on their faces that induces the ordinary citizen to
cross the street.

I have no problem in nominating the single most dangerous man
I've ever come across. He didn't belong to the army of hare-brained
terrorists, who revel in the delusion that by blowing up a plane in
midair, or placing a bomb in the local supermarket, they will change
the world. This one was quite different. He had the power of
command, and the forces necessary to execute his tasks. He was a man
with the cold mind of an exterminator who calculated acceptable
risks, divided them by the men at his disposal and arrived at a formula
of maximum damage inflicted upon the enemy. The allies were
worried about his *oeuvres de guerre* and called him *Commando
Extraordinary*. Enter: Colonel Otto Skorzeny of the Third Reich.

I made contact with him in Madrid, and arranged for the interview
to take place at his country retreat in the Republic of Ireland. He
received me with great courtesy, and gave me a tour of his castle, a
museum of World War Two mementos. He was a dyed-in-the-wool
fascist and made no bones about it. His prized possession was a piece
of marble from the Führer's desk, which had come from the bombed
Reichskanzlei in Berlin and somehow had found its way into
Skorzeny's possession. After my initial talks with him, I began to
understand the fascination his scenarios held for people like Fidel
Castro. His planning was meticulous, and his motto: *Rely on surprise.
Don't fire and the enemy will not shoot back.*

The filmed interview was not great: he didn't deliver the real goods,
so to speak. He talked about his brownshirt days in pre-Nazi Vienna,
where he was instrumental in the 1934 attempt to overthrow the
Austrian government and went to jail for it. He then outlined his most
daring exploit, the liberation of Mussolini from the mountaintop of
Gran Sasso. In the summer of 1943, Mussolini had been overthrown
by General Badoglio and interned. Hitler was furious, and ordered his
liberation. Before his friend's abduction had become general knowledge, he interviewed four German commando chiefs.

On Hitler's question: 'What do you think of the Italians?' the three

Germans present replied: 'They are our allies.' Skorzeny said: 'Mein Führer, I am an Austrian.' That remark, referring to Italy's betrayal of the Austrian emperor in World War One, clinched it for Hitler, and Skorzeny was picked for the task. German intelligence had discovered that Mussolini was kept prisoner at an alpine hotel on a mountaintop with only one means of access, a cable car. The mountain range was located in the very centre of an Italian army now hostile to the Germans. Skorzeny and a handpicked group of German commandos used gliders to crash on to the tiny meadow in front of the hotel-prison, liberated Mussolini without firing a shot and then flew him out in a single-engine short-take-off plane.

In the Battle of the Bulge, Skorzeny's commandos, dressed in captured American uniforms, redirected the flow of badly needed Allied supplies and reserves away from the American fighting men. After the war he was captured, tried and found innocent when, as his surprise witness, the head of British commandos came forward, and testified on his behalf.

The really interesting pieces he saved for when the camera was turned off. Because of my father, I was most interested to find out about the ill-fated army putsch of 20 July 1944, instigated by disillusioned German officers against Hitler.

'What went wrong? Why didn't they get Hitler?'

'*Stümpers* ... rank amateurs. Stauffenberg, placing a bomb under a table and then walking away.'

'What would you have done differently?'

'If you want to eliminate someone, you face him, and shoot him – twice, just to make certain. The bangs will create such confusion, that you can simply walk away from the scene. By the time the guards wake up to what has taken place and move into action, you're miles away, and the job is accomplished.'

For him, everything was simply a job, and a job to be executed well.

PART THREE

HOMECOMING

What did you do in the Great War, daddy?

1914–18 poster

1

CHERCHEZ LA FEMME

---

*'Love is like the measles; we
all have to go through it.'*

Jerome K. Jerome, 1859–1927

The centre of my working day in Paris was a rosewood desk on which
stood a truly antique Underwood typewriter. After two pages of
banging at the keys my fingers would be numb. The telephone was my
link to the wider universe. When it rang it usually meant either that a
revolution had started and I was expected to head for it, or that a girl
couldn't make it for dinner. The flat in the Avenue de Villiers was a
comfortable place for a comfortable life. It represented a fixed point of
return. I was never long enough in Paris to get on anybody's nerves.
Some of my loves performed miracles in my tiny kitchen to prove that
amour was connected with the palate. Some girls stayed over, others
went home before the last Métro. That suited me fine.

My semi-steady was a very attractive French aristocrat. She was a
model, and worked as a supervisor in one of the leading haute couture
houses. This gave her access to the latest in fashion. She was
spectacular company, a beautiful ego trip. When she walked into a
room she invariably became the centre of attention, if not because of
her looks then because of her caustic humour. Everybody thoroughly
disliked her.

In the course of a snobbish dinner I met the wife of a senior British
diplomat. Brigid considered my choice of girl friend simply not good
enough. Her first impression of me must have been that of a charming

personality. Whatever the reason, she intended to improve my situation. She had a weakness for intrigue. One day she invited me to a party she had specially arranged for 'intimate friends'. This turned out to be a crowded affair in a flat overlooking St Germain-des-Prés: champers, cold canapés and potted palms, and half of the diplomatic community of the city. I felt lost in the crush. The apartment was not big and people were pressed up against each other, trying to balance their champagne glasses on their plates and keep up witty conversation without dropping pickled herring down their partner's décolletage. The conversation ranged over Freud, Marcuse, Karajan and all the other people nobody has ever met. With a brutal movement which she must have learned from the French police during diplomatic riot training, Brigid managed to separate me from my French aristocrat and I found myself pressed against a tall blonde. We exchanged a few meaningless niceties, like, 'Hello, great party,' or 'Have you read Josef Stalin's memoirs?' and that's where it would have ended. But cunning Brigid had other plans. With a devilish twinkle in her eye, she squeezed through the crowd and started our conversation rolling.

'Erik darling, I would like you to meet my very good friend Annelise.'

'Hello Annelise,' I said, and it was only then that I threw more than a cursory glance at the blonde creature. She was tall, five foot ten if she was an inch, with ash blond hair, blue, blue eyes, suntanned, a strong face, with a generously filled body and a pair of slim legs that never seemed to end. In other words, she was gorgeous. I judged her to be in her late twenties. I couldn't figure out why she was hiding her charms under a Bedouin tent.

'Very fashionable,' Brigid told me and I thought it a crime. My first guess was Swedish, definitely Scandinavian.

'I am Danish, I have two children, and I go with Brigid to a cooking school.'

Annelise's clear voice and laugh were utterly captivating. There was nothing fake, her candid eyes couldn't have invented a lie to save herself from an embarrassment. She was without a trace of *la vie mondaine*. This special quality made her stand out, and disqualified her from a pick-up. I simply had to improve Danish-Canadian relations without being a bore to her or to my hostess. My French girlfriend was hovering nearby and had begun sending hostile vibes our way, and so Brigid drifted away from us and ran a beautiful interference. I did not see my French friend again that evening. As a matter of fact, I never saw her again.

There is a tide in the affairs of men, which, taken at the flood ... how do I start? Why not a straight-out invitation?

'Would you like to have lunch with me tomorrow?'

'I'd love to.'

'Where would you like me to meet you?'

'Why don't you come over to our place. I'll make something. I don't want to leave my girls.' As simple as that, no suggestions of fancy restaurants, just: come over and meet the family. Who was this family? The more I looked at her, the more intrigued I became. A beautiful woman without pretence – no-nonsense – straightforward – the mother of two girls – that much I had found out. Where was the father? Why had she come alone? I was curious. The party started to circulate and I did not wish to monopolize her. I scribbled my number on a cocktail coaster. She would have a chance to reconsider and, if she wished, cancel the invitation. She took the paper, not palming it out of sight secretly but quite openly, and said, 'Thank you, we'll see you tomorrow. Here is my address.' I went home alone.

Next morning the phone rang. I was sure she had changed her mind.

'Could you please pick up a baguette on your way?' And, I wanted to add, flowers for you and a cake for the kids. How old were they?

The phone rang again. 'Hello, Erik darling, how did you enjoy my party last night?'

'Well, actually, it wasn't bad.'

'I hear you have a luncheon date with Annelise – such a sweetheart.'

'How do you know?'

'Oh, you know, we chat a lot. I gave her a call this morning, just to find out if she would see you again. You know, girls do like to talk.'

'Did you arrange this whole thing?'

'Darling, how could you possibly accuse me of such scheming,' she said, followed by a giggle.

'Don't I know you. Now tell me, who is she, where is her husband or whoever? She doesn't look like someone without attachments. Why me?'

'Why don't you find out for yourself, darling, and give me a call afterwards to let me know what you think of her.' Always the matchmaker, cunning Brigid.

At the appointed time, with a baguette under my arm, and a rosebush clutched in the other, I made my way to the Latin Quarter. It was an old house with an old door that opened into a dark staircase. Nailed to the wall were a few mailboxes and her name was on one of them, *cinquième étage*, no elevator. On the fifth floor were two doors, and standing at attention in front of one small door was a wooden soldier of the Danish Royal Guard presenting arms. I rang the bell and could hear frantic activity. Then the door opened, and my life was changed forever.

'Come on in,' she said, 'did you have trouble finding it?'

'Your soldier was a bit too obvious.'

'Do you want red or white?' came a female voice from the kitchen.

'Meet Liller.' Liller was several inches taller than I, and very, very blonde. The typical Valkyrie. But not from a Wagnerian drama; this one was nice. She was eighteen, the Danish au pair girl, who had everything under control. Right now she was conducting an orchestra of casseroles in the kitchen. The whole place smelled of Baltic Sea and pinewood. There were bottles and spices and flowers on the table. Steam was rising from a pot. The red and white she had referred to earlier was not the Danish flag, but wine. And to honour the invited guest she had posed her question in English. We moved to the 'salon', a small, neat room, with a table on trestles, covered by a tablecloth with a design of little dwarfs. Like everything in Denmark, even the gnomes were red and white. Pinned to the wall were sketches of operatic costumes.

'*Rigoletto?*'

'No, *Amlet*. The prince of Denmark whom Shakespeare called Hamlet.'

The bedroom door made a squeaking sound. Slowly it was pushed open and out came, first one, then two pairs of big baby eyes surrounded by lots of blond hair. Very shy.

'Come out you two,' said their mother. They appeared, and my goose was cooked. The elder of the two had long blond hair, a perfect miniature of Annelise. The other had curly hair and was hiding behind her bigger sister.

'This is Annemarie,' Annelise pointed out the bigger one, 'and that is Christina. And this is Erik.' It all sounded so natural, I wasn't presented as a distant uncle or a long-lost cousin from America. I was simply Erik.

'Hello,' two tiny voices and a lot of giggles crowned our introduction.

If I wanted to end it, then I should have stopped right there, left the roses and headed for the emergency exit. However something inside me clicked and I was hooked. I had no choice but to carry on. This family was like nothing I had ever met before. From the tall Viking to the tiny tots, all blondes. And real ones at that.

'How old are you?'

'I am five,' said Goldilocks, 'and my sister is almost four.'

I wanted to rush downstairs and buy up the nearest toy shop. Dumb me, not to think of it before, but this was something entirely unexpected for a confirmed bachelor. Pretty ladies I had known before, but pretty ladies with cuddly, furry little girls, that made all the difference. The little one was hiding behind a chair. I walked around it, and she scurried off like a squirrel.

'À table,' ordered Annelise in strongly accented French, and we all sat down. I was placed between the two children, and Annelise was near the kitchen. Liller was at the head and kept control over the monsters. The meal was very tasty, and I asked naïvely,

'This is delicious. Where did you buy it?'

'I made it. It is Danish beef stroganoff.'

'You made it?'

'It is not difficult.' Just like that.

I tried my best to entertain the children, but started to come out in a rash when I couldn't remember how to build a boat with my napkin. One positive act I could perform was to help them cut their meat. The atmosphere relaxed, so much so that Liller had to take a firm hand and stop them giggling and squealing and hiding under the table. And when the meal was over and I had to say goodbye, these monsters slid over to me, grabbed my legs and wouldn't let go. Child psychology can beat anything thought of by wise men. I couldn't see myself as a father, but I was going to try my utmost to be a good one. By now I had realized that there was no other man in Annelise's life and I wanted to see her again as soon as possible.

'Do you have time for dinner tonight? I know this place ... ' I had to think of somewhere quickly. It couldn't be one of my regular hang-outs, that would be an insult. The kids continued to giggle and Liller grinned. That same evening, the au pair ordered Annelise to join me and added, 'Don't you dare come home before tomorrow morning. I shall not unlock the door.' Annelise came for dinner, and stayed.

Our love did not blossom right away, at least, not as far as I was concerned. I was scared, really scared. Of hurting her. And even more scared of being hurt myself. In the beginning there was only passion. She filled in a few of the gaps in her past. Annelise grew up in a very small town on the Baltic coast where her parents owned the local cinema. When she finished high school she went to Copenhagen to study fashion design. During the summer she doubled as a tourist guide. On one of these tours she had met a well-known American civil rights lawyer and author. She was then twenty-four and he had already been married twice. Annelise became his third wife. They lived in California, where Annemarie was born. Then, while she was pregnant with Christina, he met another woman and abandoned her. Annelise was not bitter about it, and I have never heard her say a bad word about her former husband. I told her a bit about myself and my line of work. I tried to make it sound dramatic, to frighten her into a decision.

'You must realize, when this phone rings I will have to leave you. I don't know when we will see each other again, if at all.'

'You will be back, and I will be here.'

Nothing more was said about it, and we spent the next few days trying to cram as much into what we both realized was the short space of time at our disposal. We took the girls on drives and went along the Seine for long walks, and longer talks. She not only had her good looks, she was bright. These conversations with her became a necessity for me. She knew so many things I had never thought about and she pointed out what I had missed. All that time, the girls kept running up and down and sideways and often in between our legs. They put their tiny hands into mine, and I clasped theirs, strolling about with a kind of air that screams out: look at me, I am their protector. We never stayed far away from each other. Everything was so natural and unfaked. During the night I looked at her blond hair on the pillow next to me, her sleepy features, soft and lovely. I listened to her breathing. Sometimes, in the middle of the night, I would be shaken by the tiny hand of Christina, who had the habit of pulling off my blanket and saying in a sleepy voice:

'Erik, I have to pee.' I am sure that she could have accomplished the job by herself, but it was more reassuring to have the father along to protect her from evil ghosties. I took her to the bathroom, sat her on the seat, and waited patiently. Then I tucked her back into the bed she shared with her bigger sister.

On our first Sunday morning I received a shock when the kids crawled into our bed. I was naked, and had no idea how to cope with this particular emergency. Then came Liller, the tall Viking with nothing to cover her suntan. Annelise put me on the right track.

'The children have to learn sooner or later, so why hide from them?'

It represented the sound philosophy taught on the shores of a cold ocean. We ended up at breakfast swathed in towels, bathrobes, and naked kids. It took the fearless war reporter three months to gather enough courage to admit to Annelise that I loved her.

Then the Yom Kippur war erupted. It was our first separation, but not our last. This was my third Israeli-Arab war, and also my final performance for the BBC. My association with the venerated corporation had lasted twelve years, but towards the end I simply got bored being asked to do repeats of events which had excited my imagination a decade before. Whenever I returned from a war, there were always four blond heads as my special welcoming committee at the airport. When we got home I would find fresh flowers and a meal waiting for me. I wasn't used to that, but it wasn't difficult to get into the habit. I was being corrupted into domestication and I loved every minute of it. I even became more tolerant and understanding with my colleagues. I had a family, and, of course, I had become the instant expert on paternal duties. I gave advice to those who had been fathers for years. I carried photos of my little girls and bored everybody on aeroplanes or in hotel bars with stories of the 'cute little things'.

2
THE WHITE TRIBE OF
RHODESIA

'The road to freedom is via the cross.
Mayibuye!
Afrika! Afrika! Afrika!'

Albert Luthuli, Nobel Peace Prize, 1961

A vehicle was parked across the mud track. In it was a solitary figure, with a rugged, leathery face and a no-nonsense expression. He was about forty, with curly hair and was wearing a camouflage battle jacket. The vehicle was assembled from fourteen different makes, and no wheel bore any resemblance to the next, while the tyres varied from re-treads to no-treads. The windscreen was cracked and there was a slab of welded metal for a seat. The most conspicuous item was a deadly-looking automatic rifle across his knees, its muzzle pointed towards me like an angry rattlesnake.

'Hi,' he offered with a big grin, 'I am Jack Wantenaar.'

This wasn't a chance encounter: it had been carefully orchestrated from Paris, but until this moment he had only been a voice on the telephone. He was a splendid-looking specimen of Afrikaner stock, whose hard existence showed in the deep lines on his face: power-fully built and without an ounce of fat. As I got to know him better, he turned out to be an outspoken but thoughtful man with a solid grasp of life's necessities. His border existence had taught him many skills – mechanic, cook, farmer – but most of all, survival. He radiated an aura of the lion from the veldt, a combination of protectiveness towards his own clan and the killer instinct to safeguard his territory.

My first ride with Jack in his weird contraption, which he insisted on filling up with kerosene due to an acute shortage of any other combustible product, was on a foggy dawn along a dirt track through dense vegetation, a path which had witnessed the death of a farmer just the night before. Terrorists had crossed the Mozambique border and planted a mine. The farmer had been killed, together with some Africans sitting in the back of his truck. The Africans were blown to smithereens when the back wheels struck the detonator – the white farmer died in the ensuing gun battle with the insurgents.

'How does it feel to drive on a road like this, every morning?' I asked, rather timidly, since deep down I had an awful feeling that last night's mine had a brother waiting for me somewhere in the next few miles.

'Well,' said Jack, looking straight ahead for signs of footprints on the dirt which might indicate danger, 'there is little you can do. When you hit a mine, the car goes up, and you go with it. You most likely buy it, and they'll pick up your pieces in the trees. If you are lucky you only get your legs ripped off. An ambush, that's an entirely different matter, you blast away at them and make as much noise as possible and hope that you'll scare them off. Usually you do. So if you hear any strange noises, just blast. Now, point this thing out the side.' He had provided me with an Uzi submachine gun – more for personal reassurance than protective firepower – which was lying across my camera in my lap. 'Just make sure you don't blow off your balls,' he added with a wry grin.

'I'll try my best.' My attention was focused on the leaves and what might lie in wait behind them. Even the slightest movement, wind from our jeep blowing in the grass, made me bring up my gun. And then it happened – there was a definite blur, something running, and I let go with a blast. Jack hit the brakes and, before the car stopped, he had vanished into the green canopy. After some moments of crashing silence, my nerves as tight as my finger on the trigger, I heard his voice.

'Hold it – don't fire, it's me. You sure bagged one.' The leaves parted and out stepped a laughing Jack Wantenaar, in his hand a pearl hen, or what was left of it, neatly stitched by the slugs from my gun.

'Relax, they're gone.' I wasn't sure if he meant terrorists or the flock of hens.

During the previous month, his neighbour at the next farm had fallen into an ambush. His car had received forty hits. Before his wife dropped to the floor, she had been hit by seven bullets. The most serious wound had smashed her hip. In the cradle on the back seat, their little baby, Botha Junior, got one in his bum and out through his belly, but miraculously survived. A cool Botha Senior, firing with one hand while keeping the other on the steering wheel, managed to drive them to another farm. Next morning, Botha and Jack went after the insurgents. There were over a dozen altogether. In Jack's party there were only four tough hunters, going after the biggest game on earth. It took them a week.

Jack's wife was as strong as her husband, and just as hard. She never left the house without her submachine gun, or her ·38 police special, which she carried in her handbag – even to Sunday service.

'Jack, you know the old biddy in the kraal, she's got herself bitten by a snake, they've gone for the witch doctor.'

'What the hell can he do for her? What kind of snake?' asked Jack.

'Puff adder, I suppose.'

'Then she's a goner. I'd better have a look.' So we drove there to 'have a look'. I expected a corpse and found a hobbling scarecrow with a toothless grin. While collecting firewood, she had stepped on a snake. Africans do not believe in white man's medicine, and she was no different. Her grandchildren had run for the witchdoctor, who had murmured some curses, invoked strange powers, and applied po-po leaves to the wound. Although her leg was badly swollen, the leaves seemed to have done the trick, and the old woman continued to hobble, screeching something ferociously at Jack.

'What is this all about?' I was puzzled.

'The terrs [terrorists] frightened my blacks, and they've run away and abandoned the kraal in the valley – you know, the one right on the border. Makes an ideal hiding place for the kaffirs. We better take care of it.' We piled into his car and drove to the village in the jungle. I couldn't rid myself of an uneasy feeling that somebody behind these leaves was staring down at us over the open sight of a gun.

We made a hectic dash towards the empty huts, stumbling over pots strewn all about, and chasing a few hens into a thicket. Jack ran into a hut, took out his Zippo lighter, and set the roof aflame. Whoosh! The dry palm leaves exploded, and within a few moments the whole village was an inferno, sending white smoke like a beacon into the sky.

'Let's get the hell out of here, I can smell them. They are nearby.' He didn't have to repeat his warning – I made it to the jeep before him – quite a feat, considering that I was carrying my camera, my batteries and an Uzi. Jack gunned the engine up the steep road which led from the bottom of the valley, while I stuck my gun out at the side.

'Give them a fright,' said Jack, and I let go with a burst across the valley floor. We had done about three hundred yards when one of his tyres burst, whether because of a bullet or old age we didn't stop to find out. 'Shit,' said Jack, as he stepped hard on the accelerator, and kept the car rattling along the track. All the way we were accompanied by a bedlam of screeching monkeys, thunderclaps of the kerosene-fed engine and the painful whine of a deflated wheel crunching on its last shreds of rubber. We made it back in one piece.

The following afternoon we went back to the kraal, an inflated gun party made up of Botha, two other neighbours, Jack and myself. The insurgents had disappeared, but they had left us a reminder, a headless, bleeding chicken spiked onto a pole in the midst of the smouldering rubble.

'I guess they'll be back,' said Botha.

'Yeah, guess so. I'll be waiting for them.' With that Jack kicked over the pole.

During the weekend we received an invitation to a barbecue near Chippinga. We were met by a lot of noise as we drove into the courtyard. The teenage daughters of the farmer took great pride in blasting beer bottles with their submachine guns, and when a nosey black servant came too close, they let fly in his direction, and when the man fled for his life into the nearest bush they collapsed with laughter. 'He's chicken, looky looky at him run ... '

Their proud papa looked at his daughters' idea of fun, and said: 'Wherever the Afs go to, it is only rape and lust all the way. My daughters are going over the border.' The only response from his daughters was another burst of rifle fire. 'Communism is coming, with all its evil and filth.'

'Yeah, you're absolutely right,' said Mrs Wantenaar. 'They don't think like us. We should have never taught them to speak English ... now they think they're as good as we are.'

Jack's four-year-old girl pulled at her father's trousers.

'What you want?' asked Jack.

'Bullets ... I want bullets,' answered the child. Jack took his automatic rifle, injected a shell, held it for the little girl, and simply said: 'Pull.' The four-year-old infant blasted a wine bottle from a stump. Jack turned to his sons.

'Never go in front of a gun, you hear what I say? Never go in front of a gun – this thing kills, see?' and he tore the stump apart. 'That's what it'll do to you.' And to me, he said: 'It's no longer a question of fighting terrorists, it's a question of survival now, we are fighting for our lives, that's all.'

Night on Jack's farm was an experience not to be forgotten easily. When darkness fell, Jack locked his 'security fence', which was nothing more than an 8-foot high strand of mesh wire, vulnerable to an ordinary wire cutter. Confined into the perimeter was a horde of vicious dogs, let loose at night, trained to stalk and kill. Whenever they passed a perimeter light their fangs glistened evilly. Only once did I step outside. I never heard the animal, but just before I became its victim I heard Jack's voice: 'Down boy!' He smiled when he told me: 'Don't think because you're white they won't jump you.'

But the farm's real warning system was a flock of geese, the noisiest bunch of geese I have ever heard, which prevented already nervous creatures like myself from getting any solid sleep. Whenever they cackled I reached for my gun.

The house itself, with its paper thin walls, was hardly a survival shelter. There was no way that help could have arrived before daylight. Jack knew that, and so did the insurgents. That's why they mostly attacked at night. I kept my trusted Uzi next to me, with a few spare clips, and my head under my pillow.

Chippinga, some fifteen miles from the farm, resembled a border village from a spaghetti Western. It was certainly the only place I'd ever visited where the bank manager expected you to carry a shotgun while making a withdrawal. A few wooden houses, one gas pump and a beer dispensary, grandly called The Chippinga Arms, which had long ago forgotten the liquor laws and kept its door permanently open for a crowd of thirsty, darts-throwing clients. These were never short of yet another tale of horror, and I called my film *Tales from the Chippinga Woods*.

'Hear you got a good bag last night? Eight, was it?'

'Naw, that was only the beginning. We were driving over the hump with the Kevin Reed truck, and there was this hoak sitting on a branch, so I says to Kevin, What's this hoak doing here, and he sticks his gun out and the kaffir has a grenade, so Kevin revs him off the branch, and that's when the others started to blast at us. So we take care of them, eight in the first run.'

'Sounds good, anybody get hurt?'

'Naw, the kaffirs don't know how to rev properly, only Kevin's truck is full of holes.'

'What's that?' asked a new arrival, the wife of a farmer, hanging her Uzi over the coat rack.

'Too bad about the bloke that got revved last night.'

'Who's that?' there was anxiety in her voice. They looked at her with serious faces, until one of them shouted:

'A kaffir!' and everyone exploded with laughter.

One evening, after a day's patrol along the Mozambique border, there was a call for me from home. 'Yes, yes, I can just about hear you,' I screamed down the radio-link party line, 'I'm fine, yes, everything's okay, thank you.' ... 'What, what, say again, tragedy at home?' My God, it must be the children. I had an instant nightmare. 'What, say again, what happened?'

'It's the goldfish, it has died.'

My goldfish is reality. My family is my universe, which I am willing to suffer for, go to war for. Everyone has his own goldfish. And quite reasonably so; because of our own goldfish problem we retain a certain amount of sanity while faced with burning kraals and exploding mines.

The last time I saw Jack, he was kissing his family goodbye. He had received his call-up to perform his 'stint' in the anti-terrorist border unit. As his jeep pulled away from the gate, they were all standing there, waving: his wife, his two sons and his four-year-old girl.

Finally the car disappeared in a cloud of red dust and we were alone. Mrs Wantenaar locked the safety fence, picked up her submachine gun, and went on with her daily chores. I left for another assignment along another border in another war.

Two weeks later, Jack Wantenaar's patrol truck struck a mine. He was lucky, he survived. Most of the others didn't.

3

CAMBODIA 1979

'Vile Robespierre!
You too will follow me to the scaffold.'

Danton, before his execution, 1794

There is an epilogue to my Indochina days.

The historical details about the fall of Vietnam are well known. The Americans withdrew and built a stele for their fifty thousand soldiers who perished. I left a few friends and colleagues behind. They are remembered by their reports and their films.

After *Hill 943* I felt no desire to return – I had done all the talking there was to be done about Vietnam. About the hope and the failure. About pain. About joy. About fear and horror. Reflections in the eyes of children, sometimes gentle, sometimes violent, mirroring the trauma of a martyred land. But I was destined to return to this region of the world, torn apart by years of bloodshed.

And when I returned, I had the sad distinction of being the one to tell the world about a drama which had been going on while we slept ...

When I entered the torture chamber I knew that the rumours had not been exaggerated. In the middle of the cell was an iron bedstead with shackles at the headboard and at the foot. Beneath the bed was a pool of dried blood, a dark brown stain with clouds of flies feeding on it, where the life of the last victim had gushed on to the stone floor.

Christmas 1979. It is always at the most festive time of the year that things start to happen around me. One of my most harrowing stories started during the days of peace and prayer. Like so many others, this one began with a chance encounter.

Françoise Vandermeersch, a nun, was deeply involved in humanitarian actions. She never talked about it, she went out and acted. Circumstances prevailed and she found herself deeply engaged in the Vietnam war, on the side of the North. During the bombing of Hanoi she was on the spot, a miracle worker, helping to dig ditches and bandage the wounded. Her name had become synonymous with French–Vietnamese friendship. Whenever she visited Vietnam great honours were bestowed on her by the leaders of the country. She has been attacked by many for her friendly support of the socialist ideal, to the point where she was called the Red Nun. I must stand up in her defence: politically she isn't *pro* anything, but she certainly is *anti* hunger and *anti* misery. Her life has been one of compassion. There will always be a monument to her kindness in the hearts of the children of South-East Asia.

A Paris publisher introduced me to Soeur Françoise. She most certainly was worth a portrait and, since a picture needs a frame, I decided to follow her to Hanoi. I asked her to present my request for a visit to Vietnam to the authorities. Several months passed without a reply, until the conflict between the Khmer Rouge and Hanoi finally burst out in the open. The army of the new Vietnam pushed into Cambodia. Priorities changed and my proposed visit to Vietnam became a trip to Cambodia, or Kampuchea, as it was now called.

We were sitting around the family table in Denmark, with candles and carols, when the phone interrupted our Christmas dinner, and Soeur Françoise told me to present myself at the Vietnamese embassy in Paris the following morning to be issued with a visa. That permit would allow me to accompany her into Kampuchea. Once again, it became a toss-up between family and work. Kampuchea was too big a story; nobody had been allowed into the country after the American withdrawal – I simply had to go. The only way to reach Paris in time was the Scandinavian night express. I left the warm candles and the unopened presents, and rushed to the station, where I jumped into the last carriage as the train pulled out towards the wintry cold of a Baltic crossing. Next morning, Christmas Day and my birthday, I presented myself with my passport to the Vietnamese authorities, and the following day I met Soeur Françoise on a flight to Ho Chi Minh City, previously Saigon.

There is only one way to describe Soeur Françoise: an amazing person. She was tough, and she could be gentle. She could be fully understanding, and unforgiving. She was an organizer *par excellence*. In the midst of a devastating war she managed to find us a car and the petrol to run it. When we couldn't find beds, she organized military cots in a hospital. Many times I watched her surrounded by children, while their parents eyed us with great suspicion from a distance. Her kindness always broke the ice, because she gave them back the one thing they had lost: hope.

The most telling example of her organizational talent was seen on the military airfield near Ang Khor, the ancient capital of the once mighty Khmer empire. A group of high-ranking Party leaders, under the protection of the Vietnamese army, was to visit the old temples, and we tagged along. We walked around the spectacular temple site of Ang Khor Wat, the product of a civilization without comparison in Asia, up the stairs and down the stairs and through ruined porticos, until we found ourselves up outside the main complex on a vast meadow. It was here, only a few years before, that my colleagues from French television, Puissesseau and Meyer, were shot by the Khmer Rouge. For our protection, the sky was patrolled by the same helicopters the American forces had left behind during their withdrawal. How many times had I sat in a Huey chopper, flying over these ruins, looking down, next to a rear gunner from Biloxi. Perhaps even in the very same ship. Only the colour of the markings on the aircraft had changed: the white star of the US forces had become red. I stared in wonder at Françoise, who had brought a wicker basket and a picnic. After a gourmet lunch we had to rush back to the airport.

Françoise organized a vehicle which took us to the landing strip. We drove right on to the runway, where an airliner was ready for take-off. It had already taxied into position with its jets roaring. Françoise was of slight build and walked with a stick. It was astounding to watch this figure in her black pyjamas, buffeted by the jet exhausts, half running, half dragging her bad leg across a military airfield. The armed guards surrounding us were simply too stunned to intervene. Françoise came to a stop thirty feet in front of the pilot's cabin. There she waved her cane, and shouted at the closed cockpit windows above her. Lo and behold, the window opened and the head of a Vietnamese pilot peered out. She waved her magic wand and a staircase was lowered, we climbed on and I couldn't help but hug her. She had done it again.

Perhaps the one time in her life when even she came close to despair was the day we stumbled upon the first signs of what will go down in history as '*the murder of a nation*'. We were not taken by the hand and shown it, we discovered it for ourselves. Our disclosure of the killing fields was not a media attempt to spread propaganda. What we brought back from our visit to Cambodia was the shocking revelation that for four years the world had stood by while a country was slaughtered. My film report became an indictment of one man, whose name will go down in history as the butcher of Cambodia: Pol Pot.

How many had to pay for his megalomania? One million? Two million? How many vanished during the Great Terror which transformed the land of the smiling faces into an abomination which defies description?

I had been to Cambodia before, but that seemed light years ago. When the Americans started to bomb the country to deprive the Viet Cong of their supply line, the famous Ho Chi Minh Trail, it brought to power a new order, the Khmer Rouge. After their triumphant entry into Phnom Penh in April 1975, the black devils with their red headbands systematically emptied the city, killed the intelligentsia and enslaved a nation.

Whether for humanitarian considerations or simply to create their centuries-old ambition of an Indochinese empire, the Vietnamese put an end to the massacres. Their forces crossed into Cambodia in 1979. Now, I found myself back in the country alongside this latest batch of 'liberators', who had called for an independent witness. As the Vietnamese forces advanced against a completely disorganized ragtag army of Khmer Rouge, it became more and more apparent that what we were discovering were the results of the orders of a megalomaniac, who sacrificed his own people indiscriminately to prove his warped ideas of revolutionary reconstruction: 'Rebuild a new society from the ashes.'

It was on the banks of the Mekong river, near the provincial capital of Kompong Cham. We were driving along the highway towards Phnom Penh when we noticed a sweet smell of decay pervading the

Durschmied running for cover by the Suez Canal, Six-Day War, 1967

Mrs Wantenaar with automatic rifle, Rhodesia, 1976

Jake Wantenaar burning down a village in Rhodesia, 1976

The killing fields of Cambodia, 1979 – the first pictures to prove they existed – Vietnamese tank gunner during the rush for Phnom Penh – the massacre site (frames from Durschmied's 16mm film)

Opposite above: Beirut – the aftermath of a car bomb attack, 1982

Opposite below: Beirut – the US Embassy in ruins, 1983

Right: Dead Iranians in the Gulf War, 1984

Below: Battle of El Howeiza – captured Iranians, not yet teenagers, 1984

Right: Durschmied filming
soldiers celebrating after battle
at El Howeiza, 1984

Below: Battle of El Howeiza –
Iranian helmets, 1984

Right: A dead Iranian, Gulf War, 1984

Erik Durschmied's press cards

countryside. We stopped and struggled through dense brush. The stench became nauseating.

Our jungle path opened on to a Buddhist temple on a hillside. The walls of the pagoda were covered with dried blood and bullet marks. We were not prepared for the other remains.

Countless skulls – hundreds, thousands, with tufts of hair and wrinkled, sun-dried skin, with eye sockets blindfolded, littered the ground. Large trenches full of decaying corpses, most with their hands tied behind their backs with electric wire. Some bodies had heads, some did not. Nearby we found swords made from fire-hardened bamboo, with which the executioners had broken the necks of their victims. Some of the corpses had blue plastic bags tied over their skulls. I discovered a head wrapped in plastic, with bulging eyes and a mouth frozen in the silent scream of slow death by suffocation.

This presented the first visible proof of the rumours of horror which had been running across South-East Asia for years. Nobody had believed it, nobody had ever seen it. I needed to find out more about what had taken place. I couldn't simply return to the West and report that I had stumbled on to the site of a mass execution. No one would believe the enormity of the atrocities which had been committed in this place.

Our transport, sequestrated by Soeur Françoise, was an ambulance with a French-speaking Cambodian nurse as our driver and interpreter. I had to find eye-witnesses. The Khmer Rouge had made certain that there were none left. It took us several hours slogging through the jungle, but we finally located some huts hidden in a palm grove. When we reached a kind of central clearing I found only an old woman cowering in the far corner of a hut, who stared at me with great hostility. To her, I was just a new kind of evil. She had her skinny arms wrapped around a frail body and babbled to no one in particular. Our nurse translated: 'She has lost her whole family. Her last grandson, aged twelve, was taken from her last year. She has never seen him again.'

'Please, explain to her who I am and that I do not wish her harm.' It was vital to gain the woman's confidence so that I could hear her story. The old woman's tears had run dry. She resembled a little bird, sitting on a rice-mat with her feet tucked in and her frail hand resting on her latest treasure, a blanket and a bag of rice which we had brought along. Crouched down next to her was our nurse, a gentle, plump woman with an eternal smile. It took us a long time to build up a rapport, until the only survivor finally started to talk, slowly at first, then with ever-increasing speed. Finally it came pouring forth like lava from a volcano – four years of agony, a tale of horror. I was unable to record or film, feeling that respect was called for. I felt like a voyeur intruding into the privacy of a whole nation's soul.

The nurse translated and I will repeat her story to the best of my memory.

'We were simple peasants, and we lived near the highway. Sometimes the green soldiers from the army came to buy rice or chicken. Every week my sons went to the market and sold our vegetables. One day, my sons came running back to our village and told us that there was a lot of shooting in town, and that the black Khmer Rouge had taken control.

'Even before that happened, a few of the younger boys from our village had already joined the Khmer Rouge, and sometimes they stole back during the night, in their black uniforms and their red headbands. They told us all about their great leader, Pol Pot, and how he would change everything, and that everybody would get big plots to plant rice.

'That day, we saw soldiers on the road, and in the evening we heard shooting nearby. One of my sons went to look and brought back with him a badly wounded soldier. He put him up in his house and his wife bandaged his wounds. Early next morning, a troop of Khmer Rouge came and ordered us to line up in the middle of the village. Then they asked us if we had seen soldiers. My son said that he had a wounded soldier in his house. The Khmer Rouge went to my son's house, and dragged out the soldier. Then they put him in front of us and shot him.

'The leader of the Khmer Rouge pointed at my son: "You, come here."

'My son went over. "Where is your family?" My son called his wife. As she walked to join my son, the gang leader shot her, then shot my son. "That is the way we shall treat all enemies of the revolution," he screamed at us in rage. Then they burned my son's house.

'A few weeks later we noticed a large group of people, all from the city, camped in a field. The monsoon had started, and they had to sleep in the rain. They were forced to dig a large trench, and a Khmer

Rouge told us that this would be a canal to bring water to our rice fields. We told him that there was no river nearby.

'"Let them dig, they have to learn to obey their new leaders," was his answer.

'Sometimes, during the night, we would hear a scream, or a shot. We were much too scared to find out what was going on. As the ditch approached, we could hear many more screams and more shots. One morning we watched a group of prisoners being led to our palm grove, and there the black devils forced them to kneel and then they killed them with palm axes. That night, most of our men fled into the forest.

'A few days later, a band of Khmer Rouge, all very young, came into the village to round up the men. They were furious when they found out that all had disappeared. As a punishment they burned down the houses and killed all the younger women, except three, who they took with them. That day I lost a daughter. My grandson was hiding from them in a palm tree, and they missed him. He was now all I had left of my family. The devils stole our rice and the old people died of hunger. My grandson and I hid in the woods, living on berries, snakes and rats. Every night we could hear these terrible screams, like a herd of monkeys, but more frightening. Finally our hunger became so great that my grandson left to find something to eat. He never came back.' For the first time since she had started talking, a large tear ran down her wrinkled cheek.

We found the trench she had told us about, a canal that went from nowhere to nowhere. It was a gigantic cemetery. Where the rain had washed away the red earth, pieces of bones and clothing stuck from the mud. A field of water lilies, blue plastic water lilies made of plastic bags that floated on the muddy water. The stench was something which I was to carry in my memory for a long time. I stood there in morbid fascination, almost too stunned to perform my professional duties. Never before had I seen anything like it. My attempt to describe the scene in front of the camera hardly conveyed what I really wanted to express. I fumbled for words, but couldn't describe the monumental crime in all its cruelty.

On our entry into Phnom Penh we were faced with an astounding sight. What had once been a city of one million people was now populated by less than two thousand. The streets were piled ten feet high with rotting furniture. Pol Pot's insane measures to erase the bourgeoisie involved emptying the city of its population. The Khmer Rouge had thrown all symbols of comfortable living out of the windows and into the streets and four years of tropical rains had done the rest. Delicately hand-carved chairs and tables, beds and linen closets, had decayed into a quagmire and created an impassable obstacle for vehicles and people.

I stopped thinking how many lay buried beneath this rubble. We found the beds of the French hospital rusting in the courtyard, the operating theatre smashed and blasted, the floors covered with faeces. The destruction and desecration was deliberate and systematic. The Monorom hotel had no doors, no windows and no beds. The lobby was covered with bullet holes and bloodstains. We found piles of old paper money, now worthless, drifting across the rubble. On one wall was a faded NBC News sticker. The only foreigner was a German count, Wolf von Schmettau, the representative of the International Red Cross, who told me of his trip into another region, where he had discovered another execution site:

'When we reached the outskirts of Battambang in our Red Cross convoy, people streamed towards us from the surrounding country-side, all famished and in rags. We distributed rice and medical supplies and opened a small medical dispensary. That evening, a boy took us to a cave which was located underneath a Buddhist temple. Inside we found a giant stone Buddha, and piled around him hundreds of charred bodies. The massacre had taken place only a few days before the Vietnamese had reached the town. The Khmer Rouge had pushed their victims inside the grotto, threw dozens of hand grenades into the mass of people and finished them off with a flamethrower. The smell was nauseating.' He thus confirmed that our find was not unique, and that the massacres were widespread.

He told me about the horrors of Phnom Penh, and we made our way through the rubble to see for ourselves. Despite her bad leg, Soeur Françoise was never far behind. We headed for Tuol Sleng, the former French lycée. We had been told that it had served as an interrogation and torture centre but nothing prepared us for what we found. Each classroom contained a different refinement of cruelty. For the helpless victims there was pain, or excruciating pain, or enough pain to kill. We discovered pliers for pulling out finger nails, water buckets for drowning victims, heavy crowbars for breaking limbs, and iron nails for gouging out eyes. The floor was covered with dark brown stains, the blood of the wretched captives.

The main feature in the courtyard was a double gallows: two large water containers beneath dangling ropes. The executioner attached his victims by their ankles, then lowered their heads into the earthenware jars and let them drown.

The gymnasium was partitioned off into tiny cubicles, the prison cells. These measured two by three feet. Each had an iron ring cemented to the floor, to which the prisoners were shackled until they died of thirst, or were brought before their interrogators. One large room, once the conference room of the French teachers, was piled to the ceiling with clothes.

But by far the most horrible accusation against the Khmer Rouge torturers was provided by their own photographic files. Why such pictures were allowed to fall into the hands of the Vietnamese could only be explained by last-minute panic. We found boxes upon boxes filled with pictures taken by the torture masters of their victims undergoing extreme suffering, with bones broken, faces distorted by pain, eyes dangling from sockets – humans strung up like pigs, simply bleeding to death. And even some pictures of the devils incarnate – smiling, holding heads, cutting throats.

What was left of the Khmer Rouge had faded into the jungle and left its legacy of horror. The few survivors who had passed through these years of thunder were numb. They would not talk about the past. They could only stare with a smile frozen on their round faces.

The easy way would have been to air this programme with an accusing commentary. But the crimes to be reported were so gross that this could be construed as propaganda intended to score a point against socialism. I had an obligation to report what I had witnessed without editorializing. When the documentary was first shown I demanded that the producers abstain from any editorial commentary. With a minimum of words they gave the maximum of facts and left the images to do the rest.

4

IN THE NAME OF THE ONE

(IRAN, 1970–1982)

The Wine of Life keeps oozing, drop by drop.
The Leaves of Life keep falling, one by one.

The Rubáiyát of Omar Khayyám, died 1123

During the summer of 1981 I became one of the few to be given permission to visit the New Vietnam, and this trip resulted in a report which was eventually aired by CBS, with Dan Rather, their anchorman, providing the commentary. After the broadcast he asked me into his office, a well-furnished place without windows. Perhaps he had been told that sitting with one's back to a window can be dangerous.

'That was a real nice piece, Erik. You know, I still remember … ' and off he went down memory lane. Dan is handsome in a rugged kind of Texan manner, although now he tries to hide it behind a pair of red braces and a three-piece suit. He has dropped his original drawl from the ranch in favour of a flat American accent which escapes notice from El Paso to Boston.

A few months had passed when I received a brief call from the managerial section of CBS in New York.

'Mr Durschmied, we would like to discuss some permanent availabilities with you … we'll pay for the ticket.' It was the ticket that clinched it – Annelise needed some new sheets from Bloomingdale's and the network was willing to pay for the excess baggage. So, for a pile of sheets – and a handsome contract – I joined the CBS Evening News.

It wasn't the first time that I had been involved with America's most powerful TV news organization. During the sixties in Paris I had performed the occasional freelance work for them, and of course my biggest score was *Hill 943*, which was finished for US television audiences by CBS. What was new was the signature. It was the first time in my life that I had put my name on a piece of paper which tied me contractually to a network over a well-defined period.

I entered the CBS newsroom and was immediately overwhelmed by the shattering sound level. It was a madhouse of screaming reporters, shouting editors, yelling assignment-desk dispatchers, image controllers and video operators. Secretaries cupped their mouthpieces to make themselves understood at the other end of the line. Others screamed across the room: 'Rob, pick up number seven!' ... 'Hey Jimmy, for you on fourteen!' To all this were added the ringing telephones, the staccato hammer of telex machines from AP, UP, Reuters and AFP, and three TV monitors displaying the competition's outpourings, all howling at top level. The cacophony was packed into one acre of floor space covered with torn-off telex sheets, overflowing wastepaper baskets, wet raincoats and paper cups filled with cigarette stubs. An unhealthy nicotine haze obscured the view across the room. It was quite astonishing that anyone could think under such conditions, but it was precisely this pressure cooker that delivered great lines that moved a viewing nation: its stock market analysts, its hurricane watchers, its chocolate cookie manufacturers, its upward-moving or downward-spiralling political leaders and its housewives from Schenectady to Sacramento. Twelve seconds on the CBS Evening News meant twelve seconds watched and talked about by some sixty million Americans because, according to the latest Nielsen rating, Columbia Broadcasting System was watched by 21.33 % of homes in America. Nobody questioned a rating, certainly not the advertisers, and whether the viewers were illegal Mexican strawberry pickers or Boston bankers hardly seemed to matter.

We are number one! This was the slogan which carried weight and earned client bucks. Here was the most potent arsenal of the 20th century – the mind control, the hub of the TV news business. News? What was news? News was what a viewer who didn't care much about anything wanted to see. But even television had its inbuilt imperative:

to be ahead of the others. One hour or one minute ... the battle to be
number one called for brutal competition between the various networks. An item was only news until the viewer had his first look,
thereafter it stopped being news, and the story was as good as dead.
CBS was, and wanted to remain, number one, and in the quest to be
first there, first back and first on the air, huge sums were spent. I went
to see the foreign news editor, Peter Larkin, who lived just behind the
telex machines in an air-conditioned hole with three television
monitors and four telephones. He was the man with a permanent
problem. No longer men of flesh and brains, his crews were coloured
pins in a global map. He had crews in Japan covering a visit by the US
fleet, and crews with the Vice-President on a vote-getter in Germany.
Two crews were on 'death watch', one with an Arab leader scheduled
for imminent demise, and one with his counterpart, the Israeli Prime
Minister. The Paris crew were on standby in Athens, because the
Athens crew was in Rome. The Rome crew had gone with the Pope to
Africa. There was seasonal unrest in the Gulf, the Philippines and
now ...

A grey-bearded, overweight man in shirtsleeves strolled up while I
was in his cubicle and stuck his head in the door. 'Peter, we need more
coverage from Beirut.'

'I'll look into it.'

'You do that.'

The bearded man was none other than the president of CBS News,
and he paid the salaries. As soon as he had departed and Peter had
scribbled a few notes on a pad, he looked up.

'Erik, how'd you like to cover Beirut? I'd have thought you'd like
that.' He didn't even notice my failure to reply.

While I was on my eternal stakeout in Beirut, waiting for the Israelis
to invade Lebanon, a local informer walked into the mahogany bar of
the Commodore Hotel: 'Hey, mister, please go to Iran embassy
tomorrow, with passport.'

That was bad news: Iran was granting visas. All I had to do was
proceed to the Iranian consulate and ask for one. The Tehran hostage
crisis and the treatment of the foreign press – especially those
connected with American television networks – were fresh in everyone's mind, and there was no mad rush to get to the Iranian visa

section the following morning. But one of us had to go and, to our great despair, he returned with our passports duly stamped and signed. Our options had been removed, and we no longer had any excuse: now we had to go.

I had been to Iran back in the sixties. I hadn't had much luck. There wasn't much to it. The little man with the blue plastic card had come up to me as I was interviewing a professor from the University of Tehran on the future of the Iranian imperial dynasty, and informed me that it was time for me to go to the airport. In plain English this meant that I was being kicked out.

'What are the charges?'

He didn't need any charges to kick me out of the country, but he wanted to justify his action. 'You have slandered our divine majesty, the Shah-in-Shah.'

I knew there was no use arguing. He represented the sole law. Only a miracle could save me from expulsion, and the Shah had outlawed miracles.

'I will drive you directly to the airport.'

'But what about my luggage?'

'Oh, do not worry, we are not thieves. Your suitcases will follow you on the next plane.'

This was my inglorious exit from the Empire of the Peacock Throne.

The next time I visited Iran the country was under a different ruler. My involvement with the insanity which over the next decade was to tear the Middle East apart, bring one American president to his knees and embarrass another over a shady arms deal, a madness which resulted in the death of millions, began on a winter's morning in a small village on the outskirts of Paris.

The hamlet of Neauphle-le-Château, situated astride a major highway, made only local headlines when a contingent of French riot police cordoned off a zone around a suburban bungalow in the centre of the village. That changed rapidly, because within a few months the cream of international journalism was to make the pilgrimage to France to talk to an old man. Hardly anybody had ever heard his name pronounced outside Iran. Neauphle-le-Château housed a holy man called the Ayatollah Khomeini.

We drove towards the little town and were stopped at its limits by a gendarme who politely but firmly demanded to see our identifications. There had been rumours of an assassination attempt on the aya-tollah's life, and security was tight. After having established that we were bona-fide television folk and were expected, we were allowed to proceed to the insignificant, dull grey house with its brown-shuttered windows. The only noticeable difference from its neighbours was the group of three French cops posted outside the gate, armed with sub-machine guns. A bevy of supporters of the new movement milled around in the small garden. From time to time a neighbour strolled past the house, carrying a baguette under the arm, to catch a glimpse of the person who had so upset the tranquillity of their community.

A young, unshaven man in an open-necked shirt came to greet us at the door, and asked us to remove our shoes. He then led us into a smallish room, empty of furniture. A naked bulb spread a garish light on yellow-flowered wallpaper and a psychedelic rug, green with red dots, which covered the floor. Interior decorating was definitely not a priority for exiled mullahs. We installed the camera and sat cross-legged on the carpet. Then we waited. I passed the time staring at a hole in one of my socks. Why had I chosen today, of all days, to pick one with a hole?

The door opened, and in came the man. He wore a black robe over a grey waistcoat and a white shirt. His head was covered by a black turban. I was struck by his dark grey, bushy eyebrows, and flowing white beard. He kept his eyes to the floor, even during the intro-duction. The young man mumbled something that sounded like: 'rakbaktak mister arriik barrap.' We had been asked to show him reverence, and I addressed him as 'Your Holiness'. He proffered a limp hand, and we all sat down again. When he started to speak, his voice was monotonous and quiet, his eyes still on the floor. He never raised his pitch, never showed any kind of emotion. Next to him sat his interpreter, Qutbzadeh, a former journalist, who was destined to become a minister in the new revolutionary government, before being accused of treason by the Ayatollah, and ending up on the gallows.

After the usual, 'Thank you, Your Holiness, for giving us this opportunity' etc., the interview started with a question about the Shah. His answer, delivered almost in a whisper, was an attack. 'The Shah sounds more and more like a broken man, he feels he has lost everything but he doesn't want to confess it. He admits to some of his mistakes, but doesn't yet want to realize that the whole nation is against him. No matter what he does, or what his supporters do, there is no way that he will be saved.'

Only once did the old man glance at the camera, but I could find no emotion in his face. 'The Shah must go! The Pahlavi dynasty must go! The monarchy must be eradicated! A new Islamic republic must be established through the vote of the people in a general referendum. If the Shah is wise enough to leave the country he may be able to save himself and his family. If he stays on, then the future will be agonizing. He has committed heinous crimes. The people will grab him and you may imagine what his fate will be.'

With a slightly nervous gesture he pulled up his black robe to cover his stooped shoulder. The room was cold, and only the strong television lights provided some warmth. But the chill went much deeper than the room. The atmosphere was frigid and I could feel that our presence was considered an unwanted Western intrusion.

There was an aura of hatred for everything foreign and non-Islamic. If ever this man was to gain power, it would be only a matter of months before he launched a holy crusade against the infidels of the Occident. The green flag of the Prophet would be hoisted and carried into bloody battle. The sacred fire was in him.

'Your Holiness, can you see the possibility of a military coup to overthrow the Shah?'

'A military coup d'état will not solve the problem. The age of the military coup is over. The British tried it and the Americans did it: it has failed. If such a coup takes place in Iran, it will only intensify the power vacuum, not solve it. The army must come to their senses and realize that the people they are fighting are their own brothers and sisters. They must join the people. They must join us in our process to achieve an Islamic revolution.'

And with a wave of the hand, he indicated that the interview was over. We were dismissed. He got up and walked out of the room. As I moved away from the house I had an icy feeling in my back: his eyes were still staring me down.

Meanwhile, back in Tehran, the Shah was entrenched in his splendid palace, protected by his praetorian guard. He could count on an army he had pampered, corrupted and provided with sophisticated toys. But the legions of the armed were facing up to the one messiah, fortified with the spirit and the fire of Allah. Events were heading for a climax. Once again, God with His almighty word was to smite the temporal powers of a Caesar.

The Shah-in-Shah's future ran out (which confirmed what the professor in Tehran had once told me) and a religious zealot made his triumphant entry. Within a short time, the messenger of God had replaced the imperial idolatry with a more heaven-directed spiritualism. The despotic rule of the Shah was replaced by the equally despotic rule of the Ayatollah. The prisons were overflowing and opponents of the religious revolution faced the firing squad by the thousands. Then followed the attack on the US embassy and with it the ensuing hostage crisis which humiliated a superpower and brought down an American president.

Iran's neighbours and hereditary arch-enemies, the Iraqis, had assumed that the mullah's regime was vulnerable. They had embarked on an ill-advised blitzkrieg, spearheaded by a large tank force, across their common border. Their aim was to grab some of the oil-rich provinces and to gain sole control over the Shatt-al-Arab, the vital waterway flowing into the Gulf which forms a long-disputed part of the frontier between the two countries. At first they were successful, then they got bogged down in the vastness of Iran. This war was now in its second year.

We chartered a Lear jet which took us to Damascus. There the authorities kept us sitting in the sterile airport lounge until the Iranair 'Ayatollah special' was ready for boarding. The plane from Mecca had a *Hadj* configuration, which meant there were twice as many pilgrims aboard than it was legally permitted to carry. It was a no-liquor flight with a full recital of the Koran. On arrival at Tehran's Mehrabad airport we were greeted by banners announcing that US imperialism would never win over the revolution by the truly faithful. There were equally explicit posters of women in Islamic headdress, exhorting the gentle sex to 'cut off the hand of the United States devil'. In simple words, we were not welcome.

The customs inspectors, all young and revolutionarily unshaven, proved non-committal and thorough. We were searched, ordered to declare our money and, four hours later, allowed to leave the airport.

At the gates to the Iranian capital there stands a white pyramid built by the Shah to glorify his dynasty's eternal empire – which didn't last much longer than Hitler's Thousand Year Reich. The sides were now plastered with revolutionary posters, every one with a stylized Yankee Doodle Dandy spearing a child. The Intercontinental Hotel was cavernous and empty. Since its heyday during the American hostage crisis, with obligatory daily coverage by an international press gang, the place had died a slow death. The rooms were drab and the food drabber. To leave the hotel was out of the question and with a camera it would have been suicide. In any case, there was little to be discovered in the streets, apart from a lot of black-veiled women queuing for food. Tehran was suffering from an acute shortage of everything, including petrol, which is after all Iran's main export. To buy a few gallons took an hour's wait in a line that stretched for blocks as drivers pushed their vehicles towards the only pump still operational. The black market was rampant, only nowadays it was no longer controlled by corrupt imperial officials: the ayatollahs did the skimming now.

That evening, a revolutionary guide came and ordered us to be ready for an early start. We had no idea where or what they were taking us to see. It took a bumpy plane ride to find out. As our transport rolled towards its take-off position, our guides from the Ministry of Religious Guidance recited the Koran and invoked the names of the martyrs – loudly, so that God would hear. It was a good idea to ask for Allah's protection, because the aircraft could certainly have done with a little help from above. It was a clapped-out Hercules which stayed in the air on a wing and a prayer. The spare parts embargo by the United States had had visible effects. During the flight, I had a chance encounter with one of the pilots, formerly a captain in the Shah's air force, who had joined the new rulers to defend his country against the invading Iraqis. He told me that the only source for spare parts was the devil itself: Israel.

Half an hour after take-off, a bearded revolutionary mechanic took my camera box and stood on it. I expected a soapbox declaration, but instead he started to take the plane apart. He unscrewed some of the panelling and smoke poured out. When the air cleared, I could see a profusion of colour-coded wires, which he strummed like a balalaika. Throughout this highly technical operation, the prayers from our

religious zealots increased in volume. As it turned out, it was nothing –
well, almost nothing. One of the elevator guide cables had snapped,
but thanks to American engineering, which had taken Iranian main-
tenance into consideration, there was a spare cable which kept us on
our righteous path.

We landed at an airfield in Ahvaz. Near the runway I noticed five
helicopters, most without rotors, some riddled with bullet holes, all
out of commission. That the Iranian air force was being hurt became
painfully clear. Outside the terminal building I spotted twenty trucks,
all piled high with coffins.

Our guides made us climb into several jeeps, and within a few hours
we had reached the battlefield of Dezful where the tide of war had
turned. In September 1980, Iraqi armour had brushed aside the
Iranians, whose front line had collapsed. Beset by heat, swamps and
lack of purpose, the Iraqis had ground to a halt. And now it was their
turn to be annihilated. We rode to the top of a hill overlooking a vast
plain. The first reaction was incredulity: I was confronted by a
graveyard of Iraqi armour. I looked down upon hundreds of smashed,
burnt or abandoned tanks. The Iranian revolutionary guards had
launched wave after wave of humans into the Iraqi fire. They had
overrun the defenders, and by sheer self-sacrifice had put an army of
tanks out of commission. Boys with limpet mines had thrown themselves against steel. Within a few hours a modern Iraqi army had
ceased to exist.

The plain was dotted with mastodons stuck in the mud. Some had
been swallowed up by the bog so that only their guns protruded from
the swamp, marking the wet grave of fifty tons of iron and four bodies.

A battery of Frog missiles had been abandoned in firing position.
An Iraqi was slumped dead over his launching console. He did not get
the chance to push the button: a bullet had smashed his neck. Now the
rockets were harmless, three dead whales loaded with dynamite. The
dimension of the disaster was made clear when we came upon a group
of six tanks with their gun-barrels literally stuck into each other. In
their panic to escape the onrushing human torpedoes, they had piled
full speed into each other. The rout had been complete. Now they
looked like jousting knights in armour who had fallen off their horses
and were speared by their own lances.

Our hosts loaded us into a helicopter and the pilot took us on a low-level ride across an area of utter desolation. Wherever we flew, there were abandoned tanks. We had just cleared a high dune and climbed to one hundred feet, when I heard a roar and spouts of sand erupted just in front of our path. An Iraqi MiG had skimmed the battlefield and had found another moving target, a tank creeping across the desert floor. In panic the pilot dived our helicopter towards the dune, landing us on a pile of corpses bloated by the sun, a ghastly sight and a nauseating smell. We jumped out from our aircraft and expected the worst. Nothing happened.

This incident brought the Gulf War into perspective. This was not just a minor shootout with light weapons, this was a jet age conflict with megadeaths on both sides. Not since the colossal tank battles which raged near the Russian town of Orel during the summer of 1943 had such a concentrated tank force been annihilated in a single day. Each time we approached yet another group of abandoned tanks, we were immediately surrounded by rifle-wielding revolutionary guards, who took great pleasure in climbing on to the dead monsters. Under the well-orchestrated leadership of the ever-present mullahs they yelled for the benefit of my camera and the viewing millions in the West.

'*Maghbar-Am'rica, maghbar-Am'rica. Death to America, Death to America.*'

There were thousands of them, all wearing headbands imprinted with holy scriptures. They were fierce, fired with adrenalin, with a madness in their eyes – these were the survivors. They were instilled with the holy fire I had noticed in Neauphle-le-Château during the interview with the Ayatollah. The infection had spread, the green flag of the Prophet was being carried high. We came upon a destroyed radar post on a hill, crawling with soldiers. The girders swayed dangerously with the tons of flesh it was carrying. A human antheap, all chanting their war cry: '*Death to America, Death to America.*'

The helicopter took us back to Dezful, where we met the unit commanders. All had been regular officers in the Shah's army. When their homeland was in peril, they had joined forces with the new Iran, and performed their patriotic duty vital to its survival.

Although history repeats itself, no nation has ever learned from it. Iraq's aggression on the young and internally divided Islamic

Republic of Iran gave the ayatollahs their rallying cry. The whole
nation united against the external enemy, and the mullahs consoli-
dated their power.

Our guides brought us to a prison camp, where we were shown the
remainders of an Iraqi army corps. In the broiling noonday sun we
found rows upon rows of dejected and tired Iraqis, but certainly happy
in the knowledge that they had survived the murderous onrush of
Islam's suicide battalions. A mullah harangued them and made them
shout slogans glorifying the Ayatollah and the leaders of the new Iran.
Guards passed out posters and water. I assume the kindness was for
the benefit of my camera. A ladle of cool water and the prisoner waved
the portrait of Khomeini, although without great conviction. To press
home the Iraqis' utter defeat, they were guarded by children
brandishing new Kalashnikov assault rifles. With moist eyes our
interpreter led us to a child, twelve or thirteen years old at the most.

'Look at this young boy, he is a hero of our new nation. His belief in
Allah is so strong, that he captured single-handedly all these big men.'

Not a likely story, but great propaganda. As long as they themselves
believed in it, it created the climate for future sacrifice. A thought too
horrible to contemplate. It reminded me of Germany's last stand in
front of the gates of Vienna, fourteen-year-olds against tanks. Nothing
had changed.

Back in Tehran, I applied to the Ministry of Religious Guidance for
permission to visit Evan prison, the huge penitentiary complex on the
outskirts of the town.

'Why do you want to see the prison?'

'I have been told that there are many cases of torture and execution.
I would like to disprove it.'

'We do not torture and we only kill our enemies.'

'I understand, just let me see for myself.'

'We have to get permission from the general prosecutor.' He had
been described as a psychopath, enjoying a cruelty which made even
the ayatollahs shudder. It would be fascinating to meet the monster.

The next evening, a guide came to the hotel and told us that the visit
to the prison had been arranged. We passed through an iron gate
which was guarded by three revolutionary guards brandishing submachine guns. They inspected my equipment, and counted the
videotapes. Only after every piece of tape, tripod and camera had

received its proper chalk-mark were we allowed to proceed. We entered a long, dimly lit corridor, where a 'rent-a-prisoner' chorus greeted us with the by now familiar: '*Maghbar-Am'rica ... Death to America...* '

The hallway gave on to a cavernous hangar. The wall behind the speaker's podium was covered with a monumental portrait of a benevolently smiling Ayatollah Khomeini, hand raised in heavenly blessing. The hall was filled to capacity by hysterically screaming prisoners, all wishing America an everlasting death. Most were in their early twenties, the age of university students, and all had shaved heads and stubbled chins. None of them wore prison garb. There is only one way to describe the scene: insanity. Our guides cleared a path through the pandemonium, and we were escorted to the dais.

When I climbed on to the podium I saw that the hall was divided by a steel barrier into two separate sections, one side reserved for the nasty boys, the other for the screeching girls. The female section was a scene from Dante's *Inferno*, black-shrouded houris of hell.

'These miserable criminals are thieves and murderers and homosexuals. The girls have kissed in public for pleasure, and some have even committed adultery.'

'Are there any political prisoners amongst the crowd?'

'A few.'

'Where are they?'

'Oh, here and there, we will show you some who have confessed to their sins and are now repenting.'

A young man was brought forward to stand next to us on the elevated platform and he addressed the crowd in a demure voice. We received a simultaneous translation. 'My sins are that I have had no belief in the One, the Almighty, in Allah, and I have spoken out against His Holiness the Ayatollah. Now I have seen the light, now I know that I have been wrong. Now I am very satisfied and happy to be here. These men here, these foreigners have been told that there is torture in this prison. Let us all show them that this is a lie.' And with these words, like a conductor addressing his violin section, he brought up his hands.

There was a howl throughout the hall.

'Is there any torture in this prison?' he shouted.

Up came his hands and a thousand clipped voices screamed: 'NO!'

'Why do the foreigners say there is torture?' he continued.

His hands came up for the second verse, again the well-rehearsed roar in unison: 'Lies!' His little speech may have saved the young man from a walk to the shooting gallery early next morning – I shall never know. I can only hope that our presence did some good for him and for the rest of the inmates.

Our guide hustled us into a bare room. Leaning against a naked wall was the dishevelled, unshaven figure of a smallish man with steel-rimmed spectacles. The reflection of the strip-lighting in his glasses gave him the appearance of a cobra. When he opened his mouth, his yellow, tobacco-stained teeth looked like poison fangs. He threw us a wicked grin, as he sized us up. He pointed to the floor, not in invitation, but in command.

We plonked down. Our guide introduced us: 'Gentlemen, this is Assadollah Lajevardi, the general prosecutor of the Islamic Republic.'

He barked at us in Farsi. Perplexed by his fury, I asked the guide: 'What did he say?'

'He said, you have seen there is no torture in Evan prison. I say no to all the lies, there is no torture. No, the word torture does not exist in our language.' Having pronounced his maxim of truth, Lajevardi, a sly grin distorting his mouth, dared us to reply.

There had been consistent reports of as many as ten thousand executions in the previous year alone, statistics confirmed by independent research groups such as Amnesty International. 'What about the many reports that you execute without a trial?'

His face went red, but the cynical smile never left his face. 'Lies, lies! All lies made up by America to discredit our faith in the Koran.' He nodded to one of his bodyguards hovering nearby, and a few sad-looking prisoners were paraded before my camera, each of them claiming new marvels of generosity by their gaolers.

'We are here because we have sinned against the revolution … '

'No, there is no torture … '

'Yes, the Assadollah is a just man, he wants only our rehabilitation for our own salvation … '

Some read their statements from scribbled notes. They made the prison sound like a Florida beach resort. And always, hovering in the background, with the smile of the Cheshire Cat, Lajevardi. Any slip-up by the accused, any admission to the Western media that all was not as he wanted it to appear, and it would be the rope or the bullet. I came away from this meeting with the strong impression that Lajevardi wanted his name engraved on the honour scroll of the Nobel Peace Prize for his contribution to justice and human rights.

He did not invite us to stay on ... once the prosecutor had made his point, we were escorted past the same screaming masses towards the exit. Our tapes were again counted, then confiscated. 'Gentlemen, you will get these back as soon as we have made sure that you do not try to smuggle out false impressions.'

I did not feel comfortable and passed a sleepless night. In my mind I went over all the shots I had collected with my camera, but I could not remember one which should upset our hosts. We were still their 'guests', and I did not fancy trading the Intercontinental for the Evan. Our plane, so aptly called the 'freedom bird', was not due for another three days. True to their promise, they gave us back our tapes, with only a few items wiped. I could not work out which shots had been erased.

A year passed, and I was at home to arrange the confirmation of my two daughters. It was not a drama covered by the world's press, just a holy event within the family, arriving from California and Copenhagen. The girls had lovely white dresses, and I had bought a new tie. My wife had a wide-brimmed hat and something frilly in polka dots.

The goose was in the oven when the call came from the Iranian press attaché, 'Mr Erik,' he said, 'we have been told to issue you with a visa.' I was expected within twenty-four hours in Tehran. The Iranian forces were set to launch their attack on the port city of Khorramshahr on the strategic Shatt-al-Arab waterway. I was in a quandary. I wanted to stay at home, but I had to let New York know about the unexpected invitation. I called CBS.

'I've got a visa for Iran.'

'Great, go right away.'

'Day after tomorrow is the confirmation of my two daughters.'

'Too bad. I have no daughters, go right away.'

My wife took the half-cooked goose from the oven, I put my tie in the wardrobe and set off for Tehran with Christophe Planchais, my new sound man. To drown my disappointment, I took along a shampoo bottle full of cognac.

This time there were no customs formalities. We were expected and whisked directly on to another flight to Ahvaz. There they stuffed us into a hot bus and we raced towards Khorramshahr. The city had been taken only the day before. We passed the first Iraqi defence lines, huge earth walls with a delicate system of interlinking tunnels and artillery positions. There was death everywhere. A group of prisoners shuffled through the heat towards us. One carried a soup-plate with a picture of the Imam Ali, the saint of all Shias, and kept on screaming: '*Allah akhbar, Allah akhbar,* God is Great … '

Now, Christophe was a newcomer to the war scene, and didn't realize that peeing in a minefield can be downright explosive. The area was cobwebbed with trip-wires and Christophe almost stumbled over one when he tried to relieve himself. I just had enough time to scream 'Stop!!!', and added: 'Remember, in war always pee behind your vehicle, never beside it.' Survival lesson number one, always walk, stand, or sit in tyre tracks, preferably those of heavy tanks: they will have exploded the mines for you.

'It's only a telephone cable,' said he.

'Do you really want to find out?' We left it at that, and he is still around to tell the story.

As far as the eye could reach lay a monument to all the ancient cars in Persia. The Iraqis had upended hundreds of automobiles in the sand to prevent paratroopers from landing on the sand flats behind their lines. The centre of the town had been razed to the ground to provide a free-fire zone for a secondary line of defence. A no man's land truffled with mines. Our jeep driver hurtled along a narrow track across this death strip, oblivious to my terror. Soldiers played a game of drop, pop and laugh. They would toss pieces of masonry into the fields, watch the mines explode, and roll over in stitches. It had been considerably less amusing yesterday. During the initial attack the mines had been cleared by teenage revolutionary guards, running across the minefields. They had all gone to heaven.

We reached the bridge. The slender concrete pillars which had supported the giant span crossing the Shatt-al-Arab were now reduced to mutilated stumps, sticking out of the muddy water. All that remained of the splendid riverfront mansions were piles of dusty bricks stretching for a mile. It was here, pushed into a small pocket with their backs against the water, that the defenders had made their last stand. Thousands of spent rifle bullets reflected the strong sunlight. A shoe stuck out of the debris. A soldier kicked it, and a foot came out of the ground. In an underground shelter near the waterfront we found corpses. It had been a makeshift shelter for wounded. In the final rush to reach the bridge, the Iranians had fired bazookas into the hole, killing every single Iraqi.

There was ample evidence that hand-held rockets had been fired from distances as close as five yards, signalling instant destruction both of the man it was aimed at and the man who pulled the trigger. An officer showed me where the last Iraqi defenders had tried to escape by swimming across the river.

'We were standing here,' he lifted his Kalashnikov and pointed at the lazy, murky waters, then he pulled the rifle to his cheek. 'Bang! Bang! We shot them, one by one. Nobody made it across.'

It was evening in Tehran, and a sunny Sunday afternoon in Paris. At the moment I transmitted our pictures of the conquest of Khorramshahr via satellite to the world, my daughters received their first Holy Communion.

5

DEAD MAN'S ZONE

(BEIRUT, 1982)

After we raced across the dead man's zone we crashed into a room
and were confronted by two ashen-faced, praying women.
'By all the holy saints, what were you doing out there?'
'Taking pictures.'
They crossed themselves. To them we must have appeared madmen.

The first bomb smashed through the bleachers of the Camille Chamoun stadium at about three o'clock in the afternoon. Several television crews rushed there to cover the event. Then the second bomb fell.

The French cameraman was instantly crushed to death by a slab of concrete. My colleague Alain Debos was more fortunate, as he had been further away from the impact. He received shrapnel wounds and a gash in his forehead. His soundman Sammy was also injured and the microphone smashed. Somehow the camera survived and kept running. Bleeding, Alain continued his television coverage of the carnage.

While this drama was being played out, I was in Paris with my family. I was sitting in a hot tub when the call came. It was Peter Larkin, the CBS foreign editor, who had me under contract.

'I want you to return to Beirut right away.'

'No way,' I dared to reply. 'I've just spent three months in that shitplace.'

'Alain has been hit, we don't know how badly, you simply must go.' A few hours later I was on a plane. As our Air France Boeing was approaching Beirut, the airport came under renewed Israeli air attacks and our flight was diverted to Cyprus. Later that night the pilot got us into Lebanon. As it happened, our flight was the last plane to land there for many months. At about the same time as we disembarked at Beirut International Airport, the first Israeli tank crossed into Lebanon. The long-expected invasion had finally begun. Its codename: Operation 'Peace for Galilee'.

I was no newcomer to Beirut. The civil war and the daily diet of horrors had been going on for years, and I had frequently been assigned to cover the continuous violence. Beirut held special memories. It was into this paradise of luxury hotels and sandy beaches that I had escaped from the horrors of the Mosul massacre in 1959 – it was my stopover on the way back to Europe from the Vietnam war. The setting was lovely, the girls divine, the climate just right and the food a gastronomic delight. I would stay at the Hotel St Georges on the shore of the azure Mediterranean, in a room with a view – especially on the bikini-clad vixens around the swimming pool. It was uncomplicated: with an eagle's eye I would spot a bird, go down to the poolside and invite her up, spend the afternoon with her and next morning continue my flight to Paris. A nice break in a long, tiring trip.

Lebanon was the cedars and the slender columns of a Phoenician past, it was conspicuous wealth, numbered bank accounts, casinos and nightclubs. It was women in Dior dresses and Cartier necklaces. It was oil sheikhs seeking relief from their dry desert at the most famous watering hole in the Middle East. It was noisy, gaudy and great fun.

In 1976 this *joie de vivre* came to an abrupt end. The peace was shattered, and a paradise turned into hell. The hotels along the beachfront, the Phoenicia, the Vendôme, the St Georges with its spy-infested bar, went up in flames and became burnt-out shells. Gone were the spies and the girls. Gone was the fun. Now the sandy shore where svelte creatures had roasted in the sun was turned into a garbage dump where the debris of three years of brutal civil war was unceremoniously dumped into the ocean. The palms along the waterfront had been shredded by bazookas, the water pipes for the swimming pools riddled by bullets. The restaurants were closed, or serving greasy junk food. The wealthy had taken up residence in Paris at the

Hotel Prince de Galles, the poor stayed behind to be bombed and shot and blasted.

For reporters Beirut became a matter of daily survival. It produced a special kind of photo-journalist, tough men, who went out every single day to risk their lives for a picture or a videotape. They did not feel like heroes, they were professionals doing a job and doing it well. This was no film set, there was no glitz to bloody, deadly Lebanon, where street battles could not be covered from the safety of a hotel room. Christians against Muslims, Muslims against Muslims, Druzes against everybody – all the warring factions were mixed into an unholy brew of interests by neighbouring Syria and Israel, were funded by Libya, Iran and the United States. Although there was a lull in the open war, terrorism against the civilian population continued. The city was divided by a strip of no man's land into two sectors, the Christian East and the Muslim West.

Almost no day passed without its minor bloodbath. In West Beirut this was the time of the Palestinians, as I found out rather abruptly. A car bomb had exploded along the Coral Beach road. My sound man and I were cruising the city in our camera car, listening to the *Voice of Lebanon*, when we heard the newsflash. Ahwad, our driver, kept his hand on the horn as we raced across town. It took five minutes, and then we stumbled on to a scene of blood and bricks and trampled fruit. A car packed with a hundred pounds of explosives, parked near a busy intersection, had taken down half the crowded market. The street was littered with limbs, oranges and screaming women. A house was on fire and a man rushed into the burning timbers trying to rescue his wife and child. Hell had descended. It was also descending on me. I felt a gun in my back. Two Palestinians were right behind me.

'What are you doing here?'

'I film for American television.'

'Americans and their Israeli dogs are the criminals,' he screamed at me. 'Give me your film.'

With that he pointed his gun at my video camera. The man was not only livid with rage, he had no idea about modern technology. He was plain dangerous. Recently, while on a similar exercise, Alain Debos had received a bullet through his tape recorder. That incident had shaken all of us. When we had complained to Mahmoud Labadie, the spokesman of the PLO, he had simply denied that the shot had been fired by a Palestinian. He had even gone so far as to accuse us of having deliberately destroyed the machine to create an incident. There are easier ways to create a diplomatic incident than to shoot oneself. But it was now my turn.

'I have no film, this is a video camera, it takes electronic impulses and through this cable,' I pointed to the umbilical cord which connected me to my sound man, 'he records the images on tape.'

He screamed: 'I want your film.'

I quickly turned to my sound man, 'For God's sake, give him the tape before he shoots us.'

My sound man fumbled with his machine, finally got it open and took out the cassette. As he tried to hand over the plastic box, the gunman struck him with the barrel of the gun and the tape fell to the ground. The Palestinian stepped on the case and the magnetic tape spilled out. The gunman was growing more furious by the second.

His pent-up hatred spilled out: 'You kill innocent people and then you take their pictures.' With a rapid movement he turned on us, and fired a burst from his rifle. It cut clean through the video cord. We were out of business, but at least not dead. 'Get out of here, never come back, or we will take care of you!'

Our Lebanese driver was white as a sheet. 'Please, sir,' he said imploringly, 'please, we go now.' And turning to the Palestinian he said a few humble phrases in Arabic. Pale with fright and fury, we flopped into our Mercedes and slowly escaped.

When we returned to the CBS office, news of the incident had preceded us. The CBS bureau manager, a Lebanese, was quite upset. 'Why did you start a fight with the Palestinians?'

Now it was my turn to explode: 'You son of a bitch! What do you mean, pick a fight? You sent us there to get pictures of the bomb and that's what we did. We didn't talk to anybody, we didn't place any bombs, we didn't antagonize your fucking countrymen, we only did our job. Our only problem seems that we are foreigners working for an American television network!'

From then on he carried a grudge against me, and the hostile mood between us continued throughout my remaining time in Lebanon. It was one thing to fight Palestinians and Israelis and Muslims and Christians, it was another thing to fight your own bureau manager.

***

When Peter Larkin called from New York to tell me that Debos had been wounded by an Israeli air attack, I realized that this was no longer a 'minor bloodbath', as a *Times* dispatch had described a car bomb which had killed fourteen passers-by at a jostling crossroads. This time, Lebanon was headed towards a full-out war, with every sophisticated way for man to do in his fellow man. This would involve planes and tanks and heavy artillery – meant to wipe out the Palestinians and anything that got in the way of the army which was bound to invade Lebanon.

Fouad, the manager of the Commodore Hotel, had recently been offered a bargain and had purchased a fleet of London taxis which he had painted white. (Not one of them was to survive the next three weeks.) He had dispatched one to meet us. The local fixer arranged our smooth transit through customs in the usual way, piastres changing hands and we were whisked from the airport. The city was dark and subdued, still suffering from the shock of the aerial bombardment. Twice our ride was halted by Palestinian gunmen. Fortunately, I still had my old PLO press card, and on both occasions we were waved through the roadblocks.

The Commodore was not particularly charming; it offered no view across the blue Mediterranean. What it did offer was relative safety, which meant a night's sleep. It was a nondescript concrete building, with a swimming pool, invariably without water, and a few potted plants. The Commodore was adopted by the international press corps the day all the posher seaside hotels had gone up in smoke. Its main attraction was a telex that somehow continued to function, and a bar where liquor flowed freely and where drinks could be charged to the telex bill. It also had an internal power plant which assured electricity, vital for recharging camera batteries. In the lobby resided a parakeet who loved to frighten the uninitiated with the whistle of a falling bomb followed by a snatch of Beethoven's Fifth Symphony.

'Oooooiiiiiiiiiiiihhhhhhh. Boom! Da Da Da Daaaaaaa … '

When the room clerk asked you to sign in, he always asked politely: 'Car bomb side, or shell impact side?'

Room prices were adjusted to what rich American television was willing to pay – most major networks had hired entire floors. CBS had the seventh floor, one down from the bombs. We didn't have to schlep our cameras far to get to the roof in order to witness the awesome spectacle of the divebombers. The disadvantage was that during the many power cuts we had to climb seven flights of stairs, not to mention the nearness to the heavens, but we had convinced ourselves that the Israeli pilots wouldn't miss, that we were not on their target maps, and in that feeble hope we fell asleep. Actually, when the hotel was finally hit, it was by a shell from the Lebanese army's artillery, which smashed in the middle of the building and shortened the hotel by one floor. Evil tongues claimed it was not a stray round, but a consequence of the owner's falling behind with his 'risk tax'.

On the night of our arrival there was none of the high activity of the months to come. The major television networks hadn't as yet managed to get their regular hordes into position. The airport was closed, trucks were blocking the landing strip and the only way to join the fun would be by slow boat from Cyprus. That night the lobby was quiet. The few Beirut regulars silently nursed their drinks in the bar, shocked by the death of their French colleague. Even the pet goony-bird refrained from his imitation Beethoven. Fouad had told me that my usual room was ready. I found it as I had left it. Next to the double bed with the sagging mattress was the video with pirated versions of *Gone With The Wind* and *Deep Throat*. The curtain hadn't been fixed, but the fridge had been refilled with beer. I took a shower and went downstairs. Fouad rushed up to us, red in the face and excited: 'The Israelis are invading – they're already on the road to Beirut.'

The CBS fixer got us a car and our usual driver, and we headed into the night along the coastal highway to the south. We didn't get very far. Bombs had cratered the road, there was panic and confusion, people fleeing in our direction, and shadows with guns. By now it had dawned on the Palestinians that they were headed for a showdown with the main bulk of the Israeli Defence Force. Soon we collided with a mass of frightened and trigger-happy people. I didn't take it personally when a fifteen-year-old pointed a gun at my navel. I just tried a grin, to show that I was thoroughly impressed with his authority. When our car was stopped for the fifth time, I realized that it was senseless to continue on the main road. This was not the moment to violate Erik's law: never argue with a man with a gun!

'We must find another way,' I told the driver. 'Try and somehow get us through to Damour.' A good driver makes the difference between success and disaster. A good driver never ventures on to a road where the shops are shuttered during business hours. There is always a good reason for that, usually unpleasant. A good driver knows the back roads to the destination and, what is even more important, his way back.

'We will have to go through the Palestinian camps and over the mountains,' he said, and off we went. We had no alternative, the network was clamouring for pictures, and New York would never have understood why we had failed to deliver. My view is that cameramen don't die by driving across dangerous landscapes, but because somebody has decided to shoot them.

Once through Sabra camp, we found ourselves alone on the road, with no more gun-toting youngsters eager to stop us with a bullet. By early morning we had reached our destination. Damour was a quaint little town, perched on a hill overlooking a luscious coastal plain and the deep-blue Mediterranean. But, as well as its picturesque setting, Damour had an added attraction: it was a strategic strongpoint which controlled the main coastal road – in this particular case, the invasion route along which a regiment of Israeli tanks was at this moment thundering towards Beirut and the Palestinians.

The village was located on a south-facing cliff. Its northern approach, towards the airport of Beirut, was a gentle rise covered with white stucco houses. There were window-boxes, and clotheslines from house to house. Long ago the PLO military strategists had decided to make a stand in Damour. They had tunnelled into the rock and honeycombed the place with underground bunkers. They were ready, should an invasion occur. Now this situation was at hand.

The place had an eerie aura of impending death. The population had fled, abandoning the houses and making way for men in olive uniforms and checkered *keffiyeh*, some of the best fighters the PLO could muster. Jammed in the narrow streets were ammo trucks, machine guns, stalin-organs and even a truck with anti-aircraft missiles. It was an unhealthy place to camp down; the first Israeli strike was bound to come after these tempting targets.

Many years before, my father had shared a piece of great military wisdom with me. 'The best seats in a battle and in a cinema are at the back.' Strategic withdrawal was the only valour called for in this situation.

Situated half a mile to the north was a hill with a rocky plateau which was ideal for a camera platform. We installed our gear, plugged in the video machine and sat down with our lunch boxes to fortify ourselves while we still had time. The sun was gaining in strength, a breeze wafted across the sea, the hills were quiet. Under normal circumstances this would have been the ideal spot for a family Sunday picnic. The atmosphere of peace didn't last.

Our first indication of trouble came from high up – the single vapour-trail of a reconnaissance plane. Then all hell broke loose. It caught us completely by surprise.

'Up there,' I yelled, 'turn on the sound, he's coming in for a run.' The first jets dived on Damour, releasing anti-missile flares to test the defences. The first bombs shrieked earthwards on their glide to obliteration. A yellow flash turned a neat white house into a cloud of dirty grey dust. The Palestinians were replying with every gun in the place, an ear-numbing crescendo. Out to sea, Israeli gunboats joined in the bombardment, lobbing heavy shells at a rapid rate into the hapless town. Wave after interminable wave of jets swept in, annihilating the Palestinian positions under a carpet of explosives. Tracers rushed towards heaven, white puffs on a deep-blue sky.

'On your left,' I whipped the camera around. A pair of Syrian MiGs raced in low across the hills. One disintegrated like a starburst. A reflection in my eye, my camera was not on it. The other jet, enveloped in a ball of fire, disappeared over the hill.

Our full attention is focused on the inferno unfolding in front of us, a few hundred yards from our position. My eye is glued to the finder, capturing the terrifying spectacle which unfolds across from us in the doomed village. I do not notice the missile truck which has crept up near our position into a cluster of trees. Suddenly there is a blast followed by a roar, and a missile streaks skywards after an Israeli jet.

'Grab the recorder and run,' I scream. My one thought is to get away. Automatically I snatch the camera. Normally its weight slows me up, but right now I hardly feel it. I race across the rock-strewn slope, towards a small hollow in the ground, with only one thought – to get away from the missile truck. I can feel the Israeli is coming in for the kill. Run, run, run … stumble, hit the ground. Then I see it, the ugly snout of the air-intakes, a whistling of compressed air preceding the diving jet, the hungry eye of the jet's plastic bubble searching out its prey. I see it, my mind takes it in and there is nothing I can do. I imagine the pilot's thumb on the red button, pressing, and the load disconnecting.

Two black dots detach from its belly, falling, racing straight for us.

'Down, head down,' I scream. My fingers dig into hard baked earth, nails scraping dry ground. I focus my eyes on a pebble in front of my nose. It becomes my universe.

Whooosh! Whoosh! The bombs pass over me, there is a deafening shriek, and then – nothing. A moment of brightness and searing heat. No noise – the impact was too close. The sky goes black with flying rocks and dust and debris. I try to focus my eyes – everything is blurred, covered by a dirty grey mist. Next to me lies a ragged piece of iron, a metallic gleam. I reach for it, scream and drop it. It sears my skin, a red-hot bomb fragment. I can feel. I am alive. Where the cluster of trees had been there is now a large crater, deep red earth ripped open. Where we had been standing there is not a single blade of grass. The shrapnel has cut through it like a scythe, big clumps of red earth cover the ground. I notice that I am lying on my camera. My sound engineer comes out of the dirt cloud like a white ghost. Where is the car? Has the driver been hurt? No, that must be him, a figure running towards us, calling out, pointing. I see a small tear in his flak jacket, right over his breastbone; he indicates that he is all right. I can't hear a thing. I can see and I can point. He takes us to the car wedged against a mud wall. We drive home, very shaken, very quiet.

The impact of what had happened didn't hit me until we reached the hotel. I handed over the tapes and let someone else decide what to put on the air. This was no time for heroics, some events remain better untold. I went up to my room and quietly vomited into the toilet bowl. Then I pressed my forehead to the cool porcelain to clear my thoughts. Fear is a reaction which follows the lessening of danger. I am a prisoner of that cold fear.

The end of this story is relatively simple; the way to unwind was found for me by my little daughter. Early next morning she called from Paris and wailed down the line:

'The puddgy bit me in the finger.'

With a simple phrase, Operation Peace for Galilee was put into its right perspective. There is a tendency among those who have passed a tense moment to exaggerate the danger they have been in. For me, now was a time for reflection, perhaps it hadn't been as bad as it seemed at the time ...

A few hours later we stalked again from our hotel, wearing our flak vests, to cover yet another battle.

The next few months passed like a bad dream. After the Israelis bombed the city and the PLO left, there was the massacre in the refugee camps, and then came the arrival of the US peacekeeping marines. Until they too were blasted away. Sometimes I was there to cover the happenings, sometimes I was not. There was always a journalist or a cameraman in the firing line. Simply to walk around town became a game of chicken. Once, when we raced across the dead man's zone between the Muslim and Christian sectors, a vicious killing ground known as the museum crossing, we were caught in crossfire. I switched on the camera, kept my head low, and dashed into the shelter of a house. There my soundman and I were confronted by two ashen-faced, praying women. 'By all the holy saints, what were you doing out there?'

'Taking pictures.'

They stared at us in disbelief, then crossed themselves. To them we must have appeared madmen.

Journalists and camera-teams became targets. A Canadian correspondent was shot. Then a television crew was killed. Still reporters went out every morning. Until the day the first hostages were taken. That changed everything. We faced the threat of having to spend the next few years with paper bags over our heads, chained to radiators as guests of some fanatical faction, whose demands would invariably begin with the words:

'In the Name of the One ... '

The corridors of the Commodore buzzed with the latest black joke: 'Do you know what a Lebanese flak jacket looks like? A paper bag!'

In covering the news, we were now faced with a question of morality. By reporting the kidnappers' demands, the media was actually providing a platform for terrorism. Worse yet, the various print and television organizations began to compete for scoop values, which sometimes directly endangered the lives of the hostages. So-called press conferences, with gun-wielding terrorists hiding their faces behind cut-out shopping bags, were orchestrated immorality, and we were ordered, not asked, to cover them. Those gangsters pontificated in a roomful of serious reporters. During each new hijack the number of television crews increased, until the regiments of cameras and directional microphones looked like the spears of a Roman phalanx.

Terrorism is a new kind of war, and the media could provide a powerful weapon if the various publications presented a united front: strict censorship, no self-defeating scoop competition. If twenty of the major newspapers and television networks adhered to such self-restraint, and accepted one single pool crew to provide a bare minimum of coverage of acts of terrorism, rather than having print and video hordes scrambling over each other to get *the* story, or image, then that in itself would deprive the criminals of a platform in hundreds of millions of homes around the world. And if the message released by the media is totally negative, it will soon starve the hostage-takers of that vital tool: global recognition for their 'cause'.

By the same token, however, governments must not be permitted to censor the reporting of acts of terrorism. Hostage-taking does not pass unobserved. It is much better to report the story in its criminal context than to let rumours spread. We must report the news as best we can. We must never play into the terrorists' hands by competing with each other, because then the criminals will use us. We must show the real image of terrorists and provide them with enough rope to hang themselves. That, and only that, is our duty.

The remaining months were plain nasty. Safety could no longer be guaranteed. When a French television team was kidnapped, the networks finally packed it in. I made plans to get out. A boat to Cyprus, a plane to Paris. The call from New York woke me about three minutes into a comatose sleep. 'Erik, how are you?'

'Who's that ... ?' It had been a tiresome twenty-four hours, my brain wasn't plugged in.

'I want you to go to Baghdad.' The voice sounded familiar, and the demand got into focus.

'What about going home for a while?'

'Next week, okay? Right now, we want you in Iraq. We've heard the Iranians are planning an attack.'

Fucking marvellous!

The prediction was wrong, nothing much happened and the major offensive failed to materialize. I was delighted.

They had brought us to the front line, and it was a remake of *All Quiet on the Western Front*.

When we piled out of the car, our guides had a surprise in store for us. 'You are not allowed to take pictures. This is a military restricted area.'

'But we are television. The general said we could … '

'Our instructions are that you cannot.'

It was like a conversation between two deaf people. For all our pleading and threatening, nothing worked until Christophe, in a flash of intuition, said: 'As long as we are not connected by cable we cannot do anything. Erik has the camera, but I have the tape. At least let us carry the gear.'

That face-saver was finally accepted. However, a major wedged himself in between Christophe and myself just to make sure that our cable remained disconnected. We walked along a trenchline, a permanent fixture of solid concrete, with traces of blood on its white walls, towards a point on a ridge, overlooking the Iranian town of Khorramshahr.

Right in front of us, a mere eighty metres across a ditch, was the Iranian line. A small bird landed on a sandbag near me. The war didn't concern it.

The stench of death permeated the hot air. I peered through the slit in a bunker and saw several dead Iranians hanging in the barbed wire, their corpses roasting in the heat only twenty metres from us. Nobody was willing to go out and remove them, it would have meant an instant bullet.

Our colleagues from Jordan and Kuwait wanted their pictures taken. Behind the protective sandbags they struck heroic poses with rifles and helmets. Excited by the presence of the 'world's press', a soldier raised his rifle and fired over the parapet. A shot came back. Another soldier picked up a rifle and fired a short burst. A burst of fire came back. The heroic journalists dived for cover, and our obstructive major headed for a foxhole. Christophe hooked his recorder into my camera, and we managed to get some pictures.

By now it had turned into a free-for-all: mortars, artillery and small-arms were firing more and more bullets, bombs and shells at each other.

'*Yalla, Yalla*' (which means 'let's get the hell out of here'), yelled our gallant major and we scrambled for the vehicles. There was a slight delay because our colleague from Kuwait had lost his shoe. A few shells came mighty close. My colleague from TASS took great umbrage at the shoe-delay: 'Get in here, you stupid son of a bitch, you get us all killed.' Even in Russian-accented English, the message got across.

After three frustrating weeks, we were ordered home. Without argument we obeyed the command and took the freedom bird to Paris. I was looking forward to embracing my menagerie.

6
THE CONFESSION

---

2 April 1793. The public prosecutor Fouquier-Tinville:
'Parle lui un langage qu'il puisse entendre ... address the jury in a language it understands.'

Danton, accused of treason:
'A man accused as I am does not address himself to a jury, he answers before it!'

It had been an extremely slow month newswise. We had parked our
sun-starved bodies along the poolside of a hotel in Lome – a noted
capital somewhere in Africa – drinking lemon juice, spending the
company's money, waiting for the rain to start. Since this was the
middle of the dry season, we expected a long wait. My wife phoned.
'We have new birds, you know, the little ones have hatched a batch,
and are they ever noisy!'

'That's great.'

'Yes, and I'll be going to London next week, Maggie got us tickets
for a new musical.'

'That's great.' She had still not asked after my welfare.

'Christina has been invited for a ski weekend, is it all right if she
accepts?' I am sure that the decision has already been taken, courtesy
alone demands my okay. I give it. 'Oh, yes, before I forget, the
Afghans called. You've got a visa.'

'I've got a what?' I screamed down the line. For the past three
years, every hack from Fleet Street to Times Square had been trying
for a glimpse behind the closed curtain put up by the Soviets. 'Why
me?'

'They didn't say, they only said you were expected.'

'Please call them. Say I'm on tonight's flight to Paris.'

I couldn't believe it, the network in New York couldn't believe it, but I had the OK stamp in my passport.

On arrival in Kabul, I was expected, greeted courteously, and installed in the Intercontinental Hotel. I was given a choice of 136 rooms: the hotel was completely empty. For the next three weeks I was driven around the city, looking at this and interviewing that. I was given the tour of the Red Flag Djangalak machine shop, and had to listen to a gruelling four-hour speech by comrade Babrak Karmal. I was invited to a women's congress, featuring delegations from Romania and East Germany. There I was fed sweet tea and cookies. I was even allowed inside an Afghan army base to inspect the valiant troops, poorly motivated recruits marching through ankle-deep slush. I still hadn't figured out why I had been chosen.

How much impact does television have? More specifically, can governments use television to manipulate international opinion? They draw attention to their cause on the assumption that the audience's reaction will be favourable, that the viewing millions will say: 'It was a fair judgement.' But this logic has its limitations, as the Afghans were about to discover. It was to be a show trial, where the accused publicly denounced himself for acts he had not committed. The proceedings were such an obvious replay of Stalinist show trials that the ploy backfired. For reasons best known to themselves, I was picked as the international observer.

The scene was unreal, a gruesome pageant staged for effect. The accused, wearing a scuffed green anorak, zipped up to protect his frail body from the cold in the hall, sat under the stale glare of electric lamps. The judges, in pin-striped suits with grey waistcoats, hovered high above the prisoner on the stage of a gloomy cinema, hidden by a table covered with black cloth, which left only their faces visible, severed heads on a mortuary slab – dispassionate masks against a black background. The indictment was comprehensive. The accused was charged with four major crimes: illegal entry into Afghanistan, contact with the counter-revolution, providing help to the counter-revolutionaries and, finally, photographing strategic military installations. If convicted – a foregone conclusion – the penalty was death. By rope or by firing squad, that was up to the judges to decide.

It is difficult to describe a man forced to bow and to beg. Such pictures are always painful to look at, those of a man who has learned a line by heart, a succinct phrase of public denial which might save him from the executioner's axe. They had prepared him well. He was ready to confess to any crime. With the exception of the prisoner, my sound man and I were the only Westerners in the room. We had been brought there by direct order of the revolutionary council of the People's Democratic Republic of Afghanistan. Not even a representative of the French government had been admitted to the trial, although the accused was a French national. By the presence of my camera, the Afghans intended to prove to the world that they conducted a fair trial. Prison pale, moist blue eyes, a straggly red beard, hands trembling, the slight figure sat in the box. He looked what he really was: a frightened, innocent young doctor, caught in something which was too big for him, and who had been forced to interpret a role in a drama which was way beyond his capacity to comprehend.

At 10.15 a.m. the trial got under way.

'Your name?'

'Philippe Augoyard.'

'Your profession?'

'Doctor, at a children's hospital in France.'

'Are you a member of any political party?'

'No.'

Once the formalities had been complied with, the three judges turned to each other and ignored the defendant. Augoyard had shrivelled into his corner, sandwiched between two husky armed guards with Kalashnikov assault rifles. His story was simple. The Soviets had gone after bigger game, a notorious leader of the rebel movement. Instead, they had stumbled on a young French paediatrician. He was a chance substitute and not the man intended to go on trial. Nevertheless, he would be crucified as a warning to other foreigners. He had come to Afghanistan to care for the sick and wounded – and perhaps for a touch of adventure in the far-off hills. One thing was certain, he was a naïve young man, without any idea of the consequences his actions could carry. In Paris, he had joined a group called AMI, Aide Medicale Internationale, which dispatched young doctors, and medicine to the mujahedin, who were fighting Soviet forces in the rugged mountains and trackless deserts of

Afghanistan. From Pakistan he had crossed the hills into Logar province, where he joined up with the rebels.

They were an unruly bunch, sharing no political vision for their country other than killing their occupiers, the Russians. Their hide-out was betrayed and the Soviets captured the French doctor. They handed him to the Afghan authorities, along with a demand that he be put on public trial. His captors had found a camera on him to provide final proof of his espionage activities. Other than wild goats and bombed villages, there was nothing of strategic value to photograph in the mountains. Kabul intended to make the trial work to their benefit, to show that allegations of Soviet troops unloading poison gas on hapless villagers were completely unfounded. As a medical expert, he was to provide proof that this was a 'vicious lie spread in the Western media by the enemies of the Saur (Afghan) revolution'. Augoyard knew his life depended on what he said to this court and to the world via my video camera. I had finally found out why I was allowed into the country.

The prosecutor read the accusation, which was translated for Augoyard by his court-appointed lawyer, and to me by my interpreter. The state prosecutor demanded the death penalty.

'What do you have to state in your defence?' asked the judge.

Shaking uncontrollably, Augoyard stood up, took a sheaf of papers and started to read his prepared defence in a robot-like monotone: 'I have taken note of the act of accusation, and I have nothing to add to the accusation brought against me. I admit having entered the country illegally and that I have collaborated with the counter-revolutionaries. But now I realize the grave error which I have committed, and I repent of my actions. Before I left for Afghanistan I fell under the influence of imperialistic propaganda in favour of the counter-revolutionaries. During my stay with them, I became aware that they were committing incredible atrocities of banditry and terrorism.' He added that the mujahedin forced the local population to join their ranks against their will. He put down his paper, folded his hands across his chest to keep them from trembling, and ended his plea: 'I have completely changed my opinion about the actions of the Democratic Republic of Afghanistan and those of the counter-revolutionaries. I ask the tribunal for clemency.'

With that, he made as if to sit down, but the icy stares of the three judges forced him into an unrehearsed addition to his confession: 'If I am permitted to return to France, I promise to tell everyone about the real conditions in this country. I promise never again to act against the law of this democratic republic.' This still did not seem to satisfy the presiding judge, so the little doctor continued: 'Please believe me!' Exhausted, he was allowed to sit down, and the interrogation began.

His audience was a hall filled with tribal chieftains, brought in specially for the occasion. It was a colourful collection of cutthroats, whose loyalty could be hired by the month, on a pro rata fee per rifle pledged. Most had a foot in both camps. A few government officials and two Soviet observers made up the rest. There was none of the bustle so typical of our court proceedings, no outburst in favour of the defendant or the prosecution. The room was cosmically silent, a cold and hostile atmosphere. It was trial by terror.

The judge wanted to know if the medical aid association was connected to a foreign power.

'Yes, it is highly possible that persons working with it will furnish information to foreign countries and perhaps even to the CIA.' This, and his admission that he had never treated, nor ever seen, any local people injured by chemical weapons, saved his life. 'Before I went there I was told that chemical weapons had been used in September '82. I was in the Logar in October '82. I didn't see any proof of any such use of chemical weapons, and people told me it was wrong. So this is completely wrong information, this is completely wrong information,' he kept muttering, 'used for propaganda against the Afghan government.'

The judges retired for three minutes, then came back with the verdict. It took five minutes to read it. The judgement was pronounced in Pashto by the chief revolutionary judge. His monotonous voice showed a total absence of compassion. Augoyard stood frozen in his box, his face drawn and twitching. He didn't understand a word of what they had decided. Was it to be life – or death? Finally, his lawyer bent over and whispered: 'Eight years. Eight years prison.' There was monumental relief in the young Frenchman's eyes.

'I thank the tribunal for its clemency!' were his final words, before he was led away. Thus ended the trial of a dreamer, whose only crime was that he had combined his duties as a medical man with the search for a little adventure. For that, and his two minutes of self criticism, they nailed him to the cross.

A few days afterwards, during an interview with the Afghan Prime Minister, Kestmand, I asked him about the fate of his prisoner. He hinted that if an organization 'friendly to our government were to forward a request' Augoyard's case could be reviewed. As soon as I returned to France, I contacted the French Communist Party. Their First Secretary forwarded a message. One month thereafter, Augoyard was freed. Although he mentions me in his book, I have never heard from him again.

This episode made me the centre of a polemic about the moral aspects of reporting. I was variously described as 'independent observer', 'progressive fellow traveller' and 'voyeur in search of sensation'. Everyone agreed that my journalistic assignment had yielded gripping pictures, and that I had provided information about a black comedy in which a world-wide public showed immense interest. Newspapers and television shows spent almost as much time on the 'moral stand' of my coverage, as on the trial itself. I was hammered with such questions as whether I was allowed into the forbidden country by making a deal with the government and why I had turned into a 'willing mouthpiece' for a communist masquerade? This was in reference to a television interview during which I repeated a warning given to me by the Afghan Prime Minister. 'The next one we catch,' he had told me, 'we'll keep.'

The interviewer who had put me in the hot seat kept pounding away: 'And you believe him?'

'That's what he told me, and it makes sense. At least from their perspective. Augoyard is supposed to be a warning to others not to try it again.'

'Are you taking the line of the Afghans?'

'Repeating a warning does not necessarily imply that I agree with their political ideas.'

'What can a doctor possibly have to tell?'

'A lot. These French doctors are the only independent observers to have come out of the Afghan mountains. They are highly qualified to specify how the mujahedin were wounded, by poison or by bullet, how villages were bombed, and how much resistance there is.'

'So, you admit the communist rulers in Afghanistan have things to hide?'

'I wouldn't know, I wasn't in the mountains.'

'But they did give you a free run of Kabul.'

'Free run? I don't know what you mean by that. Yes, I was allowed to drive through the city, before curfew hours, in a government-supplied car, with a government-supplied interpreter ... '

'Why you?'

'They gave me a visa.'

'What does it feel like to film a man accused of crimes he didn't commit?'

'Are you trying to ask me why I did my job?'

'All right, why did you?'

'In your opinion, should I have walked away?'

This was no longer a question-and-answer forum. It had become trial by television, conducted by an investigator whose trademark was aggressiveness. In his defence I must admit that I had known this before I walked into the studio. 'Haven't you done that before?' he asked.

'Yes, but the circumstances were quite different.'

'Like what?'

'Like, my presence might have caused a riot to start, or I felt that my camera wouldn't add anything positive.'

'What is so positive about the Augoyard show trial?'

'It was a show trial. I believe that the audience recognized it as such.' In my years behind a camera, I had observed that the easiest way out of a grilling is to repeat the questions and turn them around. He changed tack.

'This is not the sort of thing you usually cover. You are better known for your war films. What are you going to do when you run out of wars?'

'Do you think there is a chance of that?'

'Well, thank you for having been with us ... ' We left it at that, and the programme's announcer came to the rescue: 'Next week, ladies and gentlemen, we'll have in our studios ... '

However one looks at it, the Augoyard trial was a farce. Personally, I did not enjoy watching someone being degraded. I am also not denying the obvious political motive behind permitting my coverage. I knew from the very beginning that I was in Kabul to serve a purpose. Until the trial came up, I didn't realize what this purpose was to be. Suppressing the news does not provide a solution. Ultimately, my coverage of the Augoyard trial was a self-defeating platform for Afghan propaganda, since nobody in the West believed in the truth of the accusation or in the fairness of the judgement. Or, as a leading newspaper editorial, under the title: 'Horror movie from Afghanistan,' put it: 'The judgement of Kabul has been passed. We must ask ourselves why the Afghan authorities were silly enough to let such a filmed document out of the country. The pictures make it clear that Augoyard never lost his dignity. It will take a long time for the justice of Kabul to recover hers.'

Afghanistan is a wild and beautiful country. Its people are made up of the tribes which once formed Genghis Khan's hordes. They are fierce warriors, forced to live in a hostile environment. Their laws are brutal. Being tribal, they always fight, mostly with each other, unless – unless there is an intruder. They will not be subdued. The world has never fully understood this. It is best to leave them alone, as the British found out when their army was annihilated. From an expeditionary force of 10,000, there was but one survivor. To a shocked England, Rudyard Kipling sent a message:

> *When you're wounded and left on Afghanistan's plains,*
> *And the women come out to cut up what remains,*
> *Just roll to your rifle and blow out your brains*
> *And go to your God like a soldier.*

7

DEATH IN THE MARSHES

(IRAQ, 1984)

At 10 p.m. GMT on 25 February 1984, a human tidal wave crossed the Howeiza marshes in southern Iraq and rolled up to the front line defences of the Iraqi army. The opening shot was fired of one of the most senseless slaughters since World War One.

The week got off to a lousy start. My daughter received bad marks in philosophy, my wife had the 'flu, and I got a visa for Iraq.

'We want you to go right away,' were the instructions from the network. I called Christophe, my sound engineer. 'Please come and pack the cases, we're off.'

'Where to this time?'

'Baghdad.'

'Oh no.' His suffering voice gave me the impression that he wasn't overly fond of the capital of Iraq, the city which had given birth to such tales of oriental wonders as *A Thousand and One Nights*. 'Why are we going there?' He had a point.

'Because we have a visa and New York wants us there.'

He packed the cases, not forgetting the *choucroute* and the *cassoulet* and a few cans of *pâté du foie de volaille*, because he knew Baghdad and its culinary delights. Better be prepared, it might be a long trip. I added a jar of instant coffee, since, contrary to what one may have heard about Arabian coffee or Mocha, this brand name has to be an invention by Italian expresso-machine makers. Coffee in Iraq ranges from bad to undrinkable. We moved our luggage to the airport, a caravan of orange cases. With our hefty excess baggage, we are a delight to airline companies. Airlines are a chapter in our lives in themselves: some are nice, some are not so nice, and some are outright awful. Whenever their planes are empty they will promise trips to Hawaii for two, with beach bungalow and free pineapples, but when their fortunes move into the black, it's a seat in the back of the bus.

The problem of lost luggage is an eternal nightmare. Our equipment is arranged in such a way that the contents of our boxes interlock. If we miss just one case, we cannot operate. Several days after the flight, while parked in a hotel in Manila or Moscow, the airline will advise us that they have located the missing piece in Rio. Once we recover our fifteen pieces, we face endless customs formalities, stamp in, stamp out, 'are all the numbers on your list correct?' How can we make our TV audience understand that it was because of a customs paper that they couldn't witness the bombing of Tripoli? This time we found ourselves at Charles de Gaulle Airport, boxes and all. Air France managed to put Christophe in the back of the plane and me halfway up the middle, to make certain that we couldn't talk to one another. They were probably right. I was asked to stop reading and turn off the light, since this would interfere with other passengers wanting to watch the movie. At least the plane was not shot down by an Iranian missile or hijacked by Islamic freedom fighters.

In the dim and distant past, Baghdad may have held the mystery of the Orient, of spices, veiled beauties in transparent gowns and flower-scented sherberts. Since those times it has evolved, not always to its advantage. Today it is just one more dusty, hot place. The quaint old caravanserais have been turned into high-rise concrete slabs called hotels: they accept credit cards, the telephone is on the right and the light switches on the left, the telex machine is located on the ground floor in a glass cubicle called 'business centre' and the key-rings are so heavy and so ugly that nobody will attempt to steal them. The hotel's transient population are no longer mysterious Arab princes and their vast retinues, but arms salesmen from Yugoslavia and France, or oil buyers for a Japanese firm. There is no poetry in their daily conversations and telexes. The glamour that was Arabia is strictly for the story books. Our hotel in Baghdad was clinical and had a nice view across a mostly dry and hot riverbed, the Tigris. Sometimes it carried water, especially when it rained, which wasn't very often. Along the riverbank was a mudflat where the rose of Baghdad must have blossomed. Now it was covered with plastic bags and old tyres. Across the river, as a reminder that all was not well, was a quadruple machine gun which protected the presidential palace from aerial intruders. And to prevent swimmers from diving into the muddy floods, they had erected a ten-foot link fence, topped by barbed wire, which gave the river front the look of a concentration camp.

During the summer months the air superheated, creating a turbulence. Hot sandstorms would blow in from the desert, covering everything with an inch of fine white sand. This hurt the eyes.

The traditional Arab *soukh* offered a mix of medieval market goods and modern Formica. The rugs were not cheap, but were of good quality. The spice merchants displayed their wares in all the colours of the rainbow. The fabrics were garish and cheap, and made in Korea. In the midst of this bazaar was a wonderful coffee-house, which didn't serve coffee but sweet tea and a hookah. The bubbling noise of this waterpipe was quite soothing. Old men sat there, and waited until sundown, when the muezzin called the faithful to prayers.

The food was strictly shish kebab, followed by shish kebab, and Pepsi. Sometimes the chef added a few tomatoes to improve the taste. Dining in the big hotels was prohibitively expensive, but it was the only way to get alcoholic drinks.

It was to this pearl of the Orient, now in its sixth year of war against the arch-enemy Iran, that we were expedited. We got our room, with balcony, on the fifteenth floor. The nail which I had driven into the wall to spear incoming telexes on my previous visit was still there. So was the blue wallpaper. And the print of a fat woman by Renoir. All very familiar, almost a home from home. But so was the war – familiar, I mean. Six long years of it, and the world was getting tired of hearing about the Gulf War.

'Welcome, Mr Durschmied, why have you come?' This was the hotel staff's main worry, like: here comes bad news. We always arrive just before trouble starts.

Actually, this time I had been phoned by the Iraqi embassy in

Paris, who wanted to know why I was no longer covering the war. The press attaché had received instructions from Baghdad to drum up some interest in the conflict. Iraq was on a peace offensive and needed publicity.

'Do you have anything new to offer?' I asked. 'Can we interview the pilots who are bombing the oil installations at Kharg? Can we have a look at the air force? Will you take us to the front line?'

'I am sure that this can be arranged to your complete satisfaction by our authorities in Baghdad.' With that promise, lots of cash from our office and a call from New York, we went to Iraq.

Upon arrival I made phone calls to my usual 'independent observers', military attachés at the various embassies, salesmen for armanents companies and the chambermaid, whose niece was having an affair with a supply sergeant, and could tell me which way the cigarettes went. Then Christophe and I paid our respects to the director general at the Ministry of Information.

'Mr Erik, we are very pleased to have you back,' he said in welcome.

'Can we go to the front?'

'There is very little to see: all is perfectly calm and we have everything under control. Should the enemy attack, we will defeat him, as we have done so many times in the past.'

'Can we visit an air base?'

'I am afraid this falls under military secrets – however I will ask the military authorities.' Which, translated into plain English, meant that nothing would be done about it. We were assigned our guide. He visited us at the swimming pool of the hotel to tell us there was nothing arranged, had lunch and left.

Mr Hamza, our guide, was not tall, but what he lacked in height he made up in width. He preferred to wear baggy corduroy trousers which made him look even wider than he already was. He had oily black hair and a Hitler moustache. He was nice, but totally ineffective. He spoke passable French.

'*C'est très bien*, that is very nice,' was his standard reply.

'Have you heard that oil has dropped below the price of extraction?'

'*C'est très bien*,' and I couldn't help feeling that he didn't grasp the significance of oil exports, or that their whole war effort was based on the exchange rate of oil for guns.

'We want to go to the front.'

'*C'est très bien.*'
'We are bored.'
'*C'est très bien.*'

Every morning we made a pilgrimage to the ministry. We were
received by various officials defended by stacks of paper, mostly
correspondence from other journalists requesting visas. They smiled,
offered us tea and invariably said: 'Welcome, Mr Erik, no, nothing
today. How would you like to visit Babylon?'

I love excavations, but that was hardly what I had come for. Ruins
weren't on my most wanted list. I wanted to see the troops and the air
force. The war had ground into a stalemate, and I did not feel that I
would give away a strategic secret by reporting that the war was going
nowhere.

'Welcome, Mr Erik. What do your American satellites say today,
where is our enemy? Are they going to attack?'

'I was actually hoping that you might be able to tell me.'

'All is well, Mr Erik. We have a football game between the Danish
national team, and the World Cup squad from Iraq. We have reserved
two tickets for you and Mr Christophe.'

'Can we tape it?'

'No, I am afraid that isn't possible.' No further explanation was
offered as to why the football game was a national secret.

We went, we saw and we were bored by an uninteresting game of
soccer. My telex headline to New York read: DENMARK TWO, IRAQ ONE,
ERIK ZERO.

Ten days later my visa ran out. I had a gut feeling that something was
about to happen. Old reporters can smell a storm brewing. The daily
war communiqué had announced a rapid increase in air activity. I had
nothing definite to go on, just a premonition that the shores of the
Gulf were about to explode again. I called the foreign desk in New
York: 'I want to stay on, something is up.'

'What?' was the dry reply, and : 'How much will it cost us?'

'To the first I have no answer, and to the second: plenty.'

'All right, stay another four days.' I renewed my visa. Then, in a
change of mind, New York recalled me. I was booked out for next
morning.

That night, the Iranians struck across the water dividing the two countries. The silent war of the trenches erupted into full-scale bloodshed.

For millennia the mighty Tigris and Euphrates, twin sisters of Mesopotamia, had washed half a continent into the Gulf. The fertile earth of Turkey and Kurdistan was transported by the red waters towards the delta. There was too much water and too much earth. The outlets became blocked, the water backed up, and a vast marsh area was formed. These swamps were colonized by the Marsh Arabs. They traced their ancestry to biblical Babylon: when hordes of looting marauders invaded the fertile lowlands, the families escaped into the safety of the marshes. They built islets just large enough to house one or two huts, built of mud and reeds. The only means of transport was by boats made of reed. Their life centred around harvesting reed and catching fish both of which were provided in abundance by the rich waters of the Tigris. Wars and history had passed them by – they lived undisturbed, a gentle, carefree people.

In 1980 this changed. The day that Iraq moved its armies across the Shatt-al-Arab into Iran, their peace was shattered. The marshes were no longer a refuge, but were turned into one of the principal battle-fields in a bloody conflict.

I had visited Al-Beida before, taken there by an Iraqi colonel to inspect the invulnerability of their forward defences, which were indeed formidable. The village itself was a cluster of thirty mud huts with one central concrete building, which housed the village's most precious possession: a television set. Women did their washing in front of their doors, men floated their livestock from isle to isle to let them munch on the fresh green shoots. The economy of the village was provided by an abundance of reed, so thick that it hid the hamlet from view. But it also made them vulnerable to an attack, as any size of enemy force could approach undetected. The village itself was lightly defended by a company-size force and one multi-barrelled machine gun on top of the concrete building. The artillery batteries and the tank reserves were held in position some five kilometres to the rear.

'How far is the enemy?'

'About ten kilometres. Close enough for artillery.'

'Do they ever shell the village?'

'Once in a while, but they only hit the water.'

Killing fish with thousand-dollar shells was getting expensive, so the Iranians had packed it in. Women were washing, cows were munching, and all was quiet on the southern front.

Towards the end of 1983 and on into 1984, mullahs had been scouring the schools of Iran for volunteers. The boys were inducted into the Kerbala Wayfarers Volunteer Brigades, and told that they would have the singular honour of carrying the flag of Islam into the heartland of their mortal enemy. They received more religious indoctrination than military training. They were told that their ultimate sacrifice would lead on to eternal glory. Each was then given one weapon, such as a limpet mine, a grenade or a recoilless rocket. The children under thirteen never had a chance. The teenagers, fourteen to sixteen, received a Kalashnikov assault rifle made in North Korea. Each was handed his personal key to the kingdom, made of plastic, which they wore on a string around their necks.

On the evening of 25 February, this fanatical horde boarded a collection of assault boats and pleasure crafts, and the flotilla set out across the shallow waters of the swamps. Altogether they represented two divisions, close to twenty-five thousand armed children. They were led by a sprinkling of regular army and by mullahs.

The first wave washed over the small Iraqi army unit holding the village of Al-Beida, and massacred the native population. Only one soldier got away but he was able to set off the alarm. By daybreak, the Iraqi heavy armour had established a *cordon sanitaire* around the invasion force. The Iranians were faced with only two choices, drown in the swamps, or surrender. They did neither. They dug in, and fought. The first military communiqué about the battle came from Radio Tehran. I listened to it on my shortwave radio.

'In the Name of God, the Merciful, the Compassionate.

'Please pay attention to a news which has just reached us from the Islamic Revolutionary Guard Corps joint operational headquarters:

'The brave combatants and the heroic men of the liberating Islamic army and the self-sacrificing Kerbala Wayfarers, following their complete surrounding of the strategic island of Al-Beida and in a battle against the dying, helpless enemy, are now in complete control of this important island. The vital road leading to the island has been captured by the brave self-sacrificers of the Islamic army. In the Name of God ... '

Within a few hours, a similar communiqué was issued by the Iraqi high command:

'Here is the latest communiqué issued by the Armed Forces General Command:

'Early this morning, our triumphant forces continued to pursue the wretched remnants which the Khomeiniites used in their new aggression against our country. As a result of our armed forces' precaution against any eventuality and as a result of the crushing blows and prompt reaction by our armed forces, whether in defending their positions or in massing the necessary forces to pounce on the enemy, your brave sons, O glorious Iraq, managed to achieve the following:

'After the enemy thrust was completely halted in the heroic VI Army Corps (East of Tigris) operational sector and after the enemy had sustained thousands of dead or wounded and many others captured, our men repulsed and destroyed all successive human wave assaults.

'With the help of Allah, and the efforts of the zealous, the impact of the enemy offensive was absorbed completely so that the counter-offensive forces could pounce on it and pound it with the shells of our artillery and armour and the bullets of our heroic infantry forces. The enemy's end would be miserable, Allah willing.

'O proud Iraqis, wait for the glad tidings of a final and decisive victory which will break the backs of the enemy and reduce them to the lowest level. Blessed be the men of our gigantic air force, the men of VI Army Corps, and the knights of the helicopter gunships.

'We thank Allah for supporting us against the unjust clique of warmongers.'

That announcement was followed by hours of heroic songs from the army's glee club. Contrary to the early victory bulletin, the Iranians held out for another forty-eight hours. Then they were dead. Their souls had all entered the special enclave in the sky reserved for martyrs.

The first day after the battle had started we spent in great frustration locked up in our hotels. We were handed official bulletins, checked with our own 'independent sources', like the telephone girls coming to work from the gossip mill in Baghdad. Every half-hour we received a telex from the foreign editor, mostly worded like: 'PLS ONPASS MESSAGE TO DURSCHMIED OF CBS NEWS IN ROOM 1536. 26114 DURSCHMIED WHAT IS OUTLOOK FOR COMBAT PIX? CAN YOU GET NEAR BASRA? CALL URGENT.'

Yes, we could get to Basra whenever the military were willing to take us there. As to calling the office, this was not downtown Manhattan where an understanding operator and twenty-five cents will connect you to any place in the world, except Baghdad. This was an emergency in a press-censored country, where everything from an eye operation in a hospital, to a street scene in the local soukh was considered a military secret. The telephones did work, but the wait was three hours, and then the line would be cut after six minutes.

Baghdad was quiet and sunny. My telephone rang.

'Mr Durschmied, here is the Ministry of Information. The minister wishes to give a statement to the press. A car will be at your hotel in a few minutes.'

The press corps, that meant myself, Christophe, two French stills photographers, some reporters from the local newspapers, and the correspondent from TASS.

We wore running shoes and Lacoste shirts, the locals arrived in dark blue worsted and highly polished pumps. They had experience of what to wear at a ministerial reception in wartime Baghdad. We were uncouth foreigners. The minister arrived in battledress.

'*Marhaba*, gentlemen,' the minister addressed our hastily assembled gathering, 'our glorious forces have defeated the cowardly aggression. We will show you the proof.' And with that, we were whisked on to a bus. The vehicle had curtains over the windows and I wondered where we would end up. It stopped in front of a very large Russian-made helicopter, best compared to a flying supertanker.

'Please gentlemen, get on, we will take you to the front.'

I always knew that running shoes can have a decided advantage. The helicopter was covered in fine dust, and our esteemed *confrères* covered their blue serge behinds with white imprints. The engine coughed, the blades turned, we lumbered off. The centre of the ship was taken up by a big tank filled to the brim with kerosene. A sign, in Russian and English, announced: *Danger – Inflammable*. That warning did not faze our colleagues from having a last smoke. I could see it, one hit and we would turn into a towering inferno. Christophe gave me a piece of Kleenex to stuff into my ears, which brought down the infernal racket by several decibels. We landed at an airfield near the front line, and were greeted by a colonel. Night started to fall as a bus took us to corps headquarters. Along our route we could see the powder flashes of heavy artillery pounding away at the encircled invaders.

Our final destination was the corps HQ at the village of Al-Azair, where the commanding general of the southern front received us. First he gave us a situation report. The offensive had been halted (true), all the aggressors had been wiped out and there was no more fighting (untrue).

'General, what sort of an attack was it?'

'It was senseless. They came in waves and we killed them. Those Iranians treat their people like a herd of cattle they lead to a slaughter. When I gave the order to counterattack, it was like giving a command for a mass execution. Come, I'll show you what we've captured.'

His office opened into a dark, underground hallway. Huddled there was a truly pathetic sight: about a hundred frightened little kids.

'Look at this one,' said our colonel, with which he grabbed the child's hair and lifted his head, 'eleven, twelve at the most.' The child had round, terrified eyes, his rumpled uniform splattered with blood, too large for his puny body. 'When we found him he was hiding under two dead bodies.'

The rest of the prisoners were not much older, except two men in their late sixties.

'Who started this war?' I asked one of them. He only shook his head. A translator stepped in.

The old man mumbled words in Farsi, then looked at the ceiling. 'He says the war comes from Allah.'

Will it never end? How long have people been killing each other for the sake of some Allah or God? Religious zealots, fanatics, crazies. This old man wasn't one of them, he had been told what to say. He sagged back into his shell, a forlorn look in his eyes, realizing that he might have lost it all, his family, his home, his farm – but at least he was alive. The little kids, the brainwashed fanatics, had just lost it. In their twisted minds they felt that they had betrayed their loyalty to their Allah, their mullahs, and their motherland. They had not died like heroes. Shame would come on them, and their families.

'Do you believe me now?' asked the general. I could only nod.

'Would you like to report what you have just witnessed?'

'Yes sir, but how?'

'Let me help you.' With that he gave instructions to his ADC, and we returned to his office for sweet tea. The thunder of heavy artillery continued unabated, the windows shook, some cracked, and glass trickled to the floor.

The colonel returned and waved to me. 'Would you please follow me, all is set for your communication.' He brought me to a tent where it was hard for me to hear my own words, let alone those of the colonel. The roar of the 155mm gun batteries was deafening. He pointed to a field telephone. 'Over there,' he mouthed. I picked it up and had New York on the line.

'Can you hear me?' I screamed down the line.

'Who is this?' a girl's voice.

'This is Erik, I'm calling from the Iraqi front-line.'

'Who did you say you are?'

'Erik!'

'Erik? From where?'

'From Iraq!'

'Who do you want to talk to?'

'Anybody at this point, just tell them to put some tape in the machines and start recording.'

'I'm sorry, I cannot understand you, there is too much noise in the office.'

'Please, get Peter, get anybody, just get them.'

'Peter is at an important meeting, he told me not to disturb him. Can you hold?'

'Lady, I'm sitting in a front trench, there are guns going off, I am the only Western reporter, this is a military line, and I have an exclusive war report.'

'Who else do you want? Peter cannot be disturbed. Just a moment, please,' with which she put down the phone. Such are the joys of modern reporting. An exclusive held up because of total incompetence.

A familiar voice came on the line, with something like, 'Stupid bitch, she's new – all right, we got it under control, just go whenever you want, we're rolling.'

I said anything that came to my mind, and my impressions of the past few hours spilled across the wire. Sometimes my voice was audible, and sometimes it was drowned by the crash of the cannons. In any case, the report was authentic and effective.

'It seems, that for the last several days, the human wave attacks coming from Iran into Iraq were made by children and led by mullahs. There were no regular forces, there were no regular army units confronting the Iraqis. And the Iraqis were sitting with their highly trained army, with their modern weapons in fixed positions, and they just mowed them down as they came, wave after wave. Very few survived, and the ones who did are frightened little children. I mean we found some today that were ten years old, and they were just huddling in a corner, terrified.'

The report was first broadcast by the CBS evening news, and then relayed to many other countries in the world. A viewer from the States called my home to let my people know that they had heard me on the news. My family knew – they had watched my report on French TV in Paris.

Early next morning we were driven to the battle front. During the night, the Iranian survivors had regrouped and were getting ready for their last hurrah, their ascent to martyrdom for that thing called ultimate sacrifice. We had just approached a solid phalanx of tanks, lined up turret to turret on a causeway, when all hell broke loose. Guns to our left and to our right, machine guns, tracers. In the far distance we could see them rising from their trenches. It was an unbelievable sight. They were running into their death. It was a shooting gallery, only here nobody was giving out prizes. Some were blown into the air by exploding shells, others ran and fell. It didn't last long. Then an eerie silence settled over the desert, the silence of death, and a stink of cordite and fresh blood. Iraqi soldiers were running towards the camera, rifles high in the air, chanting. They danced around us:

> *'We've cut off the arm of the enemy,*
> *we've cut off the arm of our enemy,*
> *we've cut off the arm of our enemy ... '*

They found three survivors, dragged them out of a foxhole. Those poor devils shook so badly they could hardly put their hands up. The Iraqis tied their hands, with strips of cloth. Then they told them to sit. The three tried to disappear into the ground. One of the Iraqis spoke Farsi.

The first Iranian was an elderly man who couldn't open his mouth. A soldier offered him a canteen with water. 'My name is S...S...SS...Sura ... ' he couldn't pronounce his name. Shellshock.

One of them was a child, fourteen, one of the army of misguided. As they led him away, he yelled: '*Magh'bar Saddam* ... Death to Saddam [Saddam Hussein, President of Iraq]. Long live Islam!'

An ill-advised defiance that would certainly have cost him his life, had we and our camera not been present. They grabbed him by the hair and dragged him to a jeep.

We walked towards the village. The first obstacle was a solid wall of corpses. They had piled up on top of each other when they ran into a hail of machine-gun bullets. In the water, off the causeway, floated corpses, one with only his face sticking out, the mouth open, clustered with flies. The village was in a shambles and aflame. The corpses of Iranians were everywhere, here a head sticking out of a foxhole, there a hand protruding from beneath a slab of concrete. I counted up to two hundred, then gave up. There simply were too many. A smell of blood hung over this charnel scene. I found it difficult to breathe, and even harder not to vomit.

Coming in low over the village, a flight of Gazelle helicopter gunships had discovered some stragglers hiding out in the swamp and now loosed off their rockets, which streaked over our heads. I could see the impacts several hundred yards away. Fountains of mud and water rose into the air, marking the watery grave for a few poor men out there, in front of my camera.

There was one unforgettable image: as background a burning village, red flames roaring into the sky. In between the fire and us, a waterway reflecting fire and smoke. And right in front of me, in a foxhole, with only their upper bodies sticking out, two dead Iranians. One had holy scriptures wound around his head. This image, captured by the two French still photographers as well, was featured on the cover of every publication in the world. Both got an identical exposure; one of them, François Lochon, won the Photo of the Year award with it. My tape was replayed in seventy countries.

We walked away from this village of death. Its fate was sealed, the general had ordered the destruction of the place, house and bodies turned to ash in a monumental Viking funeral pyre. For the next four agonizing miles, we found a corpse every few yards. First a hundred, then a thousand. A boy, serene in death, a small trickle of blood from the side of his mouth and a grenade in his hand, with the pin removed. Deadly, very deadly.

The causeway was covered with corpses, and Iraqi soldiers were dragging them over the side, dumping them unceremoniously into the swamp. They had to, there was acute danger of contamination in this heat. When they tried to lift one mangled corpse, it came apart in the middle.

Near a cluster of heavy tanks we were met by the brigade commander. He was beaming.

'What were your casualties?' we asked him.

'Not very high.'

'And the enemy's?'

'Look for yourself.' With that he pointed across the field of slaughter strewn with corpses. The military communiqué had mentioned twenty-five thousand dead. They were probably not too far off the mark. 'When you see this, you must believe we make war on children,' he said, with a sad smile, almost as if searching for an excuse for his action, 'but they are fanatics. They jump on our tanks and blow themselves up.'

I had seen such a tank, without a turret, blown apart by a human mine. 'General, is this the end of the war?'

'No, not the war. But it is the end of the battle.'

When the shooting stopped, and survivors had been counted, we were told that the Iraqis had captured 250 out of a force of two divisions, some twenty thousand. The rest were lying out there in front of the Iraqi machine guns at the still smoking village of Al-Beida.

That night, Dan Rather opened the CBS evening news with a warning: 'War is ghastly. That means, accurate reporting about war includes grisly photographs ... '

8

THE HOME MENAGERIE

'Go directly – see what she's doing and tell her she mustn't.'
Punch *cartoon, 1872*

First there were only the girls and Annelise, then the goldfish, followed by a rabbit named Réglisse from its black fur which was like the girls' favourite sweet, liquorice. Réglisse ate the electric wiring, chewed holes into the leather sofa, and peed on the rug. When I gave them an ultimatum – either he goes or I go – guess who won? Réglisse munched on some more cables and put the whole building into darkness, lift and all. Our zoo expanded and he was joined by Papageno, a noisy parakeet.

Annelise had issued strict instructions: no more birds. While she was on vacation, I had found Papageno abandoned in the street, and when I picked him off a garbage crate where he had been munching on a banana, he bit me on the finger. It was infatuation at first sight. I had to break it gently to the family that we had an addition in the house. So I called Christina:

'We have a new bird, but don't tell mother.'

'Mother, Erik has just called, we have a new bird, he is grey and we have called him Papageno.' Child's psychology.

I put him in a cage and when he seemed to succumb to heart-break, we found him a tender young mate which the kids christened Papagena. This revived Papageno's spirits, and their love, or fights, turned the apartment into a screeching match, always at about six in the morning. Only a generous ration of kernels would shut them up.

Then came the kids' first day of school. I went to meet the teacher and all the other equally nervous parents, all proud fathers showing off their proudest production. I even wore a tie and a jacket as is proper in the posher districts of Paris. I stood there with the grin which says, look at the girls in those pretty red dresses – these are my daughters.

Another memorable moment was the day we let them go to school on their own. For us parents it was sheer panic and we passed a sleepless night. They had to cross a busy intersection, controlled by traffic lights. Previously I had found out that thirty per cent of the drivers in Paris are colour-blind. The morning came, and Annelise and I stood on the balcony, terrified, holding each other. We watched the girls reach the intersection. They stopped, waited for the little man on the traffic light to turn green, and then crossed. When they had reached the other side we both collapsed over a cup of strong coffee.

Our two girls had few problems adjusting to life in Paris. French came to them as naturally as any other language, and before long we conversed in a funny mixture of several tongues, a truly polyglot family.

'Veuille-tu me passez the salt please.'

When I suggested that Annelise and I should take a short holiday, her standard reply would be: 'I can't leave the kids.' At first I thought it was a mother's sacrifice. Slowly it began to dawn on me that being with children is much more fun than being away from them. Once we did leave them. We made a combined business trip-cum-shopping spree.

The first day we received a call: 'Mummy, where's my green woollen scarf?'

The second day it was: 'Mummy, the toilet doesn't flush.'

On the third day Annelise went back to Paris to be with the monsters.

The children loved their school, they found it easy to learn their lessons, and to make friends with their little French comrades. They were constantly invited to chocolate-and-cookie parties. Sometimes we gave parties. Réglisse hobbled around, and when the kids chased him they spilled chocolate and cake all over the floor. I had to serve more hot chocolate and clean up the mess.

Their teacher was a young man, a gifted amateur pianist, who played for the children in their lunch break. He got them started on Wolfgang Amadeus and Johann Sebastian and Frédéric – Chopin that is. One day he told Christina:

'Please ask your father to come and see me.'

'He isn't my father.'

'So who is he?'

'He is the man my mother loves.' It was intended the way she said it, a compliment, and it was the most wonderful way to pass my graduation into 'our family'. The schoolteacher has since become a good friend, and we have spent many evenings listening to his imitation Horowitz.

Eventually the girls needed a bigger place, Réglisse needed a bigger place, Papageno needed a bigger cage as Papagena was laying more and more eggs, and the change had to be made. We moved into a loft in the centre of Paris.

It is a nice place with two telephones. The lines are always busy – after all, my daughters have to call up their girl- and boyfriends to exchange the latest gossip which has happened to them on the way home in the five minutes since they have been out of touch with each other. To tell a five-minute adventure takes them half an hour. When I try to point out that I may have to call a news editor in New York, I am instructed, with a sweet smile, to get lost.

When the girls aren't arranging dates with their boyfriends, Annelise has to call somebody about the latest restaurant or dress. *Eh bien, plus ça change, plus c'est la même chose* say the French. It is a reminder of my wild bachelor existence. Only if I beg very nicely will they allow me access to the phone, for a short time. However, this is a rare event.

We have a big terrace which Annelise has covered with trees, flowers and herbs. Our life has become a multi-coloured garden of happiness and bright blossoms with many birds fluttering around.

When it rains they watch television and I can't see my football game, because they have discovered a rock concert on another channel. Their boyfriends play big men, drink my beer and I am allowed to take out the empties. So what else is new in the average happy family?

What started at a party on a crisp autumn evening many years ago became a never-ending love story, and we have not once spent one single morning, noon, or night apart from each other. That is, with the noted exception of the two hundred days per year which I have to spend in the Gulf, or other assorted beauty spots.

Annelise has transformed my life. When I first met her I had reached a point when I had abandoned hope of ever having a family of my own. She opened my windows to let love enter the empty rooms. It goes much deeper than that. She showed me the way to get out of the doldrums of my profession. I had grown tired of the endless reports from practically nowhere. I dissolved my commitment with the BBC, and began to produce films on my own. She helped, she advised, but she never pushed. These films gained a certain amount of recognition. In the wake of the initial successes, I became more easy to live with. During the struggle to build up my company's reputation, she got involved, with solid advice and direct help. Now she runs the company, and when I am away I know that everything will be taken care of. We never discuss business on the phone, we talk about school, the family, the weather and our friends. To my way of thinking, to talk business would show a lack of confidence in her capabilities, and she is very efficient indeed. The people who work for us call me Erik and her *La Patronne*.

When we face a family problem, we solve it ourselves. We keep it inside our walls. That is, almost always. There was one noted exception.

I kept them standing as long as I dared, nursing their drinks and making polite conversation around our fireplace. When I noticed that some were directing hungry glances in the direction of my wife's foie gras, I had to ask them to the table. What had prevented me from ringing the dinner bell was that my daughter Annemarie still hadn't come home from wherever she had gone, and my wife had set a place for her.

It wasn't an important party, just one of Annelise's biannual 'who-do-we-owe-a-dinner' affairs. We all resembled penguins expecting a cold winter, and even I had succumbed to my wife's insistence and had hung a tie around my neck. Annelise stood out: her black sheath made her look even taller, and her blond head towered over the petite French ladies. However, this is not to be a celebration of my wife's grace, but the description of a catastrophic dinner party.

The goose liver and the smoked trout had been served when our elder daughter finally made her appearance. I was not pleased and my face obviously showed it, because my wife threw me a pleading glance which said: please, please, not now …

I looked sternly at my daughter: 'Annemarie, you have kept us waiting.'

Violently, she pushed her chair back. First she stared at me, mouth agape, then she screamed: 'You have kept us waiting all our lives! Isn't there a war you can go to?'

With that, she stormed out of the room, followed by Christina. Around the table there was pained silence, followed by embarrassed smiles. By the time our guests picked up their forks the soufflé had collapsed. The ensuing conversation was laboured, and the dinner talk centred on such vital issues as what to do about the grasshoppers in Senegal. It was a great relief when our guests opted for an early goodnight. Once alone, Annelise busied herself with the dishes, and I didn't even attempt to help her clear the table. I was furious, fuming and boiling – in other words, I was upset. I was not paying attention to whatever my wife had to say to me.

Annelise picked up a glass, held it high, then quite deliberately dropped it on the floor. 'I am sorry,' she said, not to apologize for the shattered glass, but to catch my attention: 'The party was not an overwhelming success.'

'Damn those kids,' I muttered under my breath.

'Erik, have you ever considered that it is not the children, but you? Annemarie is studying for her final exams; she is scared and needs help, not screams. And you are never around long enough to talk to her.'

'I have my work to do!'

'At the price of alienating your own family?'

'What do you mean? Am I an outcast in my own house? Just because a teenage girl throws a hysterical tantrum, does that mean I don't care about my family!'

'She simply said out loud what all of us have been thinking for a long time. Erik, they need you, just as much as I need you. You should take more part in our lives.'

I didn't bother to close the door behind me as I stormed out. Ungrateful monsters …

***

The more I appeared on television together with 'grisly photographs', the more pressure was put on my family. They couldn't escape the television pictures pumped into our own living-room, night after night. Not that they ever said so out loud, but it was there, a deep fear, the uncertainty: is this the last time we are going to see him? There was a long trail of friends that I had left behind, from Algeria to Israel, from Vietnam to Chile, from Cambodia to Lebanon, Belfast and El Salvador. This loomed like a dark cloud over our ever more infrequent family reunions.

During the summer of 1986, on my return from North Korea, where I had been offered the unique opportunity to visit that strange and isolated socialist kingdom, I was called into the inner sanctum of the mighty CBS anchor man, Dan Rather.

'Well done, another first: we are really proud of you.' For a starter. Then the heavy stuff. 'You know, there has been a change in network policy. We may have to accept cuts, but whatever happens, we don't want to lose you, or people of your specific talent.'

'Thank you,' I said. 'That is most reassuring.'

Two weeks later the foreign news chief visited me in Paris. My contract had been cancelled. It was the start of a series of lay-offs that hit all networks. The triumvirate of CBS, NBC, and ABC no longer ruled an exclusive domain. Independent stations, network affiliates, cable television, home video and even books had cut into their profits. Staff became more preoccupied with survival than production. Company 'human resource departments' cut staff with the sensitivity of a chain-saw. Decisions were taken by computer printouts: 'The list! Who's on the list?' went up the anxious cry. Long-termers in seemingly untouchable positions walked into their offices to be told by their secretaries that they had to clear out their desks by noon and hand in their credit cards. The catch-phrase was 'Lean and mean', and it meant: 'I want it closed – now!' In many ways it was better to be fired – you could re-enter society, as it were.

A period had come to an end. Once the money-changers took over from creative talent, stock market reports replaced the importance of news reports. A heritage was squandered. Without fanfare, the beacons of information were laid to rest, and with them the influence the networks exerted over millions of faithful viewers. The once supreme CBS lost its number one rating, but its share price doubled within a year.

In a sense, it hasn't affected general news coverage. The vacuum left by the big networks has been filled by other less ambitious organizations, where an hourly rehash of news can be watched around the clock. Coverage has become a bit more sketchy, with a touch of the sensational. What sells advertising time today is ratings and they come from a combination of entertainment and news. It doesn't need to be too accurate as long as it is violent. There are actually people who measure fires on the nightly news, and report on the size of the competition's flames. 'Why are Channel 2's flames higher than ours?' Violence! 'Anybody who wants television's favour can have it in five minutes with a pistol,' wrote hostage psychologist Dr Hubbard in *Television is a Whore*.

Manipulation of the media by presidents and terrorists will always exist. Television demonstrates every day that it can start or stop social and political trends. It can force a head of state or a nation to take a stand. It can send shareholders in New York into a panic at the sudden drop of shares in Tokyo or Paris. Recently, in London, the BBC's weatherman came under fire when he failed to predict a devastating storm.

Talent will always play its role in this most advanced means of mass communication since the invention of the printing press. The one single factor which sets television apart from all the other media is the need for usable pictures. An army of willing cameramen is there to provide the material. For many years I was one of them.

I recalled the disastrous evening of that big family scream-up, a year before. The misery of high-tech food in sterile hotels, even being paperbagged and chained by terrorists – nothing could be as bad as being a loving father scorned. Those ungrateful monsters –

'Leave me alone, go away – I never have enough time to be with myself,' I hollered at my for once united family, only to be answered by peals of laughter, before I slammed the door. It was a miserable, stormy night, but I felt neither cold, nor rain. Lightning flashed messages from the Great Beyond, thunder reverberated in the glass-walled canyons of empty office blocks, the wind whipped through trees, leaves and discarded newspapers sliced through the air. People

descended into the womb of the Métro. I was numb to my surroundings, crossing streets as cars skidded on brakes, drivers spitting venom
at me. I didn't hear and I didn't feel, I just trudged on until I ended up
on the banks of the Seine. There were shadows lurking in the dark,
glows from cigarettes, *clochards* scurrying into niches and under
bridges to escape the downpour.

One constant thought kept pounding my veins: my family was so
unjust, after all I had done for them ... It was outrageous how wrong
they were! Ungrateful ... and how ungracious, to say it out loud ... or
had I ... ? Could it – just possibly – be me? Had I forsaken my family
for the doubtful pleasure of chasing bombs in far-off places? That
stormy night, I had a long conversation with a stray dog. We sat on the
river bank, I stared into the slow passing darkness of water, he licked
my hand, and nodded compassionately. Slowly, my fire was put out by
a deep realization: it was I who had to change. A rude awakening, but
suddenly I could feel the rain, running from my hair into my collar
and down my skin. When I returned home, I was cold, but calm. My
wife had left a thermos of tea, together with a note: *We all love you very
much. Now come to bed.* I knew the time to quit had finally come.

Of course, it wasn't quite that simple. But, come the holidays, we
packed the family wagon, and for the first time it was I, and not my
poor wife, who drove the suitcases and the birds, the dog and the kids
to our log cabin in Denmark. There, I talked with Annelise and
chopped wood, I talked with Annemarie and cut the lawn, and I
talked to Christina and together we picked mushrooms. And when I
did not talk with my family, I retired to my cabin on the water's edge,
cut off from a noisy cocktail of daughters, boyfriends, and record
players which they insisted on playing at the well-known teenage
level, a sound which makes windowpanes shake and fathers flee. The
little cabin provided a wonderful haven of silence, surrounded by wild
roses, the waters of the Baltic lapping at its pillars. A smell of
pinewood filled the room, I sat at a roughly hewn wooden table in
front of a bay window. Annelise never missed placing a vase of wild
flowers on it. There was no television, no newspapers, and no
telephone. The only sound was a noisy argument by a family of
seagulls and the rustle of rosebushes in the breeze coming off the
ocean. Most of all, there was peace. I unpacked my old typewriter, the
machine on which I had kept a record of my exploits, from minor

bloodbath to full-blown holocaust, and, with Pirate across my feet, let my fingers wander across the keys: 'I was twenty-eight and about to die. Don't shoot the Yanqui ... '

Annemarie had passed her final exams with honours, and had been accepted into the Sorbonne. Christina had decided to become a photographer. I could have made it easy for her, but she wanted none of it. In any case, it was better for her to find her own beginning. She got a job in a photo-agency – carrying suitcases and filing slides. She had chosen the rocky path which I had travelled thirty years before her. Now Annelise and I had to contemplate our future. Very soon there would be only the two of us.

'You are not capable of just raking the leaves and chopping wood. Go back and produce documentaries which mean something to you.' With a simple phrase she put me back on the track for a new beginning. I contacted *National Geographic* magazine, and my project was accepted.

The rain that remade the future started on 28 April 1986, more precisely, at 6.28 in the afternoon. It fell on the Swedish provinces along the Baltic coastline. It was now exactly forty-one hours since the Number 4 nuclear reactor at an obscure village named Chernobyl had exploded. The atomic fire spewed forth a poisonous cloud – a cloud that would kill one day.

My involvement in this drama started the moment when my parents-in-law called from Denmark, to tell me that half of Denmark was rushing to buy iodine pills at the nearby drugstores. A panic had gripped Scandinavia, and rumours spread.

'There has been a radiation leak at the Swedish nuclear power station at Barsebaek, right across the bay from Copenhagen ... ' – 'No, it's north of Stockholm, at Forsmark, where a reactor has exploded ... ' – 'According to the East German news agency the leak does not come from their plant at Rügen, on the Baltic ... ' By the time my plane touched down in Denmark the Soviets had finally admitted to a 'minor mishap in a nuclear power station in the Ukraine'. That announcement had taken them three days. No details about the dimensions of the disaster were provided by the Russians. Radiation protection institutes all over the North of Europe went into high gear, tests were performed, and a rapid increase in radioactive isotopes was detected. 'How bad is bad?' This nagging fear was on everybody's mind. The scientists didn't have the answer.

During the summer of '86, Aunt Heddalisa came for a visit. As her name suggests, she is a Viking from Vesterbotten in northern Sweden. The good lady is eighty-five. Her greatest pleasure is to immerse herself in cold water, and of that there is plenty in the Baltic.

'We cannot bathe any longer in our lakes,' lamented Heddalisa in her singsong Swedish.

'Why not?' asked Christina.

'There are too many becquerels in the water.'

'What is becquerels? Some sort of man-eating shark?'

'No, it is not a dangerous fish, it is more serious than that. Becquerels are a means of measuring radiation. That accident in Russia has contaminated our lakes and forests. We cannot eat the fish, we cannot eat the berries and the mushrooms, and we are not even sure about the elk and the reindeer.'

'So, why doesn't somebody talk about it?' the professional in me wanted to know.

'Well, you know we are a small neutral nation, we have to live in peace with all our neighbours ... '

As I researched into a suitable subject for a documentary, I recalled this conversation. I checked, and discovered that the situation was of more concern than any government was ready to admit. That autumn I went to Lapland. If the good Lord has ever created His paradise on earth, He must have picked Lapland. Rocky outcrops form tableaux like prehistoric beasts locked in deadly combat, streams cascade into pristine blue lakes, immense herds of reindeer graze on gentle pastures. Tens of thousands, munching lichen. The day that I reached my destination was the day when Adam and Eve had been kicked out of paradise. The Lapps had been told that their herds had been contaminated by radiation. They would have to be destroyed.

There had been heavy snowfall in early April which made it most difficult for the reindeer to reach their favourite food. Then, as Chernobyl was about to explode, a thaw set in, and the hungry animals got through to the grass. The warm rain melted the snow and irradiated the lichen. Thornbjorn Baer, a Lapp herdowner, first heard about the accident over the local radio. 'It's just another one of these sensational reports, why should I care? We are so far away from the

Ukraine.' A week went by, he and his two sons lived on what nature provided, they fished and they drank the spring water. When he returned into the valley to fetch supplies, he ran into a group of Swedish scientists with geiger counters who told him that it was dangerous to drink the water. They didn't tell him about the lichen. That came much later – six months later, the day that I arrived. The first Lapp I met was his niece, Lillemor, a pretty girl in her early twenties, cutting up a side of reindeer for lunch.

'Aren't you afraid to contaminate your family?' I said.

'There is no food without meat and fish.' And she continued, in a halting voice, trembling with emotion, 'I can't explain my feelings … it is a tragedy for the Lapps … I don't find the words.'

'What about your children, what about a generation from now?'

'I don't think any person can speak for the future.'

When I returned with this film documentary I was questioned by a reporter from a New York tabloid: 'Why should we care what happens in Lapland?' Why indeed? Unless you consider that radiation knows no national boundaries. I can recognize danger when I am up against it. But there, for the first time in my career, I had been confronted with something I couldn't put on film. Radiation is invisible, you can't smell it, it doesn't go Boom! to warn you. It is just air, a cloud of concentrated poison. Above the Arctic Circle, where the air is normally crisp and pure, I had sat on a rock and stared at the sky. I didn't notice the thousands of reindeer. I just looked at passing clouds. I reminisced about my past, and I tried to imagine my future. When will there be the next lethal cloud, and where will that one go to? I felt a presence; I looked down, and saw a dewy-eyed, velvety reindeer nuzzling on delicious, juicy lichen. Ultimate innocence munching the dew of death.

I don't think any person can speak for the future … I could not erase this phrase from my mind. The past stared me in the face. A circus filled with vicious lions and silly clowns. An arena of trumpets and drama. The audience gaping. A young man on the flying trapeze, mostly without a net: myself. Let me not claim an impact on history. I have had none. I have not built a mighty pyramid to reach for the sun. I did not smite the dark armies of evil. I have added little to the fountain of wisdom, nor have I dared to cross the uncharted seas in search of

Xanadu, or reach for the stars, like a heroic explorer remembered for ever. For ever? How many minutes is for ever? At best, I have added to the book of statistics – to what others considered, momentarily, important. So and so many kilotons dropped to wipe out a corner of humanity, so many souls perished to make it an interesting disaster ... how do we measure suffering?

'Gimme a time! ... fifty-seven seconds ... good pictures, good pictures ... a minute five ... come on, this is a good earthquake, it'll get high ratings, what am I bid for this good disaster ... a minute twelve seconds in fifth slot ... yes, what was that? Come again, please ... a minute twenty-four right after the weather forecast ... one ... a minute twenty-four ... two ... no other bids? ... three – sold to the network man in the third row.' C'mon, cash in, you won ... you are still around to tell the story. Lucky bastard? ... Luck is but a passage of time. In the beginning we were more than we are today.

There was Philippe Letellier and Gilles Caron, Paul Schutzer, Sean Flynn, Nick Tomalin, Michel Laurent, Larry Burrows. For them luck had run out.

There was the cameraman on the Plaza de la Moneda whose last picture was down the barrel of a gun. Why him, and why not me across the street? Luck was a thick brick wall.

There was the girl in the bomb cellar, Mossman, and a boy called Jim Buchner.

There is fuzzy Christina and her black rabbit, temperamental Annemarie and her boyfriends, and Annelise, the first woman to make me realize that life is not only conflicts, but love.

There is happiness in the form of a warm puppy. My girls had grown into svelte creatures with a healthy dose of their own opinions. I found myself outnumbered by the females in my domestic menagerie, and constantly overwhelmed by their utter disregard of logic. When I ran out of stamina to fight three women all by myself, I found Pirate. First and foremost, he is male, and he doesn't watch television. He is cuddly and furry and built very square, a shaggy-haired sheepdog from the Pyrenees. Now Pirate and I sit in our designated corner and commiserate with each other. Whenever the three graces in my life formulate one of their many unreasonable requests, and in a loud voice, he growls. The only time he agrees with them is when I am being ordered to take down the garbage. That means, he can come along and sniff his well-marked street corners. He adores me. At last, I have found my true love.

And *there will always be a tide*, a future, as long as I am not content with the present ...

EPILOGUE

There was a knock on my door. Two gentlemen I had never met before.

'Mr Durschmied?'

'Yes?'

'Permit me to introduce myself, I am the ambassador from Cuba.'

'Please, do come in ... '

And so began the closing of the ring.

The Cuba I rediscovered – thirty years after I had fled from the sugar island with the police of dictator Batista in hot pursuit – had changed. Nowadays, slogans exhorted the people to achieve more productive enterprise to aid a sagging economy. There were long lines in front of the Centro market, and the Bodeguita del Medio had East German tourists nailed to its famous bar, talking sunshine and socialist achievements, scribbling graffiti beneath the yellowed picture of Hemingway. The bordellos along the Malecon had been converted into respectable Party headquarters, where block wardens kept the local gentry on its righteous path towards a socialist tomorrow.

The iron bridge at Cauto Cristo was like Cuba, a bit more rusty and tired. When I strolled across it, I could hear a ghostly voice. '*No maten al yanqui!*' echoed down from the girders. It was only the wind, but to me, it sounded like ghosts conjured from the thirty years of a parade gone by. The spot where I had stared into the gaping gun barrels of Ugly-grin, Scarecrow and Baldhead had been turned into a playground, with voices chirping beneath young trees, innocents chasing each other in clean uniforms, white shirts and red neckerchiefs – children being groomed for leadership. All the heroes had vanished long, long ago, replaced by an insignificant plaque in memory of a faded glory.

This then was the New Cuba, after thirty years of revolution. It was not at all what the revolution had promised, or what I had expected. In a way it was quite sad.

It finally happened during a massive party with two thousand selected guests, digging into canapés, chocolate mousse and local beer in celebration of *la victoria gloriosa*. The larger populous masses had been barred from the festivities: they were kept at a safe distance from the upper echelons of party bosses and foreign dignitaries. Not even foreign journalists received a gold-embossed card, but I did – number 1930, my birthdate. The hall was large and they were all present: two foreign prime ministers, six party heads from brotherly socialist countries, a Nobel laureate and all those others who had received the invitation to make a pilgrimage to the Bethlehem of *el socialismo latino*. Some, such as the head of a European Communist Party, simply happened to be in Havana because the weather was awful in his country and he wanted an expenses-paid holiday on some sundrenched beach in Cuba. I was lost in the midst of this moving sea of diplomacy and freeloading. I had focused my attention on the sandwiches, when somebody came, took me by the arm and ushered me into the presence of the host, the one who had started my career, the man they call Fidel. Fidel Castro Ruz. The absolute monarch of *socialismo*. It has been said that he never forgets a face.

'*Como estás … dame un abrazo …* let me embrace you.' With a great smile he enfolded me in a bear-hug. His whiskers tickled. His legendary beard was now a bit more salt than pepper. To all outward appearances, the man still carried his revolutionary pugnacity, expressed by a simple olive uniform without medals, kepi and boots. His charisma seemed unchanged.

And yet. There was a change. Those eyes that had fascinated me in

the Sierra Maestre had lost their fire. Now they told of disappointments and frustration. Eyes that signalled a loneliness at the top, a
solitude of power, if not the solitude of a dictator. The Autumn of the
Patriarch ...

I recalled what the defiant young revolutionary had said when he
stared at my lens and dismissed the impertinent query by a young
cameraman. Thirty years later, and I was no longer certain. Did the
façade of the nationalist actually hide a determined communist?

'*There is no Communism or Marxism in our ideas* ... ' That was thirty
years ago. Castro had changed. Now, the same person ended his
speeches with: '*Today, with more vigour than ever we say: Socialismo ou
Muerte! Marxismo-Leninismo ou Muerte!*'

And the crowd would go wild: '*Viva Fidel!!!*'

A lifetime had passed, and then two men met once more. So much
had happened. The man who hugged me was no longer the Fidel I had
known. He knew that I could tell. But then I was no longer the same
either. We both had shed our innocence. He kept me for a long time in
his embrace and then, after a long pause, he said: 'Thirty years ...
you've had to wait thirty years for international detente to come back
here.'

'That's right ... but you had once told me to come back so that you
could shake my hand before I had become an old man – and now we
are both ... '

His eyes looked over my head, focusing on a memory a thousand
miles and thirty years away, on green mountains and clean air, on
youth and a hill with a gnarled tree. A hill he was never to visit again.
When he descended from his memory mountain, his index finger flew
up in the gesture I remembered so well.

'Yes, and I have kept my promise ... I must watch my words, you
are not an old man. Now we have shaken hands, and you are still a
young man ... ' There was just a little too much emphasis on the 'you'.

The following day I received a call from the Palacio de la Revolución. The president had put his private plane at my disposal, to carry
me back to the Sierra Maestre. A strange premonition took hold of me,
an anxiety, a troublesome worry. Certainly, I wanted to go back,
retrace the past – but the place held too many memories, too many
ghosts.

At a military airfield outside Havana I joined a select crowd, some of the original Castro bunch who had survived. Not all of them did: some had died, and others had not weathered the turmoils of Fidel's changing politics, and were either in prison or in Miami. Reaching Fidel's revolutionary headquarters, the comandancia at La Plata, was a simple matter of three hours instead of the original three weeks.

A special memorial highway, most certainly the best-kept road on the island, and completely deserted, led to the plateau some three kilometres from the top of the Sierra. The last portion was on foot, a steep climb for the ageing and overweight heroes of yesteryear. With great nostalgia they walked the ground that once gave them shelter.

'Faustino,' I asked the leader of the Popular Front of Cuba, 'Is this your house? *Su casa?*'

'*Mi casa? No mi casa, la casa de la administración del territorio libre* ... the house of the civilian administration which I founded, here on this chair.' Yellowed papers on a shelf, and a rusty gun. From the palm-thatched hut where I had spent my nights, a hurricane had taken down the roof. Insects crawled along the rotting beams. It made me shiver. The place had an aura of fetid decay.

I walked away from the group and their memories; I felt the need for solitude and reflection. Within twenty minutes I had reached the top of the hill. The view from the spot where my camera had stood, and from which I had stared at the silver sea and fantasized of a bright future, was now obscured by shrubs. The gnarled tree had been uprooted by some tropical storm, and was nothing but a pile of mouldy mush. Covered by lianas I discovered the remains of a wooden shack – Radio Rebelde. Timbers, a gaping black hole ... I lit a match and stumbled into the shadowy interior. The radio transmitter, that magic spark machine which Orlando Payret had kept alive with ingenuity and hope, was covered by green fungus. A few wires dangled from the rafters, interlaced by a jumble of cobwebs. A large, hairy mountain spider stood guard over some cocooned victims. I groped my way underneath – and froze!

In the midst of the rubble from some nebulous past, among naked wires and mouldy radio dials, distant voices, memories and dust, was my old camera! I stared at it for a minute or two, before I reached for it and hugged it like a long-lost child. Tears came to my eyes.

'I can't believe it ... I haven't touched this camera since the day that changed my life,' I said to no one in particular. I pressed it to my cheek and then kissed the cold metal. I turned it over and found that its footage counter was still on the last frame that had run through its mechanism, thirty years before.

Some sacred gate of forgetfulness was thrown open, turning the past to pain, and happiness. Through the fog of remembrance I heard his voice: '*I hope that I shall shake hands with you before you become too old a man.*' His last words before we shook hands, before he wished me well for the future. I tried to prise the camera door open. It was stuck. Just as well – now, the Genie of the past would never be released. Gently I put it back where I had found it, and walked out into the sunshine. Let it rest for another two generations, untouched by unrest in Yemen and the madness of Vietnam, sinking oil platforms and a poison-gassed Orient.

In this shelter it had passed, unscathed, a lifetime of tropical rainstorms, torrid heat and humidity, falling trees, and a hurricane.

But, even more important, it had survived …

PHOTO CREDITS

SECTION I

Hitler's arrival on the Heldenplatz *Wiener Library*

Bomb damage to the Albertina *Wiener Library*

SECTION II

Hill 943: Durschmied and Sepp Thoma interviewing Sergeant Joseph Coons *Hubert Le Campion*

With Sepp Thoma after he was wounded *Hubert Le Campion*

Durschmied and Col. Jim 'Grizzly' Hendrix *Hubert Le Campion*

Into the jungle *Hubert Le Campion*

The last cigarette *Hubert Le Campion*

Durschmied filming the attack *Hubert Le Campion*

After the battle of Hill 943 *Hubert Le Campion*

Bruce Black *Hubert Le Campion*

Joseph Coons *Hubert Le Campion*

Jim Buchner *Hubert Le Campion*

SECTION III

Beirut: aftermath of car bomb attack *Fadri Mitri/SIPA Press*

US Embassy in ruins *Auque/SIPA Press*

Dead Iranians in Gulf War *Al Talia Arabia/SIPA Press*

Battle of El Howeiza – captured Iranians, not yet teenagers *François Lochon/Frank Spooner*

Durschmied filming soldiers after battle at El Howeiza *François Lochon/Frank Spooner*

Battle of El Howeiza – Iranian helmets *François Lochon/Frank Spooner*

A dead Iranian, Gulf War *François Lochon/Frank Spooner*

All other photographs are from the author's collection

INDEX

Aden, 96–7, 109–10

Afghanistan, 285–6; show trial in, 286–92

Aide Medicale Internationale (AMI), 287

Al-Azair (Iraq), 302

Al-Beida (Iraq), 298–9, 306

Algeria, 85–6

Allen, Norman, 56

Ang Khor Wat, 249

Augoyard, Dr Philippe, 287–92

Austria: Germany occupies, 21–3; in World War II, 24; post-war conditions in, 49–51; *see also* Vienna

Badr, Imam, 97

Baer, Thornbjorn, 316

Baghdad, 282–3, 293–5, 301; *see also* Iraq

Basra, 301

Bathiscombe, Brigid, 233–6

Batista, Fulgencio, 68, 70, 76, 79, 81–2, 83

Beirut, 258, 272–7, 281

Ben-Gurion, David, 84

Black, Sergeant Bruce: in action, 181, 187–92, 194–5, 199, 202, 205–9; wounded, 212

Brede, Stanley, 56

British Broadcasting Corporation (BBC), 86–7, 239, 310

Buchner, Private James Irving: in action, 180–1, 183, 186–96, 199–202, 205–6, 209–10; killed, 213, 318

Burgess, Guy, 114, 223; author meets and interviews in Moscow, 224–8; death, 228

Burrows, Larry, 170, 318

Calcutta, 119–21

Cambodia (Kampuchea): massacres in, 248–55

Canada, 53–4

Canadian Broadcasting Corporation, 146

Caron, Gilles, 318

Castro, Fidel: character and style, 65, 74–5, 77–8; author contacts and interviews, 66, 71–5, 77–81; revolutionary movement, 70, 73–4, 79–80; broadcasts, 76; denies

communist influence, 80, 322; enters Havana, 82–3; author fails to reach again, 84; on author's later visit to Cuba, 321–4

CBC Close-Up (TV programme), 65

Chernobyl, 315–16

Chiang Kai-shek, 84

Columbia Broadcasting System (CBS): Evening News, 256–8, 304, 306; cancels author's contract, 312; changes in, 313

Conde, Richard (Abdul Rahman), 107

Coons, Sergeant Harry Charles Joseph ('JC'): in action, 180–1, 189–93, 196–202, 206–10; wounded, 202

Crawley, Budge, 56

Crawley, Judy, 56

Crawley Films Ltd (Ottawa), 56–7

Cuba: author threatened in, 3–7; author visits in 1958, 66–81; revolution in, 73–4; author revisits, 320–4; *see also* Castro, Fidel

Czechoslovakia, 23

Dak To (Vietnam), 178, 182–3

Damour (Lebanon), 278–9

Danang (Vietnam), 132–4, 140

Davidson, Casey, 61

Davidson, Joyce, 63

Debos, Alain, 272, 274–5

Democracy on Trial (TV series), 215

Dien Bien Phu, 128

Dollfuss, Engelbert, 16

Dulles, John Foster, 62, 76

Durschmied, Annelise: author meets, 234–9; marriage to author, 269, 285; home life, 307, 309–10, 314–15, 318; runs author's production company, 310

Durschmied, Carl (author's father): and author's birth and childhood, 15–19, 23; and pre-war political situation, 18, 21, 23–4; military exploits in World War I, 16, 28–9; skiing, 19–20; serves in World War II, 24, 28–30; opposition to fascism, 31, 41; death, 36; relations with son, 39–41

Durschmied, Erik: birth and childhood, 15–19,
  39–40; schooling, 18; skiing, 19–20, 26–7,
  51–2, 54; in World War II, 24–5; at officer
  school, 25–6, 31–2; in bomb-disposal, 33;
  sexual initiation, 34; home bombed, 35;
  wartime escape from Vienna, 37–8, 41–5;
  relations with parents, 39–40; meets US
  troops, 46; returns to Vienna, 47–8; resumes
  schooling, 48, 51; musical interests, 50;
  romances, affairs and amours, 52–3, 85,
  114–17, 128–9; migrates to Canada, 53–4;
  first marriage and divorce, 54–5, 64, 85; first
  film job, 56–7; in Hollywood, 57–60; begins
  as news cameraman, 61–4; success from
  Castro interview, 83; attacked in Macao, 88;
  lost and saved in desert, 105–7; arrested at
  Ku Klux Klan rally, 122–3; injured in
  Vietnam, 137–9; field equipment, 179;
  approached by North Koreans, 220;
  photographed with woman in Moscow,
  221–2; meets Annelise, 234–9; joins CBS,
  256–8; and moral aspects of reporting, 282,
  290–2; on air travel, 294; home and family
  life, 307–15, 318–19; produces films, 310,
  315; CBS contract cancelled, 312
Durschmied, Helene (author's mother), 15,
  47
Dwyer, Major, 133–40

Earle, Tom, 62
El Alamein, 31

Flynn, Sean, 318
Fouad (Beirut hotel manager), 276–7
Fox, Beryl, 146
Fox, Paul, 86–8, 92, 218
Foyt, Captain, 180, 186, 188, 190, 193–4,
  199–200, 202–3

Germany: pre-war expansion, 21–3; in World
  War II, 24–5, 31; invades Russia, 26;
  bombed, 31–2
Glynn, Tom, 56
Goering, Hermann, 31
Guevara, Che, 82
Gulf War, 262, 264–6, 270–1, 293, 295–302

Hamza (Iraqi guide), 296
Han, 220
Hansson, Louis, 215–17, 219
Harib (Yemen), 98, 107–8

Hendrix, Lieut.-Colonel Jamie ('Grizzly'),
  185–6, 190, 203–4, 207
Hill 943 (TV documentary), 181, 213, 247,
  257
Hitler, Adolf: visits Vienna, 20–1; in World
  War II, 24–5, 30–1; plot on life, 33, 230; and
  Skorzeny, 229–30
Ho Chi Minh Trail, 250
Hollywood, 57–60
Howeiza marshes (Iraq), 293, 299–300, 302–6
Hubbard, Dr David: Television is a Whore, 313

Iran, 258–9, 261–8, 269–71; attacks Iraq,
  298–300, 302–6
Iraq: war with Iran, 262, 264–6, 270–1, 293,
  298–306; author visits, 283–4, 293–7, 301
Israel, 239, 263; attacks Lebanon, 272–3,
  277–81

John R (reporter), 171–4

Kabul, 286
Kampuchea see Cambodia
Karmal, Babrak, 286
Kerbala Wayfarers Volunteer Brigades (Iran),
  299
Kestmand, Sultan Ali, 290
Khmer Rouge, 248–55
Khomeini, Ayatollah, 259–62, 265–7
Khorramshahr, 269–71, 283
Khrushchev, Nikita S., 83
Kim, 220
Kipling, Rudyard, 292
Kompong Cham (Cambodia), 250
Ku Klux Klan, 121–3

Labadie, Mahmoud, 274
Lajevardi, Assadollah, 268–9
Lane, Annemarie (author's stepdaughter), 237,
  269, 271; schooling, 308, 315; home life,
  310–11, 314, 318
Lane, Christina (author's stepdaughter), 237,
  239, 269, 271, 285; schooling, 308; home life,
  309, 311, 314, 318; career, 315
Lapland, 316–17
Larkin, Peter, 258, 272, 275, 303
Laupenheim, Major, 131–2
Laurent, Michel, 318
Lawrence, John, 213
Lebanon: war in, 272–81; terrorist demands in,
  281–2

Le Campion, Hubert, 178–9, 185, 188, 197–202, 210–11
Letellier, Philippe, 318
Liller (au pair girl), 236–9
Lime Grove Studios (London), 86
Lochon, François, 305
Lome (Togo), 285
Loy, Mr (Saigon), 141–3, 145, 166, 211

Maclean, Donald, 114, 223–7
Mao Tse-tung, 69
Marib (Yemen), 97–8
Matthews, Herbert, 66
Metrotone News, 61–2
Meyer (cameraman, French TV-ORTF), 249
Mills of the Gods, The (TV film), 146
Mira (of Moscow), 221–3
Mogadishu, 111
Mohammed Reza Shah Pahlavi, Shah of Iran, 260–3
Moscow, 221–4
Mossman, James: work and friendship with author, 87–8, 91, 92, 112, 115–17, 122–3; character and style, 87, 89–90; in Yemen, 92, 95–6, 98, 101, 103–8; purchases watch in Aden, 111; food-poisoning in Somalia, 111–12; intelligence background, 113–15, 216; interviewing technique, 117–18; at Ku Klux Klan riot, 122–3; moral values, 123; home, 123; on Vietnam war, 127–8; reports Vietnam war, 129–31, 136–40; leaves Panorama, 214–15; and Louis Hansson, 215–17; death, 218–19, 318; Lifelines, 217
Mosul massacre (1959), 273
Mussolini, Benito, 229–30

Nasser, Abdul Gamel, 84
Nehru, Jawaharlal (Pandit), 118–19
New York, 61
North Korea, 220, 312

Palestine Liberation Organization (PLO), 274–8, 281
Panorama (BBC TV programme), 86, 90, 109
Paris, 85–6, 233, 308–9
Paulus, Field Marshal Friedrich Wilhelm Ernst, 31
Payret, Orlando, 76, 323
'Peace for Galilee', Operation, 273, 280
Perez, Faustino, 82
Philby, Kim, 114, 116, 216, 223

Phnom Penh, 250, 253–4
Planchais, Christophe, 269–70, 283–4, 293–4, 296–7, 301–2
Pol Pot, 250, 252, 254
Premier Plan (Canadian TV programme), 85
Puissesseau (reporter, French TV-ORTF), 249

Qutbzadeh (Iranian interpreter, later foreign minister), 260

Radio Rebelde (Cuba), 76, 323
Rather, Dan, 256, 306, 312
Renner, Karl, 49
Roosevelt, Eleanor, 75
Russia: Germany invades, 26

Saigon (later Ho Chi Minh City), 128–32, 140–3, 145, 162, 167–8, 171, 211, 249
St George, Andrew, 66–8
Salzburger Nachrichten, 211
San'a (Yemen), 93, 95, 102
Sanchez, Celia, 72, 74–5, 77, 81
Schmitt, Dana, 107, 217
Schmettau, Wolf von, 254
Schuschnigg, Kurt von, 21
Schutzer, Paul, 318
Shah of Iran see Mohammed Reza Shah Pahlavi
Shatt-al-Arab, 262, 269–70, 298
Skorzeny, Colonel Otto, 229–30
Somalia, 109–11
Stalingrad, 29, 31
Stauffenberg, Colonel Claus Philipp Schenk, Graf von, 230
Stokes, Frank, 56

Tales from the Chippinga Woods (TV film), 245
Tehran, 258, 262–3, 266
terrorism and terrorists, 281–2
Tet offensive (Vietnam), 213
Thoma, Sepp: in Vietnam, 175–6, 178–9, 187, 191, 193; wounded, 195–7, 201, 202, 204; in hospital, 207, 210; leaves for home, 211–12; drafted into Austrian army, 212
Tomalin, Nicholas, 318

United States of America: presence in Vietnam, 131; US withdrawal, 247
Urrutia, Dr Manuel, 80
US Military Advisory Group – Vietnam (US MAG–V), 174

Vandermeersch, Sister Françoise, 248–51,
  254
Vienna: pre-war life in, 14–17, 20, 22; in
  World War II, 30; bombed, 33–7; author
  escapes from, 37–8, 41–5; captured (1945),
  45; author returns to, 47–8; post-war
  conditions in, 49–51; author visits to
  interview Chancellor, 117
Viet Cong, 133–4
Vietnam: nature of war in, 127–8; US military
  advisers in, 131, 174; 1962 situation in,
  133–4; conduct of war, 135–6, 173–4, 213;
  children in, 144; filming and reporting in,

146–62, 167–8, 175–211; drugs in, 163,
  165–7; psychological warfare in, 177–8;
  numbers of US troops in, 180; US
  withdrawal from, 247; see also Saigon

Wantenaar, Jack, 240–6
Watson, Patrick, 65–6
Wessel, Horst, 22
Williams, Sergeant, 183–4, 188, 207–8

Yemen, 92–108
Yom Kippur war, 239

Zurich, 115